# The Old-House Journal

# 1982

# YEARBOOK

A one-volume compilation
of all the editorial pages
printed in The Old-House Journal in 1982

This **Old-House Journal Yearbook** is a one-volume compilation of all the editorial pages printed in The Old-House Journal in 1982.

*Subscriptions* to The Old-House Journal are available in the United States only. Use the order form at the back or mail $16 to The Old-House Journal, Subscriptions 69A Seventh Avenue Brooklyn, N.Y. 11217

# Contents

# Not A Collection Of Handyman Projects

The how-to information in this Yearbook is quite different from that in any of the "handyman" publications. We're not going to tell you how to make a colonial spice rack, or how to transform an old Clorox bottle into a watering can. Countless do-it-yourself books and magazines do that.

Rather, we focus on information you can't get anywhere else . . . information about how to fix up and keep up your pre-1930 home without sacrificing its charm and character. For example, where the handyman magazines show you how to put aluminum siding on your house, The Old-House Journal tells you why that's a *terrible* idea.

In these pages, you'll find the emphasis is on *sensitive rehabilitation*. This means retaining as much of the original material in the building as possible. Not only does this help preserve the home's architectural character, but it can also be cheaper than going out to buy new material. And if your house has been badly "remuddled," The Old-House Journal shows how to recreate the original decorative detail.

Today, many magazines talk about self-sufficiency and do-it-yourself to save money. We agree with that point of view, but we go a step further. We believe, as do our 70,000 subscribers, that old houses are a national heritage. Every old house has its own special history . . . its own story to tell. The ornamental detail, the evidence of past generations, the historical style — it's all part of your home's story. When you learn to hear what the house is telling you, the joy of old-house living really begins. By preserving the home's basic character . . . while at the same time making it fit your needs . . . you have the best of both worlds — the richness of the past combined with the comfort of the present.

If you want to do a "gut renovation" and make a starkly modern statement, you won't find any help or encouragement in these pages.

But if you love old houses, and are sensitive to the special emotional warmth they possess, then you'll find the information in this Yearbook (and in the entire Yearbook series) tailored right to your needs.

*The Editors*

# The Old-House Journal

**Vol. X No. 1**                                    **$2.00**

**January 1982**

A New Look At Linoleum............9
Roof & Chimney Work..............13
Refinishing Clinic...............16
Helpful Publications.............20
Ask OHJ..........................21
Turn-of-Century Products.........23

NEXT MONTH....Rehabilitating A Stair

### Restoration and Maintenance Techniques For The Antique House

# THE COMFORTABLE HOUSE
## Post-Victorian Domestic Architecture

### By Clem Labine & Patricia Poore

MOST OF US live in houses that, though old, don't even get mentioned in architectural stylebooks. This article is an appreciative look at the most familiar old houses in America--houses found on the East Coast and the West, in semi-rural areas and small cities, in revival neighborhoods as well as old ethnic ones. These houses have a history we need to understand, and so come to respect, if we want to preserve the familiarity of most of the country.

"POST-VICTORIAN" is an umbrella term for the styles we'll describe on the following pages. Rather than conjuring up a single image, Post-Victorian refers to the era, and a changing attitude that affected the look of built America in the decades around the turn of the century.

THE POST-VICTORIAN building boom introduced the house as we know it today. These homes were built with amenities we take for granted, and with an emphasis on serving utilitarian needs. It was an era of pattern-book designs, mail-order houses, and speculative building, but methods and materials were generally of better quality than post-World-War-II houses: Walls were plaster, doors were solid wood. Many of the selling points recognized by today's home-buyer appeared in the builders' ads 75 years ago.

THE PLAN of the early 20th-century house was "open" and "comfortable;" large windows, pergolas, and porches provided "plenty of sun;" the indoor "sanitary bathroom," closets, and a kitchen with built-in cupboards became standard features. For the first time, too, central heating was designed into the new house; basements were equipped with laundry areas and clean-storage coal bins.

ON THE EXTERIOR, ornamentation far plainer than that of the Victorians made simple statements of "honesty" or nostalgia. The squarish dignity of many of these houses can be quite charming, especially when history is read into their appearance: The apparent plainness might express the faint stirrings of the Modern movement; it might be the stripped-down result of a generation fed up with the conspicuous, overworked, expensive decoration of the Victorians; or it might just reflect economy.

DECORATION was by no means gone, though. We have only to think of architect-publisher George Barber's lavish late Queen Anne houses (1888-1915, see Dec. 1980 OHJ), or the half-timbered and rusticated Tudor Revival houses, to remember that ornament, if diverse, was still around.

*continued next page*

1

# The Old-House Journal®

*Editor*
**Clem Labine**

*Managing Editor*
**Patricia Poore**

*Assistant Editor*
**Cole Gagne**

*Editorial Assistants*
**Joni Monnich**
**Stephanie Croce**

*Circulation Supervisor*
**Joan O'Reilly**

*Circulation Assistants*
**Margaret Scaglione**
**Barbara Bugg**
**Jean Baldwin**

*Office Manager*
**Sally Goodman**

*Office Assistant*
**Rafael Madera**

*Sales Promotion*
**Joel Alpert**

*Circulation Director*
**Paul T. McLoughlin**

*Technical Consultant*
**Alan D. Keiser**

*Architectural Consultant*
**Jonathan Poore**

*Contributing Editors*
**R. A. Labine, Sr.**
**John Mark Garrison**

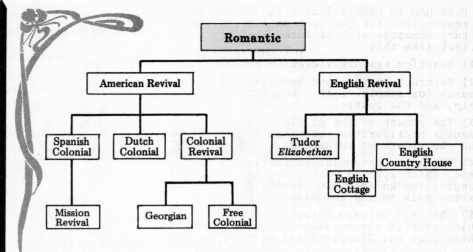

THE CHARTS on this page are an attempt to bring some order to the multitude of styles in domestic building around the turn of the century. Style names at the top of each chart represent major architectural categories or movements; as you read down the charts, you will find sub-categories of the major house types.

IN OTHER WORDS, these are not lineal charts. Sub-categories are not necessarily later ver-

sions of the style above. For example, Mission Revival actually predated Spanish Colonial Revival houses.

KEEP IN MIND that within many of the broad style categories, there might be three expressions of the style: (1) The cottage, a one or one-and-a-half storey house; (2) The villa, a house that might belong to a prosperous businessman; (3) The mansion, a big, rich house.

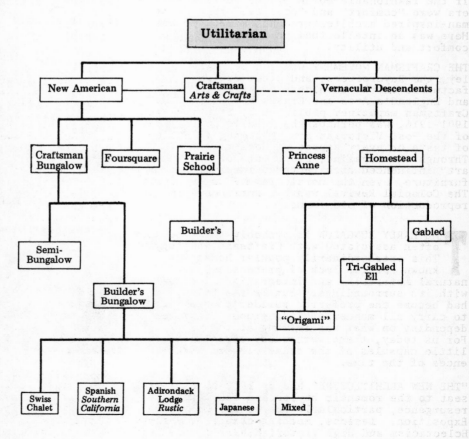

IF WE HAD TO CREDIT just a few of the forces responsible for the look of early 20th-century domestic architecture, the list would look like this:

(1) Reaction against Victorian excess.

(2) Return to nature and basics--a renewed search for simple truths, honesty in workmanship, and the rustic.

(3) The growth of the middle class, which meant a proliferation of single-family houses and the growth of suburbia.

(4) The 1876 Centennial Exhibition in Philadelphia, which spurred patriotism and a nostalgic longing for an American identity that would extend back to the Colonies.

(5) The 1893 Chicago Columbian Exposition, which created the passionate desire for anything that was Classical and white.

NOSTALGIA came in two flavors just before the turn of the century: English and American. The English Revival styles carried a connotation of taste and wealth, while the American, or Colonial Revival, styles were associated with patriotism and restraint. Nevertheless, plenty of English-inspired cottages were built by speculators, and the millionaire class often chose Colonial Revival for their mansions. These romantic revival styles had emotional appeal for almost everybody.

ADHERENTS of the Craftsman ideal, however, were not "everybody." They went in quite the opposite direction from the romantic revivalists. If the fashionable words of the Post-Victorian era were "comfort" and "utility," then Craftsman-inspired architecture epitomized the era. Here was an intellectual philosophy based on comfort and utility.

THE CRAFTSMAN MOVEMENT was led by Gustav Stickley, the Roycrofters, and other designer/manufacturers on the shoulders of William Morris and England's Arts and Crafts movement. The Craftsman magazine, published by Stickley from 1901-1916, was perhaps the intellectual leader of the Post-Victorian era, becoming an arbiter of taste on every aspect of domestic life. Through the magazine, proponents of "the new art" influenced architecture, interior design, furniture, even the moral climate of America. The Colonial Revival was its antithesis in its reproduction of old forms.

THE EARLY BUNGALOW is probably the type most often associated with Craftsman ideology. This extraordinarily popular house was known for its lack of pretension, use of natural materials, and integration of house with its surroundings. But by the 1920s, it had become the preferred builder's model, made to carry all manner of incongruous "features" depending on what was selling at the time. For us today, these vernacular structures are little capsules of the criss-crossed influences of the time.

"THE NEW ARCHITECTURE" had by 1920 taken a back seat to the romantic styles and the Beaux Arts resurgence, particularly due to the Columbian Exposition. Besides, nothing changes overnight: Eclecticism and High Victorian hadn't been left far behind. For example, after the Centennial Exhibition fostered patriotic consciousness

## THE COMFORTABLE HOUSE

" The idea in planning a house is to make it comfortable.

"Comfortable" means that the arrangement of rooms should be convenient, that the heating system should be so that the house can be made warm when one wishes, that the plumbing system should never fail to give hot water, that the windows should not leak, and that the cellar should be dry.

These things when well done give bodily comfort.

There is, however, another comfort which has been called a "comfort of the eye."

Though your plumbing system is perfect, and your cellar dry, and your house warm, we still ask: "Is it attractive? Does it please the eye?"

The houses in which we live must not only answer the conditions of efficiency, but of good taste also. "

From: *The Honest House*, by
Ruby Ross Goodnow, New York, 1914

and the Colonial Revival, it wasn't uncommon to see a High Victorian drawing room with a spinning wheel in the place of honor. The spinning wheel was the reminder of the simple life, honest work, and the beginnings of America. The most important thing--then as now--was the symbolism.

MANY MORE THINGS INFLUENCED domestic building than just revival styles and the honest new architecture of utilitarian beauty, of course. By the time the Colonial Revival, Craftsman-inspired houses, and all the imported styles had filtered down to those vernacular houses a generation later, they had been transmogrified into something very different indeed.

A NEW HOUSE often spoke the answer to the builder's own question: "What's selling?" It could be the sweet appeal of an English Cottage, or the more ridiculous Craftsman Colonial, a sure-fire seller that neither builder nor buyer realized was a contradiction in terms. Now that time has blurred some of the philosophical distinctions, we can ask: Did it matter if its proud new owner didn't understand Stickley's principles of usefulness and beauty, or the antecedents of real colonial homes? Both Craftsman-inspired honesty and the nostalgia for early America appealed to the buyer, and the house he bought is our record of what people wanted in 1915. Vernacular styles had become something in their own right.

## The Styles

WE'LL FIRST BREAK Post-Victorian houses into two major philosophical movements, both of which were born in the Victorian era: Romanticism and Utilitarianism. Romantics, or Revivalists, felt that houses should evoke an emotional response, based upon association with historical events. During the 1800s, the Greek Revival, Gothic Revival, Italianate, and Queen Anne styles were all associative romantic styles. In the early 20th-century, the Colonial Revival, Spanish and Mission Revivals, and the English Cottage and Country House styles continued the tradition, using symbols and archaeological references which summoned certain emotions in the viewer.

WHAT WE'LL CALL Utilitarian was reformist, rebelling against the emotionalsim of the Romantics. Led by William Morris and the Arts and Crafts movement in England, and publicized in this country chiefly by Gustav Stickley through his Mission furniture and The Craftsman magazine, the Utilitarians sought to eliminate what they saw as useless decoration, and to focus instead on that which combined usefulness and beauty. This intellectual/philosophical movement had a great influence on the architects of the Prairie School and Southern California, and also affected almost all of America's domestic architecture to this day.

THERE ARE MANY WAYS to reshuffle houses into "style groups." Architecture is not like biology, however; we can't assign every house a genus and species name. Categorizing buildings is arbitrary. All we can do is group houses according to certain physical similarities, taking into account the events, people, and ideas that made them look they way they do. To that end, following are the major post-Victorian house types we've isolated.

## Romantic Styles

### Colonial Revival

WITH THE CENTENNIAL EXHIBITION of 1876, America began a romance with it architectural roots that continues to this day. People were seeking a purely "American" architecture to nourish their patriotic pride. It was natural that they should look back to the houses constructed by the Colonists, houses which had been standing on American soil for 100 or 150 years. These models for the Colonial Revival, of course, had been built on English prototypes. But the Post-Victorian Colonials that were built were interpretive, and themselves became a very American house form.

THERE ARE TWO basic types of Colonial Revival buildings. First are the historically accurate reproductions. When well done, they are difficult to distinguish from the originals. Needless to say, this variety of Colonial Revival house is a rarity.

THE SECOND, more common type of Colonial Revival house was created when freely interpreted colonial motifs were applied to house types that were clearly Victorian or post-Victorian. For example, a very popular Colonial Revival house is really a large, asymmetrical Queen Anne house with grafted-on Georgian details, such as Palladian windows, quoins, swags and garlands, and classical columns. Such "free Colonial" houses are found all over the country.

THE DUTCH COLONIAL HOUSE is an important part of the Colonial Revival because it pre-dated other revival styles and became extremely popular for a long time. Its distinctive gambrel roof makes the Dutch Colonial instantly recognizable. A very flexible design feature, the gambrel roof was grafted onto everything from tiny cottages to voluminous two-storey homes. The Dutch Colonial style, unlike the more formal styles, reminded people of early farmhouses, giving the style a cozy, informal intimacy that's popular even today.

The true Colonial Revival Style was marked by a faithful adherence to the symmetry, proportion and restraint of the 17th century prototypes. This early 20th century house has the symmetry and window placement of a simple early Georgian Colonial house. The doorway, with its fanlight and sidelights, is more characteristic of the later Federal houses.

The Dutch Colonial's most recognizable feature is the gambrel roof, which has been used here both for the main roof and for the front dormer. Wood shingles were a favored material for roof and siding. The fieldstone foundation adds a note of cozy informality. Colonial details, such as a Palladian window and classical porch columns, were often added to lend grace notes of elegance.

ON THE EAST COAST, the return to architectural roots meant a return to the English-based prototypes of the 17th and 18th centuries. On the West Coast, and in the Southwest, the colonial precedents were Spanish. The Mission Revival--based on re-use of the architectural forms of the Spanish missions-- had taken hold in California in the 1890's. However, the much broader-based Spanish Colonial Revival was given a major boost by the Panama-Pacific Exhibition held in San Diego in 1915.

THE SPANISH COLONIAL HOUSE is most readily recognized by its low irregular massing, stucco walls, and red clay tile roof. High walls topped by a red clay tile coping, enclosing a garden or patio, are another popular feature.

THE SPANISH COLONIAL REVIVAL, of course, was most often built where its prototypes were found: California, Florida, and the Southwest. However, home-buyers with a taste for the exotic had Spanish houses built all over the country--even in the Northeast, where low-pitched red tile roofs are hardly ideal for the harsh climate.

# The English Styles

EVEN AS SOME ARCHITECTS in the U.S. were striving for an "all-American" architecture, others in the romantic movement were looking back to the Old World for a sense of tradition and cultural values. Although there are some French, Italian, and Spanish prototypes that served as models for the revived interest in European architecture, most of the models came from England (as they did in the Victorian era). The new interest in English architecture began around 1910, after the crusade for an all-American architecture had peaked.

THERE WERE THREE basic English housing styles that found favor in the U.S. during the Post-Victorian era: (1) Tudor; (2) Cottage; (3) Country House. All can be termed "picturesque," but they differ significantly in the details.

## Tudor Revival

THE TUDOR REVIVAL HOUSE is readily identified by its half-timbering. Other features include numerous prominent gables, large medieval chimneys, and large, expansive windows with small panes set in lead casements. The nomenclature can get a bit confusing, however, since this house style can also be called "Elizabethan" or "Jacobean." One architectural historian threw up his hands and settled for the tongue-in-cheek term "Jacobethan."

A MAJOR ATTRACTION of the Tudor house was its picturesque composition, coupled with its association with the "Merrie Olde England" legend that had been fostered by numerous writers throughout the 19th century. The Tudor house began attracting attention from American architects as early as the 1880s, four decades before the English Cottage and Country House styles reached equivalent popularity in this country.

THE MOST PROMINENT TUDOR DETAIL was the half-timbering, which suggested rugged, hand-hewn strength. Since in the Tudor originals, the half-timbering was part of the actual framing system, this gave the Tudor house the added modern virtue of "honest expression of structure." (Of course, in the Tudor Revival buildings the half-timbers were merely decoration applied over a conventional frame. But at least the Revivals gave the illusion of honesty.)

## Cottage Style

LIKE THE TUDOR REVIVAL HOUSE, the English Cottage style is picturesque, but its prototypes are the all-masonry rural farmhouses of England rather than the larger timber-framed Tudor houses. The English Cottage house is described with words like "charming" and "quaint," and by emotional association embodies all the rustic honesty and simplicity of the English yeoman. It is a truly "homely" dwelling, suggesting hearth, family and all the domestic virtues.

THE ENGLISH COTTAGE looks as if it grew organically, suggesting that the owner built the house himself using stones that he tore from the land with his own two hands. Surrounding gardens and shrubs tie the cottage even more closely to the land.

The half-timbering and massive medieval chimneys are the hallmark of the Tudor Revival houses. They often have slate or tile roofs; entrance doors are frequently of heavy plank construction, with only a small window—perhaps protected by bars. The pediment over the front door recalls the attempts by designers in Elizabethan England to adapt Renaissance forms to their medieval buildings.

The English Cottage Style is meant to be quaint and charming. Often of stone, stucco or brick construction, the cottage is dominated by its roofline, which frequently has soft, flowing curves that recall the thatch roofs of the originals in the English countryside. As with this house, there are usually large expanses of wall space, pierced by relatively few windows. There's very little overhang to the roofs.

The English Country House Style is a sophisticated and stylized rendition of traditional English vernacular shapes, especially picturesque rooflines pierced by prominent gables. There is usually very little roof overhang. The broad bands of windows in this home recall the fenestration in Tudor houses. The pergola porch to the left is a design idea borrowed from the Craftsman movement.

## Country House

QUITE DIFFERENT from the Cottage style is the more polished and sophisticated English Country House style. In England, during the period from the turn of the century right up to World War I, there was a great flowering in the architecture of country houses. Country seats, once the province of the aristocracy, became affordable to the newly prosperous business class. Edwardian architects such as Edwin Lutyens and Ernest Newton designed self-assured if unintellectual houses for their well-to-do clients.

FOR SOME IN AMERICA, the English country house was the ultimate in good taste, traditional values, solidity, and old world charm. Little wonder, then, that many well-to-do Americans in the 'teens and 'twenties had their architects design for them a North American version of the English country house.

The modest second storey marks this as a semi-bungalow. The broad sloping roof recalls a Swiss chalet, while the knee braces on the eaves and the exposed rafter ends show some Craftsman influence. The large elephantine columns on the front porch are characteristic of many bungalows.

## Utilitarian Styles

### Craftsman

UTILITARIAN HOUSE STYLES can be split into two broad groups. First are those that sprang from a well-articulated philosophy, such as the Craftsman movement. Then there are those houses that evolved from vernacular American building forms.

STICKLEY PUBLISHED plans for many types of houses in his magazine. Because of this, strictly speaking there is no single "Craftsman" style--although there is a type of house that has come to bear this title. "Craftsman" was more a philosophy than an architectural style, and many houses, from simple cottages to large two-storey dwellings, can rightly lay claim to being "Craftsman."

THERE IS ALSO a philosophical and stylistic connection between the "Rectilinear Style" of the European Art Nouveau and the Craftsman/ Mission design that was being done in America. The work of architects like Mackintosh in Great Britain and Frank Lloyd Wright of the Prairie School bears a striking similarity to the work of Craftsman designers, the Roycrofters, and to the appearance of the bungalows built in Southern California around this time.

### Bungalow

CRAFTSMAN ARCHITECTURE has become identified with the bungalow. But the ubiquitous bungalow spread far beyond the confines of the Craftsman philosophy. The term "bungalow" can be applied to any picturesque one-storey house with a low-pitched roof and surrounding porches. Although Craftsman-inspired bungalows were common, it adapted well to the Spanish Colonial style for California, the Southwest, and Florida. The bungalow also appeared in such styles as Prairie, Swiss Chalet, Japanese, Adirondack Lodge--and even Greek Revival!

This particular bungalow has been rendered in the Craftsman style, but you could find bungalows interpreted in just about any style you might fancy. The basic bungalow was a picturesque, one-storey house with a low overhanging roof and broad porches. Here, the fieldstone column bases, exposed rafter ends, knee braces under the eaves, and natural shingle siding all proclaim the Craftsman influence.

CONSTRUCTION MATERIALS for the bungalow tended to be of the "natural" and "honest" variety. Fieldstones, shingles, stucco and the like were popular. Part of the bungalow ideal was an integration of interior space with the surrounding landscape. So in addition to broad porches, you often see attached arbors and pergolas; climbing vines reach up to embrace the bungalow. Fieldstone foundations and porch columns also enhance the illusion that the house sprang from the soil.

ALTHOUGH THE BUNGALOW was unpretentious, its rambling, spread-out floor plan made it a more expensive house to build than a two-storey house of comparable floor space. Some wags termed the bungalow "the least house for the most money." Nevertheless, the open floor plan and convenience of having everything on a

This simple two-storey house exhibits many of the features of the Craftsman Style: Expressed structure in the exposed rafter ends, prominent beams, knee braces at the eaves and large porch columns. Natural materials, such as fieldstone and wood shingles, relate the house to the soil; the expansive porch integrates exterior and interior spaces.

Combining simplicity, economy and versatility, the American Foursquare was one of the most popular house styles in the early 20th century. It's characterized by a two-storey boxlike shape, topped by a low hipped roof. There is usually a dormer in the front portion of the roof, and a porch extending across the full front of the house.

Emphasis on the horizontal line distinguishes houses influenced by the Prairie Style. Broad cantilevered roofs with flat eaves, solid walls with horizontal openings, and windows set in wide horizontal bands all heighten the effect. Stucco or Roman brick were favorite materials. In this example, the porch columns are much thicker than pure engineering would require, adding a note of solidity to the structure.

single floor made the bungalow extremely popular. The bungalow has disappeared from the builder's repertoire. A descendent, however, has replaced it--the modern ranch house.

## American Foursquare

IF THE BUNGALOW turned out to be the least house for the most money, then the popular American Foursquare was surely the most house for the least money. Not only did its box-like shape and hipped roof provide ample room for America's growing family, but it also epitomized the Craftsman ideal.

ALTHOUGH we don't today associate these unpretentious houses with the "Craftsman Style," Foursquares did in fact appear regularly in Stickley's magazine. And going by Stickley's dictum that "The ruling principle of the Craftsman house is simplicity," the Foursquare measures up admirably. The American Foursquare is simple, honest, substantial, practical and economical.

BUILDERS had a good time with it, too. Put an ersatz Palladian window in the dormer, and you could advertise "Colonial styling." Make the all-important porch of fieldstone, shingle the sides and call it "artistic." Extend the roof eaves, stretch out the porch, stucco the exterior and you've got a Prairie Style house.

BECAUSE THE FOURSQUARE was so adaptable and so practical, many thousands were built from the turn of the century through the 1920s. You can find this house in practically every neighborhood.

## Prairie

OFTEN ASSOCIATED with Louis Sullivan and Frank Lloyd Wright, the Prairie style flowed from the same reformist wellspring as Bungalows and Craftsman houses. It is identified by its emphasis on the horizontal line. In its classic form, the building is low and spread out, with broad low roofs cantilevered over walls and porches. Solid walls around porches and walks, as well as the massing of the house, create deep recesses and shadows.

STUCCO was the most common material used for siding on prairie houses, followed by Roman brick, coursed stone, and wood. With the exception of stucco, all siding materials were arranged in ways to emphasize the horizontal. In brickwork, for example, often the horizontal joints are deeply raked (creating dark horizontal shadow lines), while the vertical joints would be flush.

MATERIALS generally had an integral finish. That is, if the stucco were to be colored, the coloring agent was added to the stucco mix, rather than applying paint after the stucco had dried. Wood siding was often stained, rather than painted.

## Homestead House

IN ADDITION to the styles that had firm intellectual foundations, another type of house was popular in the early 20th century--the Homestead House. Its various forms derived not from philosophical theories printed in monthly magazines. Rather, it was an evolved style, having developed over a century of trial-and-error building by owners and contractors alike.

HOMESTEAD HOUSES had been built throughout the 19th century as farmhouses--the most utilitarian of all house types. The rectangular shape of the house body made it easy to frame and sheathe. The straightforward gable roof, lacking hips and valleys, was likewise easy for the country carpenter to lay out. And two storeys under one roof provided an economical ratio of floor-space to building shell.

THE HOMESTEAD HOUSE variants here, therefore, came from the suburbanization of the ubiquitous country farmhouse. Its distinctive shape, along with a lack of pretense to any "style" at all, makes the Homestead house a recognizable style all its own.

The most basic of all the house styles of the early 20th century is the Homestead House—a style that had evolved on numerous farms in the U.S. in previous decades. The body of the house is square or rectangular, topped by a simple gabled roof. The unselfconscious absence of any "style details" makes it a style unto itself.

A familiar variation of the Homestead House is the Tri-Gabled Ell. Here, the house takes on a simple ell shape, and the roof now has three gables instead of two. In some versions, the porch is tucked into the space formed by the two legs of the ell.

The Princess Anne house is a direct descendent of the **Queen Anne** style. It retains the asymmetrical massing, complex roofline and large chimneys of earlier Queen Anne houses. In keeping with the early 20th century desire for simplicity and restraint, however, the **Princess Anne** house exhibits little of the exterior ornamentation of its more exhibitionistic parent.

## Princess Anne

BY CALLING this style Princess Anne, we're emphasizing that it is a direct lineal descendent of the Victorian Queen Anne style. Queen Anne houses were immensely popular during the 1880s and '90s, but by the turn of the century, the style was falling out of favor because of its elaborate exterior.

TASTEMAKERS at the turn of the century were urging simplicity and restraint as the hallmarks of good taste. When they railed against the vulgarity and pretentiousness of earlier decades, the Queen Anne house was one they had in mind. Nevertheless, the asymmetrical plan of the Queen Anne allowed a lot of flexibility, and its ample interior space was still popular with home-buyers. So it was updated: Builders stripped off much of the ornamentation and simplified the exterior. This way, the house was also cheaper to build.

---

This survey article is only the beginning! In the coming year, we'll be running a whole series of articles about Post-Victorians, with more pictures that show variations of each style. Next month: The American Foursquare. *A book about early 20th-century houses will be published by The Old-House Journal this year.*

---

## A New Look At

# LINOLEUM

## Preservation's Rejected Floor Covering

By Leo Blackman and Deborah Dietsch

INOLEUM DESERVES renewed atten-
tion as a floor finish in its
own right, reflecting an important period of American taste
and history. Although it was a
commonly used floor covering in
turn-of-the-century houses, it
is rarely considered in today's
interior restorations. Viewed as an enemy by
restorers searching for hardwood finishes,
countless yards of linoleum are enthusiastically ripped off floors. Discarding it in
favor of tile or carpeting, many homeowners
fail to realize its historic importance.

THE ORIGINAL APPEAL of linoleum was based on
its qualities as an inexpensive, adaptable, and
resilient flooring. Patterned to resemble more
expensive finishes such as tile, wood, stone,
mosaic, and carpeting, it was offered in a
myriad of styles. By 1918, it was being marketed for use in every room of the house. Not
only was linoleum used to cover existing floors,
but it also became standard flooring in new construction. Its popularity stretched from its
invention in 1863 until 1974, when Armstrong
discontinued its production.

## Floorcloths

PAINTED FLOORCLOTHS, the precursor of lino-
elum, were used throughout the 19th century.
The earliest description of a floorcloth
dates from 1760; as late as 1909, similar
oilcloths were still being offered in Sears
catalogues. Floorcloths were made by waterproofing coarse fabric, woven of hemp or flax,
with oil paint. First, the fabric was stretched and coated with hot starch to stiffen and
seal it. Once dry, the surface was smoothed
with a pumice stone and paint was thickly applied to both sides of the fabric. After
several applications, a final coat of higher
quality paint was brushed on. Colored patterns
were painted by hand, stencilled, or stamped on
the surface with wooden blocks. After drying
for several days, the cloth was varnished. This
made the floorcloth waterproof and relatively
easy to maintain, but its painted surface wore
off quickly.

EXPERIMENTS IN THE MID-19TH CENTURY were tried
in order to develop more durable and resilient
floor coverings. Exotic combinations, such as
coconut fibers impregnated with cement and
shredded sponge mixed with paper pulp, met
with little commercial success. An exception
was Kamptulicon, invented by Elijah Galloway
in 1844. It was produced by heating India rubber, mixing it with granulated cork, and forcing the mixture between smooth cast-iron
rollers. Although more permanent than its
predecessors, Kamptulicon was very expensive
to produce, so it was used only by the wealthy,
or in public institutions. Linoleum was an
outgrowth of this search for a more substantial
and less expensive floorcloth.

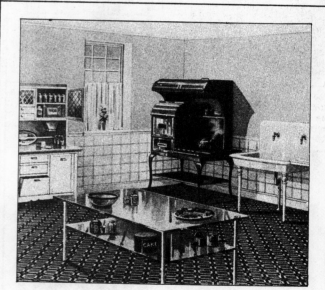

The modern dream kitchen after the turn of the century—
complete with a linoleum floor

THE WORD "LINOLEUM" comes from two Latin
words: linum, flax, and oleum, oil. Linseed oil, a heavy, amber-colored fluid
pressed from flax seed, is linoleum's chief
ingredient. When exposed to air, it begins to
thicken, changing into a tough, elastic material. Recognizing this quality, English

manufacturers applied linseed oil and fillers to a cloth backing in hopes of creating a superior floorcloth. Frederick Walton was the manager of Staines Co., a rubber and linoleum factory in England. While it's not clear who the original inventor of linoleum was, Walton can be credited with bringing the process and the product to America.

WALTON'S PROCESS used linseed oil and gum mixed with ground cork or wood flour, pressed onto burlap or canvas. He obtained an American patent for this process (but not the name) in 1869, when he formed the American Linoleum Manufacturing Co. in New York. (If Walton's name sounds familiar, you might recall his famous wallcovering--Lincrusta-Walton.)

THE ARMSTRONG COMPANY in Pittsburgh, Penn., founded in 1860, was primarily a manufacturer of cork bottle stoppers when it began production of linoleum at its Lancaster plant. Linoleum manufacturing, first thought to be an easy way of using leftover cork, soon became the company's most profitable line. Other companies were involved in the early manufacturing of linoleum: Michael Nairn, a Scottish manufacturer of floorcloths who started a plant in Kearny, NJ (1870), and George Washington Blabon, who installed the first linoleum calendering machine in the U.S. in his Trenton plant (1886).

## To Market, To Market

MARKETING GENIUS was partially responsible for the popularity of linoleum. Prior to 1917, linoleum was generally considered a sanitary flooring for use in kitchens, bathrooms, and public institutions. In an attempt to change linoleum's drab, utilitarian image, Armstrong staged a massive advertising campaign after World War I.

A sanitary bathroom

THE COMPANY provided its salesmen with pocket-size pattern books containing color plates of available stock and offered courses in "constructive linoleum sales." Advertisements were placed in magazines such as Ladies Home Journal, Women's Home Companion, and McCall's to acquaint the woman of the house with the decorative, economic, and labor-saving potential of linoleum. It was promoted as an "artistic" yet "sensible" flooring that would blend with any color scheme or decor. It was easy to clean because, unlike wood, it contained no cracks or crevices to catch dirt, and was promoted as sanitary for the kitchen or bathroom. Linoleum patterned to look like Brussels carpet, encaustic tile, or wood parquet was considered suitable for living rooms, dining rooms, or bedrooms. The perfect "modern" material, it was also used for auto running boards, countertops, and boat decks.

**Examples of printed linoleum patterns**

Pattern No. 7061

Pattern No. 7055

Pattern No. 7062

Pattern No. 7057

Pattern No. 7056

Pattern No. 7063

**Inlaid linoleum patterns**

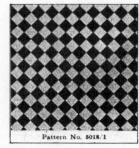
Pattern No. 5018/1

Pattern No. 5045/6

An ever-popular floral pattern

A later pattern from the 1950s

## Its Manufacture

LINOLEUM MANUFACTURING changed very little during the hundred years it was produced. It required the assemblage of raw materials from distant lands and their transportation to American factories. Linseed oil, pressed from Siberian flax; cork, stripped from trees in Spain; kauri gum, unearthed in New Zealand; and jute, harvested in Indian swamps, were the chief ingredients.

Mowing Flax in Western Siberia—Linseed oil is made from flax seed

RAW LINSEED OIL was boiled, pumped into conveyors, and dripped onto sheets of scrim, or gauze, that hung from ceiling to floor in oxidizing sheds. The oil thus absorbed oxygen from the air, achieving the consistency of caramel candy. The oil-soaked scrims, called "skins," were reduced to pulp. The pulp was heated with resins and kauri gum (fossilized sap from pine trees) to form a "cement." After cooling, chunks of this mixture were ground with cork flour.

The calendering machine

THE RESULTING PLASTIC MASS, resembling wet clay, was transferred to a calendering machine, which consisted of a series of heated rollers. The cork and the cement mixture were fed into the top of the machine, burlap entered at the bottom, and the materials were pressed tightly together. The linoleum was then hung in drying rooms and "seasoned" for three to four days before being printed and throughly inspected.

## Linoleum Types

SOME PATTERNS were available throughout the history of linoleum, others changed with current styles. "Hooked rug" and "wood planking" linoleum became popular during the Colonial Revival period; the 1930s and '40s saw the advent of Moderne-inspired patterns. A linoleum catalogue from the 1950s, while offering the mock-Jackson Pollock spattered effect, still featured standard Brussels carpet, jaspe, and wood designs.

OFTEN LINOLEUM was manufactured to a specific size, and printed to resemble a bordered carpet. Called a linoleum "rug," it was popular after 1910. Linoleum was also sold to be placed between a rug, either fabric or linoleum, and the walls. These linoleum borders were usually printed to resemble wood parquet or planking, and were sold in narrow rolls.

PRIOR TO 1927, linoleum was never textured and had a backing of canvas or hemp. In 1913-14, several manufacturers patented a process for calendering cork and linseed oil onto asphalt-impregnated paper. These products--such as Congoleum and Quaker rugs--were less durable and less expensive than canvas-backed linoleum. They were intended to make resilient flooring available to lower income groups.

UNTIL 1930, when embossed linoleum was introduced, five types of linoleum were available, each distinguished by the way it was manufactured. PRINTED LINOLEUM was patterned by machine painting with oil paints--one block for every color--on sheets of plain linoleum, typically brown. Printed linoleum was considered lower quality because the pattern was on the surface only. Many of the floral patterns were done in this manner.

PRINTED PATTERN

WOOD PARQUET

PLAIN LINOLEUM was manufactured in various thicknesses and solid colors such as grey, brown, brick red, and olive. The heavier grades of plain linoleum, known as BATTLESHIP LINOLEUM, ranged from 3/16 in. to 1/4 in. thick and were primarily used in public institutions.

INLAID LINOLEUM has a simple geometric pattern which goes through to the backing. Two types were produced. STRAIGHT LINE INLAID, identified by its sharply-defined pattern, was made by mechanically cutting sheets of plain linoleum into solid color "tiles." These were reassembled as a mosaic on burlap and bonded by heat and pressure. To produce GRANULATED INLAID, plain linoleum was pulverized into a colored powder and sifted through metal stencils onto an oiled paper sheet. This was repeated for several colors, then a canvas backing was placed on top and calendered. Next, the paper was peeled off, revealing a geometric pattern with soft, fuzzy borders.

JASPE LINOLEUM has a striated pattern, typically in two colors. It was most popular after 1900; it's described in advertisements as having the appearance of moire silk. Early jaspe was produced by rolling two sheets of colored linoleum up like a jelly roll, slicing it, and then calendering these pieces together.

GRANITE LINOLEUM was a staple of the early 20th-century catalogues. Described as appearing "like Terrazzo," it has a mottled surface and was produced by rolling out various colored chips of linoleum.

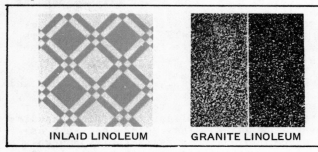

INLAID LINOLEUM          GRANITE LINOLEUM

## Vinyl Flooring

TODAY, VINYL FLOORING PATTERNS are still imitative of tile, stone, and wood--but there is a significant difference between vinyl and linoleum. The linoleum manufactured in the late 19th and early 20th century had a flat surface. In the search for verite and with the development of embossing machines, textured floors were introduced. Modern resilient flooring almost always has a sculpted surface to emphasize the pattern and

to camouflage scuffing. Gone are the more charming attempts to capture the look of plush carpeting, encaustic tile, or oak parquet on a two-dimensional plane. Solid color and simple geometric patterns, resembling plain or inlaid linoleum, are also absent. However, faux-marble vinyl is standard and similar to jaspe linoleum. Armstrong has re-issued its most popular linoleum pattern, in vinyl, #5352, a red flooring used primarily in kitchens. Perhaps they could also be encouraged to revive other 19th and early 20th century patterns. In the meantime, some contemporary vinyl patterns can be adapted to resemble linoleum in old houses.

## Linoleum's Fall--& Rise?

MATERIALS WHICH GAVE LINOLEUM its strength and resiliency also imparted certain problems of longevity, and use. As linseed oil continues to oxidize over time, the material tends to grow brittle and crack. Its amber tint also restricted the color range of linoleum--whites, rich blues, and purples were impossible to achieve. Staining was caused by the tannic acid in cork reacting with iron furniture. Linoleum's canvas backing made it sensitive to standing water.

PLASTIC PRODUCTS developed after World War II were rapidly applied to flooring. Vinyl, a colorless, waterproof, and monolithic material, could easily be patterned and textured. It was composed of synthetic materials and could be given a permanent no-wax shine. By the 1960s, linoleum was seen as an inferior product. It could no longer claim to be the most inexpensive, maintenance-free, durable, and resilient flooring it once was.

IN 1974, ARMSTRONG DISCONTINUED manufacturing linoleum because of reduced demand. However, the current high cost of manufacturing petroleum products makes an organically-based flooring more appealing and could prompt new interest in linoleum.

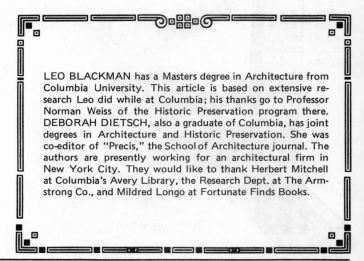

LEO BLACKMAN has a Masters degree in Architecture from Columbia University. This article is based on extensive research Leo did while at Columbia; his thanks go to Professor Norman Weiss of the Historic Preservation program there. DEBORAH DIETSCH, also a graduate of Columbia, has joint degrees in Architecture and Historic Preservation. She was co-editor of "Precis," the School of Architecture journal. The authors are presently working for an architectural firm in New York City. They would like to thank Herbert Mitchell at Columbia's Avery Library, the Research Dept. at The Armstrong Co., and Mildred Longo at Fortunate Finds Books.

# Rack On A High-Pitched Roof

## & Some Tips On Chimney Care

By Joseph V. Scaduto

HAVING ONLY TWO HANDS becomes quite a problem when you find yourself precariously perched on a roof. This fact was pointedly brought to my attention several years ago. I had been thinking about repairing the chimney on my home. From the street, it was evident that the mortar joints between the bricks had eroded and a dangerous condition now existed.

IN THE PAST, I had done several pointing and repair jobs on the chimneys of buildings that I owned. But there was a major difference between my home and those apartment buildings: The apartment buildings all had flat roofs. These flat roofs did not pose the gravity problem that I was now facing on my own residence.

GETTING UP ON THE RIDGE of my roof was not a major problem. The real difficulty would be how to maintain my balance and at the same time use both hands to work on the chimney.

I also wanted to keep the bucket of mortar and all my various tools from falling off the roof. I figured that I would need one hand to hold the pointing tool and another to hold the trowel with the mortar. But I'd also need a hand to hold the bucket of mortar and possibly another hand to help me maintain my balance. If my arithmetic serves me correctly, I would need a minimum of three hands!

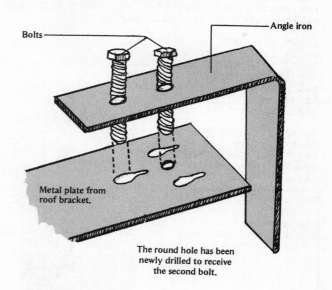

Bolts

Angle iron

Metal plate from roof bracket.

The round hole has been newly drilled to receive the second bolt.

I HAVE ONLY TWO HANDS, so I decided to ask for advice from the experts. I checked with several local masonry dealers and contractors, and received many different suggestions. Some told me to hang the bucket of mortar from the chimney. Others suggested that I build staging adjacent to the work area. A few told me to hire a mason to do the job.

NONE OF THESE ANSWERS satisfied me. It would be difficult to work on the chimney and at the same time have the bucket of mortar hanging from it. Moreover, the chimney was directly in the center of the house, and so building staging would not serve my purpose. This job became a challenge to me, and I decided to create my own extra hands.

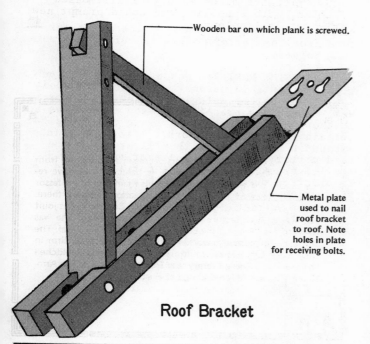

Wooden bar on which plank is screwed.

Metal plate used to nail roof bracket to roof. Note holes in plate for receiving bolts.

**Roof Bracket**

**W**HAT I CAME UP WITH worked better than I had anticipated. I hope that some of the readers can use it not only for work on their chimneys but for any repairs that have to be performed on a high-pitched roof.

MY CREATION WAS SIMPLE. I merely took an existing item and slightly modified it. I used two roofing racks or brackets (the type used by roofers when they plank a roof). I made up two pieces of angle iron that I bolted to the metal ends of the roof brackets. With the addition of the angle irons, the roof brackets could now be hung securely on the ridge of the roof. They could also be adjusted to any pitch that might be required. I then added a short plank across the two mounted roof brackets, screwing it onto both wooden bars. Voila! I had solved my problem. I could safely set on the platform not only my mortar, but also any tools that I might need. The possibility of anything sliding off the roof was now eliminated. And there was no potential for an accident from having tools underfoot. I only needed two hands after all-- and a little imagination.

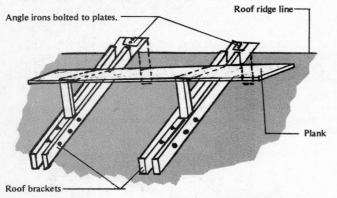

Angle irons bolted to plates.
Roof ridge line
Plank
Roof brackets

### The Finished Product

THIS RACK IS INTENDED to hold only tools and supplies, not people. DO NOT STAND ON IT. If you need a larger platform to support yourself as well, and you're willing to spend some money, then a chimney scaffold such as Gold-blatt's is an excellent idea. Or you could hire a mason--many people find it far more pleasant to remain on the ground than to climb around on the roof. But if you're a do-it-yourselfer who is not at all squeamish about heights, then I think you'll find that this portable rack can be a great help. It's certainly been a help to me!

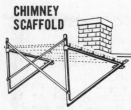
# Chimney Tips

## On Repair

**1** SAFETY FIRST: When working on a roof, wear soft-soled shoes--preferably high-top sneakers with good ankle support. If the roof is especially steep, lay a ladder on the roof and secure it with a safety bracket hooked over the ridge. You should also wear a nylon safety belt with a nylon lanyard. But if heights frighten you, have someone else do the job.

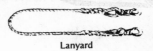
Belt                Lanyard

**2** CUT IT OUT: Repointing a chimney involves the removal of all loose mortar, to a depth of at least an inch, and replacing it with new mortar. Once the defective mortar is removed, be sure to brush out all dust and loose material.

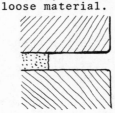
Using a hand chisel, rake out the mortar joints to a depth of at least 1 inch.

**3** DON'T FORGET TO FLUSH: Be sure to hose down all areas that will be repaired. Flushing with water will help get rid of any remaining particles of mortar, as well as moisten the areas that will be receiving the mortar. Failure to wet down these areas may result in the adjacent bricks absorbing moisture from the mortar. This in turn can create weak joints.

**4** MATCH THE MORTAR: Nobody can really see the joints in masonry way up on the roof, so why bother matching the existing mortar? Well, there's a practical reason as well as an aesthetic one. Some mortars are too rigid for certain types of brickwork. When the bricks expand in hot weather, they'll break on the hard mortar; when they contract in the cold, they'll crack away from the mortar. For more information on matching mortars, consult The Repointing of Historic Masonry Buildings by

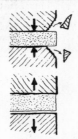
The hazards of using a too-hard mortar. Top: Breaking of bricks when they expand in hot weather. Bottom: Cracking caused by the contraction of bricks in cold weather.

Robert Mack and James Askins. It's available for $3 from Preservation Resource Group, 5619 Southampton Drive, Dept. OHJ, Springfield, VA 22151. (703) 323-1407.

**5 USE THE RIGHT TOOLS:** I use two trowels, a broad one to hold the mortar and a thin one to push it in. Don't be afraid to use a lot of mortar and really pack it in hard. You should strike the joint for weather-tightness and a neat appearance. I prefer concave joints, which should be made with a convex jointer.

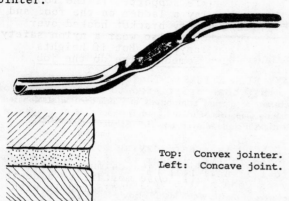

Top: Convex jointer.
Left: Concave joint.

**6 PRE-HYDRATION?:** Many masons pre-hydrate the mortar to prevent it from shrinking excessively. To pre-hydrate, you first have to mix up your ingredients with just enough water to produce a damp mass that will retain its form when compressed into a ball. Then let it set for an hour. Afterwards, mix it with the amount of water required to produce a stiff but workable consistency. This technique is still rather controversial, however. Conservation experts and professional masons say that pre-hydrating is an unnecessary procedure that weakens the mortar. Today's Type S lime has many advocates; it's already pre-hydrated and so doesn't require this procedure.

**7 CURE IT:** Concrete work is usually cured; that is, the cement is kept moist until it develops its maximum strength. I think even mortar joints should be cured as well, to ensure that they don't dry out too rapidly. There are a couple of ways this can be done. One way is to hose down the chimney for 3 consecutive days. Another way is to keep the chimney draped in damp burlap for at least 3 days--but don't do this if the chimney is in operation!

**8 MURIATIC ACID:** No matter how diligent you are when you work with cement, you will get some stains on the bricks. Wait a day or more after working on the chimney repairs, and then use a solution of 1 part muriatic acid and 10 parts water. This solution should remove any cement stains. Please note that this acid is strong, so carefully read and follow the directions on the container. Be sure to hose down the chimney afterwards, to remove any remaining salts.

# On Maintenance

**1 TV ANTENNAS:** Don't use your chimney as an anchor for a TV antenna. A great many chimney problems are directly related to the structural stress placed on them by the antenna's movement in strong winds. An additional problem occurs when the rusting metal starts to stain the chimney.

**2 FLUE LININGS:** Many older homes do not have chimney flue liners. Mortar and bricks in an unlined flue are directly exposed to the action of flue gases and will disintegrate. This disintegration, along with harm caused by temperature changes, can open cracks in the masonry. These cracks will reduce the draft and increase the fire hazard. They also permit poisonous flue gases to escape into the house. If you presently have a chimney that is not lined, then you should seriously consider having a liner installed.

**3 CHIMNEY FIRES:** If you are burning wood in either a fireplace or a wood-burning stove, then the formation of creosote is unavoidable. The chimney should be cleaned frequently; never wait more than a year between manual cleanings. Some people clean their chimneys by burning a very hot fire for a period of time each day. If you are burning wood in an air-tight stove, then consider cleaning after every 3 or 4 cords of wood. Failure to clean out creosote buildup will result in a fire. A professional chimney sweep will clean your chimney, fireplace, and stove for a very reasonable fee.

**4 CHIMNEY FLASHING:** You should have strips of metal around the chimney/roof line. This flashing sometimes pulls away from the chimney. Many chimneys have lead flashing, which can be gently tapped back into place. Other types of metal flashing can be repaired by applying roofing cement both under and over it. *(This procedure is what we call "the black-gunk solution." It works--at least for a while--but you have to check it and maintain it diligently. At some point the metal flashing itself will require replacement. Just remember never to use the black-gunk solution on visible areas of the roof.--The Editors)*

**5 ANNUAL CHECKUP:** Go over your chimney once a year. Repair those minor problems before they become major headaches. If you have any suspicions about the safety of your chimney, then consult a professional. Check your local directory under the headings for masons, chimney sweeps, or a professional group such as the American Society of Home Inspectors.

JOSEPH V. SCADUTO is a general contractor, builder, and home inspector working in the Boston area. He is Secretary of the New England chapter of the American Society of Home Inspectors, and President of Tri-Value Consultants, a firm that deals with the inspection and renovation of older homes. He's worked on a lot of roofs, too.

# Refinishing Clinic
## Using The Right Products

HOMEOWNERS WORKING WITH WOOD frequently feel that they are confronted by a multitude of fillers, sealers, stains, dyes, putties, shellacs, lacquers, waxes, oils, and varnishes, each potion with its own devotees and detractors. This Refinishing Clinic should help to demystify these products. We'll be examining what they are, what they can do, and which woods they're appropriate for.

### Filling Compounds

SOME WOODS, such as oak, mahogany, and ash, have an open grain. These "large-pored" woods have an exposed cellular structure and will need to be filled with paste wood filler prior to varnishing. Without this filler, a smooth finish is difficult to achieve. Generally, filling will not be done if you'll be using an oil finish. Sometimes renewed old wood doesn't need filling the way brand-new, unfinished wood does. Test in an inconspicuous place.

FILLING COMPOUNDS come in three varieties: paste wood filler, putty, and plastic wood.

PASTE WOOD FILLER is used before varnishing, but not with penetrating oil finishes. It packs the small, exposed cell structure of open-grain wood in such a way that finish varnish flows over the surface. (It's very difficult to get a smooth varnish job on open-grain wood without filling.) Be sure to read the label: Some paste wood fillers are supposed to be applied after the stain; others, prior to staining. It's generally recommended to choose a product used prior to staining, as it avoids the greyness that occurs in certain woods. Paste wood fillers also come in many colors. In making a selection, you should try to approximate the basic color of the wood. This stuff is not intended for use as a crack filler; there are other compounds for that purpose.
**Manufacturers of paste wood filler include Daly's, Behlen, Zar, Gulf, Duratite, and Elmer's.**

PUTTY is best for filling nail holes, and is to be used after staining and sealing. Use it last of all if you're doing an oil finish. Use it after the first coat of varnish, but before the last coat. If you use it before the finish is applied, you may stain the wood. There are two basic types of putty.
(1) NON-HARDENING OIL-BASED: This kind is tinted to the final color by the user. It is the same as the putty used for glazing windows.

In a pinch, synthetic glazing compounds work as well.
(2) WAXY FILL STICKS: These are crayonlike sticks that come pre-tinted to the final color. **Manufacturers of glazing compounds and non-hardening oil-based putty include Dap, Bix, Rutland, and Durham's. Manufacturers of waxy fill sticks include Minwax and H.F. Staples & Co.**

PLASTIC WOOD is a hard-drying cellulose compound used to fill larger voids. While often sold to fill nail holes as well, it is not nearly as good as the softer putties. **Manufacturers of plastic wood include Boyle-Midway/3-in-1.**

### Interior Prime-Sealers

WOODS SUCH AS pine, fir, hemlock, and maple are close-grain woods. They have a smooth texture and need not be filled prior to the staining and finishing steps. Old, previously finished wood which has been stripped probably won't need prime-sealer either. New wood or heavily-sanded old wood should be "sealed" prior to staining or finishing.

A NOTE ABOUT interior prime-sealers: The word "sealer" is somewhat misleading. In the context of priming surfaces, these products should not be confused with finishing compounds such as penetrating oil finishes, which actually "seal" the surface with a coating. What these products do instead is set the wood grain prior to the application of stains or finish coats. Without priming, the final result can be rough and uneven (especially when bare or sanded wood is stained). Without the prime-sealer, dark, spotty areas can appear where wild-grain areas absorb more stain or finish than the rest of the wood. **Manufacturers of interior prime-sealers include most major paint companies.**

### Interior Stains

THERE ARE TWO GENERAL TYPES of interior stains: surface and penetrating. Surface types come in either a brushable varnish base, or a spray lacquer. Both surface types are hard to handle when working on fine pieces, so this discussion will center on the penetrating types, which can be applied with a rag.

PENETRATING STAINS are available in two types.
(1) PIGMENT: The major advantage of this type is that it is colorfast and easier to wipe.
(2) DYE: This type has excellent color depth and brilliance, but sun-fades badly. Dye stain is available in both a water-soluble

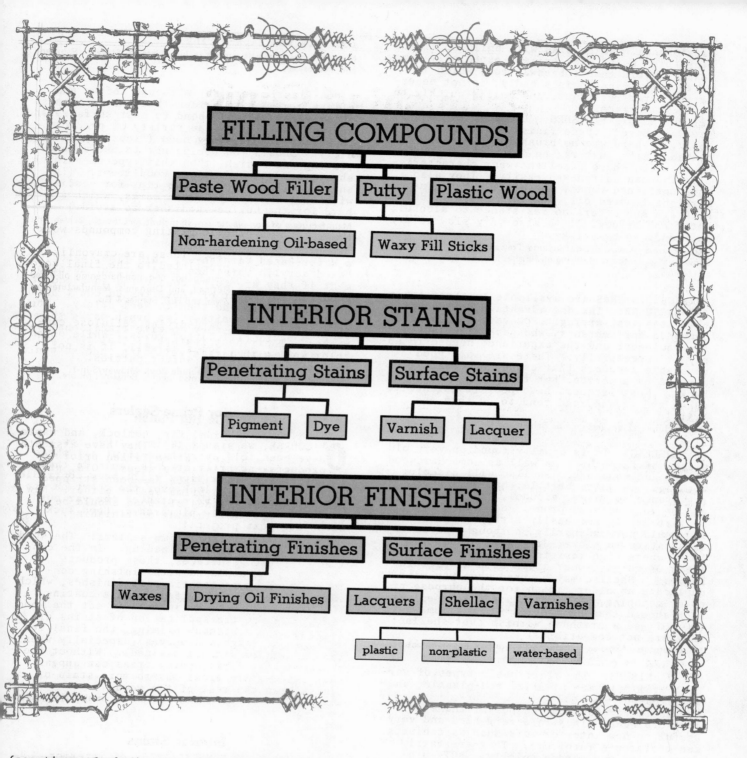

**FILLING COMPOUNDS**
- Paste Wood Filler
- Putty
  - Non-hardening Oil-based
  - Waxy Fill Sticks
- Plastic Wood

**INTERIOR STAINS**
- Penetrating Stains
  - Pigment
  - Dye
- Surface Stains
  - Varnish
  - Lacquer

**INTERIOR FINISHES**
- Penetrating Finishes
  - Waxes
  - Drying Oil Finishes
- Surface Finishes
  - Lacquers
  - Shellac
  - Varnishes
    - plastic
    - non-plastic
    - water-based

(sometimes alcohol) and an oil-soluble base, both of which are non-grain-raising. Because of their depth of color, dye stains are often used in advance of a pigment stain as a pre-color and then treated with the pigment type for colorfastness and durability. In most instances, dye stains are best finished with a varnish system.

Manufacturers of pigment stains include Daly's, Behlen, Benjamin Moore, and Zar. Manufacturers of dye stains include Behlen.

**Interior Finishes**

INTERIOR FINISHES come in two major categories: penetrating and surface. Penetrating finishes are usually dull or satin; surface finishes, gloss or semi-gloss. Surface finishes include lacquers, shellac, and varnishes.

PENETRATING FINISHES come in two types. (1) WAX: Because waxes remain very light in color over a long period of time, they are excellent for panelling. They're also useful as a final polish to varnished wood. However, waxes tend to waterspot, and so require maintenance. Waxes also will build up if too many thick coats are applied--especially spray waxes. Avoid these; beeswax too, which is quite soft, fingerprints badly, is not necessarily water-resistant, and builds quickly to a sticky surface.

(2) DRYING OIL FINISHES: Usually tung and linseed oil-based, these finishes are easy to apply. (There are no brush marks or dust to contend with; just rag on and wipe off the excess.) They have excellent wear characteristics and can be renewed easily. They also tone unstained woods. We don't suggest using straight linseed oil, however. It will darken with age and offers no resistance to alcohol, water, or mildew. It's also very slow to dry and tends to be sticky.

**Manufacturers of wax finishes include Trewax, Butcher's Wax, and Minwax. Manufacturers of drying oil finishes includes Daly's, Hope's, and Minwax.**

SURFACE FINISHES are available in three types.
(1) LACQUERS: The one advantage of lacquer is that it's fast-drying. However, it isn't recommended for amateurs, who generally lack both the equipment and the experience needed to apply it successfully. There are some good brushable lacquers that can be successfully applied by a novice, but there are still drawbacks. Most lacquers have poor resistance to water and grease, and tend to be thin and brittle.

**Manufacturers of lacquers include Behlen and Deft.**

(2) SHELLAC: It is usually found on very old pieces of furniture, as well as some hardwood floors and woodwork. Shellac will discolor with age, is quite brittle, has very poor resistance to water, alcohol, and abrasion, and is very scratch-prone. So even though it is fast-drying and easily stripped and renewed, it should not ordinarily be thought of as an alternative to slower-drying varnishes--at least where high resistance to wear is needed. (It's OK for non-wear items such as picture frames.) Shellac may be used when you wish to duplicate an older finish for the purpose of color-matching, but a standard oil-based varnish should then be applied for maximum wear. (DO NOT use a urethane varnish over shellac; they are not compatible.)

**Manufacturers of shellac include most major coatings manufacturers.**

(3) VARNISHES: The three basic types of varnish available are plastic, non-plastic, and water-based.
● Plastic Varnish--called polyurethane or just urethane. These are very hard and very useful on new interior work such as cabinets and children's furniture. They are fairly fast-drying and harden quickly. BUT--urethanes may not bond well to older surfaces, especially if the older surface was shellacked (which is very common on antique wood). If the item has an older shellac job, and you plan to use varnish, then don't use urethane; use a standard oil-based varnish instead.

Urethanes do not do well on areas exposed to weather, especially direct sunlight. Thus they should never be used on front doors, exterior smooth siding, window trim, railing, or marine surfaces. The proper treatment for varnishing exterior surfaces is to use a standard marine spar. But don't use a spar varnish on interior items because the product is too soft and slow-drying.

**Manufacturers of plastic varnish include Pierce & Stevens (Fabulon) and McCloskey.**

● Non-Plastic Varnish--Although softer and slightly slower to harden than the urethanes, these varnishes will bond to most surfaces and are available in a wide variety of products to answer almost every need (floors, panelling, etc.). Should you decide not to use a penetrating oil finish, then this type of varnish should be used on antique wood items. (In another clinic, we'll give tips for dealing with dust specks and brush marks, which are hard for the novice varnisher to avoid.)

**Manufacturers of non-plastic varnish include McCloskey, Behlen, and Hope's.**

● Water-Based Varnish--At this time, water-based acrylic varnishes need further development if they are to be considered an adequate wood finish. Most of those tested don't harden well enough and tend to feel sticky. They don't level well either, so brush marks show up even more than they do with traditional varnishes. Their best feature is that they hold color well with little yellowing, and so would be good for panelling.

**Manufacturers of water-based varnish include Benjamin Moore.**

## The Big Finish

OF COURSE, we aren't claiming that now you have been told everything about all these products--no brief article could do that. If any of the definitions still seem contradictory or confusing, look over the chart on the previous page: We've presented the various products in a simple hierarchy. Good luck with your next project!

---

PRODUCT INFORMATION

You can go into any hardware store and find fill sticks and plastic varnish without any difficulty. Obtaining certain other filling compounds, prime-sealers, stains, or finishes can be more problematic. If the regular hardware or paint stores don't have what you want, then try a building supply store or a lumberyard. You can also approach these manufacturers directly: Behlen, McClosky, Daly's, Benjamin Moore, Deft, Minwax, and Hope's are all listed in the OHJ Catalog.

---

MUCH OF THIS ARTICLE was adapted from a booklet written by Jim Daly, president of Daly's Wood Finishing Products. For a free catalog detailing his full line of products, write to Jim Daly, Daly's Wood Finishing Products, 1121 N. 36th Street, Dept. OHJ, Seattle, WA 98103. (206) 633-4204.

# Restorer's Notebook

## Cheap Alcohol

**B**ECAUSE YOU ARE my favorite, most useful magazine, I thought I'd share a tip with you.

DENATURED ALCOHOL is used by the gallons when restoring. I use it for taking off old shellac and rinsing off paint remover. It costs about $8 per gallon, so I'm not surprised that so many old houses are left to crumble.

MANY GAS STATIONS sell gasahol, a mixture of gas and denatured (or "wood") alcohol. I asked a gas station owner if I could use gasahol. When he found out that I was restoring a 10-room home full of golden oak woodwork, he understood my cost-conscious attitude. It turned out that he mixed his own gasahol, as many gas station owners do. He had plenty of denatured alcohol on hand, and sold it to me dirt cheap: I saved about $5 per gallon!

SO ALL YOU HOME RENO'S, stop going to your hardware store and start going to your nearest gasahol station instead--and save a bundle. If more old homes are to be saved, let's spread the news of cheaper ways of doing it before it turns into a rich person's game instead of the average person's dream.

Karen Lang
North Judson, IN

## Sculpture & Paint

**W**E HAVE FOUND THE ULTIMATE SOURCE for tools to pick paint out of mouldings, carvings, etc. It's a sculptor's supply house. They have literally hundreds of high-quality metal tools in every conceivable shape. We've also used some of their small files for reshaping replacement details in plaster.

OUR FAVORITE TOOL has been the "#155 Wax Tool" (page 18 in their catalog) which we've used to scoop paint out of all the mouldings on our parlor floor. The tool cost $7. The company also stocks polishing compounds and buffing wheels for refinishing marble; we've put them to good use too.

THE ONLY CAUTION is that many of the tools are imported, which means that sometimes they are out of stock and it takes a while for replacements to arrive. It's best to visit the store and see what's available, but they also do a brisk mail-order business. You can get their catalog by sending $1 to Steve Eisenberg, Sculpture Associates, 114 East 25th Street, New York, NY 10010.

Elliott Gerber & Helene Greece
Brooklyn, NY

## Remote-Control Inspection

**T**HERE IS A WAY to examine closely the steep, high roof of an old house without climbing up there and risking damage to both the roofing material and yourself: Use binoculars. Just go across the street, a good distance away so you can get a good view of the roof. (An upper-storey window of a neighbor's house is ideal.) You can then easily sight roof details close-up through the binoculars.

Maxine J. Kyle
Decatur, IL

## Defeating Contact Cement

**A**FTER I REMOVED THE LINOLEUM from my kitchen countertops, I discovered that there was contact cement underneath them. Every flooring store in town told me that it was impossible to remove contact cement, and that some kind of covering would have to go back on. I tried using paint remover, mineral spirits, lacquer thinner, and shellac thinner, all to no avail. But I finally came upon the answer: isopropyl alcohol, which is available at any local grocery or drug store. Just pour on a couple of coats--each coat about five minutes apart--and the contact cement will lift up.

Kris A. Layman
Cheyenne, WY

## Polishing Screw Heads

**H**ERE'S HOW I POLISH brass screw heads safely and rapidly. I insert them in short lengths of rubber tubing, about 3 or 4 in. long, and hold them thus secured against the buffing wheel or wire brush. (The tubing has to be of a diameter that will just accommodate the shaft of the screw.) After polishing, I place the screws, heads up, in a length of wood 1 in. x 2 in. x 3 ft. long, in which I have bored a series of holes, 1/8 in. and ¼ in. in diameter and all ½ in. deep. Then I spray them with spray lacquer or clear spray. When they're dry, I tip the board over and all the screws fall out, ready for assembly in the proper place.

Mark E. Leistickow
Green Bay, WI

### Got Any Tips?

Do you have any hints or short cuts that might help other old-house owners? We'll pay $15 for any short how-to items that are used in this "Restorer's Notebook" column. Send your hints to: Notebook Editor, The Old-House Journal, 69A Seventh Avenue, Brooklyn, N.Y. 11217.

# Helpful Publications

The Antiques Book of Victorian Interiors
Compiled by Elisabeth Donaghy Garrett
1981  (160 pp., profusely illustrated)  Cloth

FOR EVERYONE INTERESTED in the interiors of Victorian houses, this colorful, pictorial account features the interiors of America's most famous Victorian homes.  These opulent period rooms include those of Olana in Church Hill, New York, the Mark Twain house in Hartford, Connecticut, Biltmore in Asheville, North Carolina, Chateau-sur-Mer in Newport, Rhode Island, the Theodore Roosevelt Birthplace in New York City, and selected early interiors of designers Carrere and Hastings.

THE ARTICLES are a compilation from the magazine "Antiques" and focus on Victorian architecture as well as furnishings, wall and floor coverings, fabrics, window treatments, and other decorative ornaments.  Also included with the historical descriptions are insights into the lives of the people who lived in them. The full character of these homes is revealed by 240 color and black and white photographs.

To order, send $19.95 plus $1.50 postage to:
      Crown Publishers, Inc.
      One Park Avenue--Dept. OHJ
      New York, New York  10016
      (212) 532-9200


American Architecture 1607-1976
Marcus Whiffen and Frederick Koeper
1981  (495 pp., generously illustrated)  Cloth

American Shelter: An Illustrated Encyclopedia of the American Home
Lester Walker
1981  (320 pp., profusely illustrated)  Cloth

THESE BOOKS ARE VALUABLE additions to the resources in the vast and varied field of American architecture.  The chronological survey format of each book is, however, characterized by a wholly different view of America's building heritage.

FOR THE STUDENT of architecture, American Architecture 1607-1976 is a comprehensive scholarly examination of America's building periods and styles.  The emphasis is on examples of American architecture which have a certain historical and architectural significance, and as a result, forgoes other examples of the built environment. The text is detailed and authoritative; its straightforward, building-by-building survey is an excellent basic reference source.

MARCUS WHIFFEN examines America's buildings from 1607 to 1860 with an historical perspective, adding many comparisons of American and European architecture.  Frederick Koeper studies the works of individual architects to describe the period 1860 to 1976.  The book, amply illustrated with black and white photographs and line drawings, is "...likely to become one of the standard works on the subject for some years to come."(William Morgan, University of Louisville)

AMERICAN SHELTER IS A USEFUL resource for the architect, designer, builder, and others interested in the different major and minor styles of the American home.  It centers on the importance of the free-standing single-family dwelling as shelter and as a symbol of American culture.  The text briefly outlines the basics of the origin, evolution, architectural detail, and construction methods and materials of each major style and vernacular variation.  The book is primarily a picture book, one which depicts the American home as a three dimensional object through the use of 1000 exploded diagrams, floor plans, and side elevations.

LESTER WALKER, architect, teacher, and author, portrays 110 kinds of single family homes, from conventional styles (Saltbox, Georgian, Italianate, and Shingle), to more uncommon types (Inflatable, Fantasy, Underground, and Floating). Quips architect Charles Moore, it's "...a genuine feast for the eyes and mind."

To order American Architecture, send $30.00 plus $2.25 postage to:
      The MIT Press--Dept. OHJ
      Massachusetts Institute of Technology
      Cambridge, Massachusetts  02142
      (617) 253-2884

To order American Shelter, send $22.95 plus $2.00 postage to:
      The Old-House Bookshop
      69A Seventh Avenue
      Brooklyn, New York  11217


New Energy From Old Buildings
National Trust for Historic Preservation
1981  (208 pp., illustrated)  Paper

THIS BOOK, THE RESULT of a national symposium on energy conservation and its relationship to preservation, gathers together the ideas and recommendations of nationally known preservation architects and energy professionals They suggest ways to reduce energy consumption (by combining the innate energy efficiency features of old buildings with new energy conservation systems) while retaining America's architectural heritage.

THE ARTICLES include discussions of the inherent energy saving features of old buildings, the concept of embodied energy, passive and active retrofit techniques, and the legal implications of using solar devices in historic buildings.  Especially helpful is the article entitled, "How to Save Energy in an Older House which contains an exhaustive chart of conservation techniques.  Also included is an energy glossary and energy information sources.

To order, send $9.95 plus $2.50 postage to:
      The Preservation Bookshop
      1600 H Street, N.W.--Dept. OHJ
      Washington, D.C.  20006
      (202) 673-4061

# Ask OHJ

## Scagliola

**D**O YOU HAVE ANY INFORMATION on a process called scagliola? I believe it is the art of hand-painting plaster to resemble marble. I would like to know how to do it, and what tools and materials will be required. Unfortunately, my library has not been very useful.

--Maureen Wilke  Buffalo, NY

**S**CAGLIOLA is a specialty plastering method that uses colored plaster to create the appearance of marble. The color is part of the material itself in this method (as opposed to marbleizing, where the color is painted onto the surface). Scagliola is a highly-specialized finish that is rarely practiced today. It's very difficult to do, and so is not generally a do-it-yourself craft. There are plastering books that can be found in libraries and technical schools which will give you more information about this process. But we don't know of any book currently in print that describes the process in any detail.

*(As you can see, we don't have a great deal of information ourselves. Can any of our readers recommend a good craftsperson who still practices scagliola? How about an authoritative book on the subject?--The Editors)*

## Insulating The Attic

**M**Y HOUSE IS 60+ YEARS OLD, with a well-ventilated, wooden-floored attic. Under the floor there is about 3 inches of rock wool insulation, with no vapor barrier. The attic is unheated and unused, and will remain so for at least another 15 years. I have purchased enough 6-inch, foil-backed insulation to cover the attic. My question is, where should I place it, on the floor (foil down) or in between the roof rafters?

--Glenn Stein  Great Neck, NY

**Y**OU WON'T BE HEATING THE ATTIC, so you might just as well lay the insulation down on the floor. The problem here is that you shouldn't put foil-backed insulation down over the other insulation; the vapor barrier will trap moisture in the house. See if you can exchange the foil-backed for the unfoiled kind. If you can't, then slash the foil before laying down the insulation. When you are ready to heat and use the attic, you can reuse that insulation with a new polyethylene vapor barrier facing indoors.

## Cracked Houses

**H**ERE'S THE PROBLEM: My house is made of wood and has a painted brick foundation wall; there is a 2-foot crawlspace under the entire house and verandah. There are two downspouts at opposite ends of the northwest wall. For years they have emptied out onto two splash blocks. But midway between these splash blocks is a depression in which a large puddle has settled. I believe it has caused the brick foundation behind it to settle and leave a 3-inch x 8-foot space between the top of the foundation and the bottom of the wooden sill. Recently, the interior wall along the stairway has begun to show signs of stress: cracks and falling bits of plaster. What can I do about this nasty gap between the sill and the foundation?

--Kenneth Koskela  Zephyrhills, FL

**F**IRST YOU HAVE TO WEDGE THE CRACK. (The December 1981 OHJ explains this procedure.) Then dig a hole to check the foundation. After redirecting the water flow away from the house, use telltales to see if the crack is still moving. If it has stopped, then fill in the space with drypack mortar; if it hasn't, then you'll have to have an architect go over the house.

## Rescuing Lincrusta

**I**S THERE ANY SAFE WAY to remove layers of paint from Lincrusta-Walton? The exquisite details of this beautifully-patterned material in my entryway are obscured by several layers of paint, including the "classic" glossy dentist-office green!

--K.E. Possler  Lancaster, PA

**T**HERE IS NO SAFE WAY THAT WE KNOW OF to completely remove paint from Lincrusta. The methylene chloride in chemical strippers will dissolve the linseed oil in the paper; and you certainly don't want to use heat on paper. But you can safely remove some of the paint by applying lacquer thinner and rubbing with 0 steel wool. (We'd still recommend trying this out on an unobtrusive test patch, however.) When you've removed enough paint to have restored some of the detail, you should refinish the Lincrusta. First put down a ground coat of oil-based paint--one which simulates the original look of the Lincrusta. Then apply a glaze over it, as the original owner would have. Glazes are available from Wolf Paints, 771 Ninth Avenue, Dept. OHJ, New York, NY 10019. (212) 245-7777.

General interest questions from subscribers will be answered in print. The Editors can't promise to reply to all questions personally—but we try. Send questions with sketches or photos to Questions Editor, The Old-House Journal, 69A Seventh Avenue, Brooklyn, NY 11217.

# Restoration Products News

## The Source for Products and Services for Old Buildings

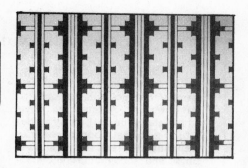

This month—a selection of products especially appropriate for the turn-of-century house.

## Help For Your Hoosier

A "Hoosier" could usually be found in turn-of-century kitchens. These handy cupboards, which often had a sugar dispenser and a flour sifter built in, are once again becoming popular. However, replacement parts are often difficult to find. One source we managed to locate was Furniture Revival & Co. Here you can find a complete selection of "Hoosier" hardware including the brackets needed to attach the top section to the lower cupboard. (They stock both the top- and side-mounted styles.) These brackets, $56.10/pair, are made of 16-18 gauge stamped steel and painted dull metallic silver. Also available are solid brass "Hoosier" door latches and hinges. And, to complete the restoration of your "Hoosier"— flour and sugar dispensers (about $63 and $56).

The company also carries many other hard-to-find hardware items including icebox and roll-top desk hardware. A catalog ($1.50) is offered. Furniture Revival & Co., PO Box 994, Dept. OHJ, Corvallis, OR 97339. (503) 754-6323.

## Keeping Warm

We have received many inquiries from readers concerning old stove and heater parts, especially radiants for the Humphrey gas heater. If you are one of the many people trying to locate a source for these and other hard-to-find replacement parts we suggest you try the following two sources: (1) Empire Stove and Furnace Co., 795 Broadway, Dept. OHJ, Albany, NY 12207. (518) 449-

5189 or 449-2590. (2) The Aetna Stove Co., 2nd & Arch Sts., Dept. OHJ, Philadelphia, PA 19106. (215) 627-2008.

These two companies—among the country's largest and oldest stove distributors—have an extensive inventory of replacement parts for every kind of stove and heater. They do not offer any literature and would prefer that you call rather than write so that they can determine exactly what you need.

An inventory of 40-50 completely restored stoves can usually be found at Agape Antiques. The selection offers parlor or cooking stoves from 1830 through 1930. Wood, coal, or gas models are available with a price range of $400-$3,700, and Dave Wells, the owner, will be happy to ship anywhere.

They also stock stove replacement parts. Although their parts selection is limited to Glenwood Stoves, it's very complete. The best way to get information is to call Mr. Wells directly. Agape Antiques, Box 43-OHJ, Saxtons River, VT 05154. (802) 869-2273.

## Craftsman Wallpaper

Richard E. Thibaut, Inc. and The Historic House Association of America have collaborated to produce a line of authentic reproduction wallpapers. All 19 designs, each available in 3-5 colorways, are very reasonably priced from $14.95 to $18.95 per roll. Many of these 54-inch wide screen prints also have matching fabric.

The patterns were taken from historic homes throughout the country, mostly from 19th-century documents; however, the early 20th century is also represented. Shown here is an Arts & Crafts pattern taken from the Roycroft Campus, E. Aurora, NY (1890s).

Each wallpaper in Thibaut's Historic House collection is accompanied by a brief history of its origins—a nice historical touch for the old-house owner. A free brochure and the name of a dealer is available. Richard E. Thibaut, Inc., 315 5th Ave., Dept. OHJ, New York, NY 10016. (212) 481-0880.

## Turn-Of-Century Lighting

Turn-of-century lighting can be difficult to find. Heirloom Brass offers two chandeliers which are reproductions, with slight changes to meet the electrical code, of 1924-1926 models. Both fixtures are solid brass, coated with lacquer to reduce tarnishing, and sold with a choice of 4 different glass shades.

Heirloom Brass supplies to wholesalers, but they will give you the name of a dealer in your area. Heirloom Brass, PO Box 146, Dept. OHJ, Dundas, MN 55019. (507) 645-9341.

*4-arm chandelier—sugg. retail $250*

*3-arm chandelier—sugg. retail $190*

## The 20th Century Bathroom

Sterline Manufacturing Corp. has established a retail subsidiary, Barclay Products, in response to OHJ readers' interest in their wholesale products. Barclay carries a full line of bathroom accessories including high-tank toilets, shower rings, and shower curtains (standard and custom sizes). Barclay's line of solid brass faucets, manufactured by the Chicago Faucet Company, are almost exact reproductions of the patterns used by Chicago Faucet in the 1920s and 30s; minor changes were made in compliance with modern plumbing codes.

*Basin cocks (sold in pairs) suggested retail—$117*

Their 10 different faucet models have a non-lacquered, polished brass finish and white porcelain handles. Barclay also sells *Never Dull* (5 oz. for $5), an alcohol-based brass polish that is alkaline and non-abrasive.

For their free catalog contact: Barclay Products Co., PO Box 12257, Dept. OHJ, Chicago, IL 60612. (312) 243-1444.

*Deck-mounted sink faucet sugg. retail—$185*

## Embossed Tiles

FerGene Studio offers embossed tiles for your fireplace and hearth. Most of these tiles have a relief design which is copied from, or influenced by, late Victorian tiles. Plain tiles are also available for those who feel that a continous pattern is too busy.

Reasonably priced stock patterns include the *Virginia Creeper*, which is designed to "grow" around the fireplace: It is comprised of running-vine tiles, corner tiles, and end-vine tiles. The cost of these and other regular relief 6 x 6 in. tiles is $10/tile. Many other sizes are available, including small hearth tiles and rectangular tiles. Prices for smaller tiles range from $3-$5.

The tiles can be glazed to match a color in your room. Another option is Crackletone glaze, which imitates the crazing seen in antique tiles.

In addition, owner Mrs. Kirtland is willing to make replacement tiles or create a new design for you. There is a design fee of about $100 for this additional custom work, which usually requires 3 months. The cost and the time depend on the number of tiles, the difficulty of the design, and the even greater difficulty of matching colors. (If your design is one that Mrs. Kirtland would like to stock, she is willing to share the cost of the custom work.)

For a free brochure, send a self-addressed stamped envelope to: FerGene Studio, 4320 Washington St., Dept. OHJ, Gary, IN 46408. (219) 884-1119.

## Overhead

The textured metal ceilings found in many turn-of-century homes are both decorative and fire retardant. Shanker Steel, who has been manufacturing tin-plated metal ceilings since 1912, is still using the original patterns and methods. Their ceilings are available in 22 different patterns, with coordinating cornices. These patterns may be purchased in 2-ft. x 8-ft. sheets, at a cost of $22.30 each.

After installing a metal ceiling, be sure to clean it with denatured alcohol or mineral spirits (a must for proper paint adhesion), and coat it with an oil-based paint or clear lacquer. A free brochure of patterns and installation instructions is available. Shanker Steel Corp., 70-32 83rd Street, Dept. OHJ, Glendale, NY 11385. (212) 326-1100.

## Fine Hardware

Horton Brasses manufactures over 500 solid brass hardware items in a variety of styles covering the period from late 1600 to about 1920.

Unlike many other companies, this one offers furniture hardware for the simpler late Victorian & turn-of-century home. Included in this selection is the *golden oak style* drawer pull ($4.50), shown here, and cast brass knobs in the sunflower design ($3.25—$4.25). They also stock an unusual item—a moulding hook (30¢). When attaching your picture hanger to the moulding, this brass-plated hook fits securely onto the moulding and is much more appropriate than a nail.

Mr. Jim Horton, the owner of this company, is willing to do custom hand-reproduction of hardware. There is an additional charge for this service, but the order will usually be completed within three to four weeks. A catalog is available for $2. Horton Brasses, Nooks Hill Rd., PO Box 95-OHJ, Cromwell, CT 06416. (203) 635-4400.

## Opinion...
# Remuddling
## — Of The Month —

THE CAPTION for this photo could be, "The siding contractor strikes again!" The makers of vinyl and aluminum siding keep insisting that their products can be applied to old buildings in a sensitive fashion. Maybe they've never bothered to point that out to the contractors who slap the stuff on buildings. Because based on the photo evidence we've seen, a sensitive job is the rare exception.

THIS SIDING contractor committed the following: (1) Removed the ornamental caps over the two central windows; (2) Covered over the corner quoins; (3) Used a "clapboard" twice the width of the original--completing his trashing of the building's exterior.

THE POOR OLD HOUSE now has a badly split personality. Anyone know a good house psychiatrist?

Submitted by: (Name Withheld)
Portland, Maine

### TAKE YOUR CAMERA ALONG. . .

. . . the next time you are strolling through an old neighborhood. Be on the lookout for harmful or thoughtless things that have been done to old buildings. We're looking for object lessons... photos that will help others avoid the same mistakes.

IF YOU SPOT some classic remuddling, snap away. We'll award $50 if your photos are selected as the monthly winner. The message is more dramatic if you also send along a photo of a similar unremuddled building.

SEND YOUR ENTRIES to: Remuddling Editor, The Old-House Journal, 69A 7th Ave., Brooklyn, N.Y. 11217.

# The Old-House Journal®

69A Seventh Avenue,
Brooklyn, New York 11217

BULK RATE
U.S. Postage
PAID
New York, N.Y.
Permit No. 6964

# The Old-House Journal

Vol. X No. 2      $2.00

## February 1982

**Restoration and Maintenance Techniques For The Antique House**

# Repairing A Stair At Our Old House

By Patricia Poore
*Illustrations and Photographs By Jonathan Poore*

EVEN WHEN A STAIRCASE is undeniably in bad shape, most of us will put off making repairs. For one thing, stairs have a mysterious hidden structure. For another, we feel sure that work will be very disruptive. This article tells how we rehabilitated a long-neglected stair right here at the OHJ offices in Brooklyn.

OUR OFFICES occupy two floors of an 1890 brownstone row-house. The two lower storeys had been converted to commercial use in a remodeling between 1900-1910. Despite major alterations, one flight of stairs remained almost intact. It was suffering,though, from all the common maladies to which old wood stairs are prone.

THE HANDRAIL was shaky because some balusters (spindles) were broken or missing; a poorly constructed, added-on newel at the bottom of the flight was loose. The stair was noticeably out of level...3/4 inch per foot! This remarkable sag did not inspire confidence--the stair's loud creaks and groans were downright ominous. And as might be expected

with such a tilt, the treads were pulling out of their housings on the wall string. (See photographs 1, 2, and 3 on page 44.)

SO WE ASKED Harry Waldemar, our consultant for an upcoming OHJ book on stairbuilding, to come fix our stair. A retired master stair-builder, Harry stabilized the structure and made cosmetic repairs with minimal disruption. He also explained all the steps to us, and shared some time- and money-saving hints on stair work he'd come up with during his fifty years in the trade. Even if your stair isn't just like ours, you'll find that Harry's techniques apply to almost any traditional wood stair.

WE MADE the assumption that the crazy tilt on our stair was caused by a type of differential building settlement. (The interior wood frame shrinks and "settles," while the masonry outer wall remains stable.) In our case, the wall string is attached to the masonry party wall, but the outside string rests on the sloping floor.

*continued on page 44*

# ANNOUNCING THE 1981
# OHJ GRANT WINNERS

Henry McCartney pulls the winner of a $1000 OHJ Grant out of the hat. With him are OHJ Editors Clem Labine and Patricia Poore.

HENRY McCARTNEY, Coordinator of the Neighborhood Conservation Program for the National Trust, was our Master of Ceremonies for the grant drawing. He picked five groups from a hat containing the names of all the preservation organizations that had participated in our revenue-sharing (group-rate subscription) program during 1981. Here are the winners:

(1) Clinton Historical Society
    Clinton, New Jersey

(2) Preserve It Now
    Fonda, New York

(3) Historic Jasper, Inc.
    Jasper, Indiana

(4) Bedford Historical Society
    Bedford, Virginia

(5) Housing Development Authority of Orleans County
    Albion, New York

THIS YEAR, 110 preservation groups participated in our revenue-sharing program by selling discounted subscriptions to their members. All of these groups made money for their preservation activities because they kept half the subscription revenue they collected.

BETWEEN the revenue sharing and the five grants, the OHJ gave over $13,000 to grass-roots preservation groups in 1981. It's our small contribution to private funding for preservation activities.

AT THE SAME TIME, OHJ gains new subscribers without dropping vast sums of money into the mail. The money ordinarily spent on direct-mail paper and postage is better given to friends whose programs spread the word about sensitive rehabilitation.

OUR REVENUE-SHARING program has been renewed for 1982. And our grant fund has doubled: We'll be giving away 10 unrestricted $1000 grants next December! For more information on how your group can participate, call or write:

Sally Goodman
Grant Program Coordinator
The Old-House Journal
69A Seventh Ave.
Brooklyn, N.Y. 11217
(212)636-4514

## The Old-House Journal®

Editor
**Clem Labine**

Managing Editor
**Patricia Poore**

Assistant Editor
**Cole Gagne**

Editorial Assistants
**Joni Monnich**
**Stephanie Croce**

Circulation Supervisor
**Joan O'Reilly**

Circulation Assistants
**Margaret Scaglione**
**Barbara Bugg**
**Jean Baldwin**

Office Manager
**Sally Goodman**

Office Assistant
**Rafael Madera**

Sales Promotion
**Joel Alpert**

Circulation Director
**Paul T. McLoughlin**

Technical Consultant
**Alan D. Keiser**

Architectural Consultant
**Jonathan Poore**

Contributing Editors
**R. A. Labine, Sr.**
**John Mark Garrison**

Published by The Old-House Journal© Corporation, 69A Seventh Avenue, Brooklyn, New York 11217. Telephone (212) 636-4514. Subscriptions $16 per year in U.S. Not available elsewhere. Published monthly. Contents are fully protected by copyright and must not be reproduced in any manner whatsoever without specific permission in writing from the Editor.

We are happy to accept editorial contributions to The Old-House Journal. Query letters which include an outline of the proposed article are preferred. All manuscripts will be reviewed, and returned if unacceptable. However, we cannot be responsible for non-receipt or loss — please keep copies of all materials sent.

**Printed at Photo Comp Press,**
**New York City**

ISSN: 0094-0178
**NO PAID ADVERTISING**

## Post-Victorian Domestic Architecture
# The American Foursquare

By Renee Kahn

THE AMERICAN FOURSQUARE is probably the most common--and least understood--of all of the houses built after the turn of the century. Most architectural style books ignore it completely. The few that take note of it refer to it merely as "the box" or "the classic box." And none have chronicled the central role it played in Post-Victorian architecture. Yet this is the house--in its several variations--that is the common denominator in countless neighborhoods across the U.S.

MANY PEOPLE REFER to the American Foursquare as a "plain" house. Yet the apparent plainness belies the richness of the philosophy and history behind the style. The American Foursquare possesses the simplicity and honesty that epitomizes the turn-of-century striving for "the comfortable house." More than any other style, this house has been "home" to three generations of Americans.

THE AMERICAN FOURSQUARE appeared during the first decade of the 20th century, and its popularity lasted well into the 1920s. During this era, although the grand public architecture still paid homage to Beaux Arts classicism, the modest homes of the middle class achieved a simplicity and honesty that had not been seen for almost 100 years. Public taste was undergoing a reaction to the decorative exuberance

of the Victorian era, and was seeking a respite in humble materials and unadorned surfaces. This new-found simplicity is evident not only in the Foursquare, but also in such other house styles as the Bungalow and Prairie.

### The Movement Toward Simplicity

PRACTICAL as well as philosophical considerations lay behind the movement away from excessive ornament, and the Foursquare was essentially an inexpensive way to provide large amounts of comfortable living space. A 30-ft. by 36-ft. house could easily contain four bedrooms, a living room, one or two baths, and ample hallways on both floors. This is to say nothing of the spacious attic under the hipped roof, and the basement.

ALTHOUGH ITS CONTEMPORARY, the Bungalow, was chided for being "the least house for the most money," the Foursquare was quite the reverse. The square plan enabled a minimum of land, foundation, and roof to enclose a considerable amount of space. Flat unbroken walls, unadorned exteriors, turretless rooflines, and gingerbread-free porches were less expensive to build and maintain than the picturesque complexities of the Victorian era.

## A Few Ornamental Details

ALTHOUGH PLAIN by comparison with its predecessors, the Foursquare was not without historic elements. Radford's "Portfolio of Plans," a popular builder's handbook published in 1909, shows a wide range of stylistic influences. Watered-down versions of Colonial Revival appears to have been the most popular, although Tudor and Craftsman styling is also quite common.

WINDOWS were one of the few building components of the Foursquare where variety was encouraged. A Palladian window could suggest Colonial restraint and elegance. Elongated, diamond-paned sashes used in combination with undivided sheets of plate glass hinted at Tudor ruggedness.

**Palladian Window**

Stained glass hall lights and dining room transoms were a hold-over from the medievalism of the Queen Anne period of the previous two decades.

FOR WINDOW TREATMENTS, the protective shutters and heavy draperies of the Victorian era were abandoned in favor of light curtains and window shades. Awnings were a common and efficient way to screen out the summer sun. In keeping with Sullivan's dictum that "form follows function," window placement reflected the needs within the structure, rather than being purely symmetrical for symmetry's sake.

### THE ESSENCE OF THE AMERICAN FOURSQUARE

The basic American Foursquare has two storeys, a square boxlike shape, and a low hipped roof with broad overhanging eaves. The exterior is unadorned, relying for its impact on its shape and proportion. There is usually a porch extending the full width of the front elevation.

Most often, there is a dormer in the roof facing front; sometimes there will also be dormers on the two side planes of the roof.

Although often devoid of any "style features," sometimes a Colonial touch has been added by inserting a Palladian window in the front facade or front dormer. There might also be a neo-Classical oval cameo window next to the front door or elsewhere. Occasionally there will be a bay window or other architectural feature that breaks up the absolute flatness of the sides.

The most common siding materials are wood shingles, stucco, and clapboards. A Craftsman styling effect can be created by allowing exposed rafter ends along the eaves. An additional Craftsman touch would be a fieldstone foundation and chimney.

Photo: Jonathan Gardner

This American Foursquare exhibits many of the basic features: Unadorned boxlike shape, low hipped roof with dormers, porch with filled-in railing and simple Tuscan columns. The most unusual feature is that the porch wraps around two sides of the house.

## Exterior Materials

ON THE EXTERIOR, the Foursquare reflected the trend towards plainness and "natural" materials. The foremost spokesman for this movement was Gustav Stickley, through his magazine, "The Craftsman." Wood, the traditional American building material, remained popular, although sometimes in the form of wood shingles rather than clapboards. Stained dark, these rough-hewn shingles were meant to create a hand-crafted appearance.

CONCRETE PRODUCTS began to challenge wood as the material of choice for exteriors. As far back as 1850, Orson Squire Fowler, the developer of the octagon house, had considered concrete (or "grout," as he called it) ideal for dwellings. "Nature's building material," he called it--cheap and inexhaustible.

BY 1905, America had a well-developed technology for making concrete blocks--usually hollow for economy, insulation, and waterproofing. Although the use of concrete dated back to

Concrete became a popular building material after the turn of the century. Among the virtues cited for it were durability, fire resistance, and the fact that it was "sanitary"—resistant to rot and vermin. The concrete blocks in this 1909 Foursquare are moulded to resemble rough-cut stone.

Photo: Steven Hirschberg

Craftsman styling marks this Foursquare: Stained wood shingles on the upper storey, rough fieldstone for the chimney and walls of the lower storey. The oriel window projecting from the side is somewhat unusual, as is the asymmetrical placement of the windows.

Roman times, it was always considered an inferior material and was covered over with "finer" substances. It was logical, therefore, that when concrete blocks began to be used for houses such as the Foursquare, they would be made to look like stone. Blocks shaped like rough-cut stone became popular, as did rusticated varieties with bevelled edges.

BY 1910, however, builders began to show increased interest in stucco. Although its initial cost was slightly more than wood, it required little or no maintenance, and could be tinted delicate pastel colors when wet. Stucco was applied over a variety of surfaces, including masonry block, brick, or wood lath. At times, a lightweight metal frame, referred to as "metal lumber," was used under stucco.

STUCCO PERMITTED considerable creativity. Its surface texture could be readily varied. No two workmen applied it alike; in fact, each mason had his own "handwriting." Shapes could be pressed into it while wet, as could colored tiles or pebbles. Although many stucco-covered houses are presently painted white, a soft beige/brown appears to have originally been the most popular color.

## The Porch: A Necessity

THE FRONT PORCH was considered a necessity for the American Foursquare. Most have a porch that runs the full width of the front elevation. Less often, the front porch will stop a few feet short of either side. The turned and chamfered columns of the Victorian porch were discarded in favor of panelled, boxed-in posts, or else the unfluted version of the Doric column known as Tuscan.

## THE IDEAL CRAFTSMAN HOUSE

THE RULING PRINCIPLE OF THE CRAFTSMAN HOUSE IS SIMPLICITY. The central thought in all Craftsman activities is the simplification of life and a return to true democracy. Accordingly, the exterior lines of the Craftsman house are very simple and its interior divisions are few.

SIMPLICITY SPELLS ECONOMY. Elaborate ornamentation is eliminated by our method of interior treatment. Post-and-panel construction replaces useless partitions. Native woods are used liberally. The fireplace is made an ornamental feature. A Craftsman house should stand for 100 years or more without requiring repairs. In fact, for many years a Craftsman house will increase in value and beauty without impairment, and use will give to it a softness and friendliness which will constantly add to its charm.

A CRAFTSMAN HOUSE REPRESENTS NOT ONLY ECONOMY IN COST, BUT ECONOMY IN FLOOR SPACE. Not an inch of space is wasted. The general living rooms are thrown together, usually including the entrance hall and stairway, so that the whole lower floor of a Craftsman house has the effect of a great living room. Post-and-panel construction and the arrangement of pleasant nooks and corners give a sense of room division as well as a feeling of semi-privacy.

BUILT-IN FEATURES ARE OFTEN INCORPORATED TO MEET SPECIAL NEEDS. Like other structural features, built-in fittings add to the interest and beauty of rooms. They are directly related to the life of the household and make for simplicity and comfort.

*—From Gustav Stickley's magazine,*
*"The Craftsman," 1911.*

The use of "honest natural materials"—fieldstone, stucco, and stained wood shingles—on the exterior of this Foursquare shows the impact of the Craftsman philosophy. Note the solid feeling that the large square columns on the front porch impart to the whole house.

Photo: Jonathan Gardner

Here is the American Foursquare in one of its most familiar variations: Shingled exterior with dormers on three sides.

Because of its small ell and the resulting complications of the roofline, this house is technically not a Foursquare. Yet you can see how the architect took the basic American Foursquare design, added Prairie-style eaves and small ells and wings, and came up with a large suburban home.

THERE WAS A PREFERENCE for slat, stick, or filled-in railings. Many of these front porches have now been enclosed and turned into extra rooms (often without adequate insulation!).

THE FRONT DOOR of the American Foursquare was in keeping with the relative plainness of the rest of the exterior. The most popular version appears to have been a bevelled panel of plate glass, with two or three horizontal wood panels underneath. Another popular door style had an elongated oval glass, bevelled and set within a delicate beaded moulding. Long rectangular panels of clear glass were also quite common.

Many Foursquares had interiors that were influenced by Craftsman styling: Extensive use of American hardwoods for panelling, simple stencilled borders, frequent use of built-in furniture, leather coverings on furniture, and the focus on the hearth as the central ornamental element.

## Interiors

ALTHOUGH Colonial influences dominated most interiors, the Craftsman style also had considerable impact. Classical symmetry was abandoned in favor of a variety of floor plans, no one of which appears to have predominated.

AMERICAN FOURSQUARES had center halls, side halls or no halls. If the stairway was off to one side, a rectangular stained glass hall window lent it an air of importance. Stairway balusters were either turned in a neo-Classical manner, or were oak sticks of the Craftsman variety. Panelled wainscotting and ceilings lent an appropriately "medieval" air, as did the highly varnished oak floors.

FURNITURE, too, was simplified, omitting the lavish pattern and ornamental detail of the Victorian period. Plain brown leather replaced heavy brocade, and eclecticism was limited to "medieval" reproductions, or quasi-"Colonial" styles.

RENEE KAHN is an architectural historian and teacher, as well as being a partner in The Preservation Development Group—a Stamford, Conn., company that consults on the restoration of historic structures.

Old-House Living...

# Renovating An Illinois Queen Anne

By James A. Gray, Assumption, Illinois

**W**HEN I BECAME PRINCIPAL of the Tower Hill, Illinois, schools in 1979, my wife Colleen and I began looking for a house to buy. Local realtors showed us houses new and old, but everything we saw was either unsatisfactory or too expensive. We decided to start looking for ourselves, and this decision led us to Assumption, the nearest town in the next county.

ONE SUNDAY AFTERNOON we came upon a large Queen Anne house that had been built at the turn of the century. The first time we saw this old house we fell in love with it, even though it had been sadly neglected. There it stood, with no paint, broken windows, and a leaking roof. Inside, the house was a total wreck. Most of the damage was caused by water entering through the roof. But nature had also added insult to injury: The house had become not just a pigeon roost, but a beehive too!

CIRCUMSTANCES COMPELLED US to live in the house while we worked on it, and so once we bought the house we moved in. The downstairs rooms were in somewhat better shape than the upstairs, and we started by organizing and cleaning that storey. But as we continued to live in the house, each room soon wound up with tools and supplies piled up everywhere. It was enough to drive us nuts.

OUR REAL WORK on the house began with the roof. It was a slate roof with a built-in tin-lined gutter around the bottom. Over the years, the gutter had gotten plugged up and all

The Grays' living room, west view.

the water had collected in it until the tin was all rusted away. The tin overhang and gutter now had to be replaced. It abutted the slate, which had begun to delaminate and was the source of many leaks. Replacing all that old slate was out of the question, so we used asphalt shingles that at least were close in color to the original slate.

## Up On The Roof

**O**UR WORK ON THE ROOF involved tearing off all the old slate, rebuilding the overhang so that it abutted the existing roof, reshingling the roof, and adding new gutters. This job would have been no problem had it not been for the weather. When we were halfway through our work, it began to rain, and it kept raining on and off for the next two weeks.

TO PROTECT THE FLOORS AND CEILINGS from any further water damage, we set up at least a dozen buckets and pans to catch the water. During each rainstorm, we'd have to empty out all this water about every three hours. Getting up in the middle of the night to do this made me feel as if I were taking care of an infant. But the worst aspect of this task was the fault of the pigeons that had been roosting upstairs: The water that seeped down from the attic was ... unpleasant. Eventually, it stopped raining and we were able to finish the roof.

WITH THE ROOF at last under control, we were able to work in earnest on the downstairs rooms. We steamed off the old wallpaper from the walls and ceilings. Then we would clean out a room, replace the broken windows, and strip the floors and woodwork. (Here is a tip I learned the hard way: If you plan to strip a large area, buy a 50-gallon barrel of stripper; you'll save money.) We would then paint and wallpaper the room and move in our furniture. Most of our furniture is antique, so it looked just right in the finished rooms.

Left: Just one of the many ceiling problems. This one was in the dining room. Right: The Solar Room. Behind that particle board is a rather sizable hole.

## Problems Upstairs

THE NEXT PHASE OF OUR WORK was the renovation of the upstairs rooms. I still hate even to think about that, so I'll start with the most pleasant memories. Before we did anything else upstairs, we stripped all the doors and woodwork. We uncovered a nice, wide yellow pine that provided a good contrast to the hardy oak downstairs. This was the best thing about working on the upstairs.

THE FIRST ROOM we worked on we called The Solar Room. It got this name because it had a section 4 ft. by 4 ft. where the wall was all but gone. You could stand in the room and look right out the wall and see the sky! So we put in new studs and then used particle board to cover this and the other holes in the wall and ceiling. (I used particle board because a person can hold and cut it without needing help.)

THE MASTER BEDROOM was in much better shape than The Solar Room. The only problem with the bedroom was that the ceiling had fallen to the floor. After putting up a new ceiling, we papered the room and moved in our furniture.

THEN WE TURNED OUR ATTENTION to The Pigeon Room. The birds had done most of their roosting here, and so the droppings on the floor had accumulated to about three inches. There was something else on the floor of this room: half the ceiling. My father-in-law gave me a number 10 corn scoop, and I just shoveled the stuff out the windows. The only health precaution I took was to limit the amount of time that I spent in the room each day. Luckily, neither my wife nor I suffered any ill effects from the droppings*. Once all that was cleared away, we fixed the ceiling and wallpapered, transforming The Pigeon Room into a study.

* For further information on the health hazards from pigeon droppings, see the following issues of OHJ: March 1981, p. 54, and June 1981, p. 137.

Two views of The Pigeon Room. Top: Prior to renovation. That stuff on the floor is the ceiling, along with a goodly amount of pigeon droppings. Bottom: After renovation. The room is now used as a study.

OUR OTHER MAJOR PEST PROBLEM was The Bee Room. From the time we began to work on the house, we had been bothered by bees. It took a professional exterminator to get rid of them. Holes had to be drilled in the floor and walls in order to spray the bees. A special poison was also placed in the holes to keep the bees from coming back. The only thing we had to do after all this was get the honey out of the house!

Top: Bees swarming at the exterior of the house. Bottom: Honey coming through the ceiling.

THE LAST ROOM that we worked on upstairs was the bathroom. It has a clawfoot tub, a wood closet with drawers at the bottom, and a rose marble basin with a foot-high marble splash-board. The only difficulty was the white wood-work, which had been painted in the old passion pink. So we stripped the woodwork and closet, redid the floor, and papered the bottom half of the walls, coating the paper with poly-urethane.

THE HALLWAY ON THE SECOND FLOOR was the only area that still needed work. It's quite large, 7 ft. wide by 20 ft. long, and has a linen closet between the master bedroom and The Pigeon Room. We repaired the ceiling, papered the walls, replaced the corner mouldings, and put up an old crystal chandelier.

## Adding Color

PAINTING THE EXTERIOR of the house was next on the agenda. I did all the painting my-self, by hand, as well as all the prelimi-nary scraping and priming. We decided to paint the body blue and the trim white. Paint-ing the trim takes time, but it makes the house look so much nicer, especially if you have an older home with attractive decoration.

WE USED 30 GALLONS of blue paint, 30 gallons of white paint, and 10 gallons of grey porch-and-deck paint. I would hate to count the number of brushes or the hours it took, but the results were worth the effort. Our next-door neighbor said that he had lived next to the house for over 25 years and had never seen anyone take a paint brush to it until we arrived.

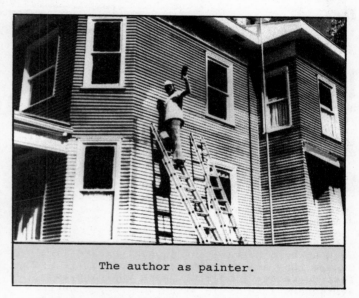

The author as painter.

THE THIRD FLOOR of the house has a finished attic and is a very unusual room. It has thir-teen walls, four dormers, and four doors (three of these doors go to unfinished closet space off the main room). The top room of the tower has a small, 4-ft. entranceway. We haven't gotten to this room yet, but we plan to make it into a study and sewing room someday. You really get a thrill going to this third-floor room and looking out of the tower window--a good 30 feet above the ground--and taking in the view.

## Last Thoughts

ALL OF THE WORK I'VE DESCRIBED may sound expensive, but we did most of it our-selves, and so managed to save a good deal of money. When we look at the houses we could have bought for fifty or sixty thousand dollars and compare them to what we have, we feel very fortunate. We have a double-corner lot, a house with over 3000 sq.ft. of living space, a full basement, solid oak floors and doors, fireplaces, and a large wrap-around porch. Can you imagine how expensive some-thing like that is on today's market?

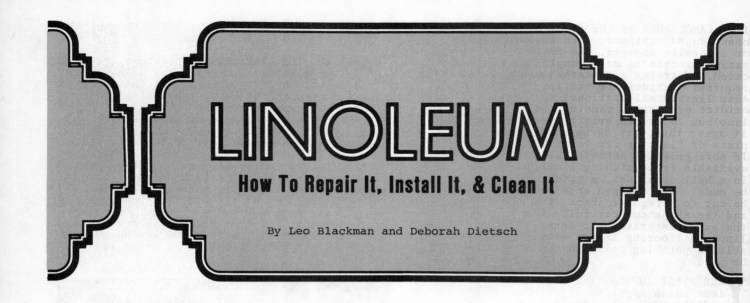

# LINOLEUM
## How To Repair It, Install It, & Clean It

By Leo Blackman and Deborah Dietsch

IF YOU'RE LOOKING for authentic flooring for a turn-of-the-century house, you might still find a roll of linoleum in the attic, a warehouse, or a carpet store basement. Or maybe you'll be lucky enough to come across a roll in an antique store. (I was!) Perhaps you already have an interesting linoleum pattern in place, or just discovered it under more recent flooring.

WHETHER your linoleum is newly installed, or old and in need of sprucing up, don't despair. This article will help you strip and clean linoleum, repair it or patch it, install it, and maintain it.

ALL PROCEDURES outlined in this article will work on both canvas- and asphalt-backed linoleum. Beware that all solvents suggested have a potential to damage linoleum. When applying any solvent be sure to do so selectively--you want to dissolve dirt and finish buildup, not the linoleum itself. Always follow these three rules: (1) Do a test patch in the least conspicuous corner of the floor. (2) Don't allow any solvent (even water) to remain on linoleum for an extended period of time. (3) Work on small areas at a time, rinsing and hand-drying as you go.

### Repairing Linoleum

ADHESIVES, OLD WAX, varnish, shellac, and other substances which obscure the surface must be removed before repairs can be made to the linoleum. Water-soluble adhesives will soften when wet, and can then be gently scraped up from the linoleum surface. Again, keep water from standing too long on the linoleum, because the canvas backing will retain water, causing the linoleum fibers and the backing to decay. This is especially true if the resilient surface has been worn or abraded., and the jute fibers are exposed.

No. 8086

IF YOU FIND WATER won't remove the adhesive, try a stronger solvent. Be careful: While oxidized and compressed oils in the body of plain linoleum are somewhat more stable than printed patterns, both can be damaged by strong alkaline solvents. Automotive asphalt removers will dissolve asphaltic adhesives, and commercial paint strippers will soften vinyl adhesives. Also, dry ice can be used to remove foreign lumps. Wearing thick gloves, place large blocks of dry ice on the floor. After only a few minutes the adhesive, tar, or chewing gum will break off with a little pressure from a thin scraper.

(STORE DRY ICE in a non-metal container, such as a cardboard box, and be sure to ventilate it well.)

WAX IS BEST REMOVED by a commercial wax stripper. The stripper you use must not contain ammonia, which is highly destructive to the linoleum surface. "New Beginnings," manufactured by the Armstrong Co. and recommended by them for stripping wax off linoleum floors, is available at most floor covering stores. If you have a printed pattern, a coat of varnish or shellac was probably applied to seal and preserve it. (As we discussed last month, printed patterns were a surface treatment; the pattern tended to wear off under steady traffic, unlike inlaid linoleum.) Shellac can be dissolved with denatured alcohol. Some varnishes can be removed with turpentine; other varnishes will only come off with commercial paint removers. After stripping, the surface is ready to repaired.

### Damaged Areas

CLEAR SHELLAC and varnish are ideal substances for repairing a torn linoleum floor. Coat the ripped edge with either one and squeeze them together. If no material has been lost, the joint should be nearly invisible.

IF A LARGE AREA of the floor has
been gouged, chipped, worn through,
or otherwise damaged, the restoration process is more complicated. Matching a patterned piece
requires considerable skill.
Also linseed oil continues to
oxidize over time, causing the
linoleum to become brittle as
it ages; thus, prying up an old
piece of flooring can be tricky.
If more original material is
available from matching linoleum
in a hall or closet, a patch can
be made. The damaged area should
be cut to a regular shape, traced,
and the shape cut carefully from
the extra material. If extra
linoleum flooring is not available, a patching compound can
be used.

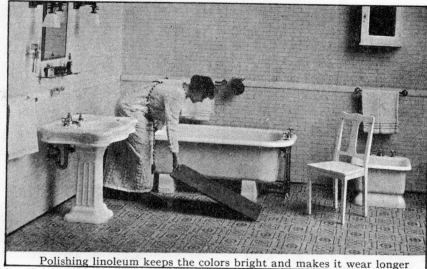
Polishing linoleum keeps the colors bright and makes it wear longer

YOUR FIRST IMPULSE for a linoleum patch might be to create
a filler from the original ingredients--cork
flour and linseed oil. Pre-polymerized linseed oil (similar to the oxidized substance),
or linseed oil plus japan dryer or cobalt, can
be purchased in an art supply store. However,
powdered cork isn't easy to obtain. And pulverizing a scrap of old linoleum requires industrial grinding tools--certainly not a job
for a Cuisinart! This home-brew has another
drawback: It would not have the durability
of the original, which was subjected to heat
and pressure in its original manufacture.

A MORE SENSIBLE PATCH can be obtained by mixing
sawdust with shellac or varnish to a dense consistency. Pigments can be added to this mixture to simulate the color of plain linoleum.
This substance is troweled into the damaged
areas and sanded smooth when dry. The surface
can then be painted with oils or acrylics to
match the adjacent pattern. Two commercially
available products might be used in a similar
manner. Artist's polymer gesso--a thick blend
of paint and plaster--or vinyl spackling compound are both slightly resilient and can be
sanded. They will provide a durable smooth-
textured base which can be painted over.

## Installing Linoleum

NATURALLY, you won't want to put linoleum
over a fine hardwood floor. In many turn-of-
the-century houses, though, linoleum or carpeting was meant to be laid directly over a
subfloor or an inexpensive wood floor. Let's
assume you're going to install some "new" linoleum you've found. Extra care must be taken
when installing old linoleum due to its tendency to grow brittle with age. Before unroll-
ing it, make sure sure it is at room temperature or warmer to avoid cracking the surface.

LINOLEUM AND WOOD expand and contract at different rates with changes in temperature and
humidity. Therefore, linoleum should not be
pasted directly to a wood floor. Turn-of-the-
century handbooks recommend laying linoleum in
place for two weeks prior to tacking it down.
This allows it to stretch, preventing any tendency to buckle or crack. The following procedure, adapted from a 1920s handbook, offers
a superior method of laying linoleum.

AFTER A WOOD FLOOR has been carefully leveled
and the cracks filled, it should be sanded and
cleaned. Strips of unsaturated deadening felt
are then cut to fit the floor. A thorough
coating of paste or vinyl flooring adhesive is
applied to the floor with a paste spreader. As
rapidly as the floor is pasted, the felt strips
are fitted into position--butted
crosswise to the floorboards. A
heavy iron roller is then used to
eliminate air pockets and aid adhesion. The linoleum should then
be fitted to the floor, leaving
a 1/2-inch expansion gap between
the linoleum and the wall. (The
gap will be hidden by the baseboard.) Next, an area (on the
felt) 4 to 6 inches
wide around the base-
board and on each
side of the linoleum
seam should be marked
using chalk. This
area should be left
unpasted; paste is
then spread on the
rest of the felt in
the same manner that

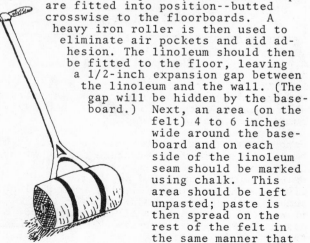

Never a complaint about linoleum that's laid like this

it was applied to the wood floor. The linoleum strips are then fitted into place, each strip overlapping the preceding one by 1/2 to 3/4 inch. Patterns for figured linoleum should be matched and the edges butted. After being rolled to ensure adhesion between the felt and the linoleum, the overlapping edges of the linoleum are cut away with a sharp knife. These unpasted edges are lifted up, sealed with a waterproof cement, and rolled flat.

IF YOU HAVE PRINTED linoleum, you may want to give it a clear, non-yellowing protective coating instead of linseed oil. Shellac, followed by wax, is renewable but brittle. Oil varnishes may be your best bet. Some product experts suggest that exterior clear wood finishes-- such as "Clear Wood Finish" (CWF) by Sherwin-Williams--can be used on linoleum without the disadvantages of linseed oil. But NO ONE recommends polyurethane varnishes because they may not not bond to the linoleum, they yellow, and they are unstrippable

## Maintenance

NOW ALL YOU have to do is maintain your revived linoleum floor. Surface dirt on linoleum can be effectively cleaned with vacuum or mop. It should be washed using lukewarm water and a mild detergent, such as Ivory Snow, followed by a barely-damp mopping with clean water. The floor should be cleaned in small areas and dried thoroughly. Scrubbing it with harsh soaps, ammonia, or alkaline cleaning agents such as sodium bicarbonate (soda) or sodium borate (borax), should be avoided because these products oxidize the oil in the linoleum, causing it to deteriorate. Waxing and polishing a linoleum floor will not only give it a longer life, but will reduce the amount of daily cleaning necessary to maintain its glossy appearance. A non-skid paste wax is recommended; follow the label directions when applying it to the linoleum. A word of caution--the wax should be applied sparingly in a thin and even coating. Excess wax will collect dirt and darken the color of linoleum.

Fig. 1

Fig. 4

**How to Scrub, Wax, and Polish Linoleum**

**Fig. 1. First Step, Scrubbing.** Pour out a small quantity of lukewarm suds, made with a mild soap, and run the machine slowly over the floor until the dirt has been thoroughly loosened.

**Fig. 2. Second Step, Removing Dirt and Water.** An ordinary cotton mop can be used, but a metal floor pan and rubber squeegee are most satisfactory. The dirty water is drawn into the pan with the squeegee as illustrated.

**Fig. 3. Third Step, Waxing.** Paste wax may be used but liquid wax is easier to apply. On a large floor, pour the wax into a bucket and immerse a clean cotton mop in it. Mop the linoleum until a thin coating of wax has been spread over the whole area. Work the mop first one direction, then the other, to insure complete coverage.

**Fig. 4. Fourth Step, Polishing.** Put the polishing brush on the machine and run over the floor slowly, first one direction, then the other. This brushes the wax into the linoleum and starts the polish. To finish, use the polishing pad.

**Fig. 5. Daily Care.** The janitor can keep a waxed and polished linoleum floor clean and bright by going over it every evening with a fine hair broom.

N. B. Electric floor machine used in these illustrations is the International, Model B.

Fig 2

Fig. 3

Fig. 5

Page Forty-one

From a 1924 Armstrong Co. booklet

## Cleaning Linoleum

ONCE YOU HAVE REPAIRED your old linoleum, the Armstrong Research Department suggests the following method of restoring and reviving your "historic" flooring. (Many of the following procedures can be used on "new" linoleum and any dull, dingy linoleum you already have in place.) After all surface coatings have been removed from the linoleum, coat a rag with boiled linseed oil, and apply it lightly to the floor. If the linseed oil is warmed slightly it will penetrate better and take less time to dry. The linseed oil will be sticky for quite a few hours while it dries, so the area will have to remain free of traffic during that time.

# Decorative Cast Iron
## Easy To Use--And Inexpensive

By Ron Pilling, Baltimore, Maryland

THAT "LOVELY OLD WROUGHT IRON" on homes in Savannah and New Orleans usually is not wrought iron at all. Most of those ornate railings, trellises, and balconies are cast iron--the products of a foundry, not a forge. Decorative casting reached its zenith in Victorian America and was widely used in all sorts of domestic architecture. Happily, reproducing these products today is easy. An enormous variety of castings is still available, and developments in electric arc welding technology has made cast iron assembly a simple process. Anyone with the proper tools can fabricate cast iron decorative items, and the cost is surprisingly low.

THIS ARTICLE makes certain assumptions. The first is that you've read the January and February 1981 OHJ articles on arc welding. The second is that you've learned to strike an arc and done some preliminary steel welding. Now all you need are the tools: a 220-volt electric arc welder, the proper electrodes (more on this later), at least four heavy spring clamps, four 90° steel corner braces (at least 2 inches on each side), a hacksaw with plenty of coarse blades, a hammer, and a power drill. There will also be grinding to do, and a portable polisher-grinder will make things easier. (I have found that the composition blades made for cutting metal with a circular saw work well on a portable grinder. Ask about them at a hardware store.)

BEGIN WITH a careful study of surviving cast iron architectural elements. Many cast iron products are basically a framework of heavy steel stock, filled with castings as decoration. Look closely to determine which parts make up the basic frame and where the castings are incorporated. The frame is generally of square stock, ½-in. square and heavier. Some fancier pieces use ornate cast corner posts as part of the frame.

Top: This 12-ft. balcony uses 1-in. square stock for the frame's bottom and vertical pieces. The top frame piece is 1 in. x 5/8 in. Close reproductions of both the corner braces and the castings are available.
Bottom: This small window balcony uses a decorative crest across the top instead of a top rail. Its corner posts are cast instead of the more common square steel. Similar castings are still available.

MEASURE THE SIZE of the frame stock, and check to see how the top of the item is finished off. Some have cresting and some have rail covers across the top. Look at the little details, like bevelled edges, that make the difference between a careful assembly and a sloppy one.

YOU SHOULD ALSO send away for the catalogs of casting houses, such as those listed at the end of this article. When they arrive in the mail, you can put your project on paper. The size of available cast elements will place constraints on your plans, so you can't proceed with your work until you know which elements you'll be using. Once you've selected the elements, you can prepare a detailed drawing of the project, with lists of each length of steel that must be cut. Starting out with such a drawing will save time and help you avoid mistakes in the shop.

EVERYTHING YOU NEED in the way of cast iron is available through the mail, and at prices so low that you won't believe it. For the window balconies used as fabricating examples in this article, the major castings cost $9.25 each. Small finials sell for as little as 40¢ each.

Here's what the window balconies will look like when they're completed. Note how the front vertical pieces extend an inch past the bottom and are bevelled on the ends. This detail is typical of old balconies.

THE STEEL FOR THE FRAMEWORK can be purchased from any local fabricating shop or direct from a steel distributor. (Many distributors have minimum purchase amounts.) Also, most steel comes in 20-ft. lengths. It can be cut at the distributor to make it easier to transport, but if you can begin with 20-ft. pieces, there will be less waste. The total cost for the pair of window balconies shown in this article (including paint and mounting hardware) was $158. Even if you have to buy the whole welding outfit, it will be cheaper than paying a fabricating shop to do the job.

## Making The Balconies

FOR A STEP-BY-STEP EXAMPLE, let's turn to the small window boxes, or balconies, seen on this page. Each of these boxes, designed to hold plants at a window, is a frame with a front having inside dimensions of 28 in. x 28½ in. tall, and sides that are 10 in. deep. A single decorative cast panel, 7 in. x 28 in., fills each side opening; three likewise fill the front. A total of ten castings, therefore, is required. Two round rods, ½ in. in diameter, run from side to side across the bottom to support the plants. The top is finished with a cover rail, mitred at the corners. The finished boxes are held to the window frames by mounting brackets made of 1-in. wide flat steel.

THE FIRST STEP is to cut each of the pieces of square stock necessary for the frame. Be prepared to go through a lot of hacksaw blades, and don't hesitate to throw away a blade as soon as it starts to dull. Clamp the steel in a bench vise for sawing. You will soon learn that you can cut about two-thirds of the way through, and then bend the bar until the rest snaps. This proce-

dure cuts sawing time but leaves ragged ends that must be ground flat. Still, I find it is easier than sawing all the way through.

WHEN ALL THE PIECES are cut and squared, assembly can begin. You must work on a large, _flat_ surface, or else the finished frame will never be true. (A flush door on a pair of sawhorses is a fine surface.) For the 5/8-in. stock used here, an AC setting of about 120 amps was used with general purpose electrodes, 1/8 in. in diameter. Ten of these electrodes were consumed on each balcony.

CLAMP THE BARS TOGETHER at the corners securely, using the corner braces to hold the assembly square. (See photograph below.) Attach the welder's ground clamp to the end of one of the bars. Spot welds will hold the corners together long enough to remove the braces and clamps. Be careful not to weld the corner braces to the balcony frames with these first tiny spot welds. After removing the clamps, run short welding beads at every joint of steel to steel to complete the corner.

## Correcting Warps

IN ASSEMBLING THE BALCONIES, the frame fronts were put together first. Then the 10-in. deep sides were attached, followed by the two vertical back pieces. The two round bars then went across the bottom. (Round bars were preferred by Victorian ironworkers.) When the welding was finished and the corners had cooled, the frame was turned up on a flat surface and checked for flush assembly.

FOR ALL OUR CAREFUL CLAMPING, the first balcony proved to be warped. When laid face up, two opposite corners on the back were high, and the frames rocked on these corners. Installing these in a plumb window frame would have been impossible; but the problem was easily rectified.

Hardware store corner braces are used to hold the balcony frame pieces squarely together for welding. The spring clamps must be strong. Here, three pieces are clamped for simultaneous welding.

TO CORRECT A WARP LIKE THIS, I always resort to cold setting. Place two bricks on a solid floor so that you can put the high corners on these bricks, off the floor. Then press down firmly and evenly on the other corners, forcing them to bend slightly. Check the adjustment by returning the frame to the flat surface, and keep pushing until the whole thing is flat. You can easily take out up to an inch of warp in this fashion.

COLD SETTING can weaken the joints, especially if the warpage is severe. But these balconies are non-structural, and I've never felt there was a problem with this procedure. If you intend to mass produce these balconies, you should clamp the sections to a jig--a rigid wooden or metal framework--and then weld them together. This method would prevent any possible warping as the metal cooled.

YOU SHOULD NOW grind the welds smooth; after the castings are in place, many of the first welds will be inaccessible. Safety glasses are a must, especially when using a portable grinder. If a joint separates during grinding, then the penetration of the weld was inadequate. Raise the amperage by about ten and do the weld over again.

Electric arc welding leaves deposits of slag and melted electrode. Here, a portable grinder/polisher with a composition metal-cutting blade is used to grind the welds smooth.

## The Castings

TIME FOR THE CASTINGS that decorate the balconies. When welding cast iron, the extreme heat of the arc can cause the iron to become brittle and break. The chance of this happening has been greatly reduced, however, by the development of electrodes that are specially designed for welding cast to cast or cast to steel.

THESE ELECTRODES OPERATE at 10% less power, thereby reducing the heat produced. So set your amperage back by about a tenth. The coating on the electrodes allows them to be used on old and rusty cast iron too, with good holding power and a minimum of slag build-up. They

also spatter less than standard electrodes, making clean-up easier.

NEVERTHELESS, CARE MUST BE TAKEN when welding with cast iron. The arc must be as short as possible. In fact, it is impossible to hold a long arc with cast-type electrodes, so you may have some difficulty striking an arc at first. Do not weld continuously, and avoid beads that are longer than an inch. Let the finished weld cool slowly, and do not peen or grind it until it has fully cooled.

## The Rail

EIGHT CAST IRON ELECTRODES were required to complete both window balconies. They are available through the foundry catalogs, but usually in large minimum quantities. Check local welding supply houses. Some have retail racks with electrodes for special jobs packaged six to a pack.

USING THE SPRING CLAMPS, hold each casting in place and spot weld it at the top and bottom where it touches the steel frame. A series of spot welds at the rear where they can't be seen by passersby will do the trick. Remember, the castings do nothing to strengthen the frame, so all the welds must do is hold them in place.

MANY OLD WINDOW BALCONIES have a rail set across the top similar to that on a fence or gate. A readily-available steel rail top was chosen for this pair. You'll find it in the castings catalogs, sold in 20-ft. lengths for about $1.25 per foot. We needed only ten feet, and by checking local metal shops we found the right lengths among their scraps.

THE UNDERSIDE OF THE RAIL is designed to sit atop a standard 1 in. x 1 in. tube. We assembled the frames of 5/8-in. stock, so to compensate we welded a 1-in. flat bar under the rail first. We then cut the mitred corners on the rail and the flat bar before we welded them together.

The top rail is made of two pieces: 1) the decorative rail, and 2) a piece of 1-in. flat steel under it. The square rod shown would be the top of the balcony frame.

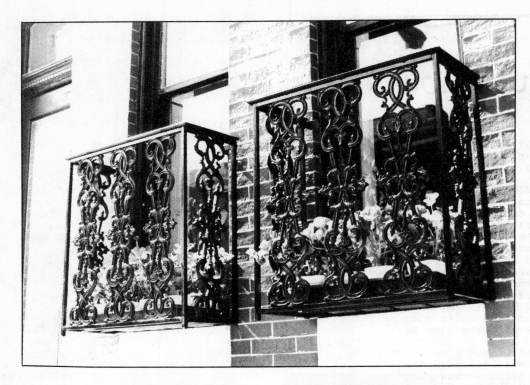

The finished balconies, complete with geraniums!

THE TOP IS STEEL, not cast iron, so we returned to the all-purpose electrode. After we ground the welds smooth, the rails were clamped atop the balconies and welded on. (You may find it helpful to use screw clamps to pull the rail against the frame top all around.)

SEVERAL COATS OF A GOOD rust-inhibitive paint will help the steel hold up to the weather. Our balconies were slightly wider than the windows, a constraint placed upon us by the size of the chosen castings. We wanted to avoid mounting them directly to the brick because we didn't want to have to chip the edges of the brick around the window. So it was necessary to weld simple brackets of angle irons to our balconies. Screws were then passed through these brackets and into the wooden window frame. Your installation will probably have special requirements too, and may need specially-designed brackets. None of these possibilities should prove to be a problem if you use the welder and a little ingenuity. 🏠

## Casting Houses

The catalogs from these casting houses will fill your head with ideas. There are flat panels of morning glory vines, oak leaves and acorns, and climbing iron roses. You'll find round iron medallions and fancy shelf brackets (like the ones used to support marble sink tops). Castings reminiscent of Gothic cathedrals, individual rails and balustrades, tiny cast finials, and cast parts for lawn furniture complete the pages. You'll recognize many as identical to old examples you've admired.

From the following list of foundries, Lawler, Fairmont, and Tennessee Fabricating have the widest selection of authentic castings. There is a great deal of duplication among their catalogs. Lawler's is the most sumptuous, but they have a $250 minimum order. Remember that in addition to the cost per casting, you also have to pay the freight, so a source closer to home may be a savings even if their catalog prices are slightly higher. The catalogs also include lots of mounting brackets for rails and posts in all sorts of situations, and probably have ideas for a tricky mounting.

J.G. Braun Company
7540 McCormick Boulevard
Skokie, IL 60076
(312) 674-2345
Catalog: free

Fairmont Foundry Company, Inc.
3125 35th Avenue North
Birmingham, AL 35207
(205) 841-6472
Catalog: free

Lawler Machine and Foundry
Box 2977
Birmingham, AL 35212
(205) 595-0596
Catalog: $5

Tennessee Fabricating Company
2366 Prospect Street
Memphis, TN 38106
(901) 948-3354
Catalog: $2.50

# Helpful Publications

## Art Nouveau Architecture
Edited by Frank Russell
1980 (322 pp., profusely illustrated) Cloth.

**M**AGNIFICENT PHOTOGRAPHS highlight this international survey of Art Nouveau architecture embracing the period from the late 19th to the early 20th centuries. The works of many celebrated architects (Mackintosh, Gaudi, Guimard, Jeanneret, Kotera, Olbrich, Wagner, Sullivan, and Wright) in eleven principal western countries are discussed in detail. Institutional, commercial, and residential architectural exteriors and interiors are treated. This oversize book is lavishly illustrated with color and black and white photographs in addition to plans and line drawings.

To order, send $75.00 plus $3.00 postage to:
Rizzoli International Publications
715 Fifth Avenue--Dept. OHJ
New York, New York 10019
(212) 397-3740

## The Antique Furniture Newsletter
Clinton Howell et al.
Bimonthly newsletter (16 pp., illustrated)

**A**NTIQUE FURNITURE collectors, restorers, and dealers will all benefit from this invaluable reference source. Veterans and newcomers will increase their "AIQ" (Antique Information Quotient) with every issue, while learning to distinguish well-designed, quality-made furniture from inferior examples. Historical information on styles, maintenance of antique furniture, and restoration techniques are lucidly explained and illustrated with detailed line drawings. A one-year subscription is $18 (6 issues); two-year is $30. Also available is the "Collector's Packet," a year's subscription plus 10 back issues for $34. Send $2.00 for a sample copy.

Send requests to:
The Antique Furniture Newsletter
Box 524, 59 Adams Street--Dept. OHJ
Bedford Hills, New York 10507
(914) 232-8687

## Furniture of the American Arts and Crafts Movement
David M. Cathers
1981 (275 pp., generously illustrated) Cloth.

**S**TICKLEY AND ROYCROFT mission oak furniture are represented in this photographic documentation of Arts and Crafts period furniture. Aimed at the collector, this book discusses the philosophic and stylistic influences of Gustav Stickley's furniture as well as the identifying characteristics and markings. The furniture of Leopold & J. George Stickley and Elbert Hubbard's Roycroft shops are treated to a lesser degree. Many different furniture types are pictured, more or less chronologically, to show the development of the Arts and Crafts movement. They include servers and china closets, sideboards and tables, bookcases and desks, chairs and other individual pieces. The text is illustrated with catalog reprints, magazine advertisements, line drawings, and plenty of black and white photographs.

To order, send $19.95 plus $1.86 postage to:
The New American Library
1633 Broadway--Dept. OHJ
New York, New York 10019
(212) 397-8000

## A Documentary History of American Interiors From the Colonial Era to 1915
Edgar Mayhew & Minor Myers
1980 (399 pp., profusely illustrated) Cloth.

**T**HIS AMBITIOUS VOLUME surveys the styles of the American interior from the 16th through 20th centuries. Old-house owners, preservationists, and antiquarians will find the capsule histories of each interior style quite useful. Clear chapter headings and subtitles provide instant historical information on furnishings, lighting, textiles, wall decorations, and color schemes of elaborate as well as humble interiors. A chapter is also devoted to American kitchens, bathrooms, and heating systems. The text is heavily illustrated with photographs and line drawings.

To order, send $45.00 plus $2.00 postage to: The Old-House Bookshop
69A Seventh Avenue
Brooklyn, New York 11217

## Neighborhood Organizing Kit
National Trust for Historic Preservation
1981 (50 pp., illustrated) Pamphlets.

**T**HIS IS A SPECIAL compilation of reprints from "Conserve Neighborhoods," a National Trust bimonthly newsletter. These materials guide you through your first organizing meeting, help you recruit members, raise money, and plan community events, and even explain such fine points as working effectively with City Hall. The packet contains an organizing guide, a bibliography of useful publications, a directory of neighborhood resource groups,

and a guide to organizing community events. The Neighborhood Organizing Kit is free.

Send requests to:
Conserve Neighborhoods
National Trust--Dept. OHJ
1785 Massachusetts Avenue, NW
Washington, D.C. 20036
(202) 673-4055

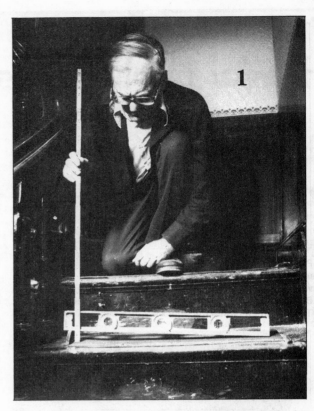

**3**

One of two things can happen. Either the wall string is pulled away from the wall, or the stair gets pulled apart, with steps coming out of the wall-string housing. The result in either case is an out-of-level stair which is awkward to use. **(3)**

IN GENERAL, stair problems (as separate from handrail problems) stem from three sources: differential building settlement, wood shrinkage, and occasionally poor detailing and workmanship. As it turned out, we had all three. Settlement had caused the slope; wood shrinkage had loosened joints and wedges in the sub-structure, causing increased deflection and creaking when anyone used the stairs. After we gained access to the underside, we found that a poor structural detail was contributing to the pronounced sag, and creating a potentially hazardous condition. **(4)**

CLEATS

CENTER CARRIAGE

NAILER

HEADER JOIST

**4**

**N**O REALLY satisfactory answer can be found for settlement problems. The dilemma? We wanted to level a stair in an out-of-level building. We did know the <u>building</u> was structurally sound. (Some fairly serious damage occurred in the remodeling 75 years ago, but stabilization work had been done when we moved in.) It had already been decided that it was impractical, if not impossible, to level the floors in the building. The question became, "To what extent should the stair be jacked up?" We couldn't have a perfect solution, so we looked for an optimum solution.

THE MOST IMPORTANT thing with stairs is that they maintain a consistent rise (height) for each step. Otherwise, walking rhythm is broken and people trip.

EXISTING LEVEL OF TOP LANDING

TOP RISER SHORTENED AFTER LEVELING STAIR

≈1½"

LEVELED STEP

EXISTING STEP

**5**

If our stair was leveled up completely, the height of the riser at the top step would be reduced by over 1-1/2 inches; a level stair meeting an out-of-level landing would present more of a hazard than a somewhat out-of-level stair. So we agreed with Harry's compromise: The stair would be jacked up only until it was comfortable to walk on, yet maintained a relatively consistent rise. Then it would be made secure. **(5)**

Above, retired master stairbuilder Harry Waldemar checks the level of the stair at the Old-House Journal offices. It had dropped 1-1/2 inches over a two-foot run, due partly to interior building settlement. Below, note treads pulling out of their housings in the wall string. "Wainscot" is just grained plaster.

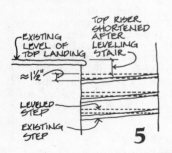

**2**

**6**

Plaster and wood lath were removed along the entire soffit under the stair. In the photo above, the cylinder braces are revealed. Ours is a typical row-house cylinder stair, or well stair. Below, the stair is braced against the partition wall opposite it. This operation pushes the steps back into their housings.

**8**

## Demolition

DEMOLITION WAS MESSY but simple--we removed the plaster soffit under the stair to gain full access to the entire sub-structure. The decorative plaster mouldings were first measured and recorded so they can be duplicated. A sample of each moulding profile was saved. The plaster cornice at the inside of the soffit could not practically be saved. Even if a neat cut could be made through the plaster and lath, it would leave a four-inch "floating" edge of lath and plaster that would be difficult to rejoin to new plaster or Sheetrock. Instead, a

new cornice moulding will be run in place; or the moulding could be duplicated with stock wood mouldings.

REMOVING THE PLASTER and lath underneath revealed that structural problem caused by poor original detailing. We'd seen it before in New York City: The carriages had merely been toenailed to a little nailing strip attached to the header joist at the bottom of the flight. (4) Now, the center and outer carriages were perched on the very edge of the nailing strip.

## Bracing

BEFORE THE STAIRCASE could be lifted and pushed back into place, all potential obstructions to the movement of the stair as a single unit had to be removed. Out came all wedges and misguided repairs from the past. (7) Misaligned treads were repositioned. Had any treads been badly warped, they would've been removed.

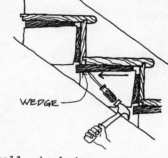

**7**

WEDGE

THE BRACING operation was simple and logical. Harry and his carpenter helper, Derek Tacon, had to push the stair back toward the wall, jack it up some, and then refasten the carriages to the header joist. (11) They placed a plank against the partition wall opposite the stair to distribute the load, protecting the plaster. Another plank was placed against the stairs. (8) Two more planks, cut slightly longer than the space between the stair and the wall, were placed in opposition. By wedging the planks in tighter and tighter with a crowbar, Harry forced the stair back into its housing against the masonry wall. (9)

PLAN OF STAIR

HALL — BRACES (PLANKS) IN OPPOSITION — FORCE

**9** CROWBAR

### Stair Scaffolds

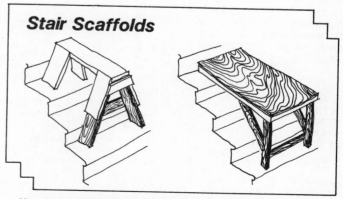

Harry uses a scaffolding set-up like the one on the left. He built an A-frame leg extension which stacks under a sawhorse. The more common stair scaffold, right, uses 3/4-inch plywood for the platform, and 2x3 or 2x4 lumber for the legs. Its height is determined by the headroom under your stair.

In the two photos at left, Harry solves the problem of the slipped carriages. First, the stair is jacked up a bit. A piece of lumber (we used left-over scaffolding planks) is wedged between the carriages and another plank laid on the steps below. After he drives in wedges to hold the carriages in place, he installs a metal joist hanger on each of the outside carriages. They make the carriages secure to the header joist.

Below left, Derek drives new wedges in the wall string housings.

## Wedging

A LL THE WEDGES were replaced to ensure that they were tight. (Glue sticks better to new wood than to dirty, previously-glued wood.) New wedges were cut from a piece of 3/4-inch pine.

They should be cut in an alternating pattern to maximize long grain. You can set up a jig on a table saw to maintain the critical dimension of the wedges. This way, variation in length doesn't matter, because all wedges will be

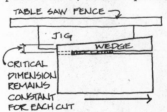

driven in to the same extent, and then excess can be trimmed off.

AT THE SAME TIME, braces were placed under the carriages at the top and bottom of the flight, to push the stair back up to a more level position. (10) To hold the stair in this braced-up position, Harry drove a wedge in between the upper end of each carriage and the joists under the landing.

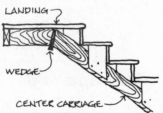

JOIST HANGERS ("Teco clamps") were used to secure the carriages to the header joist. (11) Once the carriages were secure, Harry and Derek removed the braces under the stairs. But the wall-to-stair brace had to remain until all of the sub-structure repairs were completed, including rewedging the treads and risers.

(A NOTE OF CAUTION: There's a lot of movement during all this bracing and leveling. Keep an eye on stress points, and be ready to open a joint in the string to relieve stress. Otherwise, it's possible that the string itself could crack. In our case, it was important to keep the cylinder, a weak point, from moving too much. (6)

EACH WEDGE must be glued in place. Over the years, Harry devised several tricks to save time and give him the competitive edge. One time-saver is his "bouquet of wedges." He puts carpenter's glue in the bottom of a wide-mouth container, then keeps a handful of wedges skinny-end-down. When he needs a wedge, he takes one out and spreads the glue with a scrap of wood or another wedge.

THE WEDGES are inserted from the top of the flight to the bottom, with the tread always wedged before the riser below it. The wedge must make even contact on both the surface of the step and the string. If it doesn't, the wedge won't effectively secure the step and there is a greater chance you'll split the string while driving the wedge. Hammer the wedge in until it's snug, but be careful not to apply too much force. (12) Last, a nail driven through the wedge and tread into the string helps keep the wedge in place. (13)

13

After gluing a wedge in place, Derek drives a nail through the wedge and tread, into the string. The wedges under each tread and behind each riser are what secure the steps in the string housings. The arrow in the photo above points to a wood cleat. Nailed to the center carriage, cleats prevent deflection of steps.

Below, the white pieces of wood are new glue blocks. The photo shows the front (outer) carriage and string, where glue blocks are doubled.

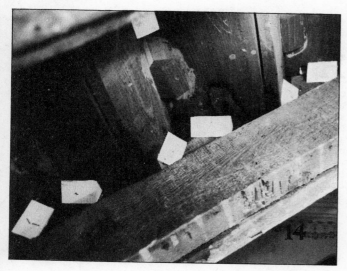

14

## Cleats

CLEATS, or stepped wood blocking, on the center carriage take the springiness out of each step and also deaden the hollow sound of walking on the steps. Even after the carriages had been braced up, the cleats were not in contact with the underside of the treads (due to wood shrinkage). This caused the unacceptable deflection of the treads when people walked on the stairs. It was also the source of the groaning. (4),(13)

THE EXISTING CLEATS were easily pried off and renailed snugly against the back side of each riser and the underside of each tread. One nail was toed into the tread, another into the riser. (Be careful to angle the nails so they don't go through riser or tread.) The cleats were installed alternating from one side of the carriage to the other. That way, the carriage won't tend to twist when load is applied to the stair.

## Glue Blocks

WHETHER OR NOT an old stair has existing glue blocks, Harry installs new ones at this point. These little blocks of wood were installed with a rubbed glue joint. (A glue-smeared block is put into position and rubbed back and forth until the glue grabs, or resists the rubbing motion.) A rubbed joint is quite strong. Two finish nails were driven into each block to keep it in position while the glue dried. (14)

GLUE BLOCKS prevent the stair from squeaking by increasing the surface area of the tread-to-riser joint. They also provide additional strength at the joints. Note that the old glue blocks were not removed. New blocks went in next to the old ones, two per step between carriages, and two more where the steps are joined to the front string.

## Nails

EACH STEP was back-nailed with 6d common nails. A nail was placed every six inches along the back side of the riser. As in all nailing operations, the nails were toed in slightly to add some strength. If a tread had sagged or warped, it would not have been forced upward for back-nailing; there's a chance the pressure of the warp would split the riser at the nail.

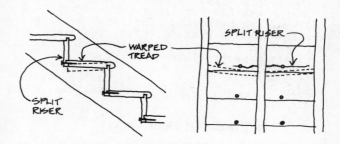

BACK-NAILING

GENERALLY, all of the fastening done on a stair is underneath--hidden from view. Face-nailing can provide additional strength, but it never looks great, so should be avoided if possible on fine stairs. Harry felt that our really shaky and not terribly fine stair would benefit from face-nailing the treads, though. He toenailed two #8 finish nails into the top of each tread, down into the riser.

FINISH NAILS TOED INTO RISER

TO COMPLETE the substructure repairs, Harry drove some #10 finish nails through the front string, into the front carriage. This helped make the flight less springy. At this point in the rehabilitation, the newel and balustrade were still loose...yet the stair felt a lot more secure!

Next month: Replacing the newel, repairing the balustrade

*Tips From Readers*
# Restorer's Notebook

### Tough Toothbrushes

REACH BRAND TOOTHBRUSHES do not disintegrate in stripper. Anybody who knows what I'm talking about will immediately recognize the far-reaching implications of this discovery.

Judee Reel
Red Hook, NY

### Restoring Marbleizing

MY 1861 SLATE MANTEL had been marbleized with brown and black paint. The paint had begun to flake off, and I felt hopeless about restoring it. But I managed to come up with a good substitute: shoe polish. It actually has the same translucent effect as glazing liquids. Using black and brown liquid shoe polish, I colored in the missing areas and hand-buffed lightly. When it was dry and hard, I followed with two applications of Butcher's paste wax for furniture (with drying time and buffing between). The final buffing brought it all to a uniform, soft, gleaming finish, and the irregularity of the paint surface is barely perceptible.

Eugene E. Smith
Philadelphia, PA

### In Praise Of Heat Guns

WE OWN AN OLD PARSONAGE. The problem is that every time a new minister arrived, the people would rip off as much wallpaper as they could and then either repaper or repaint. Removing all these layers has been a tedious job. I've tried everything to no avail (although I didn't rent a steamer). I finally tried my heat gun--what a relief! No more chipping away. I used a Red Devil P.130 scraper. All I did was hold the heat gun about 3/4 of an inch away from the wall and slide the scraper under the loose end. It softened the paste and peeled it off, with no wet mess.

*A useful hint that worked for you, but others should be aware of the potential fire hazard.—The Editors*

Mrs. Earl M. Clark
Hillsdale, NY

### Try Scraping First

THERE IS A VALUABLE paint-stripping technique that is usually overlooked: Most, if not all, of the paint can be scraped from the surface before chemical stripping begins. The more paint you can scrape off, the less gooey mess you'll have to put up with when you strip. If the surface was initially varnished, then all of the paint can be scraped off a flat surface with a sharp scraper. If the surface was initially painted, then all the paint will never come out of the pores. (Such a surface was probably designed to be painted--so it should remain painted.)

THE SCRAPER IS THE KEY. The longer the handle and the sharper the blade, the better. An old Stanley scraper with handles for both hands and a sharpenable blade has been invaluable for me. (If there are grooves to be scraped, then you can buy curved scrapers or else grind your own contours.) With some patience and muscle, I was able to scrape off three coats of paint from our oak wainscotting. All that was required afterward was some light chemical stripping to remove remnants of the varnish.

Dan Miller
Elgin, IL

### Clear Your Pipes

HERE'S A GOOD WAY to clear rust out of your pipes. Make or borrow the set-up pictured below. Attach the rubber hose with a hose clamp to the ailing plumbing fixture. Close the drain valve on your set-up and open the supply line of the sink or tub you're working on. Pump the pump--this forces air into the supply line. Leave the supply-line valve open and open the drain valve. The water in the supply line forces out the air; in a water-hammer effect, it also forces out some of the accumulated particles. Repeat the procedure several times until the water flow improves.

J. Cheydleur
College, AK

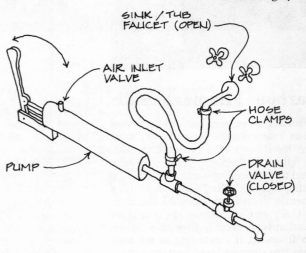

**Tips To Share?** Do you have any hints or short cuts that might help other old-house owners? We'll pay $15 for any short how-to items that are used in this "Restorer's Notebook" column. Write to Notebook Editor, The Old-House Journal, 69A Seventh Avenue, Brooklyn, NY 11217.

# Restoration Products News

## Stencils

With stencils from Adele Bishop, Inc., you can create your own floorcloth or stencilling—charming and personalized touches in your house restoration. Stencils are sold with a complete instruction booklet and drawn on Mylar (two patterns are pre-cut). Clear Mylar is available for those who would like to create their own design. Stencilling brushes and paints are also offered.

Three sets of stencils (copied from the Shelburne Museum in Shelburne, VT) were used to create the design shown here. Each set is $15.95. A color catalog ($2.00) shows the various patterns stencilled on walls, floors, furniture, and fabric. Adele Bishop, Inc., PO Box 557, Dept. OHJ-8, Manchester, VT 05254. (802) 362-3537.

## Carbon Filament Bulb

Finally—a source for old-fashioned carbon filament light bulbs. Until now, these have been very difficult to find. The glowing filament gives a special period touch to antique and reproduction lighting fixtures. The *Phoenix* bulb is an authentic recreation, manufactured in the U.S., and distributed by Bradford Consultants. A clear bulb with a carbon loop filament, it's available in 8-candle power (for signs and low-wattage lights), and 16-candle power (for wall fixtures, chandeliers, and table lamps). It operates on standard 120 volts, has a standard medium base, and works with a light dimmer. The bulb, which is said to last "forever," has a three-year warranty and is $4.50 (quantity discounts can be arranged). For more information, write to Bradford Consultants, 16 E. Homestead Ave., Dept. OHJ, Collingswood, NJ 08108. (609) 854-1404.

## A Variety Of Imports

Increasing the humidity in your house can help make it feel warmer. Litchfield House imports porcelain radiator humidifiers from England. The *Horizontal Bow Front* (10½ in. x 5½ in. x 2 in.), designed for horizontal radiators, is $26. The *Vertical Bow Front* (11 in. x 5 in. x 1 in.) is $24 and used for vertical radiators. Both styles hang over the radiator; they come in nine printed patterns, and plain white.

This company also imports English porcelain door furnishings. The designs are hand-stencilled onto heavy china and finished with a ceramic glaze. Patterns, as well as solid black or white with gold trim, are available on fingerplates, door and cabinet knobs, and florets (key hole covers). Complete sets for both sides of a door cost about $45.

Litchfield House is also selling six cast-iron firegrates, for coal or wood. These are lost-wax castings of 18th and 19th century British originals and range in price from $120 to $600. Free brochures are available on each line, so specify your interest when writing: Litchfield House, On-The-Green, Dept. OHJ, Sharon, CT 06069. (203)364-0236.

## Iron Betty, Etc.

There has been a resurgence in blacksmithing in the last decade, but Newton Millham's hand-forged work goes beyond the usual assortment of fireplace tools. Many of his designs are copies of 17th-, 18th-, and early 19th-century hardware.

A specialty seems to be unique lighting devices, such as an adjustable spring trammel candle holder ($50), and pipe or ember tongs which were used to light a pipe with an ember from the fire (a 1740s design—$225). He also has a good knowledge of early door, sash, shutter, and gate hardware. Prices range from $2 for an 18th-century sash pin (with leather strap) to $140 for a 12-in. spring latch with cast brass knobs.

Millham's ironwork can be custom forged according to measured drawings, copied from an existing piece, or taken from old builder's guides. He does offer a catalog of finished pieces, which can be reproduced or used as inspiration for your own ideas. (Allow six to twelve weeks for delivery.) Send $1.00 to Newton Millham, Blacksmith, 672 Drift Rd., Dept. OHJ, Westport, MA 02790. (617) 636-5437.

*Iron Betty ($110)*
*mid 18th-century design*

# Roofing Materials

*With spring just around the corner, this might be a good time to think about replacing or repairing your roof. Some materials listed here are superior to modern roofing in appearance or longevity; some have been around since your house was built, but are hard to find today.*

*Prices for roofing materials are usually given in dollars per square. A square is the amount of material needed to cover 100 sq. ft. with the customary lap.*

## Asbestos

If you need to replace the roof on your turn-of-century house, asbestos shingles could be especially appropriate. Supradur, one of the only companies in the country producing mineral-fiber shingles, is best known in the restoration field for their slate-like replacement shingles (*Supraslate*). They also produce *Dutch Lap*, *Twin Lap*, and *Hexagonal*—shingles that immediately bring to mind turn-of-century houses, and that have become increasingly difficult to find.

Dutch Lap                    Twin Lap

These special-order shingles are made of asbestos fiber embedded in cement. Price is about $60 to $84 per square. (The cost of asphalt shingles begins at about $30 per square, with heavier weights costing up to $80 per square.) Supradur's mineral-fiber shingles cannot rot, have a class A or B fire rating (depending on the shingle), and they have a 30-year warranty against shrinkage and warping. Thus they're a good investment, besides being unusual. The *Twin Lap* comes in a variety of colors, the *Dutch Lap* in black and in white, and the *Hexagonal* in charcoal black. For a free brochure and the location of a dealer, write Supradur Manufacturing Corp., 122 E. 42nd St., Dept. OHJ, New York, NY 10168. (212) 697-1160.

## Metal Shingles

*Metal roofing tile is fireproof, lightweight, long-lasting, and attractive. It's as historically appropriate as more expensive roofing materials in many circumstances. For more information about care and installation see OHJ March 1981.*

Conklin Tin Plate & Metal Co. has been producing a fine line of metal roofing for over 100 years. The single pattern they offer is available in 28 gauge galvanized steel, copper, stainless steel, and micro-zinc (a "self-healing" rust-proof alloy). Micro-zinc roofing is available for $341.38 per square and terne for about $182 per square. Send $3 for a brochure that describes the materials, accessories, and installation: Conklin Tin Plate & Metal Co., PO Box 2662, Dept. OHJ, Atlanta, GA 30301. (404) 688-4510.

Berridge Manufacturing Co., a large producer of modern metal roofing, also stocks three Victorian patterns. The *Victorian*, *Classic*, and *Fish-scale* shingles are available in copper, terne-coated stainless steel, and Galvalume (a "self-healing" aluminum-zinc alloy). These shingles can be shipped unfinished or with a choice of twelve baked-on finish colors; the factory finish has a twenty-year guarantee against peeling, cracking,

and fading. Galvalume costs about $125 per square, depending on the distributor and your location. For a free brochure and the name of a dealer in your area, contact Berridge Manufacturing Co., 1720 Maury St., Dept. OHJ, Houston, TX 77026. (713) 223-4971.

Well known for their metal ceilings, W.F. Norman also produces a line of metal roofing from original patterns. Several patterns are available in galvanized steel ($109 to $203 per square), or copper. For a free brochure, write W.F. Norman, PO Box 323, Dept. OHJ, Nevada, MO 64772. (417) 667-5552.

## Terra Cotta Or Clay

*Clay or terra-cotta tiles have a class A fire rating and an average lifespan of 75-150 years. This type of roofing usually brings to mind Spanish Revival houses, but there are many more tile designs besides the barrel-shaped Mission tile. The classic flat interlocking terra-cotta tile is one such style.*

Ludowici-Celadon is a major manufacturer of clay roofing tiles used in restorations. A variety of stock tiles are available; they will also do custom reproductions. They offer several flat tile styles: *Americana*, which has a rough hewn texture; *Williamsburg*, which resembles a wood shingle; *Classic*, a flat red tile that would be appropriate for the English Revival styles; *Lanai*, a textured brown tile; and *Norman*, a red/black mottled tile with an earthy, rustic look.

These tiles are hard-fired and have a low permeablity. Their promised water absorption is less than 3% of their weight, enabling them to withstand freeze-thaw

cycles. Most tiles are available in several colors, with prices ranging from $198 per square for a very plain interlocking tile to $949 for the top-of-the-line *Norman*. For a free brochure, write Ludowici-Celadon Co., PO Box 69-OHJ, New Lexington, OH 43764. (614) 342-1995.

Besides offering four patterns of clay roofing tiles, High Brooms has recently become the American importer of Keymer tiles. These flat clay tiles are handmade by English craftsmen and have been available in Canada for several years. Three finishes are offered: dark or medium antique (a mottled-weathered look), and red. They have a water absorption of 5-11% and require a minimum 40° roof pitch. The average cost is $500 per square. A free brochure is available from Mr. Tom McGrath at High Brooms, Suite 403, 24 Mount Vernon St., Dept. OHJ, Boston, MA 02108. (617) 720-1729.

# Opinion...
# Remuddling
## — Of The Month —

BEFORE: *This handsome fieldstone wall blended neatly into its surroundings. And then the painters came along...*

**N**ORMALLY, the remuddling feature deals only with harm done to old houses. But this month's "winner" raised such an interesting issue that we couldn't resist it--even though it deals more with the environment than with an old building.

FIELDSTONE was an especially popular construction material in the early 20th century. Fieldstone walls, foundations and chimneys fulfilled the Craftsman ideal of "honest materials honestly expressed." By using natural materials in a man-made construction, the builder achieved a harmony between the natural and built environments. Here, in the words of an OHJ sub-scriber, is the fate that befell the once-handsome fieldstone wall shown in the photos:

"Over the strong objections of her youthful painters, who had just finished painting the trim and stone facing of her home, the owner ordered that her multi-colored fieldstone wall and entryway be spray-painted a stark white. In a few brief hours, this beautiful wall, which previously blended into the surrounding environment, was transformed into a startling white eyesore to shock the senses of every passer-by. The only saving grace is that we currently have about a foot of fresh white snow on the ground, allowing the wall to blend into its surroundings once again--at least until spring."

FORTUNATELY, this work is reversible. Given time, Nature herself will strip the white paint and re-establish the harmony between the wall and its surroundings.

Submitted by: Roger E. Childers
Minneapolis, Minn.

**WIN FAME AND $50:** If you spot a classic example of remuddling, send us a clear black & white photo. We'll award $50 if your photos are selected as the monthly winner. The message is more dramatic if you also send along a picture of a similar unremuddled building. Send your entries to: Remuddling Editor, The Old-House Journal, 69A Seventh Avenue, Brooklyn, N.Y. 11217.

AFTER: *Painted white, the wall now looks like something made out of leftover styrofoam packing beads.*

# The Old-House Journal®

69A Seventh Avenue,
Brooklyn, New York 11217

NO PAID ADVERTISING

Postmaster: Address Correction Requested

# The Old-House Journal

### Restoration and Maintenance Techniques For The Antique House

Vol. X No. 3          $2.00

# BUYER BEWARE
## Seeing Through Bad Stained Glass

By Fred J. Gaca, Zion, Illinois

IN YESTERDAY'S HOMES, nothing bespoke luxury more than stained glass windows. Today's restorers are discovering that the addition of stained glass or the repair of existing windows brings a jewel-like radiance and a seductive warmth to the light entering a room. Fortunately, stained glass is again riding a crest of popularity. Glass artists and restorers are far more prevalent now than they were ten years ago. Unhappily, many of these people are not skilled in their craft. The demand for stained glass has created a gap in the supply--a gap too often filled with work that is poorly designed, poorly constructed, and destined for the dustbin. In the worst cases, plastics have been foisted on the unsuspecting public.

A GENUINE "BUYER BEWARE" situation now exists. Restorers who seek either new panels or the restoration of existing panels should have a basic knowledge of stained glass--what it is, how it is constructed, and how to judge its quality. Questions of style, period design, and aesthetics are best left to the perpetual debates among glass artists and glass lovers. But all styles share a common need for quality workmanship. Anyone interested in purchasing glass can learn to recognize that quality.

STAINED GLASS is made from a mixture of silica (usually fine, clean sand) which is blended with various alkalis, salts, and metal oxides. The exact composition of the mixture will determine the color of the glass. Because of variations in mixtures and manufacturing processes, each batch of glass will show slight changes in color, just as paints, dyes, or yarns vary from lot to lot. The silica mixture is heated in extremely hot kilns until it melts. The mixture is then allowed to cool, forming glass. Properly made, the colors are part of the glass and will never fade or change, except to develop a patina after several decades.

(THERE IS a growing concern that our polluted atmosphere is detrimental to glass. Many glass artists now recommend protecting stained glass panels by installing a pane of clear glass facing the outside air. The use of protective glass, while lacking historical precedence, can add years to the life of stained glass.)

WHILE STILL MOLTEN, glass can be blown or shaped to create bottles, vases, and other

*continued on page 66*

# To Dip Or Not To Dip?

**The Old-House Journal®**

*Editor*
**Clem Labine**

*Managing Editor*
**Patricia Poore**

*Assistant Editor*
**Cole Gagne**

*Editorial Assistants*
**Joni Monnich**
**Stephanie Croce**

*Circulation Supervisor*
**Joan O'Reilly**

*Circulation Assistants*
**Margaret Scaglione**
**Barbara Bugg**
**Jean Baldwin**

*Office Manager*
**Sally Goodman**

*Office Assistant*
**Rafael Madera**

*Sales Promotion*
**Joel Alpert**

*Circulation Director*
**Paul T. McLoughlin**

*Technical Consultant*
**Alan D. Keiser**
*Architectural Consultant*
**Jonathan Poore**

*Contributing Editors*
**R. A. Labine, Sr.**
**John Mark Garrison**

*Published by The Old-House Journal ©
Corporation, 69A Seventh Avenue,
Brooklyn, New York 11217. Telephone
(212) 636-4514. Subscriptions $16 per
year in U.S. Not available elsewhere.
Published monthly. Contents are fully
protected by copyright and must not
be reproduced in any manner whatsoever without specific permission in
writing from the Editor.*

*We are happy to accept editorial contri-
butions to The Old-House Journal.
Query letters which include an outline
of the proposed article are preferred.
All manuscripts will be reviewed, and
returned if unacceptable. However,
we cannot be responsible for non-
receipt or loss — please keep copies
of all materials sent.*

**Printed at Photo Comp Press,
New York City**

*ISSN: 0094-0178*
**NO PAID ADVERTISING**

WE'RE IN THE MIDST of compil-ing a major report on strip-ping paint--everything from marble mantels to wainscotting, to shutters, to.... And there is one major area in which we need feedback from our readers: dip-stripping.

WE'VE ALL HEARD horror stories about dip-stripping—fly-by-night operators, raised grain, loss of color, joints that come unglued, and the newly ap-plied finish that won't stay stuck.

YET OTHERS have used dip-strip-ping and are apparently happy. So the best way to get a com-plete picture of the pros and cons of dip stripping is to collect a wide sampling of ex-perience from the OHJ audience.

YOU MAY RECALL that last year we asked you to communicate your experiences with floor finishes. The result was the extensive report in our May 1981 issue that detailed the numerous problems people were having with polyurethane floor finishes.

OHJ READERS make up the coun-try's largest "test kitchen" --one with 55,000 cooks. So please put on your chef's cap and give us your answers to the following questions. We realize you probably don't want to cut the questionnaire out of your issue. You can either Xerox it...or use the format as an outline and jot your answers on a piece of paper. Mail to:

Refinishing Editor
The Old-House Journal
69A Seventh Avenue
Brooklyn, N.Y. 11217

MANY THANKS for sharing.

--Clem Labine

---

## My Experience With Dip-Stripping Has Been:

[ ] SATISFACTORY OVERALL        [ ] UNSATISFACTORY OVERALL

Here's my latest [ ] HAPPY
                 [ ] UNHAPPY
experience with dip-stripping:

1. Object(s) being stripped:

2. Type of wood:

3. Used  [ ] Commercial service
         [ ] Did it myself

4. What type of stripping chemical was used?

5. Do you know if and how the stripping chemical was neutralized?

6. Any problems with:
   [ ] Raised grain
   [ ] Bleached effect; color change

[ ] Joints coming unglued
[ ] Surface degradation of wood
[ ] Incomplete removal of paint

7. Type of finish applied to stripped wood:

8. Any problems with the finish?
   [ ] Yes        [ ] No
   Describe:

9. Do you have the name and address of a commercial dip-stripping service that you can recommend from personal ex-perience?

10. Any other comments, problems, or ad-vice to give anyone about dip-stripping wood?

11. Your name and address (optional).

# The Homestead House

### By Clem Labine

ALONG WITH THE AMERICAN FOURSQUARE (see last month's OHJ), there is another type of "plain" house that puzzles old-house lovers who strive to name the style of every building. A typical example of this plain house is shown below. If the house were situated in the country, many would call it a farmhouse. But if you found it on a city street or in a suburb, "farmhouse" would hardly do.

WE'VE NAMED this type of structure the Homestead House. This name recognizes both the functional and historical roots of the style. The dictionary defines homestead this way:

"HOMESTEAD: The seat of a family, including the land, house and outbuildings; especially a dwelling retained as a home by successive generations."

THE HOMESTEAD HOUSE was built as a home by successive generations of Americans. The Homestead Houses that were built in America in 1920 were not revivals; they were a continuation of a building tradition that had its beginning in the 1700's.

THE ORIGINS of the Homestead House are easy to see: It was designed to provide economical shelter for rural working families. The two-

storey construction gave maximum floor space under a single roof. The straight walls and simple gabled roof were easy for part-time housewrights to build. The lack of ornamentation reduced construction time and kept maintenance to a minimum.

DURING THE VICTORIAN ERA, the Homestead House remained a strictly rural style; its simple lines were too unsophisticated for the style-conscious urban home-buyer. But by the beginning of the 20th century, there was a massive shift in taste. Buyers were more concerned with comfortable, functional, "sanitary" houses than with the romantic structures that summoned up images of bygone days. Simplicity and honesty were the fashion.

THUS, in the early 1900's, there was a market in city and suburb for the Homestead House. Fitted up with electricity, indoor plumbing, servantless kitchen, and indoor bathroom, the Homestead House became a "modern" dwelling...and in fact displayed most of the features we find in today's new homes. So the house that had lived in the countryside for a century moved to the suburbs. It became home not only to the farmer, but to the urban working class.

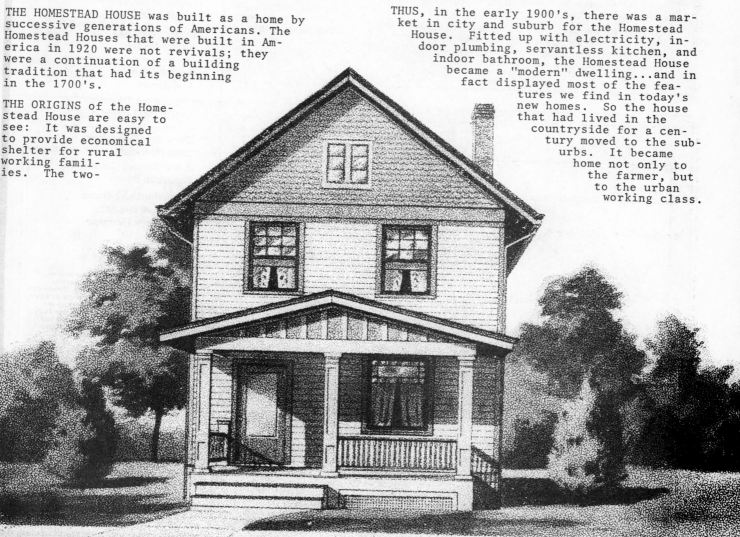

## Evolution Of The Homestead House

**1700's GEORGIAN COLONIAL**

**EARLY 1800's GREEK REVIVAL "TEMPLE HOUSE"**

**EARLY 1900's HOMESTEAD HOUSE**

THE HOMESTEAD HOUSE of the early 20th century evolved in a steady progression from the simple Colonial home of the 18th century. In the Colonial house, the accent was on symmetry, with the plan based on a rectangle. The entry door was in the center of the long side, with windows arranged in symmetrical bays on either side of the door.

The Greek Revival of the early 19th century made everyone aspire to live in a Greek temple. So the Colonial Georgian house was modified slightly, moving the entry door to the gable end of the house, and adding mouldings to the gable to make it look like the pediment of a Greek temple. On houses of the wealthy, columns, pilasters and porticos heightened the Greek effect.

The Greek mania subsided after the 1840's, but farm people continued to build houses that retained the essential geometry of the old Temple Houses—especially the entry door on the gable end. The Homestead House remained pretty much a rural style until the beginning of the 20th century....when a desire for simple, honest housing created a market for this type of home in both city and suburb.

## The Two Common Versions

THE BASIC HOMESTEAD HOUSE has two storeys, a rectangular plan, and a simple gabled roof. Sometimes there are dormers projecting from the roof. The exterior is quite plain, often just clapboard siding and simple cornerboards. In addition to wood frame construction, the Homestead House can also be built of brick or stone. On the basic Homestead House, the entry door is on the gable end. There's usually a porch extending the full width of the front facade.

THE TRI-GABLED ELL is a common variation of the basic Homestead House. Also two storeys, the plan consists of two intersecting rectangles forming an ell. The extra leg on the house provides additional opportunity for sunlight, cross-ventilation, and visual variety. The roof has three gables, hence the name. A porch may connect to one, two or three sides of the house. A common configuration is to have the porch tucked into the space formed by the two legs of the ell.

The Greek Revival house, with its emphasis on the prominent gable, was the direct ancestor of the Homestead House. This 1820 farmhouse has mouldings attached to the main gable to suggest the pediment of a Greek temple. Stripped of its Greek detailing, this same type of house was being built a century later in city and suburb. Then, they called it simply a "modern house." We are calling it the Tri-Gabled Ell.

The Homestead House is defined by its shape, rather than by ornamental details. This house has decorative details borrowed from three styles: Greek Revival cornice returns, Italianate brackets, and Gothic Revival drip mouldings around the windows. Yet the house is essentially a simple Tri-Gabled Ell, typical of the Homestead Houses built in the 1870's.

T HE CLAPBOARD EXTERIORS of Homestead Houses usually have simple vertical and horizontal boards that delineate corners, windows, eaves, etc. At the turn of the century, most Homestead Houses got a two-tone paint job so that the trim boards would stand out in contrast to the rest of the body. Often, two shades of the same color--such as green--would be used:

*The 1908 Sears Catalog showed this simple Tri-Gabled Ell. Back then, you could have built this house for $725.*

the light color for the body and the darker shade for the trim. Another popular color combination was reddish yellow for the body, brown for the trim, and red for the sashes. The book "A Century of Color " shows a number of color combinations that would be appropriate for a Post-Victorian Homestead House.

THOSE OF YOU who are lucky enough to own a Homestead House have inherited 200 years of American domestic history. It's a heritage to preserve carefully...and to be proud of.

This 1920's Homestead House is typical of thousands built in city and suburb in the early 20th century. Though partially remuddled, its relationship to the 1820's Temple House is clear. The biggest difference is the porch that extends across the front facade. Note also the triple window in the gable. Its shape suggests a Colonial Revival Palladian window, while the diamond-shaped glazing evokes the tiny panes of the earliest Colonial houses.

# OHJ Stair Repair ~
# Fixing Our Balustrade

By Patricia Poore
*Illustrations & Photographs By Jonathan Poore*

AS WE DESCRIBED last month, the stairs in the OHJ offices had been remodeled and abused. Still, the upper flight, between third and fourth floors, was relatively unchanged. We asked now-retired stairbuilder Harry Waldemar to show us how an expert would tackle these stairs.

WHILE HARRY noted with amusement some of the construction details and previous "repairs" he found, we noted with admiration his economy of means on the job: Harry completed even structural repairs without disrupting the office, and without fancy tools. Many a good carpenter would have disassembled the entire flight, but in our case, not once was the stair impassable. Happily, much of the information in this and last month's articles applies to other wood stairs, so you, too, can use Harry's practical, economical techniques if you have a staircase to fix.

THE FEBRUARY ARTICLE featured structural repairs of the undercarriage, from leveling up the stair to rewedging the steps. This month, we'll finish up our case history with work on the balustrade and newels.

BALUSTRADES (handrail + balusters) on the fourth flight and along the third- and fourth-floor hallways were wobbly and out of plumb. Changes made during the remodeling had caused the problem: The third-floor stair had been altered from its original cylinder configuration. Where there had once been a continuous curved rail, added-on newels now butted against handrails. (A partition had been built under the the balustrade and the balustrade moved closer to the stair.)

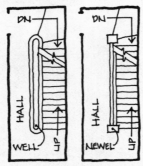

ORIGINAL PLAN OF STAIRS

PLAN AFTER ALTERATION

ALL BALUSTRADES had to be straightened and repaired. Harry also replaced both newels. They weren't original to the building, and were crudely made and poorly installed besides. Five balusters which were broken or missing were replaced with new balusters. Wherever it was possible, of course, original parts of the stair were retained, as much for economy's sake as to keep intact the history and character of the building.

SO THAT THE BALUSTRADE could be made plumb, the newels were removed and the rail bracket disconnected. A plumb bob was the most convenient tool for the leveling operation--Harry could get it in between the balusters. A level would have been awkward to use because there were no flat surfaces to rest it on.

WITH THE NEWELS removed, the balustrade could be pushed by hand into a plumb (vertical) position. (If the balustrade resists, you'll have to loosen or remove some of the tight balusters.) Now, a temporary brace was nailed in position.

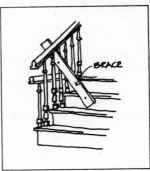

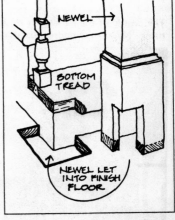

NOW WE could take accurate measurements for the replacement newels. The newels were made slightly longer than needed in order to compensate for unevenness in the floor. All of the existing cutouts in the steps and floor were squared up before fitting the newel. The newel was then cut to fit the opening as shown in this drawing and photos (1) and (2).

WHEN THE NEWEL had been fitted into the proper position at the correct height, the profile of the level rail was traced onto the newel; the newel was then mortised out for the rail. (3) Our stair rail did not have an easement (which would make the intersection between rail and newel perpendicular), so the rail was merely butted against the newel.

THE RAIL MORTISE was cut out by hand with a chisel. (4) An

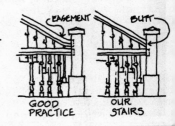

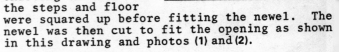

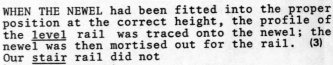

Sawn notches in the replacement newel are trimmed to fit tightly to the bottom tread and floor (above right).

The profile of the handrail is traced onto the newel for mortising. Note the temporary balustrade brace.

The poorly-constructed old newels were removed, and the openings left in the floor squared up. Each newel base was fitted into the floor and against the bottom step by trial and error: Far left, Harry chisels "a little bit more" off the newel base before installing it. If it's fitted accurately, the newel should stand sturdy even before nailing.

incannel gouge was useful for squaring up the curved profile of the mortise. Unlike a standard gouge, which cuts sloping sides, an incannel gouge will cut perpendicular sides on a mortise. (This type of gouge is very handy for stair work in general, such as cleaning out housings for stair nosings, and shaping handrail parts.)

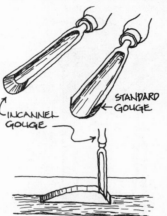

AFTER HE CUT the mortise, Harry braced the newel against the wall to hold it solidly in position for toe-nailing. (5) Finish nails were driven through the base of the newel into the sub-flooring, the bottom riser, and the front string. Likewise, finish nails were toed through the handrail into the newel. (6)

Here, Harry Waldemar cuts a mortise in the replacement newel. The end of the level rail will fit into this cut-out. Harry uses an incannel gouge to square up the edges of the rail profile.

# Shop
# Work

ALL OF THE REPLACEMENT PARTS for our stair were fabricated by Harry Waldemar, following standard woodshop procedures. Most of the repairs described in our case history are within the capability of anyone with basic carpentry skill. To do the shop work, however, you'd have to be familiar with a table saw, and a router or shaper. If you can turn and have access to a lathe, all the better.

Nevertheless, you can take an existing baluster or nosing to a woodworking shop for replication. The baluster and newel layouts drawn on this page show you (or your woodworker) what has to be considered before any wood is cut.

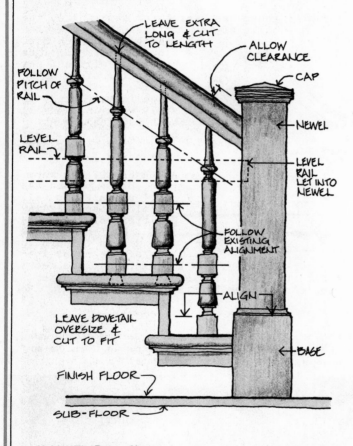

FOLLOW PITCH OF RAIL

LEAVE EXTRA LONG & CUT TO LENGTH

ALLOW CLEARANCE

CAP

NEWEL

LEVEL RAIL

LEVEL RAIL LET INTO NEWEL

FOLLOW EXISTING ALIGNMENT

ALIGN

LEAVE DOVETAIL OVERSIZE & CUT TO FIT

BASE

FINISH FLOOR

SUB-FLOOR

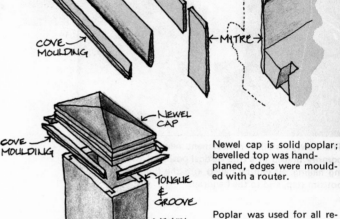

BRACKET
RETURN NOSING

COVE MOULDING

MITRE

COVE MOULDING

NEWEL CAP

TONGUE & GROOVE

NEWEL 3/4" POPLAR

COVE MOULDING

BASE 3/4" POPLAR

**EXPLODED VIEW OF NEWEL**

Newel cap is solid poplar; bevelled top was hand-planed, edges were moulded with a router.

Poplar was used for all replacement pieces. It is:
- commonly available
- relatively inexpensive
- easy to machine
- easy to stain well
- easy to match-finish

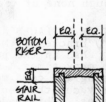

EQ. EQ.

BOTTOM RISER

STAIR RAIL

LEVEL RAIL

**PLAN OF NEWEL**

**Making The Return Nosings**

ROUGH CUT
1. Bullnose 3 sides of plank with router or shaper
2. Set table saw fence for width of nosing
3. Cut first nosing; flip plank & cut nosing from opposite side
4. Rout new bullnoses on 2 sides
5. Cut again, and repeat until plank is used up

Next, cut mitres for tread nosings.

NOTCHING
Now, notch each return nosing for the bracket to fit underneath it. Quickest way is to use a table saw—but the roundness of the blade will cause an overrun, as shown at far right. Hide the overrun underneath the nosing on its back side.

Follow same procedures for cove mouldings.

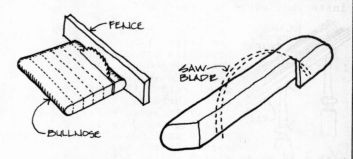

FENCE

BULLNOSE

SAW BLADE

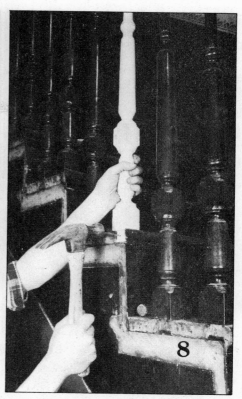

The newly-installed replacement newel is temporarily braced in a true vertical position, awaiting nailing. It will be nailed into the floor, the bottom step, and to the handrails.

Countersunk nails hold the rails to the newel. Had this been a fine parlor stair, Harry would have taken the trouble to install a hidden rail bolt. (see OHJ, June 1981, p. 138)

Balusters are nailed through the dovetail.

Harry installs the second replacement newel. (Marks in mortise are from a drill bit used to rout out most of the wood.)

THE SECOND NEWEL was installed in the same manner as the first. (7) Only the specific shape of the cut-outs varied. After both newels were nailed, the temporary brace was removed from the rail, along with the newel brace. At this point the handrails were extremely rigid, even though none of the balusters had been resecured.

WE REPLACED ALL of the return nosings and brackets. Many were split, and nearly all had in the past been whacked with a hammer too many times. Although each original return nosing and cove moulding was made in one piece, Harry cut the replacement parts as separate pieces. This made it easier to adjust the fit where existing joints and surfaces had become uneven. (See p. 60 for method used to make return nosings.) The new brackets--which, like the plain originals, were just short pieces of ¼ x 2-inch lattice--were left slightly oversize to be cut to fit later.

BEFORE ANY BRACKETS and return nosings were installed, every baluster, old and new, was

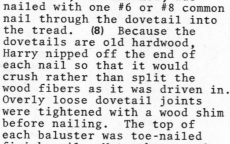

nailed with one #6 or #8 common nail through the dovetail into the tread. (8) Because the dovetails are old hardwood, Harry nipped off the end of each nail so that it would crush rather than split the wood fibers as it was driven in. Overly loose dovetail joints were tightened with a wood shim before nailing. The top of each baluster was toe-nailed with a #6 or #8 finish nail. Note that no glue was used in tightening or installing balusters.

Flat decorative brackets, return nosings, and cove mouldings are installed step by step, from the top of the flight to the bottom. Assembly order depends on each return nosing being installed after the bracket on the riser above it; then, the cove moulding goes on last because it hides a joint.

Far left, carpenter Derek Tacon—Harry's assistant—applies glue only near the mitre joint on a return nosing.

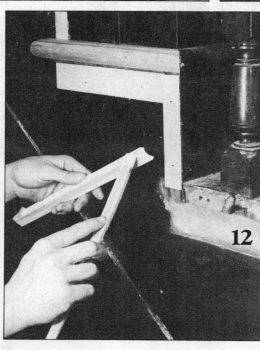

Four finish nails hold the return nosing to the tread.

The slender cove moulding—glued at mitre only—covers the joint between return nosing and bracket.

TO ENSURE neat reattachment of the nosings, cove mouldings, and brackets, all of the lumps and dribbles of old glue and varnish were scraped off the surfaces to be joined. A very sharp chisel or a small scraper works best. The chisel was dragged across the wood so that only the glue and finish were removed-- without taking any wood along.

SHARP CHISEL →

BRACKETS had been pre-cut on a table saw, including the mitre. Each one had to be trimmed with a block plane and custom fit to each step. The brackets were installed with two #4 finish nails each. Glue is unnecessary here. (9-12)

RETURN NOSINGS were trimmed and planed to fit each step. Before being nailed in place, the mitre and first few inches of each nosing were coated with glue. (9) Gluing this much of the nosing helps keep the mitre closed while still allowing the tread to shrink and swell with seasonal changes. (If the return nosing is glued along its entire length, there's a chance the tread will split, because it's being restrained by the return nosing.) The return nosing is held firmly, but more freely, to the tread with #8 finish nails. (10, 11)

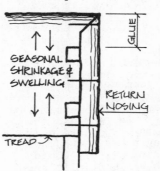

AGAIN WITH the cove mouldings, only the mitre is glued, and the rest held by #4 finish nails. Now all we have to do is match a finish on the replacement pieces to the old wood!

# Recovering An Old Silk Lampshade

By Tom H. Gerhardt
Cape Girardeau, Missouri

FROM THE LATE nineteenth
century into the early twentieth century, silk lampshades
were popular decorative items for table
lamps, floor lamps, and lighting fixtures. At
first, their use was limited, due to the danger of fire from gas and kerosene lights. But
with the advent of electrical lighting, they
became extremely popular.

MORE RECENTLY, these lampshades were considered to be quite hideous, embodiments of all
the fussy, undesirable traits of the late Victorian period. But now these shades with
their silks and trimmings are coming back into
vogue, and many homeowners are using them to
properly complement the rooms they have restored.

UNFORTUNATELY, many of these antique lamps
and fixtures are now turning up with
their shades ravaged by improper
care. These down-trodden shades
usually look as if they should
be thrown out. However, if you
want an authentic shade, then
the remains must never be dis-
posed of. Even the cloth must
not be ripped off before recovering. The best thing to do is
to place such a shade in a plastic bag for safekeeping until you
have amassed a little fund for having
it restored. Better yet, you can restore
it yourself.

## Recovering Begins

RECOVERING INVOLVES a good deal of
patience and time (usually fifty or
more hours). It's completely hand-
stitched, but can be done by a person
who is only semi-skilled in
the art of stitchery. Beginners should have no problems
with a basic project such as
the one discussed in this article. But even an elaborate
recovering need not confound
you. The most delicate panel-
work involves the same basic
operations performed in recovering plainer shades.

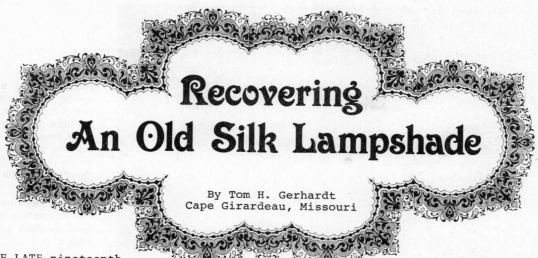

This lamp appeared in the 1922 Montgomery
Ward Catalog of Lighting Fixtures & Electrical Goods. "A lamp of rich, simple dignity
with shade of fine quality silk, fashioned and
lined with China silk in contrasting color. May
be ordered in old rose or blue, with chenille
fringe and braid edging in harmonizing color."
(By the way, it went for $17.25 back then!)

CLOSELY EXAMINE how the
shade was put together. Note
where the trimming appears, the
size of the gathering in the shirring, where the stitching is attached to the
wire frame, and in what order the material and
trimming are attached to the frame. When you
are ready to recover the frame, carefully remove the existing material. Cut the stitching
cautiously so you can save as much of the trimming as possible. Cloth samples should also
be saved to help you buy material of a similar
color.

NOW YOU'RE DOWN TO a wire frame wrapped in
cloth tape--the skeleton of the shade, onto
which the lining, outer covering, and trimming
were sewn. The cloth tape will usually be rotten by this time, and so should be removed as
well. Note how it was wound and secured on
the wire as you take it off the frame.

WIDE BIAS TAPE is a good replacement. Tightly wrap the new
cloth tape onto the bare wire
frame, sewing the seams of the
tape together at the joints of
the frame. The materials for
the shade will be sewn onto
this tape (stitches around the
wire would slip).

## The Lining

THE MATERIAL FOR THE LINING should ful-
fill two requirements. It should
have a heavier weight than the outer
covering, and its color should be a
lighter shade of the color of the outer
covering. This will help make the lampshade more opaque, thereby preventing
the outline and glare of the light
bulbs from showing through.
(Remember to avoid using high-
wattage bulbs; they become
very hot and can cause the lining to scorch.)

THE LINING is stretched tightly
underneath the frame in wedge-
shaped gores or panels. Using
a heavy-weight thread of matching color, stitch the seams on

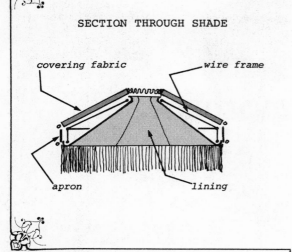

*covering fabric*  *wire frame*

*apron*  *lining*

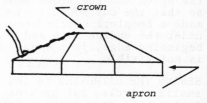

*Winding the frame
with cloth tape*

*crown*

*apron*

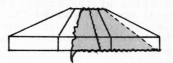

*Lining with panels or gores*

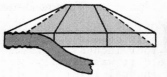

*Covering the apron
with a flat panel*

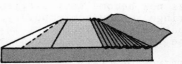

*Covering the top with
gathered material*

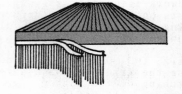

*Attaching the fringe or beads*

*Completing the other trimming*

top of the lining--the edges of the material will be hidden by the outer covering. In a basic shade such as this one, the lining runs straight from the bottom of the apron to the crown, leaving a triangular area between the outer covering and the lining (see illustration above).

THE STITCHING for the lining is attached at two places on the cloth-wrapped frame: at the outer edge of the bottom wire of the apron, and at the top edge of the crown. (Pinning the material will make sewing it easier.) The thread will be covered by the stitching for the outer covering, which in turn will be hidden by the trimming. The edges of the lining are trimmed carefully after it is stitched to the frame.

### The Outer Covering

USE LIGHTWEIGHT silk or chiffon to cover the outside of the frame. Don't despair if no clue to the original colors has survived; darker colors in shades of rose or blue look authentic and help diffuse the light. Shades with panels might use printed silk or satin, or embroidered designs on the cloth.

YOU'LL BE COVERING a circular area with gathered or shirred fabric. The length of the fabric must equal at least three times the circumference of the shade. The width of the fabric must equal the height of the frame, which is the distance from the top of the apron to the crown. When you cut the fabric, leave enough excess so that it can be trimmed after it is pulled tightly and stitched to the frame.

THE APRON IS COVERED with a strip from the material used for the outer covering. The length of the strip should be slightly greater than the circumference of the shade. The width of the strip should equal the height of the apron. Wrap the strip tightly around the apron, using one of the apron's vertical wires as your starting point. Stitch the edge of the strip to the frame; the bottom of the strip, to the edge of the lining. Make sure that the needle goes through to the tape on the frame.

THE MATERIAL for the outer covering is gathered and stitched over the top of the strip that you've just stitched to the apron. Pin the material first to ensure even gathering. The outer covering is at least triple the length of the strip, so get ready for a seemingly endless sewing session! You'll be stitching through other layers, so the needle must go through to the tape.

LIKE THE APRON STRIP, the material for the outer covering should start over a vertical wire of the frame. The edge that runs between the apron and the crown should be folded under so that the cut doesn't show. When you've made a complete circle around the frame, fold under the ending edge and overlap it with the beginning edge, just enough so that the lining is not visible.

SEWING THE GATHERING to the crown follows a smaller circle, but greater care must be taken to keep the rows running parallel to the vertical wires of the frame. Therefore, the material must be pulled tightly and the rows must be stitched closer together. At the top of the crown, the outer covering is sewn over the edge of the lining.

## Fringe Benefits

MOST OF THE FRINGE that was first used on silk shades appears to have been around four inches long. Listed as "silk chenille," it was usually gold in color and was hung in dual layers to diffuse the light. It has now become very difficult to find this fringe. Many contemporary fringes have a coarse, stiff look that in no way resembles the limpness and delicacy of original fringe.

STRINGS OF GLASS BEADS were often used instead of fringe. As you might expect, finding good beadwork today is an even more frustrating job than finding quality fringe. Fortunately, the beadwork is usually salvageable if it still exists on the shade. (Unfortunately, any surviving fringe is usually badly shedding and so cannot be kept.)

SO IT'S TWO MORE TRIPS around the shade, because the fringe is sewn directly over the stitching of the bottom edge of the strip on the apron. If beads are used, you can attach them in a similar fashion.

## Finishing Up

IF YOU'VE BEEN ABLE to salvage most of the other trimming, your work will be much simpler. These days, it's very difficult to find tapes, braids, bows, tassels, and nets that look anything like the originals.*

ON THE SHADE DISCUSSED in this article, there is only a single kind of braid. Short vertical pieces are stitched over the apron strip, onto the vertical wires of the frame, thus dividing the apron into smaller panels. Then, going around and around again, the braid is sewn over the top edge of the fringe (at the bottom of the apron) and over the bottom edge of the gathering (at the top of the apron). These horizontal tapes also cover the edges of the vertical tapes.

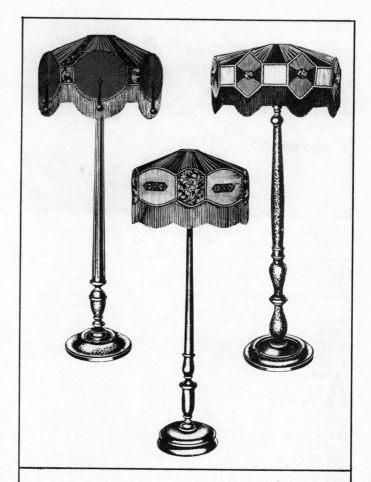

These floor lamps appeared in the 1922 Montgomery Ward Catalog. Left: Gathered silk, figured satin, sunburst shirring, silk tassels, silk braid, and 4-inch silk chenille are all elements of this shade. Center: This shade features embroidery on the plain silk panels of its apron. Right: Contrasting colors of silk gathered to rosettes on the apron of this shade are another variation in style.

TO COMPLETE THE SHADE, attach the braid horizontally over the stitching that holds the top edge of the gathering at the crown. An attractive final touch would be to attach decorative cords and large tassels to the chains on the light sockets. Such tassels, which usually matched the fringe, were frequently used to further ornament Victorian lamps.

*If you're looking for trimming, then you might want to try Novelty Trimming Works, Inc., 18 East 16 Street, Dept. OHJ, New York, NY 10003. (212) 255-7548. If money is no object, then there's Scalamandre, Inc., 950 Third Avenue, Dept. OHJ, New York, NY 10022. (212) 361-8500.

TOM H. GERHARDT is First Vice President of the Historical Association of Greater Cape Girardeau, Missouri. He has been writing for The Old-House Journal since 1975.

All glass should fit tightly into the came; there shouldn't be any gaps between glass and lead, such as the one here.

The came was too short to meet the other lead, and so a large blob of solder was used to try to hide the poor joint.

*STAINED GLASS*, continued from p. 53

three-dimensional objects. For windows, the molten glass is pressed to form large sheets. The texture of the glass varies from smooth to extremely rough, depending upon the method used to roll and shape the glass.

ANOTHER ASPECT of the glass world is painted glass, wherein the artist paints a scene onto a clear pane. Among glass lovers, there is considerable debate regarding the merits of painted glass. Opponents argue that painted glass loses its jewel-like quality. Supporters claim that painting is the only way to obtain intricate design and subtle color blending.

THE MAJOR COMPLAINT against painted glass is that most of the work is impermanent. Unless the glass is refired in a kiln after the application of special pigments, the painting exists only on the surface of the glass and so will flake off eventually. In some cases, painted glass that has not been refired cannot be cleaned without damaging the design.

CREATING A STAINED GLASS PANEL requires cutting various pieces of glass into the desired shapes and then permanently joining the individual pieces. Two construction techniques are used--lead and copper foil. In leaded construction, a length of lead, commonly called "came," is placed between pieces of glass and around the border of the entire piece. The came has channels or grooves that form an I-shape in cross-section. Each piece of glass is inserted into the channels on the side of the came. Where two or more pieces of lead meet, a joint made from solder bonds the came together.

BECAUSE THE PANEL consists of pieces of colored glass joined with lead came, it is also called leaded glass. This term is an attempt to distinguish the panel from one with pieces of glass that literally have been stained (that is, painted) with color prior to firing. The name leaded glass helps avoid confusion-- unless the panel uses copper foil.

IN THE COPPER-FOIL METHOD, the outside edge of each piece of glass is wrapped in a thin strip of copper foil. The pieces of glass are butted, and a bead of solder is then run the entire length of the copper-foil seam. Various chemicals can be used to stain the came or solder bead to alter the color as desired.

LEADED CONSTRUCTION is the older technique, dating back to the cathedrals of the Middle Ages. Copper foil was developed by Louis Comfort Tiffany during the late 1800s. Either lead or copper foil can create beautiful windows. The choice of methods is determined by the design of the window. Lead is relatively thick, measuring up to one-half inch wide. Copper-foil seams, when properly formed, are very thin. Lead is used when individual pieces of glass are large and have only straight lines or gentle curves. Copper foil is preferable in panes with smaller pieces of glass in more intricate designs. Small pieces of glass would be lost if surrounded by thick lead came.

WHETHER BUYING a new piece of glass or having an old piece restored, you have to find a good craftsperson. Always inspect actual samples; never judge quality from photographs or slides. Start by visiting local art shows. Look at various stained glass work, inspect the quality, and see if the artist works in a style that appeals to you. If you live near a large metropolitan area, check the phone book for stained glass studios. If you espy a home with attractive stained glass, don't be bashful: Ask the homeowner where he or she got the glass.

WHEN YOU ACTUALLY INSPECT WORK, you should keep certain things in mind.

● MAKE SURE you're looking at glass and not at plastic. Many of the "plastic fantastic" people will not admit to working with plastics unless questioned directly. One quick test is to hold the work up to a strong light. Glass, even the smallest piece, will show variations in color and texture, while plastic is uniform in appearance. Plastics are frequently strong, harsh colors and rarely soft, pastel colors.

● SHAKE the work gently. None of the pieces should rattle; all should be tight. There should be no gaps between glass and came in leaded construction. Any spaces indicate poor cutting and shaping of the glass.

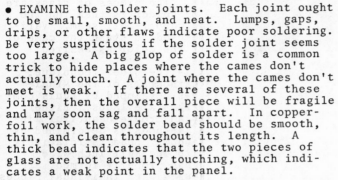

This poor-quality solder work displays all the flaws: lumps, rough surfaces, and badly-fitting cames.

A good solder joint is smooth and neat, with the glass fitting tightly into the came.

● EXAMINE the solder joints. Each joint ought to be small, smooth, and neat. Lumps, gaps, drips, or other flaws indicate poor soldering. Be very suspicious if the solder joint seems too large. A big glop of solder is a common trick to hide places where the cames don't actually touch. A joint where the cames don't meet is weak. If there are several of these joints, then the overall piece will be fragile and may soon sag and fall apart. In copper-foil work, the solder bead should be smooth, thin, and clean throughout its length. A thick bead indicates that the two pieces of glass are not actually touching, which indicates a weak point in the panel.

● LOOK for cement--a greyish substance along the came. In theory, leaded glass can be constructed so that each piece of glass is held fast by the lead. As a matter of practicality in larger panels, cement is used. After the window is assembled, the craftsperson coats the window with a mixture of portland cement and chemicals. The cement is worked into the seam where glass and came meet. The cement contracts as it dries, firmly bonding the glass to the lead. The excess is then removed from the window. Cementing is a messy and time-consuming task, one which all craftspersons hate. But it is critical to a leaded piece, ensuring structural integrity even if all the lead were to deteriorate. (Copper-foil work, of course, does not require cement.) Restoration work on a cemented window costs more because of the additional time needed to remove the glass from the came.

● INSPECT reinforcements. If any dimension is greater than thirty inches, then rebars (reinforcement bars) must be attached to the border and the glass to provide the necessary support. Skilled glass workers can shape the rebar so that it flows with the design and does not stand out from the work. For large rectangular windows, many craftspersons recommend using a border of zinc for extra strength.

NEW GLASS WORK is priced by the square foot. Leaded glass costs from $25 to $75 per square foot; prices can be higher if the artist has a good reputation and a strong following. Copper foil is more labor intensive; prices start at $50 per square foot. Red and pink glass require gold and other pre-cious metals for their manufacture, thus raising the price of the glass. Bevels, acid etching, wheel engraving, and sandblasting also increase the cost of glass work.

IT IS IMPOSSIBLE to give price guidelines for restoration work. Each job is different and must be estimated on an individual basis. For most repairs, the glass must be removed from the frame and taken to the restorer's shop. Some glass artists and restorers do remove and install work, but most do not. Any good carpenter or glazier should be able to remove and install a stained glass panel.

THE GOAL OF ANY RESTORATION is to have the finished product look as close to the original as possible. But glass restoration can only approximate the original appearance. Many people may not see the difference, but anyone who is familiar with stained glass will be able to spot the repair.

MANY OLD GLASS COLORS are no longer available. Old-time glass masters were very secretive about how they obtained their colors, and many of their formulas followed them to the grave. An old-house owner with a badly-deteriorated stained glass panel faces a dilemma. The initial desire is to restore the panel to its original condition. But how original is it if many pieces are replaced with modern glass that fails to duplicate its color and texture?

RESTORATION CAN REQUIRE a great deal of time, especially for a large piece. It is not unusual for restoration experts to have a backlog of work stretching a year or longer. Moreover, few stained glass works in residential settings have historical value worth the cost of restoration. In seriously damaged windows, the cost of restoration can exceed the cost of a new window.

THERE ARE NO EASY ANSWERS to the replace-or-repair question. But whether you install new glass or restore old glass, you will find that stained glass is one of the most charming and luxurious touches your old house can have. With a little care and attention to workmanship, you can obtain the quality stained glass that your old house deserves.

# Restoration Products News

## GAZEBOS

*Gazebos—summer pavilions—have been used since colonial times, but their popularity really peaked during the Victorian era. Listed here are companies which offer gazebo kits, many of which are Victorian inspired. The sections forming the gazebo can usually be ordered with a choice of windows, lattice, louvers, screens, solid panels, or open rails. Unless otherwise stated, they can be assembled by two people in an afternoon and prices don't include delivery.*

Two gazebo models are offered by Bow House. The *Belvedeary* below is 12 ft. in diameter and constructed of pine, red cedar clapboards, and white cedar shingles. Prices begin at $2,695 and vary with the type of section you choose—assembly time is about 4 days.

The *Shandy*, offered in 3- to 8-sided sizes, is an open lattice design with a solid roof of tan asphalt shingles. A 3-sided *Shandy* is $630; the 8-sided is $1,570. Both models are given a coat of white primer, and can be ordered with a prefabricated deck kit. Custom gazebos can also be designed. Send $2 for an illustrated brochure to Bow House, Inc., Randall Rd., Dept. OHJ, Bolton, MA 01740. (617) 779-6464.

Vintage Wood Works recently introduced three gazebo kits to their line of "gingerbread" products. The *Mary Margaret* is offered in an 8½-ft. ($1,295) and a 12-ft. ($1,695) size with optional gingerbread trim. The *Dolly Bryan*, shown here, is 11 ft. in diameter, includes lacy brackets, and is $2,995 delivered. Both models have bell-shaped roofs, are au-

*Listed here are two companies offering gazebos in cast aluminum.*

The 10-ft. gazebo shown here, $1,600, is handcrafted by Welsbach. It's painted with a weather-resistant finish, and offered with a polyester or acrylic canvas roof (in a choice of 18 colors). Custom, 8-, and 10-sided models can be ordered. For a free brochure, contact Welsbach Lighting, Inc., 240 Sargent Dr., Dept. OHJ, New Haven, CT 06511. (203) 789-1710.

thentic recreations of Victorian gazebos, and require about one week to assemble. These gazebos, constructed mostly of pine, include a "home phone numbers" guarantee: You can contact a company representative at any time (even on the weekend), if there is any difficulty with the product or its construction. Send for a catalog to: Vintage Wood Works, 66 Main St., Dept. OHJ, Quinlan, TX 75474. (214) 356-2158.

Tomaco offers a simple and inexpensive lattice gazebo kit. This 10-ft. gazebo is $495, made of pressure-treated yellow pine and fir, and should be stained or painted. For a "Gazebo" catalog ($2), contact Tomaco Wood Preserving, Inc., 1121 E. 33rd St., PO Box 55131, Dept. OHJ, Indianapolis, IN 46205. (317) 926-4535.

*Tomaco Gazebo*

Moultrie Manufacturing Co., well known for their ornamental castings, offers the 13-ft., 6-sided gazebo shown here. Available in four different patterns, it can be painted black or white with vinyl roofing in a choice of three colors. Special colors and sizes can be ordered. The gazebo, shipped in knock-down condition, can be assembled by two people in an afternoon. The cost is $2,500, includes delivery, and will be in effect until 1984. Send $1 for a catalog showing this and other decorative castings. Moultrie Manufacturing Co., PO Drawer 1179, Dept. OHJ, Moultrie, GA 31768. (912) 985-1312.

Cedar Gazebos sells three models, _agoda_, _South Seas_, and _Midwestern_. The models are made of heart red cedar, have an open lattice or a solid cedar roof, and range in size from 8 ft. to 12 ft. Accessories such as counter ledges can be ordered. Prices range from $793 to 1,479; prefabricated red cedar decks begin at $350.

SOUTH SEAS CLASSIC

Gussets (triangular wall braces) ensure that the walls are erected perpendicular. This feature makes roof installation easier and quicker. Custom orders can be manufactured in kit form. For a free brochure, write Cedar Gazebos Inc., 0432 Lyndale Avenue, Dept. OHJ, Melrose Park, IL 60164. (312) 455-0928.

*Picnic tables are sold
with two benches.*

Bench Manufacturing Co. offers an 8-sided, 8-ft. gazebo made of redwood, including a solid roof (with copper flashing). Larger sizes and accessories, such as shelves, counters, and benches, can be ordered. The gazebos, ready to be painted or stained, range from $3,000 to 57,000 depending on the options you choose. Also available—two Victorian-influenced picnic tables and benches made of fir ($1,250 or $1,600). Please specify your interest when writing for their free brochure. Bench Manufacturing Co., PO Box 66, Essex Street Station, Dept. OHJ, Boston, MA 02112. (617) 436-3080.

## Ornamental Castings

Focal Point recently introduced six new moulding patterns with four coordinating ceiling medallions. Dudley Brown, A.S.I.D., authenticated these historically documented reproductions of late 19th-century American architectural pieces. The mouldings, sold in 10-ft. sections, and the medallions are lightweight and sold with simple installation instructions. They are made of a solid, rigid polymer material which is primed in white for painting or beige for staining. The ceiling medallion ($77.61) and moulding section (about $18 per ft.) illustrated here are featured in the new "19th-century" brochure ($1.50); a catalog ($1.50) showing numerous other castings is also available. Focal Point Inc., 2005 Marietta Rd., N.W., Dept. Y2-2a, Atlanta, GA 30318. (404) 351-0820.

## Staircase Parts

*Listed here are two mail-order suppliers of replacement parts for staircases. Both companies carry an extensive selection of treads, risers, balusters, newels, and handrail fittings. These pieces are stock items and are generally available in only one size, so check the dimensions of your stair carefully before ordering.*

Taney Supply & Lumber Corp., a manufacturer of pre-built, fine hardwood stairways, also stocks a variety of replacement parts. Their catalog shows just a few of the many shapes and sizes they stock. Custom turnings and designs are also available. Stock items are made of oak, but parts can also be cut from other woods. To see if the part you require is stocked or can be fabricated, send a description and measured drawing of the piece to be replaced, and a photograph of the stair. For a free brochure, write Taney Supply & Lumber Corp., 5130 Allendale La., Dept. OHJ, Taneytown, MD 21787. (301) 756-6671.

C—E Morgan manufactures stair replacement parts in hemlock, red oak, birch, and pine. Their free catalog shows a variety of styles and sizes. These stair parts can be purchased through one of their dealers throughout the country. If it isn't a stock item, this company will try to put you in touch with someone in your area who will do custom turning. C—E Morgan, 601 Oregon St., Dept. OHJ, Oshkosh, WI 54901. (414) 235-7170.

# Opinion...
# Remuddling
## — Of The Month —

THIS MONTH's "winner" shows how a porch establishes the character of a house. When the original two massive wood columns were replaced with thin wrought-iron railing, the balance of the entire facade was upset. And it made matters worse when the wooden porch balustrade was replaced with more wrought iron.

*THE ORIGINAL: This Craftsman Bungalow retains most of its original detailing: knee braces at the eaves, elephantine columns on the front porch, narrow clapboard siding, and a delicate porch balustrade that forms a vertical counterpoint to the horizontal siding.*

Submitted by: Terry Warner
Houston, Tex.

ON ANOTHER TOPIC, a few readers have taken us to task for not including interiors on our remuddling page. We have concentrated on exteriors because they are on public view; a badly remuddled exterior assaults every passer-by. Interiors are a more private affair. If you want Danish Modern furniture in your Victorian parlor, that's fine with us. However, we do get very upset with interior remuddlings that destroy fine woodwork and other architectural details. We'll gladly consider photos of that. --C.L.

*THE REMUDDLED VERSION: The owner of this Bungalow replaced the original wooden elephantine columns and porch balustrade with thin iron railing. Now the projecting front gable seems to hang in thin air. Further remuddling took place when aluminum siding was applied: The knee braces at the eaves were removed, and the "clapboards" that were used were too wide.*

# The Old-House Journal®

69A Seventh Avenue,
Brooklyn, New York 11217

NO PAID ADVERTISING

Postmaster: Address Correction Requested

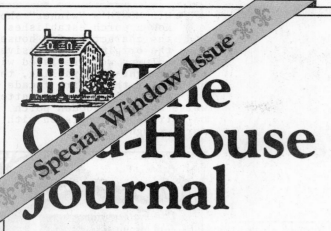

Vol. X No. 4         $2.00

**Special Window Issue**

# The Old-House Journal

## Restoration and Maintenance Techniques For The Antique House

# Replacing Old Windows
## good news & bad news

**By Patricia Poore**

INDOWS ARE SO TROUBLESOME...but they give a building its special character, and so they're worth preserving. That's what this issue is about: appreciating the variety and importance of windows, fixing and weatherizing them. So why is The Old-House Journal leading off with an article about <u>replacing</u> old windows?

WE'RE MEETING THE ENEMY head on. The advertising power of large companies is behind the sale of replacement window units, which abound. For people faced with dilapidated old windows, there's plenty of opportunity to go the expedient route. Like it or not, we know windows will continue to be eyed with replacement in mind, so we want to lay out some clear, relatively unbiased information on alternatives and selection.

TOO MUCH of the time, new windows are both materially inferior to the originals and a compromise to the appearance of the building. To be fair, some of the replacements are well made, thermally efficient, easy to maintain and to clean, and even appropriate. Nice to know if you've bought a building with truly hopeless (or missing) windows. Quality isn't cheap, however. It's almost always less expensive to recondition old windows, if that's at all practical.

GOOD NEWS: There are specific alternatives to replacement. Because old windows come in too many sizes and shapes to be sufficiently duplicated in replacement units...because of the high cost of new materials...and because of the still-growing concern with energy efficiency, some ingenious thought has gone into rehabilitating old wood windows. We've outlined a few of the unusual methods here. This kind a full-scale restoration and retrofitting of existing windows will probably become standard practice.

ALREADY, even large commercial building renovation jobs have made use of repair techniques, instead of replacement. For example, visually-important windows in the historic Colcord Building (Oklahoma City) were repaired and fitted with a kind of integral storm window--a second glazing layer set into existing wood sash. The fix-up process ended up costing less and being more energy efficient than the metal replacement units which initially attracted the owner. In addition, the historic windows were retained, and the owner qualified for a tax credit because the work was done in accordance with the Secretary of the Interior's Guidelines. (The metal units in this case would have disqualified them--see page 89.)

*continued on p. 89*

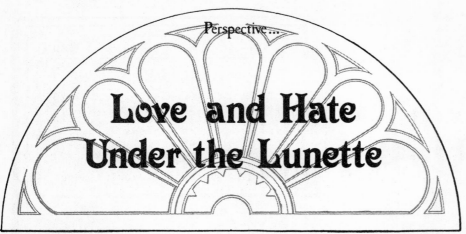

Perspective...

# Love and Hate Under the Lunette

THE RELATIONSHIP between many old-house owners and their windows can be likened to a torrid love affair. The original windows, when glimpsed from afar, seem attractive and romantic. It's love at first sight. But after living with them for a while, cold (literally) reality sets in.

OLD WINDOWS can have bad habits that make them difficult companions: They are wasteful (of energy), their beauty fades (as paint quickly peels), and they can be quite cantankerous when you want them to do something (like move up and down). So the inevitable reaction sets in: Love turns to indifference ...or even hostility.

IN SOME CASES, the relationship ends quickly with a case of "windowcide": The owner destroys the old windows and replaces them in his or her affections with new ones made of vinyl-clad aluminum (or is it aluminum-clad vinyl?).

IN OTHER CASES, the owner comes to an "understanding" with his or her formerly adored original windows: They can keep their accustomed place if they will stand uncomplaining as they are hidden from public view by triple-track storm windows.

## To Re-Kindle That Old Flame

WE AT THE OLD-HOUSE JOURNAL think it's a shame that so many beautiful relationships should end like this... because it is not inevitable. The breakup comes from a lack of caring, or an unwillingness to put some fresh energy into the relationship.

SO THAT'S what this Special Issue is all about. With the Glossary that starts on the next page, we're trying to rekindle your interest in the glamour and beauty of traditional windows. Then, with the various how-to and where-to articles, we're trying to show that there are many different ways to keep your original windows visually exciting--and easy to live with.     --C.L.

---

## And Special Thanks To...

MANY PEOPLE around the country are hard at work trying to develop practical, economical alternatives to "windowcide." Some of them, who helped us with this Special Issue, are noted below—with many thanks.

LARRY JONES is Preservation Consultant to the Utah State Historical Society. Last October, we asked Larry to send along some of his thoughts about sensitive rehabilitation of wooden windows. We heard nothing further ...until December 20, when our morning mail brought a 45-page manuscript from Larry, along with a wonderful collection of photos. As a result, you'll see his name frequently in this issue.

JOHN MYERS and CHARLES FISHER of Technical Preservation Services of The National Park Service sent along an advance copy of their case history, "Improving Thermal Efficiency: Historic Wooden Windows." They are also working on a handbook of sensitive window rehabilitation for historic structures. They encourage you to submit examples of good window rehabilitation for possible inclusion in the handbook. Contact: John Myers, Southeast Regional Office, National Park Service, 75 Spring St., Atlanta, GA 30303. (404) 246-2643.

CHARLES A. PARROTT is the Historical Architect for the Lowell (Mass.) Historic Preservation Commission. His talk at the annual APT meeting last October prompted us to ask for copies of some of the excellent photos he has of sensitive window replacement in historic buildings around Lowell.

## The Old-House Journal®

*Editor*
**Clem Labine**

*Managing Editor*
**Patricia Poore**

*Assistant Editor*
**Cole Gagne**

*Editorial Assistants*
**Joni Monnich**
**Stephanie Croce**

---

*Circulation Supervisor*
**Joan O'Reilly**

*Circulation Assistants*
**Margaret Scaglione**
**Barbara Bugg**
**Jean Baldwin**

*Office Manager*
**Sally Goodman**

*Office Assistant*
**Rafael Madera**

---

*Sales Promotion*
**Joel Alpert**

*Circulation Director*
**Paul T. McLoughlin**

---

*Technical Consultant*
**Alan D. Keiser**

*Architectural Consultant*
**Jonathan Poore**

*Contributing Editors*
**R. A. Labine, Sr.**
**John Mark Garrison**

---

Published by The Old-House Journal © Corporation, 69A Seventh Avenue, Brooklyn, New York 11217. Telephone (212) 636-4514. Subscriptions $16 per year in U.S. Not available elsewhere. Published monthly. Contents are fully protected by copyright and must not be reproduced in any manner whatsoever without specific permission in writing from the Editor.

We are happy to accept editorial contributions to The Old-House Journal. Query letters which include an outline of the proposed article are preferred. All manuscripts will be reviewed, and returned if unacceptable. However, we cannot be responsible for non-receipt or loss — please keep copies of all materials sent.

**Printed at Photo Comp Press, New York City**

*ISSN: 0094-0178*
**NO PAID ADVERTISING**

# Talk To Me Of Windows

## ...a glossary

TO THE CASUAL PASSERBY, windows provide vital clues to a house's personality, much as the eyes provide clues to human character: Some are complex and full of meaning; others are dull, or even hostile. For us inside the house, windows are frames that shape our view of the world beyond.

MUCH OF the history of architecture is told in the shapes and symbolic uses of windows. Even on a single street in America, windows appear in a dazzling variety of types. It is this complexity that makes old-house watching so much fun.

AS WITH ANYTHING ELSE, appreciation increases with knowledge. To fully appreciate windows, then, we should know the words that describe them. It's hard to get passionate about a beautiful architrave surrounding a window if we have to point a finger in frustration and call it merely "that thing."

SO WE HAVE assembled here an illustrated glossary of the most common terms used to describe visible parts of windows. (Terminology for some of the unseen elements is on page 87.) We hope that by providing a precise vocabulary for traditional window types, we'll encourage more people to preserve original fenestration. After all, how could a remodelling contractor tear it out after he learns that it's an "Elizabethan-style lozenge window"?

**APRON** — A panel on the wall below a window SILL, sometimes shaped and decorated. *see illus. on p. 87*

**ARCHITRAVE** — The moulded frame or ornament surrounding a window, door, or other rectangular opening. Also, in classical architecture, the lower division of an entablature that rests on the column.

architrave

**BALCONET** — A low ornamental railing projecting just beyond the SILL, which is made to look like a balcony.

balconet

bay window

**BAY WINDOW** — A window that projects out from the surface of an exterior wall and extends to the ground.

**BLIND WINDOW** — A recess in an exterior wall trimmed with mouldings to give it the appearance of a window. Its purpose is to add symmetry or decoration to a facade.

blind window

blinds

**BLINDS** — A rectangular frame, consisting of top and bottom RAILS and side STILES, which is filled in the center with slats. BLINDS are used as window shades and for ventilation. *see also* shutters

**BOW WINDOW** — A rounded BAY WINDOW. It projects in a semi-circle from the surface of an exterior wall. Also called a compass window.

bow window

**BULL'S EYE GLASS** — A piece of glass having a raised center as a consequence of having been formed by a blow pipe. Originally considered to be inferior glass because of its imperfection, it was used in barns and secondary windows. Now it is prized because of its obviously handmade character. *see* crown glass

**BULL'S EYE WINDOW** — *see* oculus

cabinet window

**CABINET WINDOW** — A projecting window or BAY WINDOW for the display of goods in shops.

cameo window

**CAMEO WINDOW** — A fixed oval window with surrounding mouldings and ornament. A CAMEO WINDOW usually has TRACERY or MUNTINS to divide the glass. Often found on Colonial Revival houses.

**CAMES** — Lead strips to hold small pieces of glass in leaded windows. *see* leaded glass window

**CAP** — A decorative cornice covering the LINTEL of a window. *see also* hood

**CASEMENT WINDOW** — A single- or double-sash window that is made to open outwards by turning on hinges attached to its vertical edge. This was one of the earliest types of movable windows, used from medieval times on. Often found in Gothic Revival, Elizabethan and Tudor Revival houses.

casement window

**CATHERINE WHEEL** — *see* wheel window

**CHICAGO WINDOW** — A large fixed SASH flanked by a narrow movable SASH on either side. First used by the Chicago School architects in the late 19th and early 20th century.

**CLERESTORY** — A row of windows mounted high in a wall. Most often refers to windows high above the nave in a church. Also used in Prairie Style houses. (pronounced "clear-story")

clerestory

**COMPASS WINDOW** — *see* bow window

bull's eye glass

crown glass

**CROWN GLASS** — Large panes that became available in the 17th century and were incorporated in wooden sash windows. The glass was handblown through a pipe (pontil) into a circular disc, leaving a bubble or bullion where the pipe was inserted. Also known as bottle glass or BULL'S EYE GLASS when the bullion was used in a window.

**DIOCLETIAN WINDOW** — A semi-circular window divided by wide uprights, or MULLIONS, into three LIGHTS. This ancient Roman motif was later used by Palladio for use in the 16th century. Also called a THERM. Often used in Classical Revival buildings of the early 20th century.

Diocletian window

**DORMER** — A vertically-set window on a sloping roof; also the roofed structure housing such a window. If the roof slopes downward from the house, they are known as **shed dormers**. Flat-roof projections are commonly called **doghouse dormers**. Those with pointed roofs are called **gabled dormers**.

shed dormer          doghouse dormer          gabled dormer

**DOUBLE-HUNG WINDOW** — A window with an outside SASH that slides down and an inside one that goes up. The movement of the SASH is usually controlled by chains or cords on pulleys with a SASH WEIGHT. The earliest DOUBLE-HUNG WINDOWS were known as GEORGIAN WINDOWS. *see illus. on p. 87*

double window
with oculus

**DOUBLE WINDOW** — Two vertical windows, separated by a MULLION, forming a single architectural unit. Also called a coupled window.

eyebrow dormer

**EYEBROW DORMER** — A low DORMER having no sides, the roofing smoothly curving upward over the dormer window. Also called an eyelid window. Commonly used on Shingle Style houses.

eyebrow windows

**EYEBROW WINDOWS** — Low, inward-opening windows with a bottom-hinged SASH. These attic windows built into the ARCHITRAVE of a house are sometimes called "lie-on-your-stomach" windows. Often found on Greek Revival houses.

fanlight

**FANLIGHT** — An elongated, round-topped window over a door or window with TRACERY or bars radiating in an open-fan pattern. It evolved as an economical use of CROWN GLASS, which was cut in wedge-shaped pieces. *see also* lunette

**FENESTRATION** — The art of placing window openings in a building wall. It is one of the most important elements in controlling the exterior appearance of a house.

**FIXED WINDOW** — A stationary window.

trefoil

**FOIL** — A lobe or leaf-shaped curve formed by the cusping of a circle or arch. The number of FOILS involved is indicated by a prefix, e.g., trefoil (3), quatrefoil (4), etc. FOILS are encountered in the windows of Gothic Revival churches and houses.

**FRENCH WINDOWS** — CASEMENT WINDOWS carried down to the floor so as to open like doors.

**GEORGIAN WINDOWS** — *see* double-hung windows

**GLAZING** — The process of installing glass panes in window and door frames and applying putty to hold the glass in position. Also, the glass surface of a glazed opening: "Double-glazed," therefore, refers to a SASH with two layers of glass.

**GLAZING BAR** — A vertical or horizontal bar within a SASH to hold glass. Same as MUNTIN.

Gothic-head window

**GOTHIC-HEAD WINDOW** — A window topped with a pointed arch. Same as Gothic-top window. It is not as tall and narrow as the pure Gothic LANCET WINDOW.

**GUILLOTINE WINDOW** — The first double-sash window, with only one movable SASH and no counterweights. A peg was inserted through a hole in the movable SASH and into a corresponding hole in the frame. Its tendency to come slamming down led to the colorful name.

**HEAD** — A somewhat ambiguous term used generally to denote the top or upper member of any element or structure. In windows, it refers to the top of the frame, as in ROUND-HEAD WINDOW.

**HOOD** — An ornamental cover placed over a door or window to shelter it. *see also* cap

hood

hoodmould

label stop

**HOODMOULD** — The outermost projecting moulding around the top of a door or window to discharge rainwater. Also called dripmould, headmould, label. Hoodmoulds are a prominent feature of Gothic Revival architecture. *see* label stop

**JAMB** — The top and side members of a window or door frame. *see illus. on p. 87*

**LABEL STOP** — An ornamental projection on each end of a HOODMOULD. It often takes the shape of a gargoyle or other decorative carving.

**LANCET WINDOW** — A tall, narrow window with a pointed-arch top, very often with diamond-shaped LIGHTS. Characteristic of Gothic architecture.

lancet window

quarry

lattice (lozenge) window

**LATTICE WINDOW** — A window with diamond-shaped LIGHTS. Also called a LOZENGE window. It has its origins in medieval architecture, when the lattice was formed by lead CAMES. In some revival architecture, the GLAZING BARS in a LATTICE WINDOW are made of wood.

came

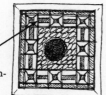
leaded glass window

**LEADED GLASS WINDOWS** — A window composed of pieces of glass that are held in place with lead strips, or CAMES. The glass can be clear, colored, or stained.

**LIGHTS** — The panes of glass in a window, as in an eight-light or twelve-light window. DOUBLE-HUNG WINDOWS are designated by the number of LIGHTS in upper and lower sash, as in six-over-six.

lights (nine-over-six)

**LINTEL** — A piece of wood, stone, or steel placed horizontally across the top of window and door openings to support the walls immediately above.

cap

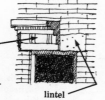
lintel

**LOOP WINDOW** — A long, narrow, vertical opening, usually widening inward, cut in a medieval wall, parapet, or fortification for use by archers. Also called a balistraria. Sometimes interpreted in Romanesque Revival architecture.

louver window

**LOUVER WINDOW** — A window having louvers, or slats, that fill all or part of an opening. It's used to provide ventilation.

**LOZENGE** — Any diamond-shaped ornament or design. Also, an obsolete term for a diamond-shaped pane of glass. A window composed of diamond-shaped panes is called a lozenge window. *see* quarry

lucarne

**LUCARNE** — A small DORMER window in a spire or steeply-pitched roof.

lunette

**LUNETTE** — A crescent-shaped window framed by mouldings or an arch.

**MEETING RAILS** — The bottom horizontal member of the outer SASH and top horizontal member of the inner SASH of a DOUBLE-HUNG WINDOW. *see illus. on p. 87*

**MULLIONS** — The vertical dividing members between multiple windows. The term is sometimes used to designate what should be called MUNTINS.

mullion

muntin

**MUNTINS** — The wood strips that separate the panes of glass in a window SASH. The term is sometimes confused with MULLION.

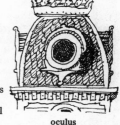
oculus

**OCULUS** — A round or oval window without TRACERY or MUNTINS. A round OCULUS is also called a BULL'S EYE WINDOW, from OEIL-DE-BOEUF. *see also* rose window, wheel window, *and* cameo window

**OEIL-DE-BOEUF WINDOW** — A small, fixed, round window without TRACERY; literally, BULL'S EYE WINDOW. *see also* oculus

**ORIEL** — A window projecting from the wall and carried on brackets, corbels, or a cantilever. Unlike a BAY WINDOW, the projection of an ORIEL doesn't extend all the way to the ground.

oriel

Palladian window

**PALLADIAN WINDOW** — A tripartite window composed of a central, main window having an arched head, and on each side a long, narrow window with a square head. Used extensively in Georgian, Classical Revival, and Colonial Revival architecture. (Also called a VENETIAN WINDOW).

**PARTING BEAD** — A vertical guide strip on each side of a DOUBLE-HUNG WINDOW frame which separates the SASHES. *see illus. on p. 87*

**PEDIMENT** — A triangle-shaped crowning ornament, meant to suggest the front of a Greek or Roman temple. Often used as CAPS or HOODS on windows in Classical Revival and Colonial Revival buildings.

pediment

**PRIME WINDOW** — As distinct from a storm window, this is the primary window in an opening, including frame and SASH.

**QUARRY** — A diamond-shaped pane of glass. Also called quarrel— the medieval term for the small panes of glass set diagonally in Gothic windows. *see also* lattice window *and* lozenge

**QUEEN ANNE WINDOW** — A window with small glass window LIGHTS arranged in various forms and usually only on the upper SASH.

Queen Anne window

**RAIL** — A horizontal member in a door or window SASH. *see illus. on p. 87*

**REVEAL** — That part of a JAMB or vertical face of an opening for a window or doorway between the frame and the outside surface of a wall. Also, the interior space used to enclose paneled interior SHUTTERS that fold back when open.

**ROSE WINDOW** — A round window with TRACERY. *see also* wheel window *and* oculus

**ROUND-HEAD WINDOW** — A window with a semi-circular or curved top. Used most often in Romanesque Revival, Italianate, and Classical Revival buildings.

round-head window

**ROUNDEL** — A very small circular window. In GLAZING, a circular LIGHT that resembles the bottom of a bottle. *see also* oculus

**SADDLE BAR** — Light steel bar placed horizontally across a window to stiffen leaded GLAZING.

**SASH** — The framework of STILES and RAILS in which the panes or LIGHTS of a window are set. *see illus. on p. 87*

**SASH WEIGHTS** — A lead counterweight that, together with the SASH CORD and pulley, holds a SASH in the raised position. *see illus. on p. 87*

**SHUTTERS** — Like BLINDS, SHUTTERS are rectangular frames consisting of top and bottom RAILS and side STILES. These are filled in, however, with a solid panel designed to actually 'shut up' the house for protection.

shutters

**SILL** — The bottom crosspiece of a window frame on which the bottom SASH rests. The SILL is of heavier stock and slopes to shed water. *see illus. on p. 87*

**STAINED GLASS WINDOW** — A window with a painted scene or pattern that has been fired into the glass. Windows with plain colored glass set in lead are most often (inaccurately) called stained glass.

**STILE** — Each vertical side member of a window or door frame. Also, a vertical side member of a SASH. *see illus. on p. 87*

**STOOL** — The STOOL caps the SILL on the inside of a window frame. Potted plants that sit "on the windowsill" are really on the STOOL. *see illus. on p. 87*

**STOP** or **STOP BEAD** — A strip on a window frame against which the SASH slides. *see illus. on p. 87*

**THERM** — *see* Diocletian window

**TRACERY** — Delicate intersecting lines of MUNTINS or GLAZING BARS that form ornamental designs in a window. Originally, the term related to the patterns in the upper part of Gothic windows, but it can also refer to the delicate glazing patterns in some Georgian and Colonial Revival houses.

tracery

transom window
transom bar

**TRANSOM BAR** — A horizontal member separating a small upper (TRANSOM) window from a larger, lower window.

**TRANSOM WINDOW** — Any small window over a door or another window, often containing STAINED, LEADED, or bevelled glass. It was usually operable, to allow ventilation.

**TRIPLE WINDOW** — Any tripartite group of windows with square heads. These are frequently found on Colonial Revival houses; they suggest PALLADIAN WINDOWS but are less expensive to build.

triple window

**WHEEL WINDOW** — A round window with MUNTINS radiating from the center, as in the spokes of a wheel. Also called CATHERINE WHEEL. Those with TRACERY are generally known as ROSE WINDOWS. *see also* oculus

wheel window

**VENETIAN WINDOW** — *see* Palladian window

*Illustrations by Leo Blackman*

The title for this glossary came from F. Palmer Cook's "Talk To Me Of Windows, An Informal History." All our readers who love the romance of old windows—old English windows in particular—will enjoy this charming and informative book. Published in 1970, it is now out of print, but you should be able to find it in your local library.

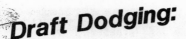

## Draft Dodging:

# How To Install Weatherstripping

By Larry Jones, Salt Lake City, Utah

**A** LOOSE-FITTING SASH is responsible for the worst energy losses a house can suffer. It will permit the entry of cold wind and the escape of heated air. If your leaky windows are creating these infiltration problems, it's up to you to stop the leaks.

THE SUREST WAY to seal a window is with caulk. If the window is almost never opened, use an acrylic latex caulk and keep it caulked shut all year long. If you want to use the window during the summer, use a good, temporary roll-type caulk such as Mortite and seal it just for the winter.

IF YOU NEED AN OPERABLE WINDOW for all seasons, then you'll have to weatherstrip. There are numerous types of weatherstripping available, and as far as quality is concerned, you get what you pay for. The plastic or adhesive-backed foam types, although cheap and easy to install, have a relatively short life span.

Above: This typical double-hung window has been painted shut. The curtains, shade, and hardware have all been removed to facilitate removal of the sash. Below: A heat gun is employed to break the paint film on the interior sash stops and the frame to which they are attached.

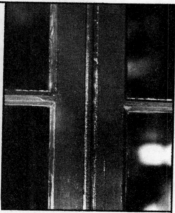

Casement windows are hard to weatherstrip. Those at left were rarely opened, and so were permanently caulked shut (right). Roll-type caulk can also be used for seasonal sealing.

THIS ARTICLE will show you how to install metal integral weatherstripping (the kind carpenters usually install) that will last for decades. See "Restoration Products News," page 92, for several sources.

routed sash
metal weatherstripping

**B** EGIN BY SELECTING one window on which you will try out the following procedure from start to finish. When removing the stops, be sure you have replacements that match the originals. If a stop is attached with, say, barbed nails, you're better off discarding it rather than attempting to remove it intact. Replacing the stops also eliminates the need to strip paint from them. You can use a thin-bladed putty knife or pry bar to separate the stops from the frame.

After removal of the left stop, the paint film holding the lower sash is broken by working a thin putty knife along the bottom, sides, and meeting rail of the sash.

Above: Outside, a thin pry bar is carefully worked under the sash to break the paint film. Paint along the edges is then removed with a heat gun. Below: Here's the lower sash after being removed from the frame. Note the old sash cord in the upper right corner of the sash.

USE A PUTTY KNIFE to free the lower sash. Do not try to force open a stuck sash; you could accidentally damage the glass or the frame. If you're using a heat gun to strip the paint holding the sash, be sure not to direct it at the pane--it can crack the glass. Remove the lower sash from inside and loosen and tie off the sash cords. Remove built-up paint on the upper sash, parting bead, and exterior blind stop. Carefully pry out the parting bead. (Don't worry if it breaks--you can easily replace it with lumberyard stock.) Once you slip out the parting bead on one side, you can slip the upper sash out of the window frame.

WITH THE SASH REMOVED, finish stripping all paint from the window, especially from the sash runs, sill, and parting beads. You now should make whatever repairs the frame and sill may require. Sand the frame and sill. If you feel a wood preservative is needed, use Cuprinol Clear; if all you need is a water-repellent without a fungicide, use Thompson's Water Seal. Allow to dry and then apply a suitable primer to all surfaces. Caulk and fill any cracks that could trap moisture. Inspect the sash cords. If they're deteriorating, remove and replace them with chains or new nylon cords. (Never paint sash cords; they work much better when they remain flexible.)

MEASURE AND CUT metal strips for the top and upper sides, taking care to mitre the corners. The weatherstripping can be cut easily with

The heat gun is used to remove built-up paint from the sash run and center parting bead. The upper sash is almost always painted shut. Use a putty knife or a Red Devil "Windo-Zipper" to break the paint seal.

Tools Required To Install Weatherstripping

1. Heat gun (for paint removal—optional)
2. Putty knives (for paint removal and loosening of stops)
3. Thin pry bar (for loosening sash)
4. Hammer
5. Punch or nail set (for driving nails)
6. Tape measure
7. Drill and small bits (for pre-drilling weatherstripping—optional)
8. Drop cloth
9. Extension cord
10. Table saw, radial arm saw, or router (for cutting channels into sash)
11. Tin snips (for cutting weatherstripping)

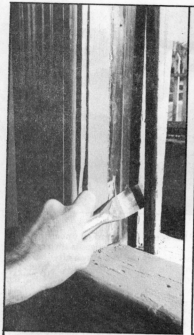
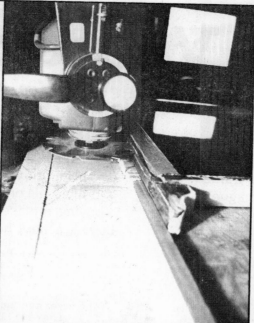

Left: The parting bead is usually nailed or just pressed into place. Carefully pry it out, starting at the sill and working your way up to the bottom of the upper sash. Then lower the sash to its lowest position and loosen the bead from the top down. Center: The sash is cut to fit the new weatherstripping. Use a carbide-tipped blade on a radial arm saw to cut the approximately 1/8-in. wide slot re-

quired to fit the weatherstripping. (The saw guard was removed in this photo to show the procedure.) Right: Space must be left for sash pulleys when installing weatherstripping. In some cases, it's possible to trim the weatherstripping in such a way that the projecting metal strip can run continuously up beside the sash-rope pulley without binding.

tin snips, or on a radial arm saw with a metal-cutting or carbide blade (not a carbide-tipped blade). Install the head strip first; then nail the weatherstripping into both sides of the upper sash run.

THE UPPER SASH is cut across the top rail and down the sides; the lower sash, across the bottom rail and up the sides. Cut them carefully so you can get a tight fit that still allows the sash to slide freely in its track. The saw is set into the horizontal position and should be set to cut a 7/16-in. deep slot. You can also use a table saw or router with a 1/8-in. veining bit to achieve similar results.

Metal weatherstripping is fitted to both the upper and lower sashes at their meeting rails prior to the installation of the sashes in the frame.

CUT THE MEETING RAILS of both upper and lower sashes. Use either a simple router cut or a dado cut on one or both rails to allow the meeting-rail weatherstripping to be attached. This stripping is then cut to length and applied to each sash rail. Check for proper meshing of the two sashes before assembling them in the frame.

INSTALL THE UPPER SASH into the frame by inserting it from the bottom. Test it for a good fit; then remove it, install sash cords, and slide the upper sash into its sash run and push it up into position.

NOW INSTALL the lower vertical weatherstripping to the sash run of the lower sash. (Needle-nose pliers will prevent mashed fingers when you're driving nails into the weatherstripping in those narrow channels.) With the sides installed, proceed to measure, cut, and install the lower sill strip. Slip the sash into its run from above and slide it down over the weatherstripping in the lower frame.

MAKE SURE the sashes slide without binding or catching. Now install the interior stop. Most stops are nailed into place, but I always suggest installing brass tapered woodscrews with tapered washer seats about every six inches in tapered, pre-drilled holes. This arrangement allows for easy window-sash removal, should it be required in the future. Also, if stops are loosened during subsequent repainting of the window and trim, they won't become attached to the window frame with a paint film. 🏛

# Storm Windows

## Do You Really Need Them ?

■ **YES** ...but should I buy

inside-mounting wood-framed
outside-mounting metal-framed
glass glazing magnetic
acrylic glazing removable
storm/screen combination fixed ...?

■ **NO** ...I'd be better off

just caulking & weatherstripping
using movable insulation
double glazing existing sash
buying replacement windows
buying a new hot water heater

By Patricia Poore

IT USED TO BE that there were two choices in storm windows. You could either live with the heavy old wooden ones that came with the house, or you could pay a handsome price for triple-track storms. If you're in the market for storm windows today, you have more choices. ("Triple-track" refers to the permanently-installed windows that have a track for the lower storm sash, another track for the upper sash, and a third for a screen.)

WE GET LETTERS from people asking "which is best?". There is no one kind of window that's best in all situations. So what this article will do first is sort out the advantages and disadvantages of each option. Then, we'll show some solutions that worked for other subscribers.

LET'S RUN DOWN the list of things you might be better off doing. First, storm windows are an awfully expensive substitute for caulk! Caulking, weatherstripping, and reglazing are all inexpensive, do-it-yourself procedures that should be done whether or not you buy storms. After you've stopped the air leaks, you may very well find that storm windows are not a high priority.

IF YOUR PRIME windows are good and tight, movable insulation could be more economical and effective than storms. The disadvantage of movable insulation is that you have to remember to move it. See page 88.

IF YOU'VE DECIDED to recondition your prime windows anyway, you might be able to rework the existing sash to accept double glazing. This of course adds cost to the reconditioning, but afterwards your second glazing layer is an integral part of the window--more effective than a storm window. (Double-glazed inserts can be purchased as a hermetically-sealed unit.)

WE FIRMLY BELIEVE that most windows can be fixed. But there's always the hopeless case. No matter how good a storm window is, it can't take the place of weathertight prime windows.

AS YOU APPORTION your energy retrofit budget, be aware that adding storm windows to existing glazing merely changes the R-value from .9 to 2.0. (The average uninsulated wood-frame wall is R-4.5.) They will cut down on drafts and make you "feel" warmer, but think hard about adding storms as an "obvious" retrofit. Let's say you spent last winter cutting down considerably on infiltration losses, by caulking and weatherstripping. If you don't yet have, say, a separate, insulated hot-water heater... storms can wait.

## Options: Inside Or Out ?

MORE AND MORE PEOPLE are putting their storm windows inside the house. This allows your prime windows to face the world in all their glory, solving the "blank stare" problem encountered with multi-light windows: The unique thing about all those separate panes of glass is that each reflects light a bit differently, so passers-by see a dancing reflection. That effect--subtle but important--is lost when a single sheet of glass is placed over such windows.

OTHER ADVANTAGES of interior storms: They're generally cheaper and easier to maintain than exterior windows, because they don't fight the weather. Storms that are stored in summer are easier to take down and put up if they are mounted inside. Exterior storms, of course, protect the prime windows from water and baseballs. And they don't interfere with any interior window decoration.

DON'T FORGET the "temporary solution": plastic sheeting stretched in a pine frame, or taped to the interior window frame. (Careful--tape may mar the paint.) If they're neat and unabused, these can become a semi-permanent solution.

## Glass Or Acrylic ?

HERE ARE the advantages of each: Glass is a proven material. We know it resists weather, dirt, and scrubbing and still stays clear. It's relatively inexpensive. It is easy to buy in almost any size. On the other hand, acrylic is very light, and it doesn't break into shards.

↓ A neoprene gasket seals between glass and the aluminum frame.

↑ When a narrow aluminum frame is "painted out" to match house trim, it's almost unnoticeable. These custom-made storms are non-operable, caulked between aluminum and wood casing.

The very best in custom-made wood storm sash, with a curved top rail, and hinged to allow ventilation on warm winter days. The top pane is fixed, but the bottom one is an aluminum-framed screen insert; a glass insert is substituted in winter. →

THE DISADVANTAGES? Glass is heavy. Acrylic is a little more expensive and, depending on the quality of manufacture, will yellow and "cloud" in more or less time. It takes special care in washing. You might not be able to find acrylic sheets locally in all sizes.

## Wood, Metal, Or Combination ?

BOTH WOOD- AND METAL-FRAMED windows have their advantages. Wood is a much better insulator than metal. It can always be repaired or partly replaced. And it's prettier. Metal-framed windows are light weight and very easy to buy as stock items.

DISADVANTAGES? Wood has to be kept painted or it will rot. It's heavier than metal—a consideration if you plan to handle the windows often. Metal is a terrible insulator, and while there are insulated metal frames available, these are costly and unfixable once the seal is broken. And unlike wood, repair of metal windows (when it's feasible) is not in the realm of the average carpenter or do-it-yourselfer. You may need parts that are no longer made.

VINYL-CLAD ALUMINUM and aluminum with a factory finish are maintenance-free for some years. But when the vinyl breaks down (and it will), the window will be a mess. Factory-applied enamel finishes will eventually need painting, just like wood.

THE OHJ EDITORS found something we really hate: aluminum-clad wood. Again, they are being sold as "maintenance-free windows with the insulating qualities of wood." They'll be okay for a while. But as soon as the aluminum is damaged, it will be a perfect water trap, unseen and unfixable. To us, these combine the worst features of wood and metal...you're stuck looking at aluminum while you wait for the wood to eventually get wet and rot!

NOW FOR SOMETHING we really like. Storm/screen inserts do combine the best features of wood and aluminum, with fewer mechanical and visual problems than triple-tracks. Interior or exterior wood frames are left in place year-round. In winter, you insert aluminum-framed glass panels. In summer, glass is replaced by aluminum-framed screens. Here are the potential drawbacks: You still have to store something, though inserts are much less unwieldy than entire storm windows. Also, gasketing should be provided and checked yearly to ensure a tight seal between the narrow aluminum frame and the wood.

## Magnetic, Removable, Or Fixed ?

NOW YOU CAN BUY a removable interior storm window that's attached to the frame or interior casing with magnetic strips. Light-weight acrylic glazing and snap-together vinyl frames are cut to exactly fit the window. They're not heavy-duty, but many immediate advantages come to mind. They are easy to install, fit most any window, do little damage in installation, and come off quickly if your window is suddenly a fire exit.

THEIR MAJOR DISADVANTAGE is lack of a track record. Will the magnetic strips stay stuck to the window, and will the magnet stay magnetized? If they somehow wear out, will the company still be around to sell you new magnetic strips? We sure don't know.

REMOVABLE storm windows give the opportunity for maximum ventilation in summer, and minimum visual impact for the months they're stored

Photo: Alan D. Keiser

Aluminum triple-track storm windows can be reasonably unobtrusive on the average window, provided they're painted or factory-enameled to match the house trim.

IN EVALUATING TRIPLE-TRACK storm windows, rarely do people focus on the spring-loaded latches. These are sometimes the troublesome component — and are difficult to judge in advance. The latches have to operate smoothly year after year for the windows to work as advertised. Often, they don't.

Seven years ago, I bought top-of-the-line black aluminum triple-tracks for my four-storey row house. I am very satisfied with the look of the windows, but dissatisfied with the way they work. Even though they were supposedly the best windows available, the latches never worked well and have gotten worse with age. (This problem may be worst on higher-priced windows, which have "hidden" latches.) To operate my storm windows, you need the deft hands of a surgeon to make sure the lugs on the latches are mated securely into the frame. Neither my family nor the fellow who washes the windows have the required touch.

This scenario has been played out at least a dozen times: Someone raises the lower storm sash and thinks it's securely latched. (It isn't.) Minutes or hours later, it comes crashing down. The result is either a broken pane or a broken aluminum frame. I also have latches that lock in place and won't release, no matter how hard I pull. On a scale of 1 to 10, I'd rate my triple-track storm windows a 2.
— C.L.

Aesthetics is not the only consideration when you buy stock storm windows — mechanical and design details count, too. Above, a tale of woe.

away. The disadvantages are obvious: They have to be fiddled with spring and fall, and they have to be stored. Fixed (but operational) windows, such as triple-tracks, are practical but in evidence all year.

YOU DON'T HAVE TO settle on just one kind of storm window. Here's an example: A three-storey house, air-conditioned only on the bedroom floor, with very pretty multi-light prime windows on the first storey. Perhaps an unused attic bedroom would do fine with plastic or an insulated panel. Second-storey rooms might take permanent exterior storms (left alone in summer because of the air conditioning). The downstairs windows could be fitted with interior combination storm/screen windows. In spring, the storm window inserts are removed and carted one flight to cellar storage and the screen inserts are installed in their place.

## Where Do I Buy Them ?

DESPITE the number of options, you may still find aluminum being offered most consistently. Before you take the word of your local window contracting place, make some phone calls and consider mail-order suppliers. On page 95 in this issue, we've listed a few reputable companies that are off the beaten path. The companies listed under "Prime Windows," too, are often manufacturing storm windows similar to their prime-window product line.

IF YOU'VE DECIDED on wood storms, by all means contact local millworks and lumberyards. In some cases, your lowest bid will be for custom wood sash built exactly to your specifications locally. An added advantage is that you can have them installed by the firm that made them. There are some custom millwork companies listed on page 93 which specialize in windows.

A WINDOW OR GLAZING contracting company is a good bet if you know what features you want. They carry and install storm windows from the big manufacturers--Pella, Andersen, Coradco, Marvin. These companies offer high-quality windows that are quite suitable for some circumstances. The average contractor may be very good at getting you "the best deal," but won't be looking out for aesthetic impact. That's up to you.

Photo: Mary C. Lambert

This 1880s Homestead/Queen Anne house belongs to OHJ subscriber Mary Lambert. For a couple of seasons, the Lamberts struggled to make a decision on what kind of storm windows to buy. Storms were deemed necessary for the northeastern Maryland climate, but none of the usual options seemed appropriate.

Glass and wood, a likely combination, would have been too heavy to handle. The Plexiglass and vinyl kits that were available in 1980 at first seemed a good idea, but Mary found the vinyl strips poorly fitted and "ghastly" with her interior trim.

A major consideration was the original wood-framed half-screens with their decorative cast-iron corner brackets. Discarding them felt anti-preservationist. Nevertheless, the Lamberts

A search turned up a glazing supplier who sold them 'Caroglaz' acrylic glazing in economical sheets. Their carpenter hand-picked clear pine for the dowelled and butt-jointed frames. The panels pop in place in winter — without obscuring the half-screens that remain — and are clipped to the exterior casing with wing nuts. Each window cost $44.80, installed. Materials cost just $18.82 per window (1980 prices).

A hint from Mary Lambert: Acrylic is surprisingly scratch-resistant and non-yellowing. But it must be washed with plain soap and water, and preferably left to air dry. Don't use ammonia or coarse cloth on it.

*'Caroglaz' is manufactured by the J.W. Carroll Co., 22600 S. Bonita St., Carson, CA 90745; 9 Headley Pl., Fallsington, PA 19055; 12337 Tullie Circle, NE, Atlanta, GA 30329. They'll give you the name of a distributor in your area who can sell you acrylic glazing in large sheets if necessary.*

got estimates on permanent triple-track storm/screen windows that would take their place. In 1980, the contractor's estimate came to $50 per window — not including installation! When she inquired whether the aluminum mid-rail would mate with the off-median meeting rails on her prime windows, Mary was told that would cost an extra $10 per window. The Lamberts decided it was too much to pay for something they didn't really want anyway.

Finally, a compromise design dawned on them: 'Why forget the wood frame because of its weight, when maybe glass was the real culprit? Using a light-weight synthetic glazing in a wood frame was the most appealing idea of all," Mary wrote to us.

The exceptional character of these Queen Anne windows is in the glass colors and patterns. Exterior wood storms, designed and installed by the owner, are nearly invisible. The house is in Havre de Grace, Maryland.

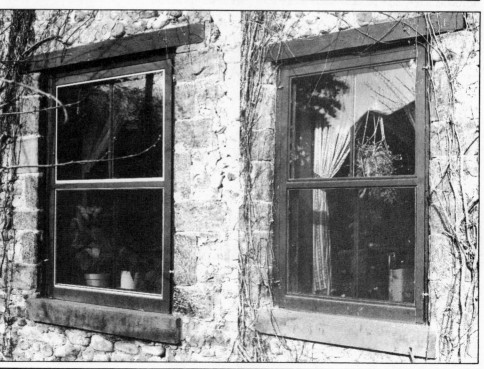

An ideal storm window for 2-over-2 sash (above) might be mounted indoors. Yet these 1-over-1 wood storms look pretty good. Right: Raw aluminum insert frames make window look as if it has dental braces, until it's painted.

# RESCUING THOSE "HOPELESS" WINDOWS

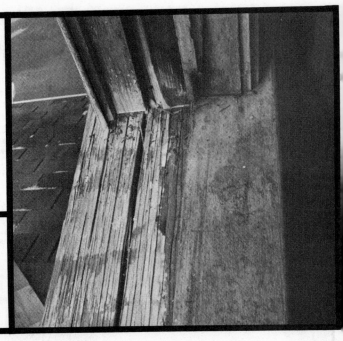

*Sills like this can be rehabilitated. Those in worse condition can be replaced without replacing the entire window unit.*

## Low-Tech Repairs

### By Clem Labine

AT THE SIGHT of peeling paint on a window sill, the typical home improvement contractor will shake his head sadly and pronounce the window "hopeless." The only solution, he will announce gravely, is to replace the old window with a modern unit. But beware: Not only may the replacement look bad, but it may also be an unnecessarily costly solution.

THE WINDOWS in my 1883 brownstone were pronounced hopeless 15 years ago. Yet, with some relatively simple repairs, these windows have served me well for 15 years. Moreover, they should be serviceable well into the next century. And since it was all do-it-yourself work, the cost of repair was only a few dollars. Even on some standard commercial jobs, those contractors who take the trouble to cost out the alternatives are finding that in some cases it is cheaper to rejuvenate the old windows than to buy replacements.

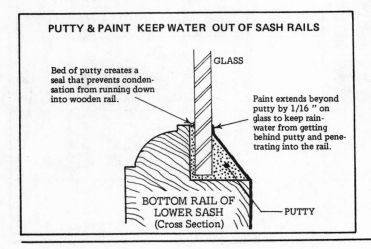

**PUTTY & PAINT KEEP WATER OUT OF SASH RAILS**

GLASS

Bed of putty creates a seal that prevents condensation from running down into wooden rail.

Paint extends beyond putty by 1/16 " on glass to keep rainwater from getting behind putty and penetrating into the rail.

BOTTOM RAIL OF LOWER SASH (Cross Section) — PUTTY

THE TRADITIONAL wooden double-hung window has some outstanding advantages: (1) The wood is a relatively good insulator; (2) The simple construction makes it forever "fixable"; (3) The wood will last indefinitely if it's properly maintained. If the wood does rot out new wood can be spliced in using simple carpentry techniques. Try to imagine locating replacement vinyl gasketing 10 years from now, or the problem of replacing a bent aluminum channel.

THE MORAL IS CLEAR: It makes sense to rehabilitate your current wood windows if at all possible.

## Dealing With Rot

MORE THAN ANY other factor, rotted and checked wood in the sill and lower sash rail leads to the verdict of "hopeless." So this article is going to focus on the rejuvenation of partially rotted window elements. A directory of how-to information for the other common window repairs will be found on the opposite page.

BEFORE PLUNGING IN to repair and consolidate wooden window elements, try to determine whether the failure is caused by normal weathering, or whether there is an unusual condition that is causing water to collect on or behind the window. Among these conditions would be defective gutters, cracks in window framing that permit water to enter, sills that aren't tipped so as to shed water, and defective storm windows.

TRIPLE-TRACK STORM WINDOWS can trap water on window sills. The installers are supposed to leave two gaps ("weep holes") in the caulking at the bottom edge of the storm window. Then, during summer when the screen section is down, rainwater that gets on the sill can drain out. But if the storms weren't properly installed, or if the weep holes have gotten plugged, you have an ideal holding tank for rainwater.

PEELING PAINT is a good indicator of where water is entering wood. Usually you'll find paint failure on the top of the sill and areas where the end-grain of the wood is exposed to moisture. Wood that is badly deteriorated is a candidate for replacement or epoxy consolidation (see section following). Wood that has only minor decay (such as the sill in the photo opposite) can be rehabilitated with low-tech repairs.

FIRST STEP is to seal the wood to retard moisture absorption. Make sure the wood is thoroughly dry. Then scrape and wire-brush all loose paint. Better still, remove all the old paint with a heat gun or by hand scraping. Complete removal enhances absorption of the water repellant and subsequent adhesion of the new coat of paint. Flow on generous amounts of water repellant--as much as the wood will absorb. Pay special attention to joints and other places where water can reach the end-grain.

**DECAY-PRONE AREAS**

Window elements start rotting at points where end-grain can absorb moisture, such as ends of sill, bottom of jamb, and joints in sash. Treatment starts by thoroughly waterproofing these vulnerable areas.

FOR THE WATER REPELLANT, you can use a commercial product (e.g., Thompson's Water Seal) or you can make your own (OHJ Oct. 1981 p. 223). Some old-timers prefer a 50-50 solution of boiled linseed oil and turpentine. Take your choice.

## Where To Find Window Fix-It Information

A directory of how-to information from two basic sources: the back issues of The Old-House Journal and the Reader's Digest Complete Do-It-Yourself Manual——a good, basic book available at most bookstores.

| PROBLEM | WHAT TO DO | WHERE TO FIND INFORMATION |
|---|---|---|
| Sticking sash | Remove accumulated paint; lubricate with soap or paraffin; plane wood only if absolutely necessary. | Reader's Digest Manual p. 119 |
| Excessive air infiltration | Caulk and weatherstrip | This issue p. 77<br>OHJ Sept. 1980 p. 128<br>Reader's Digest Manual p. 122 |
| Broken sash cord | Replace cord or chain | OHJ Dec. 1979 p. 133<br>OHJ Aug. 1976 p. 1<br>Reader's Digest Manual p. 120 |
| Broken glass | Re-glaze; while sash is out, do other reconditioning. | Reader's Digest Manual p. 123 |
| Loose and/or missing putty | Remove loose material; reputty. Paint putty as indicated on diagram on opposite page. | Reader's Digest Manual p. 123 |
| Peeling paint on frame | Eliminate unusual sources of moisture; strip or scrape loose paint; caulk; prime and paint. | OHJ Sept. 1980 p. 113<br>OHJ Apr. 1981 p. 89<br>OHJ May 1981 p. 103 |
| Loose or rotten bottom rail on lower sash | 1. Brace existing rail connection with flat angle; or<br><br>2. Splice in new bottom rail | 1. OHJ Jan. 1976 p. 10<br><br>2. Reader's Digest Manual p. 388 |
| Broken or missing muntins | 1. Repair with epoxy if possible; or<br><br>2. Make or buy new muntin | 1. This article<br><br>2. Consult local lumberyards; This issue p. 93 for custom millwork shops |
| Rotted sash | 1. Consolidate existing sash; or<br><br>2. Replace sash | 1. This article<br><br>2. This issue p. 94 OHJ Catalog for additional sources |
| Rotted sill | 1. Consolidate existing sill; or<br><br>2. Replace sill | 1. This article<br><br>2. OHJ Jan. 1980 p. 7 |

FOR BEST RESULTS, let the waterproofer dry for 24 hours, then repeat the process. After another 24 hours, fill all holes with linseed oil putty or glazing compound. Long cracks can be filled with a high-quality caulk, such as polyurethane. Also seal all joints in the window frame with caulk, especially the joint between jamb and sill. Wait at least 24 hours for a skin to form on the putty and caulk. Then prime with an alkyd primer. Finish coat can be either an alkyd or latex paint.

## Epoxy Consolidation

### By Larry Jones

 ROTTED WOOD can be detected with the "ice-pick test": Probe suspected areas with an ice pick. Those areas that break across the grain--rather than splintering--are weakened by rot and are candidates for epoxy consolidation. This is an amazingly simple technique for strengthening and solidifying decayed wood. The trick is to use the right epoxy, and knowing when it is cheaper to replace an element rather than consolidating it.

I HAVE FOUND that it is often cheaper to repair items such as deteriorated window sills than it is to pull the frame apart to replace the sill. Epoxy consolidants are not cheap--but splicing in new wood is a labor intensive (and thus expensive) process.

I SHOULD ALSO MENTION products that have NOT worked in consolidating exterior woodwork such as window sills. A spackling compound called Tuff Kote proved to be a total disaster, both when used by itself and in conjunction with fiberglass mesh. Auto body fillers, such as Bondo, and fiberglass boat repair products have not proved successful. If moisture gets behind these patches (which it has in our experience) it leads to further wood deterioration.

### One That Works

FOUND ONE FIRM, through The Old-House Journal Catalog, whose products do work successfully on wood repair: Abatron, Inc. (see p. 94). The President, John Caporaso, has been very helpful in helping us find the right epoxy (they make dozens) for our application.

EPOXY CONSOLIDATION is usually a two-step process. First, an epoxy of thin viscosity (about the consistency of motor oil) is allowed to penetrate deep into the wood. When cured, the epoxy renders the treated wood fibers impervious to moisture--and thus relatively immune to further decay. The second step is to use a thicker epoxy to fill any cracks and voids, and to build up a smooth surface for painting.

THE PENETRATING EPOXY we used for the first step was a two-part system: Abocast #8101-4 resin and Abocure #8101-4 catalyst. It has a pot life of about 30 minutes when mixed for use. (The factory can adjust set-up times to suit needs.) Resin and catalyst are mixed at a 2 to 1 ratio for best moisture resistance, or a 1 to 1 ratio for greatest flexibility.

THE PENETRATING EPOXY can be applied with a brush, making sure to get it into all cracks and voids. It is best applied to horizontal surfaces since it is fairly thin, although sloping window sills seem to pose no problem. Lay window sashes on their sides to apply.

COST is about $20 per quart (for a 2 to 1 mix, 3 quarts are required) or $50 per gallon (for a 2 to 1 mix, 3 gallons required). The material seems to go a long way, so try out the quart size first.

### Filling Holes And Cracks

 AFTER THE IMPREGNATING EPOXY has cured, thus stabilizing the rotted wood, any holes and cracks can be filled with an epoxy filler. Abatron recommends its Woodepox-1 as compatible with the Abocast impregnant used in the first stage. The idea is to fill up voids to a suitable thickness which, after curing, can be sanded and painted to match surrounding wood. Woodepox-1 can be built up to a thickness of several inches.

WOODEPOX-1 is also a 2-part system, mixed at a ratio of 1 to 1 of resin and hardener. The material may also be mixed with sawdust to extend it further. Cost is around $18 per quart (2 quarts required) or $36 per gallon (2 gallons required). As with most epoxies, you should plan on buying a quart of solvent for clean-up. Abosolve solvent costs $9 per quart.

 ONCE THE DETERIORATED WOOD has been stabilized and patched with epoxies, I favor treating the bare wood with a waterproofer or wood preservative before painting. A plain waterproofer is preferred over wood preservatives because it avoids the toxicity problems associated with preservatives. You can buy commercial waterproofers (e.g., Thompson's Water Seal) or make your own (see OHJ Oct. 1981 p. 223).

DIPPING OR SOAKING wood elements for at least three minutes is the best way to ensure deep penetration of the water repellant solution. One of the simplest ways to dip-treat wood elements, such as window sash, is to take an old piece of aluminum gutter that is long enough to hold the longest side of the sash. Cap each end of the gutter, sealing the seams with silicone caulk. Fill the gutter with waterproofer and soak each side of the sash in the trough, then set aside to dry.

TO USE THIS TECHNIQUE, the sash must be free of paint. Best results are achieved if the glass and glazing putty are removed from the sash. However, you can leave the glass in place with good results. Obviously, such areas as sills and jambs will have to be brush-treated. Allow the bare wood to soak up all the waterproofer it will hold in two successive brush applications. After 24 hours of drying, prime and paint as usual.

*COMING NEXT MONTH: Photos and text showing step-by-step procedures for epoxy consolidation of deteriorated wood.*

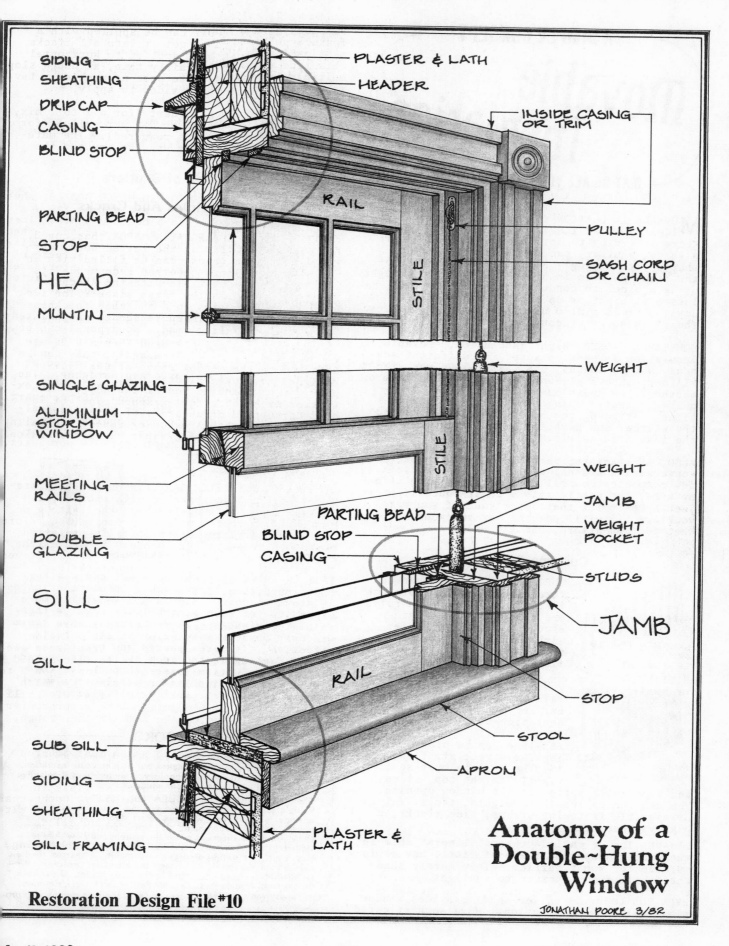

SIDING
SHEATHING
DRIP CAP
CASING
BLIND STOP

PARTING BEAD
STOP
HEAD
MUNTIN

PLASTER & LATH
HEADER

INSIDE CASING
OR TRIM

RAIL

STILE

PULLEY

SASH CORD
OR CHAIN

WEIGHT

SINGLE GLAZING
ALUMINUM
STORM
WINDOW

MEETING
RAILS

DOUBLE
GLAZING

STILE

WEIGHT

PARTING BEAD
BLIND STOP
CASING

JAMB
WEIGHT
POCKET

STUDS

SILL

SILL

JAMB

RAIL

STOP

STOOL

SUB SILL

SIDING

SHEATHING

SILL FRAMING

PLASTER &
LATH

APRON

**Anatomy of a
Double~Hung
Window**

**Restoration Design File #10**

JONATHAN POORE 3/82

# A SIMPLE CONCEPT

# Movable Insulation

## MAY BE ALL YOUR WINDOWS NEED

MOVABLE INSULATION for windows is not a new idea--just an idea whose time has come. We're referring to any opaque material, be it a shade, shutter, panel, curtain or quilt, that's fitted snugly against a window _some_ of the time. Movable insulation is usually thought of as a block to conduction and convection losses at night or on cold, overcast winter days. But it's also used to block sunlight (heat) in sunny windows on summer days.

SOMETIMES CALLED "night insulation," movable insulation is easy to adapt for different seasons, window shapes, and tastes. So why aren't all our windows already fitted with one sort or another? We guess one reason is that it requires a subtle change in peoples's expectations...it means you have to pay attention to the weather and nightfall. ("Time to pop in the insulated panels.")

ALSO, it's not yet part of the usual energy-conservation arsenal at the hardware store. A few companies do sell custom-fitted insulation or kits, but mostly it's a do-it-yourself project. Don't let that deter you; if you make your own, it will look the way you want, cost what you can afford, and fit well.

## Curtains & Shades

SAND BAG OR LEAD WEIGHT IN HEM

MATED MAGNETIC STRIPS

CURTAINS AND DRAPES can be turned into high-performance insulation. The basic rules are few: (1) The curtain should slow heat transfer with multiple layers, inclusion of a reflective foil or fiberfill-type layer, or use of a very thick, tightly-woven fabric. (2) The curtain should contain a vapor-barrier material to keep condensation off the glass. (Vinyl, foil, Mylar, or polyethylene can be used.) This impedes direct air flow, too. (3) The curtain must seal tightly to the top, sides, and especially bottom of the window opening. You can employ lead hem weights, tacks, Velcro or magnetic fastening strips, side tracks, a high valance, etc.

BEWARE: The so-called "thermal liners" sold in the drapery department are of little use as insulation or vapor barrier. They merely shade the fabric from exposure to sunlight.

EVEN THE LOWLY $8 roller shade provides window glass with some insulation. More sophisticated versions give a tighter seal on all sides, and feature multiple layering. The Window Quilt mentioned on p. 93 is a now-famous example of this type of window insulation. One of its multiple layers is a vapor barrier; it seals tightly on all four sides; and it's quite pretty (if not historical).

REMEMBER THAT a glossy white shade, or one with an aluminized foil layer facing outdoors, will turn away much radiant heat from the summer sun.

## All Kinds of Shutters

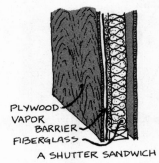

PLYWOOD
VAPOR
BARRIER
FIBERGLASS

A SHUTTER SANDWICH

TO OLD-HOUSE PEOPLE, shutters are a familiar way to block the sun or close off chilly windows. When they're designed specifically for the purpose of insulating, shutters are much more energy-efficient than their old-fashioned counterparts.

SHUTTERS can be made as loose panels that must be stored when not in use. Then again, they can be attached to the window frame or casing, and designed to hinge, slide, fold, flip up, disappear, or any combination of the above. The shutter might be a foil-wrapped panel of laminated corrugated cardboard...or bifolding, hinged panels with a mahogany veneer concealing a fiberglass insulation/vapor barrier sandwich.

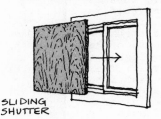

SLIDING SHUTTER

FOLDING SHUTTER

IF YOUR PRIME WINDOWS are tight and weather-stripped, consider movable insulation _instead_ of storm windows. Storms are generally more expensive yet have a much lower R-value than insulated windows. If you already have storm windows, movable insulation is still quite effective. It saves energy and creates a warmer feeling in the room as it cuts convection and conduction losses through the cold glass. Movable insulation is almost always more cost-effective than triple glazing.

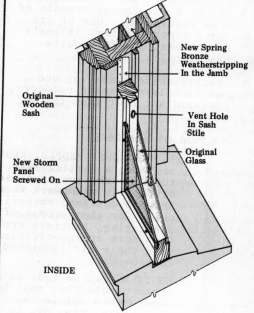

New Spring Bronze Weatherstripping In the Jamb

Original Wooden Sash

Vent Hole In Sash Stile

Original Glass

New Storm Panel Screwed On

INSIDE

## "Integral" Storm Windows

When a preservation-minded architect is charged with the rehabilitation and energy-efficiency upgrading of a landmark building, an ingenious solution is born: integral storm panels, set into a new rabbet in existing wood sash. Architect Jack Graves would not consider two overused solutions — exterior storms and solar-tinted thermal replacements — because either would have had a negative impact on the look of the ornamented, light-colored Colcord Building. The use of metal replacement windows would have cost the owner preservation tax benefits. Technical Preservation Services (National Park Svc.) ruled that metal windows would (1) alter the character of the building, and (2) possibly cause an external condensation problem that could cause the terra cotta to spall.

The storm panel used was easily installed during overall reconditioning of the window. A neoprene gasket in the rabbet behind the new glass has thus far kept the humidity in the air space low enough to prevent condensation. (In wetter climates, a vent hole could be drilled in sash stiles.) Glass was used because weight was not a problem — sash weights didn't even need to be increased. Acrylic would have been initially more expensive and might have suffered under harsh cleaning by maintenance staff. The bottom line made everybody happy: Primary wood sash, reconditioned, weatherstripped, and retrofitted with year-round storm panels, cost 1/3 as much as new metal replacement windows, and were more energy efficient than new metal windows. (Metal-framed replacements, double-glazed, non-thermal-break, $300. Repaired sash, $100. Metal as above, U=.69. Wood windows, U=.49)

*A very clear, useful report about the Colcord windows was written by Sharon Park of Technical Preservation Services. It's not yet generally available, but we've obtained a pre-print copy. We'll Xerox it (with permission) for those interested in the details of the work. Please send $2 to cover reprinting and postage costs to The Old-House Journal, 69A Seventh Ave., Dept. TPS, Brooklyn, NY 11217.*

## More Good News

**O**KLAHOMA'S COLCORD BUILDING has gotten a lot of attention, but it's not an isolated case. Repair, installation of storm windows and movable insulation, and thermal retrofitting are all good counter-arguments to window replacement. Other rehabilitation jobs have made use of hermetically-sealed double-glazing, available through window dealers and lumberyards. These glass units are inserted in existing sash after removal of the old single glazing layer. The process allows retention of the original sash and frames, but is probably feasible only for standard-size, 1-over-1 sash.

Salt Lake City carpenter Jack Churchill cuts a deeper rabbet into old sash parts. A hermetically-sealed, double-glazed unit will be installed in the reconditioned window sash.

YOU CAN GO HALF-WAY, too, and save money along with the appearance of the window: Sash alone can easily be replaced, while jamb and casings are repaired. New sash can be ordered single- or double-glazed. If counter-weighted windows are double-glazed, be aware that sash weights may need to be increased.

## Local Sources

The photo is of wood replacement windows, a specialty of Four Star Lumber in Brooklyn. Most communities have a millworks that will custom-make sash or whole window units.

For example, a recent job in Brooklyn required all new wood windows for a building being converted from light industrial to residential use. The Landmarks Commission suggested 6-over-6 sash as most compatible with the style of the building. Because of the special requirement, and because the oversize openings couldn't be fitted with stock units, the architect asked Four Star to build true 6-over-6 double-hung windows with single glass. (Double-glazed multi-light sash were considered unattractive because of the larger glazing bars, and because of expense — $250 to $300 per unit.)

Contractor cost was $150 per window, primed. (Small jobs would cost up to $190 per window.) In addition, wood frames for interior storm windows were built for $35 each, unglazed. Light-weight acrylic will be used for easy handling by the owner. So — the 6-over-6 windows with interior storms cost less than stock windows of comparable quality.

*Thanks to Cosmo and John at Four Star Lumber, 189 Prospect Ave., Brooklyn, NY 11215. (212) 768-7112.*

## Sensitive Replacement

Built in 1837, The Old Market House in Lowell, Massachusetts, was first remodelled between 1868 - 1872. At that time, a cupola was added and original 8- and 12-light sash were replaced with 2-over-2.

The Lowell Historic Preservation Commission oversaw its rehabilitation in 1981. The building had been badly neglected. Besides rebuilding the cupola and reopening bricked-up windows, workers replaced all sash and frames. New wood windows match the Victorian 2-over-2 sash, but have 7/16-inch sealed insulating glass in each light. Real 1¼-inch wood muntins were used. Sash channels have spiral spring balances. The window fabrication was handled locally, and cost was competitive with standard units.

The photo was sent to us by architect Charles Parrott of the Lowell Commission.

*Photo courtesy Lowell (MA) Historic Preservation Commission*

BACK TO HOPELESS windows--new replacements don't have to be a travesty. Recent high-visibility renovations have featured replacement of windows with new ones that are exact visual replicas of the originals. Several manufacturers, large and small, have responded to demand by introducing historically appropriate windows (see p. 94).

A SOURCE not to be overlooked is your local lumberyard or millworks. If you need special windows--say, round-heads or 6-over-6--local custom duplication is your best bet. First, write down your exact specifications. Then, take out the Yellow Pages and call every company listed under WINDOWS--WOOD, or MILLWORK, or even LUMBER. Start with the companies who advertise "custom wood sash" or "double-hung windows."

## Bad News

PROBLEMS to be wary of: Total Insensitivity, The Path of Least Resistance, and Manufacturer Mimicry. The first two are familiar and still rampant. The third, the most insidious, is gaining rapidly.

TOTAL INSENSITIVITY happens most often when a building is renovated for a new use. As a hallway becomes a bathroom, its window is blocked halfway up and turned into a blind ventilator. We've all seen these sometimes funny, always sad, examples.

**BAD NEWS**

This is a clear-cut case of Total Insensitivity — a distinctive window, visible from the street, ripped out and its opening bricked up. It's no average building, either: It was designed by late-19th-century Philadelphia architect Frank Furness.

A runner-up for this month's Remuddling Award, photo at right shows a commercial building in Portland, Maine. It was sent to us by subscriber James Munch III, who wrote, "When I look at the building, I always think of it as being sick — which it probably is since its windows were reduced in the name of saving energy." Lighting and ventilation loads have probably increased dramatically in the 1877 structure.

## The Path of Least Resistance

The Path of Least Resistance comes perilously close to Total Insensitivity in this case of window replacement. These exceptional residential windows are on a wide, parkside avenue in an historic district. Yet the contractor employed to turn two of three such buildings into multi-family cooperative housing apparently had no time to respect the wood windows — which had curved sash rails and convex glass. His standard-size, flat replacements are surrounded by black aluminum infill to make them "fit."

THE PATH OF LEAST RESISTANCE is the most common reason for ugly windows. It's taken to avoid trouble, long searches, talking back to the contractor, making extra phone calls, or waiting for delivery of a custom item. Because it's so easy to take the Path of Least Resistance, we have wood windows replaced with metal; 4-over-4 sash replaced with 1-over-1; round-head windows ripped out, their curved tops filled in with plywood or bricks.

MANUFACTURER MIMICRY is a new kind of bad news. With preservation and beauty higher in public consciousness (and with tax credits for sensitive work), window makers have begun to parrot the right words, but have missed on their meaning. Here are some things to watch out for:

● "Multi-light sash with 'muntins'." The manufacturer might mean wood or vinyl strips that snap in place over a single sheet of glass. Maybe that is what you're looking for; maybe it isn't.

● "Any size." One of the largest, best-known companies is currently promising "replacement windows to fit any size or shape opening" for old houses. Intrigued that a big company would offer custom windows, we checked it out. What they have in mind is combining their stock glass-pane sizes with thick metal mullions to infill the old opening!

● "Historic multi-light sash, double glazed." A year ago, a subscriber called us with a sad story: Her early 19th-century house has multi-light windows with narrow muntins, and she needed a few replacement sash. A seemingly conscientious manufacturer talked her into the benefits of double-glazed windows, which he promised would have "real wood muntins"-- separated panes, not just snap-ins. She ordered the sash, paying a dear price, only to realize on delivery that the muntins had been milled bulky and wide to accept the double glazing. The new sash doesn't even come close to matching original sash still on the house.

EVEN IN THE LAST EXAMPLE, it's a case of misunderstanding more than deceit. It probably never occurred to the manufacturer that the muntins had to be a certain size...just as the customer never thought to ask if the muntins would be big and fat. The moral is: Just because they use words like "old--historic-- replica--any window," it doesn't mean they know what they're talking about.

## Thank You's

The Editors would like to thank several people in New York City who "talked to us of windows."

Gary Nebiol at Air-Flo Window Contracting Corp. was a great help with product information. Air-Flo is a window supplier-fabricator–installer for the New York metropolitan area; they deal in wood and metal, storm and prime, double-hung or casement windows, and specialize in production of windows that conform to Landmarks Commission standards. Their new address is Air-Flo, 194 Concord St., Brooklyn, NY 11201.

Alex Herrera at the New York Landmarks Commission, and Laurie Hammel at The Landmarks Conservancy, inspired us with their knowledge and specific source information.

# Restoration Products News

## Interior Storm Windows

*Interior storms are becoming increasingly popular as an inexpensive solution. These storm windows are usually glazed with acrylic (making them lightweight, regardless of size); they're easily detachable in case of fire; and they can be ordered or constructed to fit any size window. They should be handled carefully to avoid scratching the acrylic or bending the frame.*

Poplar frames (usually two sections, ready to be painted or stained), acrylic glazing. Held in place by rubber tubing between the storm & interior frame. Custom made to fit even askew windows. 48 in. x 24 in. storm, approx. $85. Brochure, 50¢. McNair Construction Co., Box 6414, Dept. OHJ, Baltimore, MD 21230. (301) 539-1237.

*In-sider* available with a hinged aluminum frame, or a self-adhesive vinyl frame. Components for this do-it-yourself kit sold in most major hardware stores. Cost for 36 in. x 60 in. window, including acrylic glazing, $30-$50 depending on the frame you choose. Free brochure. Plaskolite, Inc., 1770 Joyce Avenue, PO Box 1497, Dept. OHJ, Columbus, OH 43216. (614) 294-3281.

*Magnetite*—in non-yellowing acrylic (1/8 to 1/16-in. thick) glazing with brown or white plastic frames. Attached with magnetic strip (on all four sides) to interior window frame. Can purchase components separately or have it installed to fit any size window. About $4/sq. ft. (installed). Distributors throughout the U.S. & Canada. Free brochure. Viking Energy Systems Co., 275 Circuit St., Dept. OHJ, Hanover, MA 02339. (617) 871-3180.

*Custom-made wood interior storm by McNair Construction*

*Magnetite storms shown on hard-to-fit windows
Photos courtesy of Bow & Arrow Stove Co.*

## Unusual Glass

Clear & colored hand-blown cylinder glass for restoration of old-house windows. $5.25 and $5.74/sq.ft. Free price list. Blenko Glass Co., Inc., PO Box 67, Dept. OHJ, Milton, WV 25541. (304) 743-9081.

Hand-blown bull's eye glass. 8 in. x 8 in. pane, $40. Also diamond-pane leaded casement windows. Brochure, 50¢. Kraatz Hand Blown Glass, RFD 2, Dept. OHJ, Canaan, NH 03741. (603) 523-4289.

Complete selection of glass including bent (about $75 per radius depending if stock or custom item), & glazing supplies. Free brochures on various subjects—making your own storm windows; cutting and measuring glass. Catalog, $4. Shadovitz Bros., Inc., 1565 Bergen St., Dept. OHJ, Brooklyn, NY 11213. (212) 774-9100.

Machine-made clear glass bevels. $.80-$3 per bevel piece. Catalog, $1. Whittemore Durgin Glass Co., Box 2065OH, Hanover, MA 02339. (617) 871-1790.

Several varieties of hand-blown & machine-rolled, antique styled glass. Clear & colored. Prices range from about $1-$10/sq.ft. Free information. Bendheim, S. A. Co., Inc., 122 Hudson St., Dept. OHJ, New York, NY 10013. (212) 226-6370. Also, Bienenfeld Industries, Inc., 22 Harbor Park Dr., Dept. OHJ, Box 22, Roslyn, NY 11576. (516) 621-2500. Contact a Bienenfeld distributor for your local dealer. Chicago: (312) 523-8400. Houston: (713) 864-0193. Wilmington, Cal.: (213) 549-4329. Canada: (416) 677-8600.

# Shutters, Shades, & Blinds

*Night closure of interior shutters or insulated shades can result in significant energy savings, even over single glazing. These products can be designed to fit almost any style or size window. Unless otherwise stated, literature is free.*

Custom-made insulated interior wood shutters. Pine, raised-panel shutters for 3 ft. x 5 ft. window begin at $363. Order through dealers or direct. Neilson Co., Rt. 1, Dept. OHJ, Falmouth Foreside, ME 04105. (207) 781-2160.

*Neilson's insulated shutters*

Two sources for plastic/vinyl "trac" kits for constructing your own insulated window shades. $3-$4/sq.ft. Can be purchased ready-made to your fabric and size specifications, or track can be ordered alone. Bow & Arrow Stove Co., (also distributor of *Magnetite Windows*), 11 Hurley St., Dept. OHJ, Cambridge, MA 02141. (617) 492-1411. Sold through dealers—Plum Industries, PO Box 14, Dept. OHJ, Delta, OH, 43515. (800) 537-1076.

*Insul-Trac from Plum Industries*

Complete collection of fabrics including acrylic flocking to make your own insulated shades & drapes. Average price, $4.50/yard. Stores in Belchertown, MA; Cheshire, CT; & Scotia, NY; mail orders welcomed. Home Fabric Mills, Inc., PO Box 662, Rt. 202, Dept. OHJ, Belchertown, MA 01007. (413) 323-6321.

*Window Quilt*, a do-it-yourself or dealer-installed five-layered quilted roller shade with vapor barrier. Available in three neutral colors; held in place with self-adhesive plastic tracks. $5-$6/sq.ft., also solid panels, $4-$5/sq.ft. Sold through dealers. Appropriate Technology Corp., PO Box 975, Dept. OHJ, Brattleboro, VT 05301. (802) 257-4501.

*Insulated window shade from Appropriate Technology*

*And the more traditional...*

Custom shutters (especially historical duplication). Variety of woods & styles. 36 in. x 60 in. (4-panel, ready-to-install), $275-$300. Quotes made on detailed drawings or samples. Beauti-home, 408 Airport Blvd., Dept. OHJ, Watsonville, CA 95076. (408) 724-1066.

Wood Venetian blinds, a traditional window treatment, are $8/sq.ft. Designed to fit a variety of architectural shapes. Free brochure. Devenco Products, Box 700, Dept. OHJ, Decatur, GA 30030. (404) 378-4598.

*Most lumber yards will do custom millwork. However, if you have difficulty finding one, the following companies specialize in custom duplication of wood storm & prime windows. For a free price quote, send dimensional drawings and specifications; windows can be shipped nationwide.*

Architectural Components, PO Box 246, Dept. OHJ, Leverett, MA 01054. (413) 549-1094. Brochure, $2.
Gibbons, John—Cabinetmaker, 2070 Helena St., Dept. OHJ, Madison, WI 53704. (608) 241-5364. Brochure, $1.
Hallelujah Redwood Products, Box 669, Dept. OHJ, Mendocino, CA 95460. (707) 937-4410. Catalog, $1.
Island City Wood Working Co., 1915 Sealy Ave., Dept. OHJ, Galveston, TX 77550. (713) 765-5476. No literature.
Maurer & Shepherd, Joyners, 122 Naubuc Ave., Dept. OHJ, Glastonbury, CT 06033. (203) 633-2383. Free brochure.
Michael's Fine Colonial Products, Rte. 44, RD 1, Box 179A, Dept. OHJ, Salt Point, NY 12578. (914) 677-3960. Free brochure.
Robillard, Dennis Paul, Inc., Front St., Dept. OHJ, South Berwick, ME 03908. (207) 384-9541. Literature, $1.50.
Somerset Door & Column Co., PO Box 328, Dept. OHJ, Somerset, PA 15501. (814) 445-9608. Free brochure.
Strobel Millwork, PO Box 84, Rt. 7, Dept. OHJ, Cornwall Bridge, CT 06754. (203) 672-6727. Brochure, $2.
Victorian Millshop, 4220 Milwaukee St., Dept. OHJ, Denver, CO 80216. (303) 321-3771. No literature.

*Shutters by Historic Windows*

Solid hardwood Early American interior shutters (full or half). Custom-made only. 30 in. x 60 in. shutter set, $150-$170. Brochure, 50¢; sample, $12 (refundable). Historic Windows, Box 1172, Dept. OHJ, Harrisonburg, VA 22801. (703) 434-5855.

---

# Prime (Replacement) Windows

*The #1 rule when ordering prime or replacement windows is to measure carefully. Don't assume that the top and bottom widths are equal. Custom windows CANNOT be returned. If you order incorrectly, you'll have to adjust the window opening, or settle for a window that stands apart from surrounding windows. Unfortunately, one-size-fits-all windows, being easy to find, often result in inappropriate replacements. Listed here are leading companies that will manufacture custom-size windows for you. For a 36 in. x 62 in., double-hung window, expect to pay $35-$70 for custom sash; window units (sash & frame) begin at about $120.*

Clear white pine stock parts are used (for quick delivery) to make windows to your specifications. Custom sashes & special architectural shapes. Catalog, $2. Drums Sash & Door Co., Inc., PO Box 207, Dept. OHJ, Drums, PA 18222. (717) 788-1145.

Prime & "self-storing" (upper sash storage) storm windows made of Ponderosa pine. Custom & stock sizes. Double-hung or tilt-takeout balances with 1 over 1, true-divided lights, or grill. Distributors throughout New England. Free brochure. Wes-Pine Millworks, Inc., King St., Dept. OHJ, West Hanover, MA 02339. (617) 878-2102.

Primarily Colonial reproductions, in clear white pine. 1-in. sash only. No literature. Write or call. Smith, R.W., 67 Main St., Dept. OHJ, North Orange, MA 01364. (617) 249-4988.

*Marvin's own photo of their fanlight-topped production window. (Nice hat.)*

Major manufacturer concerned with (re)fitting your windows with appropriate or custom-sized prime or storm windows (even special architectural shapes). Pine frames in a variety of styles including double-hung, casement, & true-divided lights. Free catalog. Distributors throughout the U.S. & Canada. Marvin Windows, 8030 Cedar Ave., Dept. OHJ, Minneapolis, MN 55420. (800) 346-5128.

## Wood Epoxies

*Epoxies, considered superior to oth fillers, can be used to stabilize and co solidate decayed wood. (See page 86.)*

Manufacturer of a large selection epoxies such as *Woodepox-1,* $18/q (approx. mixed cost—epoxy is a two-pa product). Mr. Caparoso will help yo choose the correct product; send a de tailed description of your requirement All products sold direct. Abatron, Inc 141 Center Dr., Dept. OHJ, Gilberts, I 60136. (312) 426-2200.

Marine supply stores are a hand source for wood epoxies. *"Git"-Rot,* two-part consolidating epoxy, is $5-$ for 4oz. Sold through distributors nation wide. Free information. BoatLIFE, Inc 205 Sweet Hollow Rd., Dept. OHJ, O Bethpage, NY 11804. (516) 454-0055.

For land-locked customers, here's mail-order source for BoatLIFE pr ducts. Catalog, $1.25. Defender Indus tries, 255 Main St., Dept. OHJ, Ne Rochelle, NY 10801. (914) 632-3001.

## Awnings

Traditional window awnings in canva and a variety of canvas-like materials About $100 (installed) per window. Fre information; they'll guide you to thei distributors nationwide. Astrup Co. 2937 W. 25th St., Dept. OHJ, Cleve land, OH 44113. (216) 696-2800.

---

*These companies custom-make windows in special architectural shapes, such as sidelights and fanlights.*

Screens, storms, & prime windows in many custom shapes, including Queen Anne, fanlights, and Gothic arches. Pine frames sold in kit form with "everything" except the glass. Also a good selection of old-fashioned, often hard-to-find window hardware—sash hinges & adjusters, channel friction controls—even brass sash numbers 1-100. Catalog, $1.50. Crawford's Old-House Store, 301 McCall, Dept. OHJ, Waukesha, WI 53186. (414) 542-0134.

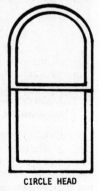

CIRCLE HEAD

Historical reproductions and custom designs beginning at about $1,000. Brochure, $2. John Lavoie, PO Box 15, Dept. OHJ, Springfield, VT 05156. (802) 886-8253.

*Cameo window by John Lavoie*

Straight transom, fanlight, & Palladia windows in single, double, or triple glaz ing. About $850 for a 5- to 6-ft. fanligh Brochure, $1. Woodstone Co., PO Bo 223, Patch Rd., Dept. OHJ, Westminster VT 05158. (802) 722-4784.

*Manchester Lite—custom fanlight priced at $224 & up*

Custom window sashes & frames Stained or antique glass is available Average price, $350. Free flyer. Man chester Lite, PO Box 143, Dept. OHJ Manchester, MA 01944. (617) 526-4706

# Storm Windows

You have many choices when selecting storm windows. Custom-sized wooden storms, often authentic to your style house, can be purchased more readily and inexpensively than you'd think. Metal storms are a popular choice, especially with baked-on finishes. We haven't listed the more common metal storms, such as triple-track, because they're so widely available. Unless otherwise stated, these windows can be purchased directly from the companies, free literature is offered, & prices for a 32 in. x 64 in. storm range from about $45-$75. The article on page 80 points out features you should be aware of before making a purchase decision.

Tubular steel-framed storm windows, flush-mounted with *Thermolock* expanders for tight fit, even in out-of-square windows. 36 in. x 64 in., about $128. Sold through dealers. RUSCO, RD 2, Dept. OHJ, Cochranton, PA 16314. (814) 724-4200.

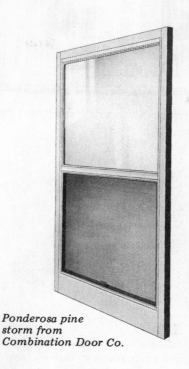

*Ponderosa pine storm from Combination Door Co.*

*Cusson's wood storm*

Pine wooden sash with storm/screen inserts in brown or white aluminum frames. Cusson Sash Co., 128 Addison Road, Dept. OHJ, Glastonbury, CT 06033. (203) 659-0354.

*Rusco's metal storms fit out-of-square windows and come in a variety of traditional trim colors.*

Custom & stock storm windows. Wooden frames with white aluminum storm or screen inserts. Sold also through distributors. Combination Door Co., PO Box 1076, Dept. OHJ, Fond du Lac, WI 54935. (414) 922-2050.

## Old-Fashioned Miscellany

*Listed here are companies which carry unusual & often hard-to-find items.*

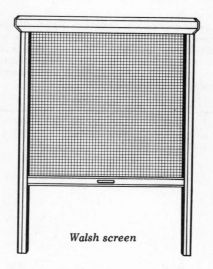

*Walsh screen*

SCREENS: Interior rolled bronze screens custom-made to fit almost any window (ideal for casements). Will also restore or replace your present unit. Prices begin at $56 for a 12 in. wide screen. Free information. Walsh Screen Products, 26 E. 3rd. St., Dept. OHJ, Mount Vernon, NY 10550. (914) 668-7811.

WINDOW HARDWARE: Numerous replacement parts for all types of windows, including casement. Catalog, $1. Blaine Window Hardware, Inc., 1919 Blaine Dr., Dept. OHJ, Hagerstown, MD 21740 (301) 797-6500. See also Crawford's Old-House Store, p. 94.

SASH WEIGHTS: One of the last sources for cast-iron sash weights. 35¢/lb.—sizes range from 3 to 30 lbs. Custom castings, too. Free brochure. Waterbury Foundry Co., 112 Porter Street, PO Box 2450, Dept. OHJ, Waterbury, CT 06722. (203)753-6680.

WINDOW CHANNELS: Replacement channels ($10-$15) available in most lumber yards, home centers, & hardware stores. Standard sizes only. Free literature. Quaker City Manufacturing Co., 701 Chester Pike, Sharon Hill, PA 19079. (215) 727-5144. See also Crawford's Old-House Store, p. 94.

GLASS BLOCKS: A variety of patterns & sizes in standard, thin, & solid blocks. About $24/sq.ft. (installed). Distributors throughout the U.S. & Canada. Free information. Pittsburgh Corning Corp., 800 Presque Isle Dr., Dept. OHJ, Pittsburgh, PA 15239. (412) 327-6100.

# Opinion...
# Remuddling
## — Of The Month —

*AFTER REMUDDLING: This Colonial house originally had windows made from small panes of rectangular glass—probably 6 over 6. Because the long sides of the rectangles were oriented up and down, the original windows had a pronounced vertical look. The replacement windows, on the other hand, unbalance the house by accentuating the horizontal look. The panes of glass in the new windows are much bigger than the originals, and the glass is set horizontally. The net effect is to give the house a vacant, horizontal stare. To top things off, the shutters on the bottom windows are clearly fake, since they are too narrow to properly close off the openings.*

*ORIGINAL WINDOWS: This stone house of similar vintage has its original windows intact. The small panes of glass and the numerous muntins give the house a safe, enclosed look. The vertical accent of the windows counterbalances the horizontal nature of the front elevation.*

# The Old-House Journal®

69A Seventh Avenue,
Brooklyn, New York 11217

# The Old-House Journal

### Restoration and Maintenance Techniques For The Antique House

Vol. X No. 5                     $2.00

# The Flowering Of The Conservatory

By Cole Gagne

"It is a real bower for a maiden romance, with
its rich green fragrance in the midst of winter.
It is like a picture in a dream.  One could
imagine it a fairy land, where no care, or grief,
or weariness could come."

THE OBJECT of such heady praise is the
conservatory, and for once, Victorian
hyperbole seems inadequate.  In its
beauty and novelty, a conservatory does
add a truly unique dimension to a house.
It needn't be an extravagant luxury, either:
There's no reason why the old-fashioned conservatory and the energy-efficient sunspace
can't be one and the same.  Building your
"passive solar addition"
as a conservatory means
you can combine charm
and historical interest
with energy conserva-
tion.  We hope this ar-
ticle will rekindle the
homeowner's love affair
with the conservatory.

ALL DEVOTEES of the con-
servatory should be
thankful that Tiberius
Caesar had a fondness
for cucumbers.  The an-
cient Romans were the
first to make a reason-
ably transparent glass,
and soon they were using
it in the construction
of greenhouses--thus

providing the emperor with a year-round supply of his favorite fruit.  With the fall of
Rome, under-glass horticulture went into decline.  The practice was finally revived in
the 16th century by the Dutch and Flemish.
The English and French quickly seized on the
idea, and by the 18th century, most wealthy
landowners had their own greenhouses.

(A TECHNICAL FOOTNOTE:  For the purposes of
this article, the term 'greenhouse' will refer to a free-standing structure in which
plants and/or flowers are cultivated.  The
term 'conservatory' will be used for a similarly used structure that is attached to a
larger building.)

THE EARLY 19th century
saw advances in the man-
ufacture of both glass
and cast iron.  As a re-
sult, greenhouse design
became increasingly
ambitious and sophisti-
cated.  This freedom of
design enabled people to
physically attach their
greenhouses to their
homes.  (Why get a chill
every time you visit
your plants?)  Integrat-
ing the greenhouse into
the home was not only
aesthetically pleasing,
but also a significant

*continued on page 108*

# Paint Strippers, Take Note

## The Old-House Journal®

*Editor*
**Clem Labine**

*Managing Editor*
**Patricia Poore**

*Assistant Editor*
**Cole Gagne**

*Editorial Assistants*
**Joni Monnich**
**Stephanie Croce**

*Circulation Supervisor*
**Joan O'Reilly**

*Circulation Assistants*
**Margaret Scaglione**
**Barbara Bugg**
**Jean Baldwin**

*Office Manager*
**Sally Goodman**

*Office Assistant*
**Rafael Madera**

*Sales Promotion*
**Joel Alpert**

*Circulation Director*
**Paul T. McLoughlin**

*Technical Consultant*
**Alan D. Keiser**

*Architectural Consultant*
**Jonathan Poore**

*Contributing Editors*
**R. A. Labine, Sr.**
**John Mark Garrison**

When you strip paint in an old house, you're a potential victim of lead poisoning — no matter which method you use. And the precautions you're already taking may not be sufficient!

YOU HAVE TO ASSUME that any house built before 1950 has lead-based paint in it. Stripping the paint, by any means, releases some lead. You can then absorb it by swallowing or breathing lead-containing dust.

OHJ SUBSCRIBERS, like OHJ Editors, already know all that. But we've heard a few recent lead-poisoning stories that scared us anew...so we're reprising and amplifying our previous warnings.

SOME WAYS of stripping paint carry higher risk of lead poisoning than others. The worst is probably use of a propane

(4) Wear a separate set of work clothes for stripping, including full leg and arm protection and a different pair of shoes. Wash all these separately from the rest of your laundry. Don't walk around uncontaminated parts of the house in work clothes.

(5) Do not eat or smoke anywhere near the stripping site-- not even after daily cleanup. Never smoke unless you've scrubbed up first.

(6) Every day, dispose of paint residue in the outside trash. Damp-mop floors and horizontal surfaces to keep dust down. Damp-mop floors, walls, and ceilings after job is completed.

(7) Treat paint scrapings, dust, chemical residue, and cleanup materials (such as rags and water) as toxic waste. Dispose of them immediately and properly.

## .....lead poisoning update.....

torch, which vaporizes lead in the old paint, making it very breathable. A close runner-up is paint removal by scraping and sanding, because a lot of lead-laden dust is created.

IN A National Bureau of Standards lead-paint hazards report (NBSIR-75-974), electric hot-air guns were rated "safer" than solvents, propane torch, infra-red heater, or dip-tank methods. No method came near the "perfect safety" rating, however; every method is risky.

### What Can You Do?

DESPITE THE HAZARD, people will continue to strip paint. If you take these rules to heart and never break them, you'll at least minimize the risk.

(1) No pregnant women or children under six should be in the house during the full period when stripping is going on.

(2) Paint-strippers should wear a respirator with a cartridge specifically designed to filter lead. An ordinary dust mask may not be good enough.

(3) Seal off the room being stripped from the rest of the house. BE THOROUGH. Leaded dust is insidious!

WATCH YOUR ANIMALS. If pets get listless or start vomiting, there's a good chance the air is contaminated with lead.

USUAL CLINICAL symptoms of lead poisoning include dizziness, aching joints or head, abdominal cramps or nausea, and a bluish line on the gums. But for reasons not fully understood, adult paint-strippers with elevated blood lead levels won't always have these symptoms.

SOME ABSORPTION OF LEAD is inevitable. So if you're doing a lot of stripping, have your blood tested for elevated lead levels every four to six weeks.

•••••••••••••••••••••••••••••••••

*The Comfo II respirator is available from Mine Safety Appliance Corp., Att. Sales, 1100 Globe Ave., Mountainside, NJ 07092. (201) 232-3490*

*You must buy the mask and a supply of OSHA approved filters. The medium-size mask, most often ordered, is Comfo II 460-968, $12.90 ppd. Other sizes are available; call and ask to talk to a salesperson if you have any questions. The filter you need is Type H 464-035. A box of ten costs $31.20. You must buy a whole box; filters are discarded when dirty.*

*The mask is much less effective if you have a beard. Those with pulmonary or heart trouble should not wear the mask — nor should they strip paint.*

*Published by The Old-House Journal © Corporation, 69A Seventh Avenue, Brooklyn, New York 11217. Telephone (212) 636-4514. Subscriptions $16 per year in U.S. Not available elsewhere. Published monthly. Contents are fully protected by copyright and must not be reproduced in any manner whatsoever without specific permission in writing from the Editor.*

*We are happy to accept editorial contributions to The Old-House Journal. Query letters which include an outline of the proposed article are preferred. All manuscripts will be reviewed, and returned if unacceptable. However, we cannot be responsible for non-receipt or loss — please keep copies of all materials sent.*

**Printed at Photo Comp Press, New York City**

*ISSN: 0094-0178*
**NO PAID ADVERTISING**

## Post-Victorian Domestic Architecture

# The Dutch Colonial Revival Style

By Renee Kahn

THE WAVE OF NATIONAL PRIDE which swept over America at the turn of the century found its expression in the Dutch Colonial Revival style. What could be more representative of our national heritage than this cross between a Dutch or Flemish farmhouse, a Georgian manor, and a traditional American barn? It was as if the Victorian era had never existed, and the Colonial period had continued unbroken.

A REFLECTION of the "back-to-nature" movement of the day, the Dutch Colonial Revival turned away from the decorative excesses of Victorianism, to a low-lying house that appeared to hug the earth. Its humbler origins not only spoke of the days when our country was young and proud, but reflected new social philosophies, and a respect for labor and democratic ideals. The conspicuous consumption that characterized the post-Civil War era displeased the intellectuals who espoused "natural" materials and rugged simplicity.

IT IS GENERALLY ASSUMED that the gambrel roof characterizing Dutch 18th- and 19th-century architecture was brought here from the Netherlands, but there is little evidence for this.

Apparently, the Dutch acquired their taste for the gambrel roof from the English, who introduced it into the Colonies in the late 17th century. What could be called Dutch (or Flemish, in this particular case) were the slightly flared eaves that extended over the front and rear of the house.

ORIGINALLY, the gambrel roof was adopted as a solution to the age-old problem of how to provide ample headroom under a pitched roof. The gambrel, like the mansard, created a full additional storey out of marginal attic space. There were several economic benefits as well. For example, shorter rafters could be used (an important factor prior to machine-sawn lumber). Roof and wall were one unit, thus offering the convenience of a 2-storey house without the expense of building it. A 1-storey house also was charged less tax than a 2-storey house.

LIGHTING THE UPPER STOREY of the Dutch-roofed houses presented problems. In Colonial times, most of the light came from gable windows at either end. Joining dormers to the roofline was difficult, and so they were rarely used. By the time of the Dutch Colonial Revival, dormers had become important and increasingly

When porches became fashionable in the early 19th century, it was easy to place columns under the already-hanging, flared eave of a gambrel roof. This use of the eave became a common feature of Dutch Colonial Revival houses. (Note the echo of the roof's flared eaves in the three dormer roofs.)

complex. Eventually, they extended along the full length of the roof in a shed design. Intersecting gables and gambrels also lit the upper storeys, creating picturesque and varied rooflines.

THE GAMBREL ROOF was abandoned by the English colonists shortly after the Revolution, but it remained popular among the Dutch until the 1830s. It reappeared in the nostalgia that dominated the country after the Centennial Exposition of 1876. In its earliest phase, the Dutch Colonial Revival was essentially a variant of the Shingle Style: low-lying, picturesque, wrapped in a skin of rugged shingles. Its giant roof sat like a cap, drawing together a variety of subsidiary units under one sheltering roofline.

## Medievalism & Classicism

DECORATIVE ELEMENTS of the Revival style were drawn originally from both medieval and classical vocabularies. Small-paned windows and stained glass transoms stood alongside Palladian windows and neo-Federal doorways; classical columns rested comfortably beneath fairy-tale turrets. But the medieval aspects began to diminish late in the 19th century, and ornament started to take on an increasingly accurate "Colonial" look.

LATE GEORGIAN and Federal influences came to dominate the Revival, as was evident in the elaborate fanlight and sidelights surrounding the front door. Early in the 20th century, the Tuscan influence was also strongly felt. Heavy, stucco-covered columns under a trellised-roof porch, or pergola, supplied the fashionable Italian "vineyard" look and provided both light and shade to the front rooms.

WINDOW STYLES VARIED with the date of construction. The earlier, more medieval versions of the Revival have small-paned windows, often used over sheets of plate glass on the lower sash. With the turn of the century, the one-over-one style prevailed, returning in the 1920s to modified "Colonial" patterns of six-over-six, eight-over-eight, and six-over-one.

This turn-of-the-century, brown-shingled Revival house has a gambrel-shaped dormer and features a stained glass hall light, Palladian-influenced columns, and porch vents. Like so many houses in this style, it is a combination of rugged natural materials and classical details.

Architect John Calvin Stevens designed this house for himself in 1884. He utilized an all-encompassing gambrel roof to draw in and order the various spaces of the house's main volume.

This typical plan-book Dutch Colonial Revival house, dating from around 1930, has a shed dormer across the front.

Tuscan columns elegantly contrast with the rough stone and shingle siding of this Revival house.

## What's Outside . . .

THE COLONIAL-ERA Dutch house and its Revival descendant both share an affinity for shingle-covered exteriors. In the 18th century, the Dutch used whatever materials were available, and so the houses were often picturesque combinations of shingles, clapboard, stone, and brick. The Revival was not limited to local materials, and so it utilized whatever skin-coverings were fashionable at the moment.

DURING THE LATE-19TH and early-20th centuries, Dutch-roofed houses were generally shingle covered, with a heavy cobblestone foundation or first storey. Clapboard, when used, was only on the lower floor, after the Queen Anne style. Stucco, and later, all-clapboard, increased in popularity further into the 20th century.

COLOR COMBINATIONS went from all-dark schemes in the 1880s to all white in the 1920s. Shingles were left to darken naturally, or stained walnut brown or dark red. Other base colors varied considerably,. including drab yellow, soft grey, light green, dark green, or Delft blue. Trim colors were generally lighter than the body of the house (except in earlier Shingle Style houses with their medieval flavor). Warm white and cream tones were the preferred trim colors, especially against a darker-bodied structure.*

This house offers an unusual and fascinating glimpse of a transition in architectural styles. A Dutch Colonial Revival, it nevertheless incorporates features of the then-outgoing Queen Anne style, such as the pointed tower.

## . . . And Inside

INTERIOR DECORATION depended greatly upon the age and stylistic concept of the house. The interiors ranged from Craftsman style, with its hand-hewn look and penchant for oak, to delicate, painted surfaces embellished with Adamesque garlands and swags. In the early-20th century, rooms often contained elements of both. But by 1920, interiors were simplified, reflecting the influence of the modernist

*Roger Moss' *Century of Color, 1820-1920*, an excellent reference source, suggests several attractive color combinations.

This Dutch Colonial Revival house, with its intersecting gables, offers a high-style intermingling of Shingle Style and neo-Georgian Colonial architectural elements.

movement. The use of mouldings and wainscotting diminished. Interiors emphasized smooth plaster surfaces and uncarpeted oak floors. The fireplace mantel and corner cupboard were usually all that remained of the Colonial Revival.

THE REVIVAL MOVEMENT was so pervasive in its influence that it survived the social and artistic upheavals of the 1910s and '20s and remained popular until the 1930s. By the 1920s, however, it had been transformed into a gambrel-roofed version of the standard "Colonial Revival." Row upon row of neat little houses appeared in America's suburbs, often with ersatz gambrels: gabled roofs with long, shed-roofed dormers creating a false gambrel line. In one fell swoop, the economy-minded builder could create a roof, side wall, dormer, and the all-American look.

## A COLONIAL HOUSE OF SOUND VALUES

The 1929 book "Small Houses of Architectural Distinction" featured this illustration of a Dutch Colonial Revival house. It described the house with the following caption: "Pleasantly informal, expressing the quality of domesticity, it is planned to make the most of the money spent."

*RENEE KAHN is an architectural historian and teacher, as well as being a partner in The Preservation Development Group—a Stamford, Conn., company that consults on the restoration of historic structures.*

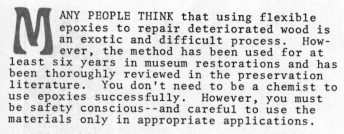

# DEMYSTIFYING EPOXY

## Using Epoxies To Repair Damaged Wood

By Alan D. and Shelby R. Keiser

MANY PEOPLE THINK that using flexible epoxies to repair deteriorated wood is an exotic and difficult process. However, the method has been used for at least six years in museum restorations and has been thoroughly reviewed in the preservation literature. You don't need to be a chemist to use epoxies successfully. However, you must be safety conscious--and careful to use the materials only in appropriate applications.

THE THRESHOLD QUESTION is why use epoxies at all? In many cases, wood splicing, inserting "dutchmen," or total wood replacement may be better in the long run. However, epoxies can be useful to the homeowner in such situations as patching decorative elements that are partially rotted, floorboards with partially rotten ends, etc. Especially if you aren't a particularly skilled woodworker, epoxies are often the fastest and most economical answer.

WE HAVE USED or have seen these materials used successfully for many types of repairs:

- Ends of porch floorboards
- Column bases and capitals
- Balustrades and railings
- Window sills, casings, shutters
- Sill plates
- Doors, trim and mouldings

CAN EPOXY CONSOLIDATION be useful to you? Here are some guidelines to help you decide:

1. Is there enough wood left to consolidate and patch? You can't consolidate thin air. If the area is large, it may be cheaper to patch with wood. Why fill a large void with something that costs $50 per gallon when you can use wood that only costs $2 per foot?

2. What are the structural requirements of the piece? Epoxies without reinforcement are generally used in non-structural areas. They can stand some compression--for example, in a column base--but we would not recommend them where the element is in tension, such as the end of a floor joist.

3. What is the historical significance of the piece? If an element is important historical-

ly, every effort must be made to preserve it. Epoxies make preservation of the original elements possible and are therefore highly valued in museum restorations.

4. What would be the visual impact of inserting a wooden patch versus an epoxy repair? For example, epoxy patches on unpainted surfaces that are highly visible are not very attractive. In this case, a wood patch may be preferable.

5. Is replacement wood available at reasonable cost? Often, decorative elements such as cornice blocks, mouldings, and column bases are frightfully expensive or impossible to obtain. Epoxies can be quite effective in these cases.

6. How much will it cost? Epoxies are expensive. But so is the cost of skilled labor. If epoxies enable you to do a job yourself, rather than hiring a skilled carpenter, then they may prove very cost-effective.

7. Will heat build-up in the repaired area cause problems? Epoxies give off heat as they cure. Although the likelihood of fire is remote, on one occasion a finial we were repairing began to smoke. If this should happen to you, cool the piece off quickly. (A $CO_2$ fire extinguisher would do this handily.) Be especially cautious if you are using large quantities of epoxy on a hot day.

8. What are your preferences? If you are a skilled woodworker, or are particularly sensitive to chemicals, you may prefer traditional wood patching methods. On the other hand, if your woodworking skills are minimal, you may find epoxies attractive.

### Getting Started

AN ADVANTAGE of epoxies is that they are portable. You can take them to the repair site and work on the wood in place. However, to gain access to all surfaces, and to better control the curing process, you may prefer to remove wooden elements and work on them in your shop when possible.

EPOXY REPAIR is usually a two-step process: (1) You first consolidate the deteriorated area with a low-viscosity penetrating consolidant; (2) You then fill large voids with an epoxy patching compound. You can omit step #1 if there is a void but the wood is sound; for example, where a piece of carving has simply broken off rather than rotted. The epoxy repair is usually followed by application of a wood preservative and then good quality paint. (Paint adheres very well to epoxies.)

IN MIXING and applying the consolidant, safety to you and the building is paramount. Try mixing the consolidant in clear plastic squeeze bottles with ounce markings on their sides. Bottles used for hair dyes (sold at drugstores) work quite well.

FOLLOW THE INSTRUCTIONS from your manufacturer carefully and mix the materials VERY WELL. Epoxies cure by chemical action and the two ingredients must be thoroughly mixed for the process to work. Since epoxies cure best between 70° and 75° F., be sure your environment is warm enough. And be sure you observe all the safety precautions.

HERE ARE SOME HINTS for applying the consolidant:

● Saturate the wood completely, leaving all deteriorated wood in place. Don't try to fill voids; the filler is designed to do that.

## SOURCES FOR EPOXIES

Epoxies have been used for some time in the repair of wooden boats, so marine supply stores are one source. Git-Rot and Marine-Tex are the brand names of two of the marine consolidants and epoxy fillers.

The epoxy consolidant used in the photos was Seep 'n Seal from Allied Resins. Seep 'n Seal costs $33.75/gal. (the smallest quantity sold) plus shipping, and can be ordered directly from the manufacturer. Call first to find shipping charges to your location. Allied Resins, Weymouth Industrial Park, Dept. OHJ, East Weymouth, MA 02189. (617) 337-6070.

The epoxy filler used in the case history shown here was Woodepox-1 from Abatron, Inc. Woodepox-1 costs $11/pt., $18/qt., or $42/gal. (Since it is a two-part system, to end up with a gallon of filler, you'd use 2 quarts of resin and 2 quarts of hardener; both parts are the same price.) Abatron also sells an epoxy consolidant: Abocast 8101-4 resin with Abocure 8101-4 catalyst. Each part costs $12/pt., $18/qt., or $48/gal. plus shipping. Absolve epoxy solvent costs $9/qt. There is free literature on all Abatron resins. Phone first for shipping charges. Abatron, Inc., 141 Center Dr., Dept. OHJ, Gilberts, IL 60136. (312) 426-2200.

● After the first application hardens, another application may be necessary if the first treatment didn't sufficiently saturate the wood to make it solid.

1. The rotted jamb on this door frame is an ideal candidate for epoxy repair: The area involved is not large, there's enough sound wood left to consolidate and patch, and it would be quite awkward to splice in a new piece of wood in this spot.

2. First step is to drill a few ¼-in. holes above the affected area so that consolidant can seep into the end grain. (DON'T drill all the way through the wood; consolidant will leak out the other side.) Holes are angled so epoxy won't run back out.

3. The two components of the epoxy consolidant are measured into a graduated plastic bottle. Thorough mixing of the resin and hardener is essential; shake the bottle for at least two minutes. Be sure to observe safety precautions in handling epoxies!

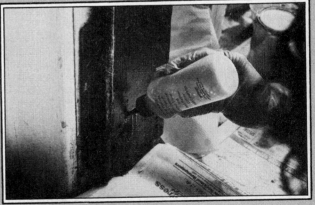

4. After mixing the epoxy consolidant, it is squirted into the holes and allowed to saturate the wood fibers completely. If the wood doesn't get completely saturated, a second application of the epoxy consolidant may be necessary.

# Working Safely With Epoxies

1. Epoxies are toxic chemicals. Read product safety warnings and directions BEFORE starting.

2. Avoid contact with eyes and skin. Use goggles, plastic gloves, and a heavy plastic work apron.

3. Avoid breathing fumes. Work outside or in a well-ventilated area. When sanding epoxy patches, wear a high-quality dust mask. For maximum protection, wear a vapor respirator with proper cartridge when mixing or applying epoxies. Respirator E-454 with cartridge E-451-6C is recommended for epoxies. The manufacturer, Eastern Safety Equipment Co., does not sell directly to homeowners. You can call the company at (212) 392-4100 for the name of your nearest distributor. You can also buy the respirator + one cartridge for $22.75 postpaid by mail from:

> Dick Jones Sales, Inc.
> P.O. Box 141 Dept. OHJ
> Hanover, PA 17331
> (717) 632-7000

A box of 6 replacement cartridges is $22.00 postpaid. Be sure to specify model numbers for both respirator and cartridge when ordering.

4. Watch out for spills. Mask areas adjacent to the repair. To clean up spills, use absorbent materials such as sawdust, newspapers and rags. Clean up spills promptly—don't let the epoxy cure or you'll never get it up. Specific epoxy solvents, such as Absolve, are also handy for cleanup. To avoid vapor hazards, be sure that all clean-up materials are placed in a trash can outside the house.

5. Use soap or detergents—NOT epoxy solvents—to wash any stray epoxy off your skin.

6. Use disposable stir sticks, dippers and gloves. Discard any used materials OUTSIDE after wrapping in newspaper. Launder soiled clothing separately.

7. Epoxies are flammable materials. Store all materials in a cool location and, of course, never smoke or have an open flame when working with epoxy resins and solvents.

5. Consolidant is also applied directly to the side grain in the affected area—although most of the benefit comes from allowing the consolidant to seep into the end grain through the holes that have been drilled.

6. After the consolidant has cured, an epoxy filler is applied to fill the voids. The filler is also a two-part system, and when mixed has the consistency of glazing compound. It can be easily applied with a putty knife.

7. The surface of the epoxy filler has to be built up slightly higher than the surrounding wood to allow for final smoothing and sanding. Don't worry about a smooth finish at this point; the filler is easily levelled after it has cured.

8. After curing, the epoxy filler can be smoothed with chisels, planes, and sandpaper; the material works easily, so use whatever tool is most convenient. A water repellant can then be applied to the surrounding wood, followed by priming and painting.

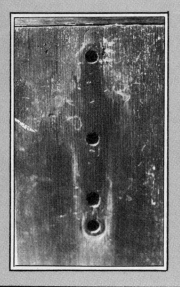 

## FILLING HOLES WITHOUT CONSOLIDATING

Because the wood around these ½-in. holes in a front door (left) is not rotted, the holes can be plugged with an epoxy patching compound (right) without bothering to first use an epoxy consolidant. Epoxy fillers offer two major advantages over other wood filling compounds: (1) They don't shrink while setting; (2) They will expand and contract with the wood, and thus won't fall out with changes in moisture content. When auto body putty is used as a wood filler, for example, it usually tears loose in 18 to 36 months as the wood expands and contracts.

The larger the hole, the greater the advisability of using epoxy fillers. Holes ¼ in. and smaller can be satisfactorily plugged using glazing putty, caulk, or other wood filler.

● In applying, exploit the end grain. The materials will not penetrate the side grain of the wood.

● If the end grain is not exposed, then drill 1/8"-1/4" holes to expose it. The holes should be staggered and at angles to the side grain to expose as much end grain as possible. But don't overdo it; you can destroy the wood with too many holes.

● Prevent leakage--especially if the elements are still attached to the building. Wax or clay plugs (plus your imagination) can help here. Epoxy dripped on brick or stone is very difficult to remove and may leave permanent stains. Try to clean up any leakage before it cures. If you're too late, paint removers containing methylene chloride will SOMETIMES remove cured epoxy.

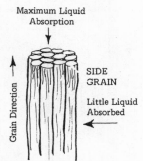

END GRAIN

Maximum Liquid Absorption

Grain Direction

SIDE GRAIN

Little Liquid Absorbed

The structure of wood can be likened to a bundle of drinking straws. Liquids — such as epoxy consolidants — are absorbed through the ends of the straws, not the sides.

## The Cure

THE HARDENING TIME for epoxies varies from product to product. We always use those which take eight hours or longer to cure. This allows the materials to soak well into the wood before they harden. After the consolidant has cured, apply an epoxy putty to fill any voids. If no patching is required, clean off any excess on the surface--sanding usually works--and apply water repellant and paint if desired. BE SURE TO WEAR A DUST MASK when sanding any epoxy material.

IF YOU'RE APPLYING an epoxy filler, it needs to be mixed thoroughly. Mix until you are sure it is OK, then mix again! Application is usually simple--albeit messy. If the area to be patched is large, you can save material by

---

### FOR ADDITIONAL INFORMATION

THE W.E.R. SYSTEM MANUAL—By Paul Stumes. Describes how to use reinforced epoxies for repair of load-bearing wooden members. $5.50 from: Association for Preservation Technology, Box 2487, Station D, Dept. OHJ, Ottawa, Ont. K1P 5W6, Canada.

EPOXIES FOR WOOD REPAIRS IN HISTORIC BUILDINGS—By Morgan W. Phillips and Judith E. Selwyn. Discusses the chemistry, theory and application of epoxies in wood repair. $4.00 from: Society for Preservation of New England Antiquities, Attn. Leslie Fox, 141 Cambridge St., Dept. OHJ, Boston, MA 02114.

---

imbedding a piece of wood in the center of the patch.

AFTER THE FILLER has cured, remove the excess. You can use chisels, planes, or sandpaper--depending on the circumstances. Then apply a water repellant (if desired) and paint.

WE MUST EMPHASIZE that epoxies are not miracle materials. They require finesse in their application, and the danger of staining adjacent material, causing a fire, or improper curing is always there. Yet you're encouraged to experiment with these materials. Considerations of cost and preservation of existing materials often make them the best choice.

FINALLY, keep in mind that using epoxies is not an either/or proposition. You can also use epoxy repair in conjunction with traditional wood splicing techniques.

Alan D. Keiser is Director of the Restoration Workshop in Tarrytown, N.Y., run by the National Trust for Historic Preservation. Shelby R. Keiser is a college English teacher and freelance writer. They own an early 20th century Cotswold Cottage in Ossining, N.Y., that has provided ample opportunity for them to hone their skills in epoxy repairs. (The photos in this article, for example, show repairs done to Alan and Shelby's front door.)

# Helpful Publications

### The Revolving Fund Handbook
Architectural Conservation Trust, and
Architectural Heritage Foundation
1981 (112 pp., spiral-bound) Paper.

**A** REVOLVING FUND CAN BE a useful tool in preserving an old building for reuse and, if successful, can help to stimulate private investment in the neighboring area. This handbook gives a comprehensive look at the mechanics of establishing, financing, and operating the revolving fund. Local community groups, state historical societies, and preservation organizations will find this clearly written book most valuable in setting up their own funds. An actual preservation development project is explained in depth and provides firsthand, practical information to novice and veteran fund organizers.

To order, send $5.00 ppd. to:
Architectural Conservation Trust
45 School Street--Dept. OHJ
Boston, MA 02108
(617) 523-8678

### Tage Frid Teaches Woodworking: Shaping, Veneering, Finishing
Tage Frid
1981 (210 pp., profusely illustrated) Cloth.

**T** HIS IS TAGE FRID'S second book in a series of three. The basics of bending, turning, veneering, carving, inlaying, and finishing are taught by the Danish woodmaster, who is also senior editor of Fine Woodworking magazine. Like his previous book (Joinery: Tools and Techniques, $18), this one follows an exceptionally clear, well-illustrated format. Hundreds of photos and drawings show you the tricks and techniques step by step, while the accompanying

text is a concise, witty narrative. For the serious (or soon-to-be serious) woodworker, these are THE essential how-to books.

To order, send $18 ppd. to: Taunton Press
52 Church Hill Road
Box 355--Dept. OHJ
Newtown, CT 06470
(203) 426-8171

### Fine Woodworking Techniques 3
Compiled by the Editors of Fine Woodworking Magazine
1981 (224 pp., profusely illustrated) Cloth.

**A** LL THE EXPERT TECHNICAL information of a year's worth of Fine Woodworking magazine is preserved in this book. Articles in Volume 3 cover tried-and-true methods of cabinetmaking, turning, carving, and coopering, as well as veneering, laminating, and finishing. Projects for making tools, toys, and furnishings are accompanied by detailed photographs. This

is a handsome, well-bound book, generously illustrated with black and white photographs and line drawings.

To order, send $17 ppd. to:
Taunton Press
(see previous review for address)

### Homeowner's Energy Investment Handbook
Michael McClintock
1982 (116 pp., illustrated) Paper.

**T** HIS GUIDEBOOK will help the energy conscious homeowner to compare the cost and savings of over one hundred energy-conserving improvements (from weatherstripping to solar additions) which can be made to your home. It is neither a how-to-do-it book, nor are all the options sensitive to older homes (replacing windows with new thermal ones), but it does give you enough information to decide which options are best. The book also explains energy tax laws and contains a useful table for calculating annual electricity costs.

To order, send $8.95 plus $1.00 postage to:
Brick House Publishing
34 Essex St.--Dept. OHJ
Andover, MA 01810
(617) 475-9568

### Shopfronts
Bill Evans and Andrew Lawson
1981 (128 pp., profusely illustrated) Cloth.

**Q** UERIES ON SHOPFRONT restoration prompted us to feature this book. It's about English shops, but it may provide some ideas for those restoring American ones. The storefronts of many merchants are recorded, including the grocer, ironmonger, florist, milliner, and pharmacist. Historical and modern photos are included and the text provides interesting bits of history and tradition about shop types. A separate chapter is devoted to the signwriter's craft and 19th and 20th-century shopfront architecture. The book is generously illustrated with 240 color and black and white photographs.

To order, send $16.95 ppd. to:
Van Nostrand Reinhold
7625 Empire Drive--Dept. RB
Florence, KY 41042
(606) 526-6600

From Shopfronts: An Art Nouveau shopfront on Market Street, Cambridge.

CONSERVATORIES, *continued from p. 97*

step toward making gloomy homes warmer and sunnier, and so the conservatory was born.

DEPENDING ON the taste of the homeowner, a Victorian conservatory was anything from an 11,000-sq.ft. winter garden to a modestly sized, sunlit room overflowing with heliotrope, geraniums, and ferns. The conservatory would go on the southern side of the dwelling, where it could receive the most sunlight. On sunny winter days, the family would open the doors that separated the conservatory from the house, and the warm air would circulate throughout the home.

THOSE DOORS were always open during any large social gathering, and the conservatory soon developed a reputation as the primary hunting ground for eligible bachelors. In People I Have Known (c. 1882), E.C. Granville Murray observed that 'spooning' in the conservatory, with all those heady exotics, and ... champaign [*sic*] afterwards, puts [men] in such a condition that any girl of sense and courage can have her way with them."

*Manistee County Historical Museum*

Several standard features of the well stocked conservatory are in this historic photo: encaustic-tile floor (ceiling too), aquarium with fountain, steam radiator for auxiliary heat, and a lot of palms, ferns, and other plants. Note the pocket door, extreme right, for closing off the conservatory.

*Mark Twain Memorial, Hartford, Conn.*

This contemporary photo shows the restored conservatory that stands at the southern end of the library in Mark Twain's house in Hartford. A good deal of research went into the task of filling the conservatory with plants that were not only of the period, but were known to have been in the Twain conservatory. The potted apidistra, the rubber trees, and the zebra plant are all documented in an old photo; the creeping fig is an actual descendant from the creeping fig grown by Mrs. Clemens.

DESPITE THIS SITUATION (or perhaps because of it!), the Victorians attached profound social and moral importance to the conservatory. A common attitude can be found in Henry Williams' Window Gardening (1875): Flowers and plants are "the best and most practical educators of healthy sentiment. ... Constant association with such objects of floral beauty, fits people to rank high as useful members of society."

THE CONSERVATORY came to be seen as an indispensable part of the social fabric, and so was sought after by more and more people. Thus, it was frequently grafted onto houses without any regard as to how energy-efficient it was. In those days, a lot of people had money to burn, and a north-facing conservatory that required its own heating system wasn't such a hardship. The rationing of fuel during World War I initiated the decline of the conservatory; its fate was sealed with the demise of the Victorian lifestyle after the war.

COMBINING beauty, nostalgia, and energy-efficiency, the conservatory has begun attracting a growing number of homeowners. Some have adapted a room into a mini-conservatory by adding a glazed frame to a window; others have restored an existing conservatory. It seems that more and more people today are getting a better education in healthy sentiment.

# Rebuilding A Conservatory

ONE OF THE LOVELIEST FEATURES of Connecticut's Lockwood-Mathews Mansion is its conservatory. In 1964, almost a century after the house was built, the conservatory was demolished when a tree branch fell on it. Subsequently, a board of trustees was established to administer the estate as a museum, but funds for the recreation of the conservatory didn't become available until late in 1979.

RICHARD BERGMANN, the architect who oversaw the restoration, was caught in a tug-of-war between historical accuracy and modern necessities. Originally, the translucent, 1 ft. by 2 ft. panes of the conservatory had been patterned and textured glass. However, Bergmann decided to replace the glass with acrylic. Stronger than glass, acrylic offered better protection from accident and vandalism. And although both glass and acrylic would have to be custom cast, the cost of glass would be triple that of acrylic--providing someone willing to make the glass could even be found!

THE GLASFLEX CORPORATION of New Jersey took up the challenge of making replacement panes of acrylic. They took an aluminum mould of one of the surviving panes and produced a copy that identically matched the original in color, texture, and bubble content. (The quality of this test pane helped persuade a reluctant Federal government to contribute funds for the restoration.) But the task of mass producing exact replicas was formidable: A tremendous number of panes had to be made in order to yield enough accurate reproductions.

ACTUAL WORK on the conservatory began with the laminating of the structural wooden ribs. These were attached to a wooden frame, which was joined to the half-dome's granite base with stainless steel expansion anchors. (Another updating: originally, the anchors had been wrought iron.)

Top: Reconstruction of the conservatory began with new pine elements in the half-dome. Bottom: The panes were made from a special formulation that gave the acrylic high strength and resistance to ultra-violet light.

The millwork was built according to measured drawings made by Richard Bergmann. He used the surviving pieces of the conservatory as the basis for his designs.

THE DECISION TO USE ACRYLIC created an entire chain of necessities. Unlike glass, acrylic expands and contracts greatly. Therefore, white lead putty, which was the original glazing compound, was replaced with a far more flexible silicone sealant from Dow. But silicone would not be compatible with wood preservatives, so the wooden ribs and muntins could only be stained with a heavy-bodied exterior stain. And to complete this round robin of requirements, the silicone used had to be one that would match the color of the stained trim.

THE FLOOR of the conservatory also had been damaged in the accident. Upon examining remnants of the tile, Bergmann found the name of the manufacturer: the Minton Tile Company of England. Research revealed that the company was still in existence, now under the name of the H. & R. Johnson Company.* The tile fragments were shown to the company, and they were able to make reproductions. These were laid after the rest of the work on the conservatory was completed.

B Y MID-JULY OF 1980, Bergmann, woodworker Siegfried Dean, and Bottone-Riordan contractors had completed their work on the conservatory at a cost of fifty thousand dollars. Their achievement is one of the high points in the restoration of the Lockwood-Mathews Mansion. The American Wood Council feels the same way about the re-creation; they gave a First Honor Award to Bergmann for the "extreme elegance" of the conservatory. 🏠

*Readers can direct inquiries to H. & R. Johnson, Inc., State Highway 35, Keyport, NJ 07735. (201) 264-0566.

The leaded diamond shapes are created by the slightly corded surface of the acrylic window panes. Centered in each of the diamonds is a blue fleur-de-lys. (Note the way the panes overlap horizontally on the half-dome.)

Norwalk's Lockwood-Mathews Mansion, built in 1864-8, is an outstanding example of post-Civil War opulence, in size, scope, and craftsmanship. Once scheduled for demolition, it has been saved for future generations.

Readers who wish to view the conservatory, along with other features of the 4-storey, 60-room house, can visit it on Tuesdays through Fridays from 11 to 3 and on Sundays from 1 to 4. For further information, call or write the Lockwood-Mathews Mansion Museum of Norwalk, 295 West Ave., Norwalk, CT 06850. (203) 838-1434.

American Wood Council

# Ask OHJ

## Humidity At Home

WE HAVE A 1910 BUNGALOW-STYLE HOME in eastern Tennessee. The outer walls are insulated with blown cellulose, but without a vapor barrier. Can we use a humidifier in our house?

--Clay Crowder  Maryville, TN

A HUMIDIFIER SHOULD BE USED only sparingly. Overusing it will probably cause water to condense inside the walls of your house. You might want to consider painting the interior walls with a vapor-impermeable paint in order to help provide a vapor barrier. You'd also want to seal around electrical outlets.

## Fill Formula

OVER THE YEARS, the ground next to my house walls has washed away. I think I need to get some fill to build it up, sloping the ground away from the house. What would you suggest as a fill? I'm afraid that just plain dirt would soon wash away. Should the fill be dirt mixed with cement and/or small stones; should it be straight cement mixed with stone?

--T. Morris  Philadelphia, PA

IF YOU DO NOT HAVE any severe problems, then the best fill for you to use is gravel with about six inches of dirt over it. Grade the topsoil away from the house, and be sure to keep the dirt at least six to eight inches away from any wood surfaces on the exterior of the house. With this method, water will be able to percolate through the gravel. (Cement would only trap and hold the water.) If you are having a serious basement water problem, then your situation should be inspected by an architect or an engineer.

## Replating Metal

AFTER STRIPPING THE PAINT from the hinges, doorknobs, and backplates of my old house, I discovered that the hardware is a plain cast metal. It had a brass (?) plating, the color of which was changed in the stripping process. Without the plating, the hardware is quite ugly. I have tried using copper and pewter tone paints, but it looked really cheap. Can the hardware be replated? If so, who does it? (This would be a lot cheaper than buying new hardware.)

--Pattye Schroder  Sykesville, MD

REPLATERS DO EXIST and are available. Consult your Yellow Pages under "Plating." (If there isn't anybody in your area, try the listings of large cities near you.) Get prices from them--in some areas, replating can be more expensive than replacing the hardware.

## The War Against Scratches

MY BEVELED GLASS MIRROR has been scratched in several places in the glass. Can anything be done to minimize or remove these scratches?

--Karen Jellum  Chinook, MT

YOUR LETTER SENT US to our friends at Atlantic Glass & Mirror Works (439 North 63rd Street, Dept. OHJ, Philadelphia, PA 19151 [215] 747-6866). They specialize in resilvering and restoring mirrors, and told us that they themselves were still looking for a solution to this problem. A scratch in the silver behind the glass is easy to repair; a scratch in the glass itself is far more problematic. They had purchased an expensive machine that was guaranteed to remove such scratches. However, in the process of grinding out the scratches, the machine created "bull's eyes" and so had to be returned to the company! Techniques in this particular area of restoration still have a long way to go.

## Rescuing Redwood

SOMEONE DECIDED TO "SMOOTH OUT" the beaded redwood panelling in my bathroom with a coat of plaster. Over and under the plaster are several layers of paint. Has anyone encountered a similar problem? How do I get it all off?

--Donna Hampton  Alameda, CA

THE PAINT BETWEEN the plaster and the wood has probably saved you from a far worse disaster. Careful scraping with a putty knife should dislodge the plaster; just be careful not to gouge the wood in the process. When this is done, then you can proceed to remove the paint either chemically or with a heat gun.

General interest questions from subscribers will be answered in print. The Editors can't promise to reply to all questions personally—but we try. Send your questions with sketches or photos to Questions Editor, The Old-House Journal, 69A Seventh Avenue, Brooklyn, NY 11217.

# Restoration Products News

## Historical Metal Fencing

Krug, the oldest continuously working iron shop in the country, is best known for their custom ornamental iron-work. They recently introduced a wrought-iron picket fence, an original design from the 1870s. Uninstalled, this 32-in. high fence sells for $30/linear ft. (posts and a gate are extra). For a sketch of the fence, send a business-size, self-addressed, stamped envelope. G. Krug & Son, Inc., 415 W. Saratoga Street, Dept. OHJ, Baltimore, MD 21201. (301) 752-3166.

Stewart has an extensive selection of metal-picket fencing, made from 1886 and later patterns. They will also custom-make replacement sections for existing wrought-iron fencing. All fences are made of rolled steel in a variety of sizes, and cost $20-$35/linear ft. An illustrated catalog showing some of their stock patterns is free. Stewart Manufacturing Co., 511 Enterprise Drive, Dept. OHJ, Covington, KY 41018. (606) 331-9000.

The 1890 Iron Fence Co. manufactures an historical hairpin fence appropriate for 1890 through 1920 houses. It's made of pre-formed steel, is sold in 3- or 6-ft. heights, and is $12/linear ft. (for the 3-ft.-high version). The fence gate can be monogrammed. Unlike the fencing from some of the other foundries, installation is geared toward the do-it-your-selfer. Free information. 1890 Iron Fence Co., PO Box 467, Dept. OHJ, Auburn, IN 46706. (219) 925-4264.

*Hairpin fence by 1890 Iron Fence Co.*

Robinson Iron stocks iron fence posts and panels, many of which are cast from original 19th-century patterns. They will also do custom castings from an existing piece, photograph, or dimensional drawing. Stock items are $20-$40/linear ft. Specify your interest when writing for brochure, $3. Robinson Iron Corp., Dept. OHJ, Robinson Rd., Alexander City, AL 35010. (205) 329-8484.

*The Victorian fence post on the left is manufactured by Robinson Iron; the post on the right—Tennessee Fabricating.*

Architectural Iron's specialty is restoration or reconstruction of iron fencing. They will fill large or small orders in cast iron, wrought iron, or a combination. Custom castings can be made from an existing piece (even if it's damaged). If you are not in the Northeast, they will work with a foundry in your area. Prices begin at $300 for a simple newel post. For a free brochure, write Architectural Iron Co., Box 674, Dept. OHJ, Milford, PA 18337. (717) 296-7722, or (212) 243-2664.

Gorsuch will do custom reproductions in cast iron. While they prefer to work from an original piece, they will produce castings from drawings and photographs. A local ironworks will be contacted to install your custom casting. Castings are $2/lb. No literature; call or write about your specifications. Gorsuch Foundry, 120 East Market Street, Dept. OHJ, Jeffersonville, IN 47130. (812) 283-3585.

## Cast Components

*The following companies sell decorative fence components, either in cast iron or cast aluminum. Use the castings as replacement pieces on an existing fence, or to create your own historically inspired design. Unless otherwise stated, these companies will sell directly to individuals or they will put you in contact with an iron-fabricator in your area. The fabricator can design and install your fence, or occasionally be persuaded to sell individual components for the do-it-yourself project.*

Tennessee Fabricating has many of the same basic patterns offered by the other foundries, but has a wider range of sizes and shapes. Included in these shapes is a circle (one pattern can be cast to include your monogram), and coordinating cresting. Three cast-metal, Victorian-style fence posts are also stocked. Components and railing sections cost $3-$25. Their catalog is $3.50 and they will sell direct. Tennessee Fabricating Co., 2366 Prospect St., Dept. OHJ, Memphis, TN 38106. (901) 948-3355.

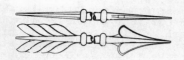

J.G. Braun features structural fence components which include balusters, baluster collars, railings, brackets, and handrail terminals in a variety of metals. Arrows and feathers are stocked in malleable iron, aluminum, and architectural bronze. Prices range from $3-$30/linear ft., and they will sell direct. Their catalog is free. J.G. Braun Co., PO Box 66, Dept. OHJ, Skokie, IL 60076. (312) 761-4600.

Lawler stocks a large selection of decorative components (spears, balls, caps, and points) which includes three sizes of the *pineapple point*, and the *Victorian*

*Crown* shown here. Traditional and Victorian castings, $7-$25/linear ft., are shown in a 76-page catalog ($5). They will sell direct; a minimum order is $250. Lawler Machine & Foundry Co., PO Box 2977, Dept. OHJ, Birmingham, AL 35212. (205) 595-0596.

The metalwork from Fairmont Foundry contains fencing panels in an assortment of traditional, Victorian, and Gothic style designs. Castings are $10-$25/linear ft.; a catalog is $5. They will not sell direct. Fairmont Foundry Co., Inc., 3125 35th Ave. N, Dept. OHJ, Birmingham, AL 35207. (205)841-6472.

## Authentic Paint Colors: Inside & Out

*To look its best, your house should be painted with colors to suit its personality. Just as you dress according to the occasion, the exterior colors you choose should be appropriate to the architectural style and age of your house. Color placement is equally important. White with green shutters is not the only choice for your old house! While this combination would be fine for a Colonial Revival house (1890-1920), it would probably cause A.J. Downing heartfailure if used on a vernacular Italianate (1840-1880). The latter style is especially attractive when painted in its original colors, such as dark brown on the body, warm brown on the trim, and a dark green door. For more information on exterior color selection and house painting, refer to OHJ April 1981.*

*In the past few years, many paint manufacturers have expanded or added "historic" colors to their paint selection. Listed here are reputable companies that offer well-researched colors. The paints are usually sold in exterior and interior formulations. (Interior colors are often "step-downs" or tints of the exterior pigments.)*

**Allentown**, the oldest ready-made paint company in the U.S., has recently reintroduced 12 colors produced and sold by them from 1867 to 1913. They will also manufacture any of their other original 54 colors upon request. These linseed-oil-based or latex exterior paints retail for $17-$25/gal. and are pre-mixed. They can be purchased through distributors, or direct. For information and a free color chart, specify *Breinig's Ready-Mixed Oil Paint*. Allentown Paint Manufacturing Co., Inc., PO Box 597, E. Allen & N. Graham Sts., Dept. OHJ, Allentown, PA 18105. (215) 433-4273.

**Benjamin Moore** offers 174 traditional 18th- and early 19th-century colors in oil/alkyd or latex. The *Historical Color*

*Collection* is $18-$25/gallon; several colors are ready mixed, others are custom-blended. This paint and a complete color chart can be found at distributors nationwide. A sample 30-color chart is free. Benjamin Moore Co., 51 Chestnut Ridge Rd., Dept. OHJ, Montvale, NJ 07645. (201) 573-9600.

**Martin Senour** manufactures paint for Colonial Williamsburg, in historically-inspired mid-18th-century colors. These latex paints are available in 80 interior and 36 exterior colors, for $21-$24/gal., ready-mixed. They can be purchased direct from the Williamsburg Craft House or a Martin Senour dealer. Both offer a free color chart. Craft House, Colonial Williamsburg, Box CH-23187, Dept. OHJ, Williamsburg, VA 23185. (804) 229-1000.

**Finnaren & Haley** produces 31 traditional colors, ten of which were authenticated, with the cooperation of the National Park Service, for use on historic Philadelphia buildings such as Independence Hall. The oil/alkyd or latex paints range from $14-$20/gallon. They are ready-mixed and sold through regional dealers or direct. For a free color chart, write Finnaren & Haley, Inc., 2320 Haverford Rd., Dept. OHJ, Ardmore, PA 19003. (215) 649-5000.

**Fuller O'Brien** offers 46 exterior-interior colors in their *Heritage Collection*. Interior paint is $13-$14/gal., exterior paint is $18-$21/gal.; both can be custom-mixed in a variety of oil/alkyd or latex bases. They are sold through distributors; a color chart is free. Fuller O'Brien Paints, PO Box 864, Dept. OHJ, Brunswick, GA 31520. (912) 265-7650.

**Stulb Paint** offers 16 colors from the first half of the 19th century. Twelve of these colors were authenticated by, and used at Old Sturbridge Village. This low-

sheen, oil-based, ready-mixed paint usually requires only one coat to cover and is $24.95/gal. It can be purchased direct or through distributors. A chart showing *Old Village* paint colors is $1. Stulb Paint & Chemical Company, PO Box 297, Dept. OHJ, Norristown, PA 19404. (215) 272-6660.

**The Sherwin-Williams Co.** features 40 historic 19th-century colors authenticated by Dr. Roger Moss, the historian who wrote the book "Century of Color." This latex or oil/alkyd-based paint is $18-$22/gal., custom-mixed, and sold through distributors nationwide. Their $2 color chart also illustrates appropriate colors for different styles of architecture. Sherwin-Williams Co., Attention: Color Studio, 101 Prospect Ave. NW, Dept. OHJ, Cleveland, OH 44101. (216) 566-2332.

**Devoe & Raynolds'** *Traditions* line is 84 Victorian-styled colors, 48 of which are reproductions of colors in "Exterior Decoration: Victorian Colors for Victorian Houses," an 1885 Devoe paint catalog. This latex or oil/alkyd paint is about $20/gal. It's custom-mixed, sold through distributors (nationwide, except for the West Coast), and colors are shown on a free color chart. Devoe & Raynolds Co., 4000 Dupont Circle, Dept. OHJ, Louisville, KY 40207. (502) 897-9861.

---

### HELPFUL COLOR GUIDE

*Century of Color: Exterior Decoration for American Buildings, 1820-1920* is a helpful and detailed book by Dr. Roger Moss. It illustrates colors which are readily available and appropriate for the major styles of architecture. For further details, see page 113E.

---

# Opinion... Remuddling
## —Of The Month—

THIS SAD STORY is best told in the words of the OHJ subscriber who sent along the photos: "This National Register building had been standing since 1846. Last year, however, it was 'improved.' The exterior was rehabilitated according to Secretary of Interior Guidelines. But little sensitivity was shown for the inside; the guts of the building were torn out to modernize it. A large center brick support wall that went from foundation to attic was reduced to three or four pillars--greatly reducing its strength. This gave each floor more open area, supposedly making it more attractive to prospective tenants. Next, concrete was poured over the old wood floors to make them more aesthetically pleasing. It was after concrete had been poured on the third floor that the building collapsed. I don't know whether you'd call this 'Technological Trashing' or 'Engineering Idiocy.' But it shows that many developers, architects, engineers, and contractors are out of touch with the hearts and souls of these old buildings."

Submitted by: R. Quentin Robinson
Lafayette, Ind.

*THE PILE OF BRICKS that fell from the front of this building undergoing renovation was an ominous sign that the gods who protect old buildings were not pleased with what was going on inside. Just a few hours later . . .*

*. . . the roof, floors, and front facade collapsed in a cloud of dust. Interior remuddling had seriously weakened the structure. The final insult occurred when workers poured concrete over the old wood floors. At that point, the building just gave up.*

# The Old-House Journal®

69A Seventh Avenue,
Brooklyn, New York 11217

NO PAID ADVERTISING

Postmaster: Address Correction Requested

# The Old-House Journal

Vol. X No. 6     $2.00

### Restoration and Maintenance Techniques For The Antique House

# ELECTRICAL CAPACITY

*Does Your House*     *Have Enough?*

MANY OF US old-house owners worry when certain fuses blow or circuit breakers trip too often. We're sure our electrical service isn't adequate. Let me emphasize at the outset: Unless your MAIN fuses blow or your MAIN circuit breakers trip, you do not have inadequate electrical service--yet.

BUT SUPPOSE you want to install a new kitchen. Your plans include replacing the old gas stove with two built-in ovens and a cooktop. And there will also be a dishwasher and garbage disposal. And while you're at it, you decide to add central air conditioning. Will you have adequate electrical service for this renovation?

THIS ARTICLE will give you a simple method for determining whether your current electrical service is adequate for present needs --and if there is any room for expansion.

MOST OLDER HOUSES were retrofitted or equipped for electrical service at a time when electricity was used for a few lighting circuits only: 15 or 20 ampere capacity was more than adequate. As more pieces of electrical equipment came to be considered indispensable in the '30s and '40s, 40- and 60-amp service became necessary. In the 1950s this grew to 100-amp service...and more recently to 150- and 200-ampere service. Skeptical of the need? Just count the number of electrical appliances you've added in recent years and add up the wattages involved. My 1903 house originally had 25-amp service; now it has 100. With my household load now totalling around 93 amps, it's obvious that I don't have much room for expansion.

TO ESTIMATE the electrical service needs of your house, we'll use the second of the two methods specified in the 1981 National Electrical Code. The Code is written and promulgated by the National Fire Protection Assn. In my opinion, the Code is one of the glories of U.S. technology. Fewer electrical fires occur in American homes than in any other modern country, and this is largely due to the efforts of NFPA through the National Electrical Code. The Code is accepted everywhere in

*continued on p. 124*

By Jeremy Robinson

# Letters

*Fred J. Gaca's article, "Seeing Through Bad Stained Glass," appeared in the March 1982 OHJ. Here are some of our readers' comments and clarifications on this popular article.*

To the Editors:

YOUR RECENT ARTICLE, "Seeing Through Bad Stained Glass," was basically useful and informative. However, it does permit certain misconceptions.

AT THE New England Home Show, readers of your article questioned the quality of my work because it used lead instead of copper foil. Their reading of the article had left them with the impression that only crude, second-rate work utilized lead.

ANY GLASS ARTISAN knows that fine work with lead indicates a high degree of technical skill. It is the beginners who usually use copper foil, because the glass need not be cut with the accuracy required when using lead. Therefore, I always caution buyers against any studio that works exclusively with copper foil. Moreover, copper is an innovation of the late 19th century; any restoration or replacement of stained glass from an earlier era must use lead if it is to be historically accurate.

ANOTHER reader misinterpretation concerned the placement of reinforcement bars. Some of your readers argued that if the bar was visible, the work was inferior. What they did not understand was that it is not always possible to bend and camouflage it. If windows of a certain size and shape are to last for decades, then the reinforcement bar must be positioned where it will work most effectively and not just where it will go unnoticed.

SOME OF YOUR READERS seem confused by the article. I hope these comments help.

Joseph Pompeii
Pompeii Studios
Medford, MA

To the Editors:

BRAVO! It is a rare occurrence for an article such as "Seeing Through Bad Stained Glass" to be written and presented to the public. I can't begin to count the number of times I've said almost exactly the same things to prospective clients, lecture audiences, art students, and club meetings. In every little art-and-craft show, home hobbyists are selling work that is not just poorly designed, but poorly copied and poorly constructed. It is so very important that the buying public become aware.

I WISH to commend the author, you, and your publication for this splendid article. I will recommend it to others.

Wesley S. Windle
Windle Stained Glass Studio
Jacksonville, NC

To the Editors:

I THOUGHT I should write and offer a point that was missed in the March issue's excellent article on stained glass.

COPPER FOIL is not waterproof and so should never be used in direct contact with weather. It can be double or triple glazed to avoid this danger. Also, copper foil (and, to a lesser extent, lead) should be used in construction only by someone who has a complete understanding of structural physics. It is not stable in large sections by itself and requires more than the average hobbyist's skill if it is to last longer than a few years.

Don Robertson--Stained Glass
Hastings, NE

To the Editors:

CONGRATULATIONS to Mr. Gaca for his excellent article on the pitfalls of purchasing old stained glass. As a co-owner of a studio that does new and restorative art glass, I am often confronted with the difficulty of explaining to a new owner of old glass why repairing the window properly will cost more than he paid for it.

I AM AN enthusiastic reader of OHJ. Keep up the good work!

Richard R. Morse
Melotte-Morse
Springfield, IL

# The Old-House Journal ®

*Editor*
**Clem Labine**

*Managing Editor*
**Patricia Poore**

*Assistant Editor*
**Cole Gagne**

*Editorial Assistants*
**Joni Monnich**
**Stephanie Croce**

*Circulation Supervisor*
**Joan O'Reilly**

*Circulation Assistants*
**Margaret Scaglione**
**Barbara Bugg**
**Jean Baldwin**

*Office Manager*
**Sally Goodman**

*Office Assistant*
**Rafael Madera**

*Circulation Director*
**Paul T. McLoughlin**

*Technical Consultant*
**Alan D. Keiser**
*Architectural Consultant*
**Jonathan Poore**

*Contributing Editors*
**R. A. Labine, Sr.**
**John Mark Garrison**

*Published by The Old-House Journal © Corporation, 69A Seventh Avenue, Brooklyn, New York 11217. Telephone (212) 636-4514. Subscriptions $16 per year in U.S. Not available elsewhere. Published monthly. Contents are fully protected by copyright and must not be reproduced in any manner whatsoever without specific permission in writing from the Editor.*

*We are happy to accept editorial contributions to The Old-House Journal. Query letters which include an outline of the proposed article are preferred. All manuscripts will be reviewed, and returned if unacceptable. However, we cannot be responsible for non-receipt or loss — please keep copies of all materials sent.*

**Printed at Photo Comp Press, New York City**

*ISSN: 0094-0178*
**NO PAID ADVERTISING**

Left: James and Meredith Boone pose before their newly-bought house.
Right: The wonders worked by repairs and a new coat of paint.

Old-House Living...

# A Victorian Dream Come True
## A Survivor In Springfield

By Cole Gagne

AT THE RIPE OLD AGE OF 87, the house at 97 Florida Street in Springfield, Mass., was still vital enough to win the hearts of James and Meredith Boone. Jim first saw this neglected and deteriorating Queen Anne in 1974 and simply could not forget it. Although he wasn't looking for a house at that time, he went home and told his wife about the house, saying, "If I ever should want a house, that's the house I'll want." When Merry saw the house, it exerted a similar influence on her. For the next two years, they drove past it every day, becoming increasingly won over by it.

EVENTUALLY, they decided that they had to have it. They began by conducting extensive research on the house, learning all they could about it and its previous owners. Built in 1887, the house had changed hands in 1890 and stayed with that family for the next fifty years. In 1941, it was sold and converted into a boarding house for the elderly, a

The second of the two porches is located on the side of the house.

role it played until the early 1970s. The Boones are grateful that the house served such a purpose; they believe that it survived in such good condition because those boarders lacked the money, energy, and interest to re-muddle it.

WHEN THE OWNER of the house died in 1975, Jim and Merry corresponded with the executor of the estate. They were not the only ones interested in the house, however, and to purchase it, they had to undergo a "very nerve-wracking experience": submitting a sealed bid and waiting for an answer.

THE ANSWER was "sold," and Merry and Jim moved into the house in October of 1976. It had been unoccupied for over a year, and so the first task facing them was to clean it. They spent two weeks cleaning in a house without gas or hot water, relying on only a used Coleman stove. To bathe, they had to pay a visit to their neighbors.

The restoration of the carriage barn was completed in 1976. Note the iron fence, which the Boones bought two years later.

## The Big Clean-Up

HAPPILY, THE CLEANING PROCESS was also the unveiling of the house's treasures. Under all that dirt and grime, in excellent condition, were original hardware, mantels, and tiles; unpainted cherry woodwork throughout all three floors; marble and slate sinks; Lincrusta-Walton wainscotting in the dining room; and 11 of the 12 original stained glass windows. "They were so dirty we couldn't distinguish most of the colors," says Merry. "It was exciting when we first cleaned the deep blues and glowing ruby colors."

IN PURCHASING THE HOUSE, the Boones bought a good deal along with it, including a half-acre lot with shrubs, fruit trees, and a 200-year-old oak, as well as a two-storey carriage barn

This photograph shows the Boones' front entrance hallway, complete with organ and newel light.

that had been converted into a six-room apartment in the 1920s. This carriage barn needed immediate attention in 1976. The Boones spent the balance of that year repairing the roof and replacing the chimney.

IN 1977, JIM AND MERRY received a grant from the City Historical Commission for exterior restoration of the house. With this money, they hired a contractor to rebuild all the porches and steps, replace the deteriorated clapboard and shingles, and repair the slate roof and masonry of the tower. The Boones made sure that the house received an authentic period paint job as well. The result of all this work was that in 1977, they were awarded the City Preservation Award.

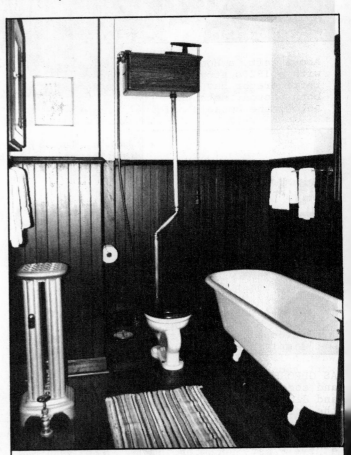

The restoration of the bathroom included the installation of a high-tank toilet.

## Restoring Rooms

ONLY THE BATHROOMS AND KITCHEN had been painted, and the Boones were determined to restore them to their original condition. From 1977 to '79, they stripped and refinished all the wainscotting and woodwork in both bathrooms. They retrieved a high-tank toilet from a garbage dump in Rhode Island and had it installed in the upstairs bathroom. (The plumber who did the job remarked, "This is the first time I ever installed one of these. I'm used to taking 'em out.")

Above left, a Hoosier cabinet side-by-side with a 1920s stove. Right, the late '20s refrigerator has cooling coils on top. In both photos, note the "linoleum rug." Below, the house's original soapstone sink.

## Proud Caretakers

THE THREE-STOREY, twelve-room house may be an exemplar of the skill and artistry of its makers, but today it is also a tribute to the taste, energy, and dedication of the Boones, who supplied these closing remarks:

"We are very settled in this magnificent house and look forward to a lifetime of satisfying projects here. We feel extremely fortunate to have acquired it in such complete and original condition, and we are committed to carrying out an authentic restoration. We feel that we are but a small chapter in what will be a long and proud history for this place. We feel obligated to pass it along to the next owner in even more complete and original condition and with more of its intrinsic beauty showing. We feel like privileged and proud caretakers, and we look forward with great anticipation to the next fifty years of old-house living."

AS OPPOSED TO so many old-house owners who gut and completely modernize their kitchens, Merry and Jim decided that the kitchen should match the rest of the house. They stripped and refinished all its wainscotting and woodwork, including six doors: "THANK GOD for the heat gun." [An unsolicited comment!] They installed a tin ceiling and added a 1920s stove and refrigerator. A Hoosier cabinet and linoleum rug* were the finishing touches in their remarkable restoration.

THE BOONES were also adamant about properly restoring the grounds of their house. After clearing out all the weeds, they began looking for an appropriate iron fence. Coincidentally, through an ad in THE OLD-HOUSE JOURNAL, they found just such a fence in Pennsylvania. They restored and installed it in 1978, along with a cast iron fountain that they discovered in Maine. Perennial beds and plantings of the house's period, as well as urns and a bench, now grace the grounds at 97 Florida Street.

From this vantage point, you can see the front and side of the house, the carriage barn, the grounds, the fence, the fountain, and a very cute dog.

*They used a modern product called Thrift-Tex—an interpretation of the linoleum rug. Both Thrift-Tex and a companion product, Manolux, are available in retail stores. For information on a distributor near you, contact Mannington Mills, PO Box 30, Dept. OHJ, Salem, NJ 08079. (609) 935-3000.

## Tips From Readers
# Restorer's Notebook

## No Plaster Marks

EVERYONE WHO REMOVES plaster lath has been bothered by the plaster marks that are left on the wood. Here's an easy solution to this problem. Use a whisk broom or wire brush to dust off as much of the plaster as possible. Then apply an oil stain to the wood. (You may have to mix a couple of stains together to get the color you want.) Plaster dust absorbs stain very readily--pretty soon, you'll forget you ever had plaster marks.

Mikki Bitsko
Dayton, OH

## The Fight Against Mildew

ONE OF THE BEST WAYS to combat mildew is to remove the cause. And for many homeowners, the cause is all the bush and tree branches that overhang the house. Prune these away from the roof, and you'll get rid of the mildew in the adjacent rooms.

William T. Farenga
Sagaponack, NY

## Removing Asbestos Siding

A MAJOR CRIME committed against our Queen Anne house was the installation of asbestos siding. Here are some tips on how to remove it, based on our experience.

YOU SHOULD SPOT CHECK the condition of the original clapboard and/or shingle siding to see if you want to expose it. Break off individual pieces of the asbestos at any areas of the house which may have been subjected to excess weathering or deterioration.

IF YOU DECIDE ON full-scale removal, do one side of the house at a time. Using light hammer blows, break the bottom row of siding and remove. You can now remove individual pieces in successive rows. Bare the nail head by pushing the piece against the house. Snip off the nail head, pull the piece out, and slide it down from the row above. This method prevents a big mess in your yard and leaves you with intact pieces of siding which you can sell to a salvage yard. It also enables you to pound and countersink the remaining shank of the nail into the wood siding. Then you can fill the holes with exterior putty. On our house, the tar paper behind the asbestos siding was installed with only a few roofing nails. We pried out these nails and filled the holes.

Steve Bibby & Gordon Huser
Minneapolis, MN

## A Ladle For Lead

TO FINISH SEALING a caulked wastepipe, I had to pour melted lead into the joint. Unfortunately, no local hardware or plumbing supply dealer had a ladle in stock. My solution was to improvise one, using a cast iron pipe cap. The cap had an inside diameter of about 1-3/4 in. and cost around $1.25.

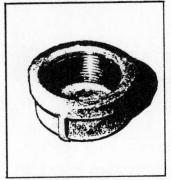

THE RIM OR FLANGE of the cap is fairly thick, and the metal can be filed easily. Using a triangular file and a half-round, I made two diametrically opposed pouring lips. To make room for a wrap-around handle, I removed about half an inch of the two lugs that run along the sides of the cap. For the shaft of the handle, I used a 4-ft. length of baling wire. I bent the wire double, wrapped the double strand around the cap, clamped the free end in my bench vise and twisted until the cap was held snug. I evenly sawed the ends of the four strands and tapped on a file handle to serve as a comfortable, heat-proof grip.

Milton Herder
Scarsdale, NY

## Rubber, Not Canvas

IN THE OCTOBER 1981 "Ask OHJ," you recommend canvas instead of tar paper on a porch floor that also serves as the roof for the porch below. Even better than canvas are some of the newer elastomeric rubber-sheet goods now used as roofing. (Trade names include Goodyear, Carlisle, and Uniroyal.) The material is almost always black, but can be painted with a Hypalon paint that is virtually maintenance free. This material can also be used to line built-in gutters, thereby saving homeowners the cost of patching in new gutter liners and replacing rotten wood, until they can afford to do it right.

Andrew B. Buckner
Blackmore & Buckner Roofing, Inc.
Indianapolis, IN

**Tips To Share?** Do you have any hints or short cuts that might help other old-house owners? We'll pay $15 for any short how-to items that are used in this "Restorer's Notebook" column. Write to Notebook Editor, The Old-House Journal, 69A Seventh Avenue, Brooklyn, NY 11217.

# Plaster Resurfacing:
# My Experience With Glid-Wall

By Norman L. Polston, OHJ subscriber, Lansdowne, Penn.

Above: When the walls and ceiling reach this condition, complete resurfacing is an answer. Below: This is the same room after the application of the Glid-Wall system.

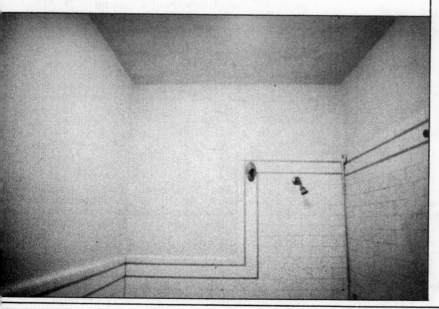

ALMOST EVERY ROOM in our old house requires some kind of attention. There are only a few minor hairline cracks on some walls and ceilings; others have whole sections of loose, crumbling plaster. We also have our share of cracked and peeling paint and wallpaper. We are repeatedly faced with the decision of whether a particular room (or portions of it) should be gutted "down to the studs" and rebuilt, or whether it should be patched and redecorated. Often, we've opted to gut and rebuild, not because conditions demanded such drastic actions, but because there simply was no way to rebuild the surface to an acceptable condition.

SEVERAL MONTHS AGO, I discovered a method that promised to fill the gap between minor surface repairs and major rebuilding. A thin, porous sheet of reinforcing material is used not as a patch, but to resurface an entire wall or ceiling. The sheet is stuck to the wall and then filled with paint. The resulting surface is strong, hard, durable, and will not crack.

I TRIED SEVERAL reinforcing materials, and the most impressive results were achieved with a lightweight sheet of fiberglass. It's made by Johns-Manville and marketed by Glidden as part of their Glid-Wall system. Fiberglass is stiff enough to bridge most cracks, dents, and holes (as large as ¼ inch), and to mask the rough edges left from scraping paint and wallpaper. It is also flexible enough to cover small bumps and ridges, and to form easily into corners, thereby producing invisible seams.

THE INSTRUCTIONS for the Glid-Wall system say to begin by applying a coat of paint to the

June 1982 121 The Old-House Journal

# Some Notes On Glid-Wall — And Canvas

Resurfacing walls and ceilings is a tried-and-true practice; traditionally it's been done with canvas instead of fiberglass. Plaster surfaces are canvassed for two reasons: (1) To provide a stable substrate for decorative finishes—so that fancy work need not be redone after minor plaster cracking; (2) To smooth out imperfectly patched or slightly damaged old walls and ceilings.

A note about the Glid-Wall system: It's guaranteed by Glidden only if their Insul-Aid paint is used and their instructions are exactly followed. As described in this article, Mr. Polston changed both the paint and the application technique. After some trial-and-error use of Glid-Wall, he found he couldn't work fast enough to apply the fiberglass to the still-wet painted wall. He used a less expensive brand of paint, which doesn't give the vapor barrier afforded by Insul-Aid. He's happy with his method, but we suggest homeowners try to work according to the manufacturer's recommendations.

Whether you opt for traditional canvassing (about $2.75 sq.yd. including vinyl paste) or Glid-Wall, plaster resurfacing may be the cosmetic answer you've been searching for. By itself, of course, it won't cure failing plaster, fill or bridge large cracks or gouges, or re-anchor plaster to lath or to studs. But you can use a resurfacing method if the plaster is sound — or can be made sound — but . . . .

- There's a thick, alligatored paint buildup
- There are numerous cyclical cracks
- There are decelerating, hairline settlement cracks
- The surface is over-patched, botched, or poorly taped
- The surface has suffered fire and smoke damage.

Canvas is preferred by professional paper-hangers because it is available in 54-inch bolts that eliminate most seams in a room. Both canvas and fiberglass insignificantly change the texture of the finish plaster — a good job is barely noticeable.

surface. This holds the fiberglass while you position, smooth, and trim it. This approach gave me problems because I couldn't work quickly enough to position the sheet properly before the paint dried. Through trial and error, I came up with an alternate method that I could use more easily.

---

### MATERIALS

You'll need fiberglass and paint, of course; just how much depends on the size of the job. If you adopt Norman Polston's modifications, you'll also need a staple gun. But whether or not you follow Glidden's instructions to the letter, the job will require the following equipment:

1) 3-in. nylon brush
2) 9-in. paint roller with long-nap cover
3) roller tray
4) drop cloths
5) wallcovering smoothing tool (or another 9-in. paint roller and cover)
6) razor knife

If you're applying the system to the ceiling, you'll also need:

1) 4-in. putty knife
2) extension handles for paint rollers

---

## How He Did It

**1** PREPARE THE SURFACE. Do as you would for any painting job: Scrape off all loose plaster, paint, and wallpaper; fill large holes and cracks; level any large, disjointed cracks, ridges, or valleys with a feather coat of plaster or joint cement. Glid-Wall will mask many of the minor imperfections you might miss, so don't waste time being a perfectionist in this step.

**2** PROTECT YOUR SKIN. Skin contact with fiberglass causes irritation and itching. Wear a long-sleeve shirt, button the sleeves and collar, and apply a skin cream or lotion to all exposed portions of your skin. [It would

be a good idea to wear a particle mask when you actually cut the fiberglass.--Eds.]

**3** APPLY THE FIBERGLASS. The fiberglass sheet is produced in rolls 36 in. wide. Cut it into strips to the height of the surface. Rather than paint the surface at this point, I used staples to hold the sheet loosely in place. I began at the center of the sheet and stapled out toward each end. From 1½ to 2 inches of overlap have to be left for the seams--and corners, if you're doing more than one surface.

**4** APPLY THE PAINT. Spread the paint on thoroughly. Be sure to force it through the fiberglass, so the sheet can bind properly to the surface. Start at the center and work toward the ends. Be very careful not to paint within 1 or 2 inches of the overlapped seams.

**5** TRIM THE SEAMS & REMOVE THE STAPLES. Make certain the sheet is pressed smooth before the paint dries. Once it's dry, double-cut the seams (and corners) and remove the excess. Be sure to cut through both layers of fiberglass. The sheet should be tight against any corners when you trim. Pull out the staples with a pair of pliers. Apply a coat of paint to the seams with roller and brush. (Notice how the seams magically disappear!) If you dispose of the excess at this point, you'll no longer be bothered by the fiberglass, so you won't need the skin cream and buttoned shirt.

**6** FINISH UP. Saturate the fiberglass with another coat of paint (more than one if you think it's necessary). Then apply a finish coat of paint. If you can't work at this full time, the process will take several days; so, at the end of each day, place the roller and brush in the pan, add a wet rag to keep things moist, and cover the pan with aluminum foil. (This prolonged soaking would destroy a cheap roller, so be sure to use a good one.)

NOW YOU'RE FINISHED. Stand back and admire that near-perfect job. With this system, even the most critical lighting will reveal--only faintly!--nothing but the most gross imperfections.

## Fiberglass & Paint

**F**IBERGLASS is the secret of Glid-Wall's success. What Glidden refers to as their "smooth, lightweight fiberglass mat (no. 70127)" should be available at Glidden outlets near you. It costs from 45 to 55¢ per linear yard, and they prefer to sell it a roll at a time (400 ft., 133 sq.yd.).

THE PAINT serves several purposes. It acts as a high-quality adhesive that binds the fiberglass to the surface. It is also a filler for the fiberglass sheeting. Lastly, it offers a tough, rigid surface that's resistant to water, soap, and steam. Glidden recommends that you use their Insul-Aid paint with the fiberglass, warning that they won't guarantee results with any other paint.

INSUL-AID is Glidden's best wallpaint, retailing for $18 per gallon. They say that one gallon of paint should cover no more than 100 sq. ft., or 11 sq.yd. Allotting for two coats of paint, Insul-Aid winds up costing about $3 per sq.yd. Another 50¢ for the fiberglass brings the cost up to $3.50 per sq.yd. That may not sound like much (especially in comparison to wallpaper prices), but the total cost for doing an entire room 10 ft. wide, 15 ft. long,

and 8 ft. high comes out to $193.50--a strain on anyone's budget.

MY ADVICE is to do what I've done almost from the very beginning: Use an inexpensive, good paint. After all, the paint only has to glue and fill. An inexpensive paint I found had the same square-foot coverage Insul-Aid had, but sold in 5-gallon containers and cost only $4.35 per gallon (and it wasn't even on sale). Except for a slight spattering problem, it was a perfectly good substitute. This change brought costs down to $1.23 per sq.yd., or $75.03 for our hypothetical room--a saving of $118.47.

## A Word Of Caution

**T**HE GLID-WALL SYSTEM is rigid enough to hold small patches of loose or weak plaster against the wall, provided there is a good adhesion to sound surfaces all around the patch. But it cannot hold sagging walls or ceilings together, nor will it mask large imperfections, such as the rolling ridges and valleys commonly found in old plaster surfaces. Fortunately, these gentle undulations add a necessary charm to an old house and should be left alone anyway.

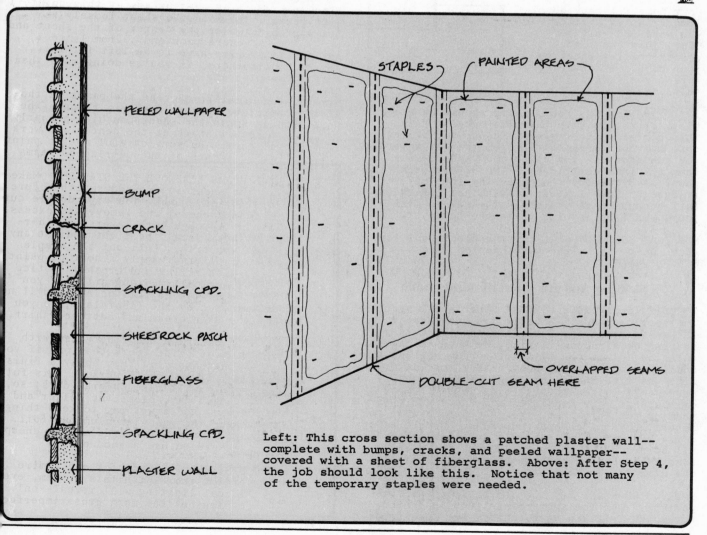

Left: This cross section shows a patched plaster wall--complete with bumps, cracks, and peeled wallpaper--covered with a sheet of fiberglass. Above: After Step 4, the job should look like this. Notice that not many of the temporary staples were needed.

the U.S., though some jurisdictions (such as New York City) have stricter requirements. You are urged to consult your local building officials to determine if variations from the code are required in your locality.

## Your Present Electrical Service

IF YOUR HOME has circuit breakers, the master switch box (if there is one) or the main circuit breaker box will probably list the capacity in amps. The master switch or the master circuit breaker toggle switch may have the amperage printed on the tip.

IF YOU HAVE 230-volt service, you'll probably find that you have two master circuit breaker switches. If you don't have 230-volt service, then your electrical service is probably inadequate. You cannot add an electric clothes dryer, an electric range, or efficient air conditioning. This may not be important to you now, but it may be important to a potential buyer of your home. If any doubt lingers as to whether you have 230-volt service, just count the electric wires entering your home. If there are three, you've got 230-volt service.

**3-Wire Entry Service Makes It Possible To Have 115-V. or 230-V. Circuits**

*+ 115 v.*    *Ground (neutral)*    *– 115 v.*

*115-v. Circuit*    *115-v. Circuit*

*230-v. Circuit*

IF YOU HAVE a fuse box, there should be a large black rectangle with a handle labeled MAIN. This contains the two main fuses, and if the fuse box door doesn't tell you the box amperage, you can shut off the power and read the amps from the fuse cartridges. (BE SURE that the power is off before touching the fuse cartridges!) You'll need a flashlight for this task because once you throw the main switch there won't be any lights in the house.

NOW THAT YOU KNOW your current electrical service, write it on the Worksheet on Line 6.

## Heating And Air Conditioning Load

THIS IS THE MOST COMPLEX item in calculating service needs. Briefly put, the Code requires that the larger of the two loads, heating or air conditioning, be used in the calculation, since you will not be heating and air conditioning simultaneously. You must determine the size and/or amperage rating of all permanently wired motors (e.g., water pumps, oil burners, air conditioners, etc.) and enter them on the Worksheet. You may not be able to determine furnace motor amperage. Use 10 amps for a hot air furnace blower and 7 amps for the oil burner motor. Figure 10 amps for a well pump. Air conditioner amperages are listed on the nameplate of the machine.

NOW YOU'RE READY for the heating/cooling comparison. Use the appropriate section of the Worksheet. If you have central air conditioning, ADD the furnace blower motor wattage to the air conditioning side to obtain the total air conditioning load. Enter the higher of the two wattages on the Worksheet at (1).

## Lighting Load

NEXT, you'll have to calculate the square footage of the living area of your house. This is calculated from the OUTSIDE dimensions and does NOT include porches, garages, and spaces not adaptable to future living areas. These excluded spaces can include basements, attics, sheds, etc. However, if your plans call for finishing a basement or attic eventually, you should include it in your calculation.

MULTIPLY THE SQUARE FOOTAGE by 3 watts and place this figure in Lighting Load section on the Worksheet. This figure may seem large to you, but it includes the demands for all lamps, radios, TV's, vacuum cleaners, hair dryers, and the like.

## Small Appliances And Laundry Circuits

ALLOW FOR TWO 1500-watt circuits for small kitchen appliances (to the Code, a refrigerator is a small appliance). The Code requires these two circuits for new construction, and you'll need them if you ever remodel your kitchen. Add a special laundry circuit of 1500 watts. These have already been placed on the appropriate lines of the Worksheet.

ANY APPLIANCE served by a separate circuit that serves no other load is called a special appliance. Examples include ranges, separate ovens and cooktops, water heaters, disposals, clothes dryers, and water pumps. Each must be entered at its nameplate wattage. If you do not now have such an appliance but are going to add

### WATTAGES OF TYPICAL ELECTRICAL APPLIANCES

| | |
|---|---:|
| Electric Ranges | 12,000-16,000 |
| Range Top | 4,000-8,000 |
| Oven | 4,000-8,000 |
| Waste Disposal | 1,000 |
| Dishwasher | 1,200-1,500 |
| Clothes Dryer | 5,000-8,000 |
| Water Pump | 1,200 |
| Furnace Blower | 1,200 |
| Oil Burner | 800 |

| ELECTRIC MOTORS: | |
|---|---:|
| 1/6 horsepower | 450 |
| 1/4 horsepower | 700 |
| 1/3 horsepower | 850 |
| 1/2 horsepower | 1,000 |
| 3/4 horsepower | 1,350 |
| 1  horsepower | 1,500 |
| Over 1 h.p.—per h.p. or fraction | 1,200 |

## WHAT'S A WATT?

FOR THOSE who are confused by electrical terminology, the "water analogy" can be helpful. Consider the flow of electricity as similar to the flow of water. Then:

VOLTS are analogous to water pressure. The water at the bottom of the lake behind a 230-ft. dam is under twice as much pressure as the water behind a 115-ft. dam. The greater the pressure, the greater the amount of work a given volume of water can do. For example, a gallon of water from a 230-ft. dam will do twice as much work turning a water wheel as will a gallon of water from a 115-ft. dam.

AMPERES or AMPS measure the amount of electricity flowing. It's analogous to gallons of water. The greater the pressure (voltage) behind a given number of amps, the more work (watts) the amps can do.

WATTS, WATTAGE is the amount of work or power available in a circuit, or the amount of power an appliance draws while it is doing its work. The amount of work available in a circuit is the total volume of electricity (amps) times the pressure (volts). If you have conductors (wires) that can safely handle a flow of 15 amps, you'll get twice as much work out of the circuit if you have 230 volts available rather than 115 volts. This becomes important when you want to install high-wattage machines like central air conditioners or electric ranges.

A FUSE or CIRCUIT BREAKER can be thought of as a safety valve. Your wires (conductors) are rated to carry a certain number of amps safely (usually 15 or 20). If there's an unusually heavy load placed on one of your circuits, and more than the rated number of amps starts to flow through the conductor, the safety valve trips, shutting off the flow of electricity entirely.

...ne, use the Table of Wattages on page 124.
...ese are high values and should be adequate
...r planning.

...W TOTAL the "Lighting & Other Load" column.
...he first 10,000 watts of this total are enter-
...d on Line (2) at full value. The remainder of
...his "Other Load" total is multiplied by 0.4
...since it's unlikely that you'd use all of it
...t the same time) and the resulting figure is
...ntered on the Worksheet on Line (3).

...DD LINES (1), (2) and (3) and divide by 230.
...Divide by 115 if you have 115-volt service.)
...he result on Line (5) is the service demand
...in amps) or capacity needed for your home.

### An Example

THE FIGURES that are written onto the Worksheet are for a typical old house (mine). It's a 2,200 sq. ft. house with a 12,000-watt range, a 2,500-watt water heater, a 1,200-watt dishwasher, a 5,500-watt clothes dryer, ...ne 6-amp 230-volt air conditioner, and two ...2-amp 115-volt air conditioners.

...HE FILLED-OUT WORKSHEET shows a current need
...or 100-amp service, which is what I now have.
...t also shows that I do not have sufficient
...apacity to add much to my electrical demand.
...hould I wish to add central air conditioning,
...r electric space heat to my cold third floor,
...'ll need to increase my service.

...OW DOES your house rate?

...EREMY ROBINSON, in addition to being Editor-in-Chief for Architecture and ...ngineering at McGraw-Hill Book Co., is an old-house owner with extensive do-it-...ourself experience. He analyzed steam heating systems in OHJ's November issue.

## WORKSHEET FOR ESTIMATING ELECTRICAL SERVICE REQUIREMENTS

**HEATING LOAD:**    Amps   X   Volts   = Watts

| | Amps | | Volts | | Watts |
|---|---|---|---|---|---|
| Blower | 10 | X | 115 | = | 1150 |
| Oil Burner | 7 | X | 115 | = | 805 |
| Hot Water Pump | — | X | — | = | — |

Total Heating Load    1955

**COOLING LOAD:**    Amps   X   Volts   = Watts

| | Amps | | Volts | | Watts |
|---|---|---|---|---|---|
| AC No. 1 | 6 | X | 230 | = | 1380 |
| AC No. 2 | 12 | X | 115 | = | 1380 |
| AC No. 3 | 12 | X | 115 | = | 1380 |

Total Cooling Load    4140

Heating or Cooling Load (whichever is higher)    4140 (1)

**LIGHTING & OTHER LOAD:**    Watts

| | Watts |
|---|---|
| 2200 sq. ft. at 3 watts/sq. ft. | 6600 |
| Two Kitchen Appliance Circuits | 3,000 |
| Laundry Circuit | 1,500 |
| Electric Ovens + Cooktops | 12000 |
| Water Heater | 2500 |
| Dishwasher | 1200 |
| Disposal | — |
| Electric Clothes Dryer | 5500 |
| Well Water Pump | — |
| Other | —— |
| Other | —— |

Total Lighting & Other Load    32300

First 10,000 watts of Lighting & Other Load at 100%    10000 (2)

Remainder at 40% ( 22300 X 0.40 )    8920 (3)

Total of Lines (1), (2), (3)    23060 (4)

**SERVICE REQUIREMENT IN AMPS:**

Line (4) / House Voltage = $\dfrac{23060}{230}$ = 100 a. (5)

**MY CURRENT ELECTRICAL SERVICE IS**    100 a. (6)

*The essential step in removing the grime that obscured the original marbleizing (left) was nothing more complicated than washing with soap and water, followed by rubbing gently with fine steel wool (above). A coat of high-gloss varnish over the renewed finish (right) heightens the marble effect.*

# Renewing A Marbleized Mantel

### By Joan Wells

ONLY ONE of the original coal-burning slate fireplaces remained in the 1881 Victorian house we have been restoring as a country inn. The mantel is quite handsome, in the "Eastlake" style with incised decorations and a marbleized finish. However, the years had taken their toll. The painted marbleizing on the top shelf of the mantel was badly worn and chipped. The thin piece of slate that was supposed to hide the bricks around the firebox was long gone. And the rest of the marbleizing on the front of the mantel looked quite dull and dreary.

ON THE PLUS SIDE, the slate that remained was in good condition, and the marbleizing on the front of the mantel, although dull, seemed to be intact.

OUR FRIEND, C. Dudley Brown, suggested that just a bit of work would renew the finish on the mantel and restore it to a showpiece once again. Following his instructions, here's what I did:

(1) I washed the entire mantel and surrounding bricks with a soap and water solution to clean off accumulated layers of soot and grime. In places where woodwork paint had splattered on the mantel over the years, I carefully scraped it off with a knife.

(2) Next, I lightly rubbed the mantel with a pad of very fine (0000) steel wool to finish the grime removal process.

(3) Then I gave the mantel a final rinse to get off all the soap and loose particles. When wet, the mantel looked wonderful; it gave me an idea of the appearance it would have after my work.

(4) The marbleizing on top of the mantel was essentially gone. Since I wasn't up to re-creating the marbleizing, I used a chemical paint remover to strip the remaining paint on the top shelf of the mantel.

(5) I painted the stripped area of the mantel top with black enamel paint. I also re-painted with the glossy black a couple of small sections that had not been marbleized originally but merely painted black.

(6) The most dramatic step was to coat the marbleized areas with a high-gloss varnish. The varnish really brightened and enlivened the colors and veining in the marbleizing.

(7) Last, I re-gilded the incised decorative panels, using a very fine brush, a straight-edge, and gold decorator's paint. Then I varnished those areas again to protect them.

BECAUSE the fireplace flues were no longer functional, the firebox got a strictly decorative treatment. I placed andirons and a dried flower arrangement in the fireplace-- just as the Victorians might have done. I added a brass fender to protect my new master-piece--and then stood back to collect compliments on a mantel that no one had ever noticed before!

*JOAN WELLS is the keeper, along with her husband Dane, of The Queen Victoria Inn in Cape May, N.J. They'd be delighted to have you stay with them and to show you the restored mantel in person.*

# Bathrooms With Character

### By Joni Monnich

*There is no such thing as a Colonial toilet (no matter what the ad might say!). But even if your old house predates 1880, an early-20th-century bathroom isn't an anachronism. That's because the indoor bathroom didn't become a standard feature in most of the country until around the turn of this century. So that's an appropriate period to consider in furnishing your bathroom. Like kitchens, bathrooms don't always lend themselves to historical restoration. If you're after an old-fashioned look, though, you'll enjoy this little tour through the old bathroom.*

AS EARLY AS 1850, a bathroom was an integral part of 'grand' houses costing $10,000 or more. Then, shortly before the turn of the century, it was transformed from a luxury to a standard feature of even the cheapest 'catalog' house. Fixtures were left exposed for a neat, sanitary and easier appearance although the cleaning, the latter was often by over-ornamentation.

'Pedestal Lion' Closet

FROM 1880 to and surface bathroom very offered in varieties paper. fixtures, made of cast coated with a porcelain glaze, were often painted to imitate wood, bronze, or gold. Even toilets were embossed or transfer-printed in 1900, embossed decoration for fixtures was elaborate, as many as wall-These usually iron

designs suitable for the Colonial Revival, Aesthetic, or Art Nouveau styles.

AT THE SAME TIME, wood-encased wash-basins gave way to open earthenware basins set on ornate cast-iron frames. These basins and their frames were often decorated to match the style chosen for the bathroom.

Early
Cast-Iron Frame

Porcelain
Pedestal Sink

A luxurious 1880s bathroom with a panelled, hooded tub.
(When the flush toilet first appeared in public buildings, operating instructions were often hung alongside.)

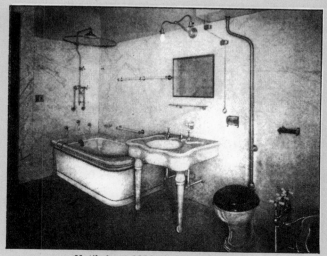

Until about 1900, bathrooms featured
all the plumbing fixtures on one wall.

WHILE EVERY HOUSE had a toilet (often called the W.C. or water closet), and a sink, not all houses had an installed bath or shower. The hip bath was still in use up to about 1925. Many a grand-parent can recall the cozy sight of a warm bedroom with a hip bath set on a waterproof sheet, hot-water cans gleaming in the light of a fire, and a thick towel warming on the fireguard. While seemingly crude, hip baths were in fact covered with a bath sheet onto which water was poured. Thus, the occupant never saw (or felt) the basic metal container underneath.

VERY EARLY BATHTUBS were usually made of sheet metal, and often enclosed in the same wood wainscotting used to protect the walls. But by 1880, bathtubs, which had been encased in panelled woodwork with elaborate woodframes and tile splashbacks, were free-standing cast-iron forms with intricate, applied exterior decoration.

WOOD WAINSCOTTING, no longer surrounding the tub, was still used on the walls. Moisture-resistant, embossed wallcoverings, such as Lincrusta, were often used above the wainscot-ting or in place of it. Hooded tubs in such woods as mahogany remained popular until about 1900.

## Sanitary & Compact Bathrooms

WHEN BATHROOMS became standard, they also got smaller--even for a large house, archi-tects began to prefer several small bath-rooms instead of one large one. Except for the occasional costly fantasy, even a bathroom in a large house was essentially the same as that in the smallest newly-built villa. By 1900, porcelain or vitreous china was commonly used for all fixtures; the various styles were discarded in favor of plain, white, san-itary atmosphere.

WOODWORK, CURTAINS, CARPETS, and elaborate dec orations began to disappear. In their place came white enamel fixtures, and polished brass and nickel-plating. (Maybe not as im-pressive but certainly more practical, especially for a house without servants.) Now and then, through the use of colored tiles, the walls and floors were of-ten as elaborately decor-ated as any other room in the house. But small hexagonal, large square, or rectangular tiles, usually all in white, we the most popular. Often, a single course of patterned or colored tiles (such as glossy bla was inserted one course below or at the top of the dado, which was about 4-ft. high. Floor tiles were generally solid colors (usually whi with perhaps a simple border near the wall. Diamond and mosaic patterns were also used.

*The compact 'bath cell', 1908*

TOILETS IN THE MID TO LATE 1800s were a comple system of noisy pipes. By 1900, the syphonic toilet was developed (a mod-el similar to the one we use today), bringing a peaceful and simple unit to the American bathroom. This advance in plumbing brought about first the high-, and then the low-tank toilet. The toilet was made of china or porcelain and featured an oak tank with a matching toilet seat. By 1927, all the fixtures in the bathroom were available only in white china or porcelain. The toilet seat was made of birch--hand-rubbed until it was ivory white for the ultimate sanitary effect.

*The 'Moreton' Chair Enclosure for the 'Optimus'*

Notice the embossed tile and the built-in sink in this 1902 bath.

A 1909 bathroom complete with scale and an early shower unit.

*(Both photos from the Byron Collection of the Museum of the City of New York.)*

A claw-foot bathtub.

The standard 1913 tub.

IN 1900, sinks were one-piece basins made of fireclay or whiteware--what we now call china or porcelain. They often featured a recess for soap and were attached to the wall with brackets and later thin, porcelain legs. (Occasionally, wood cabinets were built to surround or support them.) By 1910, pedestal sinks, always in white, were a standard bathroom fixture. Lever faucet handles were followed by cross or 'spoke' handles. Initially, they were made of brass or nickel-plated; later porcelain became popular. At this time (in keeping with the trend for smaller, compact bathrooms), corner sinks and medicine cabinets became popular.

THE SHOWER/BATH also saw dramatic changes a-round 1900. A shower enclosure was often a semi-cylinder of sheet zinc, double-shelled, and perforated inside to give a fine spray, an alternative to the overhead shower, also available by 1900. Showers as separate, free-standing units, or as cylindrical rings hung from the ceiling over the tub, were common features by 1910.

FREE-STANDING TUBS with stout legs were available in the Sears Catalog as early as 1902. By 1908, these legs had developed into ball & claw feet (sometimes whim-sically gilded). These tubs were replaced, about 1913, by a tub similar to the one we use today. A cast-iron, double-shelled, 5ft.-6in.-long tub, porcelain-enameled inside and out, was put into quantity production. It was a standard feature of every new house, often built into the wall of the sanitary, compact bathroom, and avail-able at a price everyone could afford to pay.

YOU MAY NOT BE ABLE TO OR WANT TO create a bathroom that is exactly authentic, but it's still possible to get a turn-of-the-century look. Not only can you make use of reproduction fittings...but you can also rely on fixtures that haven't changed much in 80 years.

*L. Wright's* **Clean And Decent** *is an amusing and informative history of bathing and related functions. A new edition has recently been released under the title* **Deep Fresh.** *You can order it by mail, $7.95 ppd., from Routledge & Kegan Paul, 9 Park St., Boston, MA 02108. (617) 742-5863.*

At a time when entire "catalog houses" were available by mail, the customer could buy bathroom sets, too: This one cost $37.50 in 1910.

By 1913, the bathroom was smaller, its floor and walls tiled for a "sanitary" effect.

# Restoration Products News

## Tubs, Showers, & Sinks

*There are ways to combine turn-of-the-century styles with modern convenience in your bathroom. We have selected companies that offer sinks, tubs, and shower conversions that are appropriate for a period bathroom. We have highlighted products that caught our fancy, but for their full lines, contact each company. Next month, we'll feature toilets.*

Tennessee Tub specializes in antique tubs and pedestal sinks from 1880 to 1920. Salvaged pull-chain toilets, brass and chrome fittings are also offered. All of their fixtures are reglazed and restored. For a free brochure, write Tennessee Tub, 905 Church St., Dept. OHJ, Nashville, TN 37203. (615) 242-0780.

Kohler's *Birthday Bath* is a unique adaptation of the claw-footed bathtub. The 6-ft. long, 37½-in. wide, cast-iron tub is offered in four colors, with claw-feet in chrome or 24kt. gold finishes. Prices begin at $1,456. Another item of interest is the *Marston* corner sink, $210-$270. These products are sold through distributors, but you can contact Kohler for their free *Elegance* brochure and the location of your nearest dealer. Kohler Company, Dept. OHJ, Kohler, WI 53044. (414) 457-4441.

Cumberland General Store still sells a hip bath! Similar to the one on pg. 128, it features arm and soap rests, is 30-in. tall by 31-in. wide, and costs $75. Another authentic bathtub (just introduced) is their claw-footed tub with oak feet, cradle, and rim ($450). Both tubs are made of galvanized steel and can be seen in their *Wish & Want Book*, $3.75 ppd. Cumberland General Store, Rt. 3, Dept. OHJ, Crossville, TN 38555. (615) 484-8481.

Perhaps the most flamboyant reproduction tub we came across is a copper bathtub with a cast-brass cradle and a wood rim. Prices begin at $2,800. Information is free from Walker Industries, PO Box 129, Dept. OHJ, Bellevue, TN 37221. (615) 646-5084.

The WaterJet *Nostalgia* tub is made of cast iron and has a centered overflow. Available in white and various colors, the exterior and the legs are not glazed so they can be custom painted. Prices begin at $1430, and tubs can be purchased direct or through dealers nationwide. Free literature is offered by WaterJet Corporation, 8431 Canoga Ave., Dept. OHJ, Canoga Park, CA 91304. (800) 423-5519; in Calif., (213) 998-3884.

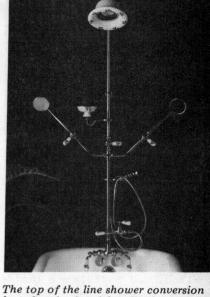

*The top of the line shower conversion from Sunrise Specialty. See bottom of the opposite page for Sunrise's address.*

Sterline manufactures *Convertos*, shower conversion fixtures such as the one pictured here, and shower rods (straight, rectangular, and corner) for period tubs. Shower curtains in white, lightweight vinyl, or plastic are $.26/sq.ft. and can be made to fit any size. Products can be purchased through Barclay, their retail sales company. For a free brochure, write Sterline Manufacturing Corp., 410 N. Oakley Blvd., Dept. OHJ, Chicago, IL 60612. (312) 226-1555; or Barclay Products Co., PO Box 12257, Dept. OHJ, Chicago, IL 60612. (312) 243-1444.

**No. 193**

SPECIAL NOTE: Montgomery Ward is currently offering the Sterline 24-in. x 42-in. brass shower ring at a reduced price of $89.98. A chrome version and the *Converto* shower are also on sale. To order, consult the phone book for a local catalog store or write to Catalog Circulation Dept., Montgomery Ward Plaza, Chicago, IL 60671.

Shower curtains to fit enclosures up to 108 in. wide and 96 in. long are sold by the Surrey Shoppe. Clear liners and matching curtains are available. A brochure, $.50, gives size, price, and color details. Surrey Shoppe Interiors, 665 Centre St., Dept. OHJ, Brockton, MA 02402. (617) 588-2525.

*Pictured above is Kohler's corner sink (left) and tub (right). To the left is WaterJet's claw-foot bathtub.*

Stringer's E.R.D. hand-crafts white
reous china pedestal sinks. The *Berke-*
*, an 1895 reproduction, is 32-in. high
d sells for $300. The *Whitney* is a
)s design, and sells for $325. (Slightly
perfect 'seconds' of these are avail-
e at reduced cost.) A catalog, $2.50,
offered. Stringer's Environmental Res-
ration & Design, 2140 San Pablo Ave.,
pt. OHJ, Berkeley, CA 94702. (415)
-8-3967.

The pedestal sink seen here is one of
e many reasonably-priced bathroom
xtures sold by Remodelers' & Reno-
tors'. The sink, complete with a brass
ik and faucet set, is $490 in hemlock
alder; $510 in oak or redwood (fit-
gs can be purchased separately). A free
talog shows this and other bath acces-
ries. Remodelers' & Renovators', 611
44th St., Dept. OHJ, Boise, ID 83704.
08) 377-5465.

For the ultimate period bathroom,
Sherle Wagner offers bathroom fixtures
such as the embossed porcelain pedestal
sink shown here ($1,200), and hand-
painted porcelain washbasins (beginning
at $350). The products seen in their 84-
page color catalog ($5) can be ordered
direct. Sherle Wagner, 60 E. 57th St.,
Dept. OHJ, New York, NY 10022. (212)
758-3300.

Known as a fabricator and importer
of brass hardware since 1857, P.E.
Guerin also carries patterned china basins in traditional designs, and embossed
pedestal sinks. These are shown in their
catalog, $5. P.E. Guerin, Inc., 23 Jane
St., Dept. BD-1, New York, NY 10014.
(212) 243-5270.

Included in Plumbing Expressions
Xtraordinaire's large selection of plumbing supplies for period bathrooms is the
pedestal sink shown here. Sinks in eleven
patterns ($835) or solid white ($745) can
be purchased direct. Matching plumbing
fixtures and accessories are also available. Their *Victorian Ensembles* brochure is free; a complete literature package is $3. **Plumbing Expressions Xtra-
ordinaire**, 3901 Rhode Island Ave.,
Dept. OHJ, Brentwood, MD 20722.
(301) 779-3775.

Bona sells oval, round, and square
drop-in sinks in fluted, hammered, embossed, or polished brass or copper. A
round, polished brass sink, 13 in. in diameter, is $135. Their catalog is free.
**Bona Decorative Hardware**, 2227 Beech-
mont Ave., Dept. OHJ, Cincinnati, OH
45230. (513) 232-4300.

Sunrise Specialty offers a choice of
three different brass shower conversions
which can be installed without 'tearing
the wall down'. The most elaborate one,
at $1000, features three independently
controlled shower heads; a simpler unit
is $450, and a combination tub-fill and
hand-shower is $425. A 12-in. round,
drop-in sink, $85, is available in white
vitreous china. A variable discount for
orders under $1000 is usually offered;
the present discount is 25% until July 1st.
Their color catalog is $1. **Sunrise Special-
ty**, 2210 San Pablo Ave., Dept. COHJ,
Berkeley, CA 94702. (415) 845-4751.

# Opinion...
# Remuddling
## — Of The Month —

**P**ERHAPS THE WINNER of this month's Remuddling Award suffers from fractoglaziphobia.* In any event, here's what the nominator has to say: "I was always disturbed when I visited a friend and saw this house nearby. It was depressing. That house was dead! Then when OHJ gave out the first Remuddling Award, I realized that what I'd been reacting to was a classic example of remuddling.

"MY FRIEND WAS INTRIGUED when explained about remuddling. Getting into the spirit of the thing, she located another hous in the neighborhood that looks exactly the way the poor house at the left used to look."

*An irrational fear of having one's windows broken.*

Submitted by: Robert Grenchik, Jr
Joliet, Ill

*The house at the left was once identical to the house above, which is a Homestead House with a somewhat unusual roofline. With aluminum siding and new windows, however, the house at the left has become an architectural style unto itself. Personal taste aside, it must be VERY DARK in there!*

![logo] **The Old-House Journal®**

69A Seventh Avenue,
Brooklyn, New York 11217

NO PAID ADVERTISING

Postmaster: Address Correction Requested

# The Old-House Journal

### Restoration and Maintenance Techniques For The Antique House

Vol. X No. 7      $2.00

# Patching Limestone & Marble

## A Step-By-Step Guide

by Lynette Strangstad

**B**ROKEN STONE STEPS are hazardous and unsightly. Believe it or not, repairing them isn't as overwhelming a job as it seems. What's needed is time, careful work, and patience; in many cases, you'll be able to tackle the job yourself. Even if you elect not to, the background information given here will help you oversee the mason who does the work.

STONE DETERIORATION is common, especially at corners and nosings (edges). A metal baluster may have rusted in the stone and expanded, causing exfoliation --the breaking away of stone layers due to pressure. Frost damage, too, is not uncommon. (After repair, you should be sure drainage is adequate to prevent ponding on or around the steps.)

YOU'LL WANT to repair damaged steps as soon as possible, not only to arrest further decay, but also for people's safety. This article will explain how to repair limestone or marble steps, corners, and nosings broken off up to approximately half the length of the step. The repair of a broken-off bottom step will be described briefly.

ON THE OTHER HAND, if your steps merely have depressions from long wear, you'll likely want to retain these as a cherished feature of your old house, one that tells of the many feet that have approached your door.

TOOLS are simple enough: several masonry chisels of varying sizes up to 1-inch, a 3-pound hammer, and some small pointing and caulking trowels. You'll also need limestone or marble dust--and getting stone dust requires some ingenuity. You can often get stone dust at quarries, stone-cutting companies, or monument (gravestone) works, where it's nothing more than the sweepings at the end of the day. For a price, artificial-stone companies may be willing to part with some marble dust.

IF YOU MUST, you can order a small quantity of stone (the smaller the blocks, the better), and break it up yourself. Just prepare to spend an afternoon in the garage with a couple of buckets, a 3-pound

*continued on page 143*

# Haunted Houses

By Henry Wadsworth Longfellow
1807 — 1882

All houses wherein men have lived and died
   Are haunted houses.  Through the open doors
The harmless phantoms on their errands glide,
   With feet that make no sound upon the floors.

We meet them at the doorway, on the stair,
     Along the passages they come and go,
Impalpable impressions on the air,
     A sense of something moving to and fro.

There are more guests at table, than the hosts
     Invited; the illuminated hall
Is thronged with quiet, inoffensive ghosts,
     As silent as the pictures on the wall.

The stranger at my fireside cannot see
     The forms I see, nor hear the sounds I hear;
He but perceives what is; while unto me
     All that has been is visible and clear.

We have no title-deed to house or lands;
     Owners and occupants of earlier dates
From graves forgotten stretch their dusty hands,
     And hold in mortmain still their old estates.

## The Old-House Journal®

**Editor**
Clem Labine

*Managing Editor*
Patricia Poore

*Assistant Editor*
Cole Gagne

*Editorial Assistants*
Joni Monnich
Stephanie Croce

*Circulation Supervisor*
Joan O'Reilly

*Circulation Assistants*
Margaret Scaglione
Barbara Bugg
Jean Baldwin

*Office Manager*
Sally Goodman

*Office Assistant*
Rafael Madera

*Circulation Director*
Paul T. McLoughlin

*Technical Consultant*
Alan D. Keiser
*Architectural Consultant*
Jonathan Poore

*Contributing Editors*
R. A. Labine, Sr.
John Mark Garrison

*Published by The Old-House Journal© Corporation, 69A Seventh Avenue, Brooklyn, New York 11217. Telephone (212) 636-4514. Subscriptions $16 per year in U.S. Not available elsewhere. Published monthly. Contents are fully protected by copyright and must not be reproduced in any manner whatsoever without specific permission in writing from the Editor.*

*We are happy to accept editorial contributions to The Old-House Journal. Query letters which include an outline of the proposed article are preferred. All manuscripts will be reviewed, and returned if unacceptable. However, we cannot be responsible for non-receipt or loss — please keep copies of all materials sent.*

**Printed at Photo Comp Press, New York City**

*ISSN: 0094-0178*
**NO PAID ADVERTISING**

*Dear Patricia,*

WE AGREE with your observations on "saving the worn spots" (OHJ, Nov.'81), and thank you for them! I don't know if you're familiar with Longfellow's lovely poem, so I've sent it along for you.  The first five stanzas will strike a chord, I think....

MY HUSBAND AND I are restoring an early 1800s landmark.  Some of the rooms have so many layers of paint on the woodwork that the paint is alligatored and the moulding details are blurred.  We intend to strip and repaint.

MY DILEMMA is this:  To what extent should we fill in the gouges, chips, drying-out cracks, etc., many of which might be relatively recent? It's easy for us to treasure a gouge in a chair-rail made by a nearby Norfolk latch, but we're not so sure about the c.1947 nicks and gouges.

CAN YOU make a statement of policy or philosophy to guide us?  We find ourselves without the time or funds to visit professional restorations, such as Williamsburg.

          *Yours sincerely,*

          *Mary Lou Charles*
          *Aurora, New York*

*Dear Mary Lou,*

PLEASE don't feel bad about not visiting large restorations.  The answers aren't there.  What's right and timely for a pure restoration, or for a history-inspired re-creation, isn't often right for a house that different generations have made a home.  There are no experts...only your sensibilities.

SOMEONE like you who stops to consider such questions probably won't make regrettable mistakes.  I think the most important advice is, WAIT.  Don't rush into anything. Live in the house; see what you grow fond of, what your favorite visitors are drawn to.  And note, too, things that become an annoyance.

HERE'S a helpful tip I heard recently.  Bill Kennedy of the Jonesborough, Tennessee, Civic Trust told me that this is the yardstick they give to contractors and volunteer workers:

> "If it's a mark of wear, leave it alone.  If it's a mark of abuse, repair it."

A RULE-OF-THUMB is no substitute for thoughtful judgement. No single rule can get you out of every dilemma, just as no single tool can do every job! I hope this "new tool" makes the job a little easier.

WHEN WE'RE sweating over a broken step or reworking a budget for the new roof, we may forget why we live in these old places. I love the poem, because it's a reminder.

*Patricia Poore*

## Post-Victorian Domestic Architecture
# The Princess Anne House

By Clem Labine

YOU'VE PROBABLY SEEN hundreds of houses like the one above--and haven't known what to call them. Don't feel bad; nobody else does either. Like most early 20th century homes, this house is a style orphan. When it was built, it was simply called a "modern house." And no architectural historian in the ensuing eighty years has attached a style name to it. So this house has lived in dignified anonymity --even though many thousands of them were built in city and suburb across the U.S. from roughly 1900 to 1920.

THESE HOUSES deserve to be rescued from obscurity because they are visually interesting, well-built dwellings with an exciting history. Recognizing this need, The Old-House Journal developed the name "Princess Anne" in our initial survey of post-Victorian architecture.

SOME NEIGHBORHOOD handbooks have called this house Queen Anne. A few others have called it an Edwardian Villa. But the designation Queen Anne is off the mark. Although the house is a direct lineal descendant of the Queen Anne house of the 1880s, it differs in several important ways from its more exuberant parent (see following page). And it is singularly unhelpful to call it an Edwardian Villa. Edwardian

merely describes the period of time (1901-1910) during which Edward VII was king of England. Many different styles of homes were built in America during this period. To call a house "Edwardian" tells you only when it was built-- not what it looks like.

### The Taste Of Two Centuries

THE PRINCESS ANNE house is fascinating be-cause it embodies the taste of two centuries. Its asymmetrical shape reflects a lingering Victorian romanticism and the love of visual richness. The relatively simple, unornamented surfaces reflect early 20th century taste: the utilitarianism of the Arts & Crafts movement, allied with the chaste restraint of the classically influenced American Renaissance.

The passions behind those conflicting turn-of-century philosophies have cooled, but the Princess Anne house remains as a tangible remind-er of that aesthetic tug-of-war.

IN ANY GENERATION, taste in archi-tecture (and everything else) is created by a dictatorship of the articulate. Those people who, through their command of language, can make a persuasive case for what they personally like create the fashions that everyone else follows. For example, in 1902 architect Joy Wheeler Dow published an impassioned series of articles in Architects' And Builders' Magazine under the title of "The American Renaissance." In these articles, Dow ridiculed the taste of the Victorian era and held up the houses of 18th century American colonists as paradigms of simplicity, restraint, and good taste. He urged all architects to journey to Annapolis, Maryland, and use the Colonial houses to be found there as models for their modern homes.

BUT THE HOME-BUYING PUBLIC always lags behind the tastemakers. Not everyone was ready for the plain simple lines of Colonial Revival homes. Some remembered with fondness the vigorous Queen Anne houses of their youth, with towers, bays, and cozy inglenooks. The Princess Anne house was perfect for this market. By retaining an exterior punctuated with gables, bays, porches, dormers, and perhaps a vestigial tower, the silhouette recalled the Queen Anne house of childhood memory. And by retaining much of the Queen Anne plan--especially the central reception hall with its prominent

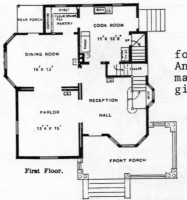

First Floor.

A Princess Anne floor plan—1901

staircase--the Princess Anne house had the homey feeling that buyers were looking for. But the Princess Anne house was not just a manifestation of nostalgia for the Victorian era; it was also a product of twentieth century rationality. By using fewer siding materials than the Queen Anne house, and by eliminating most of the ornamentation, the house looked truly "modern." And as a not incidental side benefit, the Princess Anne was cheaper to build, and easier to maintain, than its more extravagant parent.

WITH THEIR ROOMY, COMFORTABLE interiors, Princess Anne houses have been home to four generations. They have a proud history, and as more people come to understand that tradition, we look forward to hearing people boast: "I own a PRINCESS ANNE house!"

**Typical post-Victorian Princess Anne houses ➤**

George F. Barber, architect—1890

## THE QUEEN ANNE HOUSE

The Queen Anne House (1880-1900) is usually a two-storey house distinguished by asymmetrical massing and a variety of shapes and textures—all of which combine to produce a highly picturesque effect. Vertical surfaces are divided into a series of horizontal bands through the use of varying siding materials, such as stone, brick, clapboards, and shingles with differing end cuts. Steep gables, towers, dormers, balconies and verandahs further enrich the surfaces. There often is a gable in the verandah roof over the entrance. Windows often have art glass, providing a surface richness that echoes the richness of the siding materials. Porches frequently display elaborately turned spindlework, and there is sawn wood ornament decorating the verge boards and the prominent gables. Multiple roofs make a complex skyline, which is further accentuated by tall chimneys with decorative brickwork that is sometimes inset with terra cotta panels. The house often has classical details, such as swags, garlands, classical porch columns, etc.

Radford Architectural Co.—1903

## THE PRINCESS ANNE HOUSE

The Princess Anne house (1900-1920) retains much of the asymmetrical massing of its parent, but the surface treatment is much simpler. Gone are the multiple bands of shingles, each with different cuts on the butt ends. In their place are simple clapboards or straight-cut shingles—or combinations of the two. The horizontal division of the vertical surfaces is less pronounced than on the Queen Anne. Like the Queen Anne, the Princess Anne house has multiple roofs and gables— but minus the highly decorated verge boards and gable ornaments. Sometimes there will be a vestigial tower with a "candle snuffer" top. Surfaces are further elaborated with bays, oriels and verandahs—and the verandah roof frequently retains the Queen Anne gable over the entrance. The porch, like the rest of the exterior, has much less applied ornamentation than on a Queen Anne house. The Princess Anne will have an occasional classical detail (e.g., a Palladian window) which sometimes misleads people into calling it a Colonial Revival.

1909

1901

1915

1909

1902

1909

# Helpful Publications

## Victorian Gardens: How to Plan, Plant, and Enjoy Them
John Highstone
1982 (183 pp., illustrated) Paper.

GRACEFUL PATHS, twisting vines, lush green grass, colorful flowers, trellises, gazebos, and greenhouses compose the 19th century garden. This delightful book will help you incorporate these ingredients, and more, into your own special Victorian retreat. A multitude of flora types are described, along with information about their requirements and care. The appendix features useful charts of vines, flowers, trees, and shrubs to help you choose greenery most suited to your taste and region.

Bachelor's Button

To order, send $9.57 plus your local tax and $1.50 postage to:
Harper & Row, Publishers
2350 Virginia Avenue--Dept. OHJ
Hagerstown, MD 21740
(301) 824-7300

## The Windsor Style in America
Charles Santore, Edited by Thomas M. Voss
1981 (215 pp., profusely illustrated) Cloth.

THE WINDSOR STYLE, in all its variations, is studied in depth by Charles Santore, a renowned authority and true lover of the style. First popular in America between 1730 and 1830, the Windsor style has many versions. This book chronicles the comb-back, low-back, fan-back, sack-back, bow-back, rod-back, and continuous-arm chair as well as rocking chairs, settees, and children's chairs. Thoughtful, factual text and multiple photographs and line drawings make this book a must for those interested in antique American funiture.

To order, send $27.50 plus $2.00 postage to:
Running Press
125 South 22nd St.--Dept. OHJ
Philadelphia, PA 19103
(215) 567-5080

## New Life for Old Buildings
Mildred F. Schmertz, FAIA & The Editors of Architectural Record Magazine
1982 (189 pp., profusely illustrated) Cloth.

AS FINANCING AND construction costs rise, old-building owners and developers are discovering that revitalizing an old building is not only fashionable, but practical and profitable. New Life for Old Buildings is a compilation of case histories of successfully reused old structures. These adaptive reuses take all forms, from restorations to renovations and remodelings. Urban marketplaces, civic, campus and commercial buildings, restaurants and houses are some of the structures used as examples. Fully described and amply illustrated with large photographs, each case,

with its own problems and solutions, can stimulate awareness and reuse of other potentially endangered old buildings.

To order, send $32.50 ppd., plus your local tax to:
McGraw-Hill Book Company
PO Box 400--Dept. OHJ
Hightstown, NJ 08250
(609) 448-1700

## Wood Finishing and Refinishing
S.W. Gibbia
1981 (316 pp., generously illustrated) Cloth.

OF ALL THE FINISHING books in our library, this complete, unpretentious, and well-illustrated book is the best. It describes all techniques of wood finishing and refinishing, even the traditional French polish method. The step-by-step format demystifies the finish process so you can do it yourself. Coverage of filling, bleaching, stain removal, and sanding techniques, as well as paint removers, stains, finishes, and polishes are just some of the topics in this comprehensive book.

To order, send $16.95 ppd. to The Old-House Bookshop. You can use the order form in this issue.

## Architectural Photography
Jeff Dean
1981 (132 pp., generously illustrated) Cloth.

THIS IS A BOOK which every amateur architectural photographer should own. Written especially for preservationists, planners, architects, historians, and all those who need to take good architectural photographs, this is a comprehensive, readable, and personalized volume. It favors the use of the 35mm single-lens-reflex camera, rather than large-format view cameras, and explains in depth the use of the PC or shift lens to correct perspective distortion--an important consideration in photographing buildings. There is a chapter devoted to basics of photography as well as one on lighting and filters, film, and composition. Filled with useful hints, techniques, and illustrations, this book will help you plan and take better architectural photographs.

To order, send $19.95 ppd. (AASLH members, $14.96 ppd.) to:
American Association for State and Local History
PO Box 40983--Dept. OHJ
Nashville, TN 37204
(615) 383-5991

*This view of the Rittenhouse Inn in Bayfield, Wisconsin, could only be made with a very-wide-angle lens due to constricted surroundings.*

# A Victorian Pastime

## Setting Up Your Yard For Croquet & Roque

By Dan Maciejak, Landscape Architect, Brooklyn, N.Y.

IF YOU'RE LOOKING FOR a diversion from all the work your old house requires, you might consider the popular Victorian lawn game, croquet. The game has its origins in Paille Maille, a 13th-century French game. By the 19th century, it was enjoying great popularity in England as croquet. It has had famous devotees throughout the world. In recent times, enthusiasts have included Harpo Marx, Alexander Wollcott, Averill Harriman, Daryl Zanuck, Sam Goldwyn, and Louis Jourdan.

PERHAPS THE MOST WELL KNOWN croquet game of modern times is the one in Lewis Carroll's Alice In Wonderland. In it, flamingos were used as clubs and the balls were hedgehogs. But even if you use more traditional equipment, you'll find a somewhat mad quality to croquet-- especially if you're a beginner. The satisfying thunk of the ball when solidly hit, the smooth roll towards the hoop, the nudging aside of an opponent's ball--these are all elusive events. Yet the game is popular with people of all ages. Governed by finesse and strategic skill rather than strength, croquet can be played by children and adults together. It is indeed a perfect game for the whole family.

### Playing Croquet

THE AMERICAN VERSION of croquet is played on a grassy court that is, at its maximum, 100 ft. long by 50 ft. wide. There are two standard layouts for the nine-hoop game (illustrated on pages 140 and 141). The game is also played on a six-hoop court, 28 yd. by 35 yd., which is modeled after the standard six-hoop British layout. Free-style courts are laid out as dictated by space. The U.S. Croquet Association recommends a minimum rectan-

gular court that is 40 ft. by 50 ft. But whichever court you choose to use, you'll need hoops, pegs, and four balls: two per side, black and blue vs. red and yellow.

THE HOOPS, OR WICKETS, should be made of sturdy metal. Beginners should use large ones; skillful players will find narrower hoops more challenging. The interior width of the hoop can vary from five to seven inches. You can make hoops out of 1/2- to 9/16-in. diameter steel rods, about 4½ to 5 feet long. Bend them around a four-inch outside diameter pipe to shape them into hoops.

PRESS OR HAMMER the hoops into the ground so that the top is about 11 inches above ground, with each hoop leg about one foot into the ground. Mark the boundaries with white chalk, closely spaced pegs, or orange plastic marking tape.

PEGS SHOULD STAND about 1½ feet above ground. (Wooden broomsticks can be used.) Mallets, pegs, and balls can be purchased from sporting goods stores or one of the many suppliers of finer equipment. (See this issue's RPN, page 148, for equipment sources.)

FOR BOTH AESTHETIC and recreational reasons, you'll want a durable lawn, or green, for your court. You might want to consider a Shakespearean lawn of chamomile. It's low growing, dense, aromatic, and can be cut like grass. But any well established lawn will provide a good playing surface.

TO HELP YOUR LAWN establish itself, don't cut it too short; 2½ to 3 inches is a good length. Cut it often enough to encourage a strong root system. After it is established for play, it can be kept somewhat shorter. To water it properly, mist it for longer periods of time, instead of quickly flooding it. This will nourish the roots without flooding them. During the hottest parts of the summer, a short lawn can brown even if it is watered well. You may have to wait for the cool fall nights to trigger healthy growth.

IF YOUR COURT develops bare spots, rearrange it and give those areas a rest. Break up hard or crusty soil with a rigid-tined rake before you spread new seed. Don't go crazy over the lawn--a friendly game of croquet does not require a crew-cut, rolled, fussed-over, expensive lawn. And there's also no need for a perfectly flat or level surface, which is as boring for play as it is to the eye. Actually, a surface with a uniform minimum pitch of 1/4 inch per foot encourages water to run off and averts ponding. (Puddles will inhibit play and damage grass roots.)

UNDULATIONS in the playing surface help make the game interesting; a slight slope adds to the challenge. Most lawns pitch away from house foundations. A dogleg court situated near the house often has a minimum surface run-off built in. In general, courts should be sited on high spots rather than on low spots, or on areas where accumulated surface runoff from adjacent higher areas is not a problem.

ALL LAWN-GAME COURTS are best sited in full sun. This helps dry them off after rains and keeps them free of litter, twigs, leaves, caterpillars, and the other seasonal nuisances spawned by shade trees. Southern and western court locations in the Eastern states are often breezier, as long as they are not hemmed in by buildings or fences. Breezy locations are also relatively bug-free for evening play. Orientation of the long axis of the court in a north-south direction will keep the sun out of the players' eyes.

## Playing Roque

OF COURSE, you might prefer a more structured game than croquet. Or maybe you just don't have enough room for an interesting croquet course. In either case, there's always roque, a croquet and billiards derivative from the turn of the century. It uses a curbed and paved court and can be played with the same equipment used in croquet. The rules for play are a complex mixture of croquet and billiards, with a vocabulary that includes innings and home runs.

A ROQUE COURT measures 30 ft. by 60 ft., with the corners chopped off to six-ft. lengths. The hoops are located in a precise manner and in formal play can be very narrow and quite challenging. (I recommend that you use croquet hoops, unless you plan tournament play.)

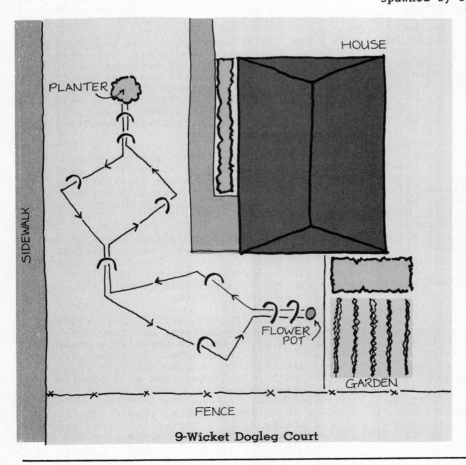

HOUSE

PLANTER

SIDEWALK

FLOWER POT

GARDEN

FENCE

9-Wicket Dogleg Court

## Roque Court Curb Detail

This illustration shows the court surface built right on the grade, with the new berm built up to the curb. If your soil conditions require that the court be built below the grade, then the excavation for the court surface can provide soil for the new berm.

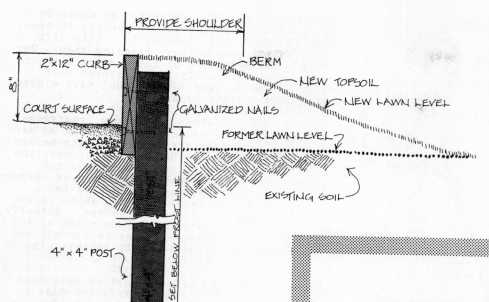

PROVIDE SHOULDER

2"×12" CURB

BERM

NEW TOPSOIL

NEW LAWN LEVEL

8"

COURT SURFACE

GALVANIZED NAILS

FORMER LAWN LEVEL

EXISTING SOIL

4" × 4" POST

SET BELOW FROST LINE

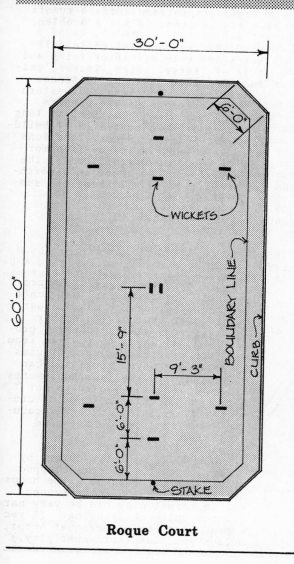

30'-0"

6'-0"

60'-0"

WICKETS

BOUNDARY LINE

CURB

15'-9"

9'-3"

6'-0" 6'-0"

STAKE

**Roque Court**

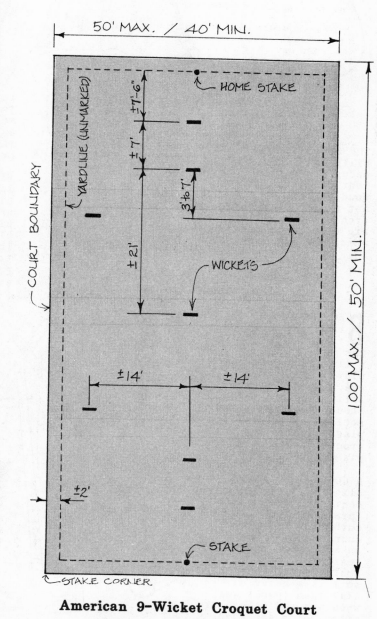

50' MAX. / 40' MIN.

HOME STAKE

±7'-6"

±7'

3' to 7'

YARDLINE (UNMARKED)

COURT BOUNDARY

±21'

WICKETS

100' MAX. / 50' MIN.

±14'

±14'

±2'

STAKE

STAKE CORNER

**American 9-Wicket Croquet Court**

THE CURBS IN ROQUE are similar to those on a billiards table, and so they have to be high enough to deflect the ball as well as resilient enough to offer carom possibilities. Wood makes a bouncier curb than concrete does, but a precast concrete curb is permanent and free of undulations. The best court surfaces are clay, compacted earth, or hard-packed sand, which are all faster than grass.

## The Roque Court

BECAUSE THE ROQUE COURT is more formal than a croquet court, care should be taken to integrate it properly into the yard. An earth court surrounded by a line of bricks may be adequate for play, but it could also offend the eye. At night, when other garden activities are under way, the area should be illuminated to prevent accidents. Victorians used to place lighted candles on the croquet hoops to facilitate playing at night.

A COURT THAT IS SET on or slightly below grade and contained with a CCA (pressure-treated) wood curb will be very economical. Pick an area that is reasonably well drained. If your soil is a heavy clay loam (packs well when wet and cakes hard after being squeezed in your hand when it's dry), build the court right on the grade. If your soil is sandy or sandy loam (crumbles when squeezed, whether it's wet or dry), set it slightly below grade because it will drain adequately.

EVEN A "SIMPLE" HAND EXCAVATION is labor intensive. For example, excavating only eight inches for an area 30 ft. by 60 ft. requires moving 1200 cubic feet of soil. Your local cesspool excavator is equipped to do this work. Chances are the expense is well worth it.

A GOOD APPROACH is to scrape off, by machine or hand shovel, the surface clods of lawn-grass roots. Level off the area and set the 2 in. by 12 in. CCA wood curbing directly on the top. Fasten it together in the shape of the court with 1 by 6 scraps, or 1/2-in. plywood planks. This will provide temporary rigidity while the construction is under way.

USING A POST-HOLE DIGGER or a gas-powered soil auger, dig post holes six feet on center below the frost line for 4 in. by 4 in. cedar or CCA posts. Set them in to the proper depths and alignment, using a mason's cord on end posts. Then pack in the excavated soil to hold them in place. Nail the 2 in. by 12 in. curbing onto the posts, using 3-inch, hot-dipped, galvanized nails.

FILL IN THE COURT AREA to a height of eight inches below the top of the curb, using a combination of materials which provides drainage and a good playing surface. Some possible combinations are: two inches of 3/4-inch crushed bluestone, topped by 1½ inches of "blend" (bluestone breaker dust); 3½ inches of basalt trap rock screenings, including dust and stone particles no greater than a half inch in diameter; or 1½ inches of clay and sand, mixed two to one, set on two inches of "clinkers" (crushed hard brick or crushed gravel).

AFTER THOROUGH SOAKING, any of the above surfaces can be either rolled with a 400-lb. roller or just permitted to weather in place. Over the course of the first year, an unrolled surface can settle and tighten from rain and use. If settling is uneven, fill in with the topping material as required. Spray paint the playing line (boundary line), using two boards placed an inch apart as a stencil.

*Illustrations by Patti Allison*

# steps continued from page 133

hammer, and some fine screening. The stone is relatively soft and powders easily. As you work, transfer the finest grains to the second bucket, so your efforts are spent on the coarser stone. You want "dust" of a uniform size.

IN ADDITION, you'll need wooden forms to help you create the final configuration of the step. These conform to the negative profile of the step nosing. Use a profile gauge (copycat) and transfer the step profile to a block of wood.

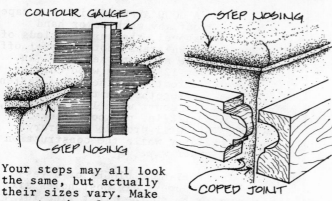

Your steps may all look the same, but actually their sizes vary. Make your tracing from the largest step. If you've got your own woodshop, you'll be able to cut it out yourself; if not, take it to a local carpenter or millshop. Be sure you have a long enough piece made up so you can cut it for corner copings, as well as a straight length for the longest nosing repair you have to make.

## Mixing the Mortar

HERE, the intention is to make the mortar look like the original stone. Experience is the key, so plan on plenty of trial time if you have no background in masonry. The mortar must match the stone in durability, color, and texture. It will be composed of portland cement, lime, and either marble or limestone dust as aggregate.

START WITH 1 part white portland cement: 1 part lime: 3 parts stone dust. Experiment with small batches (a cup or two, prepared) to approximate hardness and to determine color and texture. Hardness in this case is not a technical stone quality, but rather represents durability, or how the mortar will respond to weathering.

MIX SEVERAL BATCHES, each of a slightly different formulation, and let them cure outside for as long as possible, with two weeks a minimum and three months none too long. Then test them for hardness by scraping with a masonry chisel, comparing their resistance to that of stone.

VARY THE THREE component parts once again to get a close proximity in color. It may be necessary to reduce the white portland cement by, say, 1/4 part, replacing that with grey portland. Or perhaps an additional part of stone dust may give the right color without making the patch too soft.

AS TO TEXTURE, the grain size of the stone dust can be altered by more or less pulverizing and the size of the sifting screen you use. Beyond

Deteriorated stone steps like these are hazardous and unattractive — and they'll continue to get worse as water and debris collect in the cracks. Most people prefer to leave masonry work to the experts, but a careful do-it-yourselfer can successfully repair limestone or marble steps after a bit of practice.

that, you may attempt to expose the grain of the stone (simulating weathered stone) by lightly brushing the cured surface with a dilute solution of muriatic acid. More about that later.

## Preparing the Surface

ALONG WITH the wooden forms and mortar mix described above, you'll need reinforcing materials, epoxy, and a bonding agent, all described below. I suggest you follow this general work sequence for efficiency and best results:

(1) Prepare stone surface and armature.
(2) Mix mortar.
(3) Mix bonding agent.
(4) Spray stone surface lightly with water.
(5) Apply bonding agent.
(6) Apply mortar.
(7) Repeat water spray; shade area.

The early mixing of the mortar gives it some time to pre-shrink before use, thus reducing the degree of later shrinkage.

USE A well-sharpened masonry chisel and a hammer to cut back all broken stone faces to a sound surface. The purpose here is to create

a smooth exterior edge, at the same time undercutting the stone slightly (about 30°) to receive the mortar.

BROKEN STONE surfaces-- if they're solid and clean of dirt and debris-- may simply be washed with a dilute muriatic acid and water solution. (This provides a fresh surface to which the mortar can adhere.) A dilute solution is the equivalent of 1 acid: 6 water ratio, using a 5% acid concentration. Take care not to spill any acid in unwanted areas, as it will etch the stone surface.

WHERE DAMAGE is slight and steps require only a small repair, do not feather the edges where mortar will meet existing stone. It won't work. Mortar will soon break out at a feathered joint. Instead, cut in at least 1/4 inch, again undercutting the joint. If the deterior-

DON'T attempt to feather the edge of a shallow patch.

DO cut down to sound stone.

ated area is quite small, this may be all the preparation necessary prior to filling. In most cases, though, you'll have to use reinforcing rods.

## Reinforcing with Steel

**R**EINFORCING ROD is usually stainless steel rod, which is commonly available pre-threaded. Rods of 1/4-inch diameter are sufficient for step and nosing repair. The rods are placed in holes drilled in the stone. Holes should be at least 3/8-inch in diameter and 1/2-inch deep--large enough to easily accommodate both the rods and a thick epoxy.

THE 1/4-INCH steel rods are placed horizontally, roughly parallel to the top of the step, about 1/2 inch below its surface. A small electric drill with masonry bits easily drills small holes into marble or limestone. Take care, of course, not to drill too near the edge of the stone or with too large a bit; otherwise, you may break off more stone. Now clean dust out of holes with a small air compressor or water from a garden hose. A small spray bottle will also do the job.

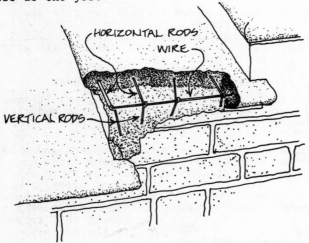

IF THE NOSING to be repaired is broken for an extended length, or if the broken corner area is large, you should supplement the initial rods with small auxiliary ones--in this case, heavy-gauge stainless steel wire set into holes drilled in the stone perpendicular (i.e., vertical) to the main reinforcing rods. These wires, when in place, will meet the main rods and can be epoxied to them for extra strength.

A broken corner is ready for mortaring, with stainless steel armature in place. Liquid soap is brushed on wood forms to make it easy to part them from the set mortar patch.

FURTHERMORE, WIRE can be stretched between rods to form an armature, as in the photo above. If the damaged area is wide, drill small holes (1/4 inch or less) at 2-inch intervals along the stone sub-surface. These provide mechanical keying for the bonding agent and mortar.

## Anchoring with Epoxy

**E**POXY is used as the adhesive anchoring the armature of reinforcing materials to the stone. Industrial-strength epoxies are formulated in a variety of strengths and working consistencies for different uses. If you're ordering the epoxy from a supply house, specify that you want a formulation for use on limestone or marble. (See the Supply Box on page 147.)

A GEL-CONSISTENCY epoxy is recommended for anchoring reinforcing rods to stone. It's a bit difficult to mix, but a small electric drill with mixer attachment works well. Measure carefully, because the proportion of hardener to resin affects the strength of the cured epoxy. Pot life of the mixed epoxy is about 20 minutes, varying with the outdoor temperature, so mix only as much as you can use in that time.

WEAR RUBBER GLOVES, respirator, and general protective clothing. Epoxies are great adhesives, but they are toxic until cured, and are strong skin sensitizers as well. Once the epoxy is mixed, use a small dowel or heavy wire to place it in the holes drilled for the rods. Put the reinforcing rods in place, checking with a straight-edge to be sure the rods don't extend above the surface of the step or beyond the corner. Once the rods are set, allow at least 24 hours for the epoxy to cure.

## Using Bonding Agents

**B**ONDING AGENTS are designed to ensure a strong bond between the new mortar mix and the existing stone. Both acrylic and epoxy bonding agents are on the market today for use on masonry. The jury is still out on whether acrylic should be used outside, so many people prefer epoxy. A medium-viscosity epoxy, specially formulated to join new mortar to old mortar or existing stone, provides a good bond. (An example is Sika Hi-Mod.)

AN EPOXY bonding agent needs to be mixed just prior to application, it's initially toxic, and it requires a solvent for clean-up. Epoxy (and acrylic) formulations present the theoretical problem of setting up a water barrier behind the patch, which could result later in spalling of patches under certain conditions.

THERE IS a traditional alternative: use of a slurry consisting of 1 part portland cement, 1/2 part lime, and 3 parts sand. This formulation allows water permeability and is weak enough not to set up undue stresses. Your choice may depend on your faith in either traditional methods or modern technology!

THE BONDING AGENT should be applied according to manufacturer's directions, just before you apply the base coat of mortar. Use a small glue brush to cover the entire sub-surface of the stone. Take care not to get any on the exterior surface of the step, as you may be left with a stain that's difficult to remove.

## Applying the Base Coat

**D**EPENDING ON the depth and complexity of the repair, a base coat of mortar may be needed under the finish coat. If the size and depth of the area to be patched is moderate and not more than an inch deep, you might eliminate a base coat and do the job in one operation. But shrinkage must be taken into account, and the greater

---

**F**OR THOSE with good masonry skills, the following is an outline of the repair sequence for return steps. Repairing broken returns at the base of steps is similar to step repair, but more difficult. A concrete base may have to be laid below grade to support the return, because insufficient support is often the reason for its failure.

If the return is broken off in a single piece, it can be reattached with a 1-inch reinforcing rod. You can use threaded stainless steel rod again, or switch to Teflon rod — if you can find it. Teflon is strong, dimensionally stable, and chemically inert. But you'll undoubtedly have to thread it yourself. Cut a spiral groove into it by hand or with a 1/4-inch die.

Drill matching holes well into the broken return and the existing step. Glue the rod in with epoxy. To make it easier to set, level, and line up the heavy stone, let the epoxy cure around the rod in one hole before coating all other surfaces with epoxy and affixing the return. Use epoxy on the broken faces and all along the rod.

If a gap exists where part of the stone is missing due to previous breakage, fill it using a bonding agent and the previously-described mortar mix. If no gap exists, an epoxy can be used to glue the two pieces together.

If the return is still there, but seriously deteriorated, it must be cut back to sound stone, and rebuilt using a stainless steel armature both for reinforcement and to approximate the shape of the return. The stone mix is built up in layers, day by day, until the final configuration is reached through hand-sculpting and carefully measured comparison with an existing return. This is all pretty complex and requires previous experience.

Matching holes are drilled in the step and its broken-off return. Then, a threaded steel or Teflon rod is used like a dowel to reinforce the connection. Epoxy acts as the adhesive for both the rod and the masonry bond.

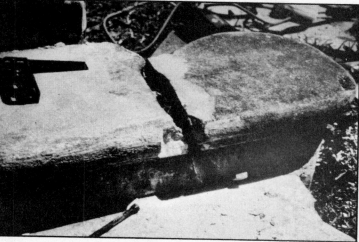

Here, the broken return has been reattached — mortar will fill the gap.

A stainless steel armature reinforces and gives shape to a badly deteriorated return step.

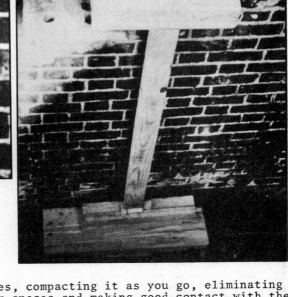

The finish coat of mortar is troweled into the wood forms, which are tamped into place on the step. Note the propping of forms, right. The block of wood near the edge is merely a spacer for a baluster that will be re-inserted later.

the volume of mortar applied, the likelier it is that shrinkage cracks will occur. They aren't a problem in the base coat, but you don't want any cracks in the finish coat.

A GOOD REASON to apply a base coat is to save on stone dust. The base coat can consist of the same proportions of the elements of the finish coat mix described earlier--but with the substitution of uniformly fine, sharp sand in place of stone dust. Always leave at least 1/4 to 1/2 inch as a minimum depth for the finish coat. Leave the base coat quite rough, or score it while still wet, to provide keying for the finish coat.

THE WET MORTAR should be fairly stiff, but still workable. It is applied directly over the wet bonding agent with pointing and caulking trowels. Take care to press the mortar into all

crevices, compacting it as you go, eliminating all air spaces and making good contact with the stone surface and bonding agent.

IF YOUR MORTAR MIX begins to dry too soon, you can add a small amount of water to re-temper it. Do keep in mind that frequent re-tempering results in a seriously weakened mortar.

IF THIS IS a base coat, it's a good idea to apply it early in the morning. Then it will have set up enough for you to apply a finish coat later the same afternoon. If instead the base coat is applied late in the day, it can be covered lightly with damp cheesecloth, and misted periodically with water. Or the area

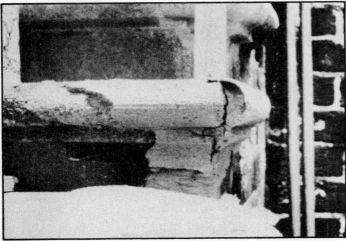

This photo was taken after the wood forms were removed from the finish coat, but before hand-sculpting was done.

Here, missing mortar has been filled in by hand, and high spots have been trimmed away.

can be covered with plastic. By retarding curing, you can apply the finish coat directly to the base coat the next morning.

IDEALLY, the finish coat should be applied before the base coat is completely cured. If the work is interrupted, apply your bonding agent again to the base coat after it's completely cured. Then trowel the finish coat directly over that.

## Sculpting the Finish

YOUR MIX for the finish coat contains the stone dust. Dampen the surface again before applying the finish coat. First, fill all voids up to the nosing level. Then, coat the wooden forms with liquid soap (as a parting agent so the mortar won't stick), fill them with mortar mix, and tamp firmly into place on the step. Leave no voids in the new patch.

NOW, SECURE the forms with clamps, props, or simply by fitting them along the existing nosing. All flat areas of risers and steps are next hand-tooled. As with the base coat, the area is kept damp and shaded, to avoid shrinkage cracks or overly rapid drying of the mortar.

THE WOODEN FORM is removed after two or three hours, depending on temperature. To remove, tap the form gently along its length to loosen it, and slide it off the new patch. You may need to add mortar even at this point. Final sculpting is done by hand.

YOU MAY well wonder why, when you've gone to such trouble to make and use wooden forms, the final effect is still achieved by hand. In fact, some people--sculptors with a steady hand and a practiced eye--can do without the forms on smaller patches. But the job is much easier with forms; they also hold the mortar firmly in place as it begins to set up, so there's no "sag" in larger patches.

THE FINAL TOUCH--bringing everything into square or round--is up to you. A quarter-inch pointing tool works well for most of this work, used with a light touch and a smooth, scraping motion to reduce high spots. Remember that you made the form to the size of the largest step. It is easier and surer now to reduce high areas than to build up low spots.

ONCE THE SCULPTING is complete, this, too, must be kept shaded, covered with damp cheesecloth, and misted for several days if the weather is hot and dry. Or cover the steps with plastic.

## Cleaning Up

CLEAN-UP IS SIMPLE, as long as excess mortar falls only on stone areas. Avoid getting even a thin wash on surrounding brick areas, and wash it off immediately if you do. Once the patch is cured, much surrounding mortar can be scrubbed off with a brush and water. If that doesn't work, remove it with a solution of muriatic acid and water. This is also the time to run a light, dilute acid wash over your patch if you want to expose the grain to match weathered stone. Follow this with water in a few seconds. A light touch is best here--begin with a sample patch of cured mortar--not the step itself!

IN NEXT MONTH'S ISSUE.........PATCHING BROWNSTONE

### SUGGESTIONS FOR SUPPLIERS

THE TOOLS you'll need are available at most hardware or masonry supply stores. We've also listed some mail-order sources for high-quality masonry tools and equipment on page 148.

EPOXY can be purchased at contractor's building-supply houses, plumbing suppliers, some large hardware stores, and through companies such as these:

Abatron, Inc.
141 Center Drive
Gilberts, IL 60136
(312) 426-2200 — call for specific information.

Sika Corp.
Box 297
Lyndhurst, NJ 07071
(Write for specific literature and name of your closest distributor.)

NOTE: Epoxies may vary slightly from one company to another in application and use, so be sure to check product literature. If you have particular questions regarding epoxy use, call a sales representative.

STAINLESS STEEL ROD, too, is purchased through commercial or contractor's hardware stores; try at local machine shops, too.

TEFLON ROD may only be available through commercial plastics companies.

**Lynette Strangstad** has been a millwork apprentice and furniture restorer in Wisconsin; a researcher for a gravestone preservation project in South Carolina; a restoration masonry artisan in New York City. During her two-year apprenticeship with the National Trust's Restoration Workshop in Tarrytown, N.Y., she was project foreman for work done at Drayton Hall in Charleston. The photos accompanying this article were taken during limestone stair-tread repair there.

We'll be running other articles by Lynette this year, including one on patching brownstone and another on cleaning marble.

A special thank you to Alan Keiser and the Restoration Workshop, National Trust for Historic Preservation.

# Restoration Products News

## Ultimate Croquet

To play croquet as described in the article on page 139, you can readily purchase equipment from your local toy or department store (for about $15-$30). When you become a true aficionado, holding Victorian tournament parties, you might opt for championship-quality equipment. John Jaques offers sets ranging in price from $350 to $1325. The sets contain four hardwood mallets (with hickory or ash handles) and balls; along with a choice of nine or six wickets, and one or two pegs. Accessories and individual items are also sold. For free information contact Croquet International Ltd., John Jaques & Son, Ltd., 635 Madison Ave., Dept. OHJ, New York, NY 10022. (212) 688-5495.

## Linoleum Today

*We never thought we'd be listing sources for linoleum flooring. But as a result of the Jan. and Feb. 1982 articles about linoleum, subscribers helped to put us in touch with suppliers of this period flooring, in addition to donating numerous samples. Linoleum may not be an historical floor covering for all houses, but it can lend the perfect period touch to an early 20th-century room.*

Tony Lauria supplies an authentic *battleship* linoleum, in six solid, inlaid colors—beige, terra-cotta, black, brown, dark green, and grey. (The color isn't printed on the surface, but throughout the material.) This durable, long-lasting flooring is 1/8-in. thick, can be cut in any length with widths up to 6 ft., and is even burlap backed. The price is $3/sq. ft. and includes delivery. Free samples are offered with a SASE. We were astonished by the quality and richness of this material. Tony Lauria, RD 2, Box 253B, Dept. OHJ, Landenberg, PA 19350. (215) 268-3441.

Mannington Mills offers two inexpensive floor coverings, with several patterns reminiscent of turn-of-the-century linoleum. *Thrift-tex* is an asphalt-saturated felt in nine oil-based painted designs and twenty colorations. A 9 ft. x 12 ft. roll is

*Manolux*　　　　*Thrift-tex*

$23-$25/roll. *Manolux* is a vinyl printed flooring that's sold in ten designs and seventeen colorations. Rolls 9 ft. x 12 ft., and 12 ft. x 15 ft., are about $10 more than *Thrift-tex*. Both of these products are designed as temporary, low-wear floorings, which are not recommended for high-traffic areas. But with their low cost and unusual patterns, they could provide an appropriate finishing touch to a room. For a free pattern chart and the location of a dealer in your area, contact Mannington Mills, Inc., PO Box 30, Dept. OHJ, Salem, NJ 08079. (609) 935-3000.

## Southern Details

When the supply of architectural antiques began to dwindle, Nostalgia decided to make their own reproductions of details common to the Savannah area. Included in this selection are two delightful *Dolphin* downspouts—utilitarian as well as ornamental. The model pictured here is a reproduction from an original 1820-1860 casting. Made from cast aluminum, it's 58 in. long, 5-in. in diameter, and is finished to resemble cast iron. The cost for this intricately detailed casting is $200. A catalog showing these and other reproductions is $1.50; the individual downspout sheet is $.50. Nostalgia, Inc., 307 Stiles Avenue, Dept. OHJ, Savannah, GA 31401. (912) 236-8176.

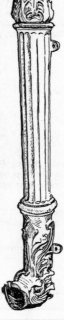

## Masonry Tools

*Trowels and other common masonry tools are generally available at your local hardware store. For those who believe that the highest-quality tools are an economical investment, though, we've listed here two mail-order sources that sell a complete selection of fine masonry tools and equipment.*

Goldblatt's trowels, shown here, feature a steel ferrule and maple handle; prices begin at $5.65. Long-time OHJ readers may remember this company as the source for the *Glitter Gun*, which can be used for sand-painted finishes. (See OHJ, Sept. 1979 for an article on Sand Painting.) In addition, Goldblatt offers other trowels, floats, brushes, scaffolding, etc. in their free catalog. Goldblatt Tool Co., 511 Osage, PO Box 2334, Dept. OHJ, Kansas City, KS 66110. (913) 621-3010.

Masonry Specialty carries high-quality masonry equipment, including Marshalltown trowels. This tuck point rake, $11.80, is made of tempered steel and can be used to clean old mortar from brick joints. A full selection of tools and equipment can be seen in their free *Tools and Equipment* catalog. Masonry Specialty Co., 4430 Gibsonia Road, Dept. OHJ, Gibsonia, PA 15044. (412) 443-7080.

*Correction...*

## Interior Storms

In the April issue we described *Magnetite* interior storm windows. These top-of-the-line acrylic storms must be dealer-installed; we mistakenly said that components could be purchased separately. Components for do-it-yourself magnetic storm-window installations are also available and can be purchased at local hardware stores or from companies like Plaskolite (also described in the April issue). For more information about the *Magnetite* brand window, contact Viking Energy Systems Co., 275 Circuit St., Dept. OHJ, Hanover, MA 02339 (617) 871-3180.

# Period-Inspired Toilets

*On this page, we continue our list of companies offering period-inspired bathroom fixtures (please refer back to last month's issue). Many companies have begun to offer high-tank toilets. Listed here are a few sources for these and other historical toilets.*

Similar to the 1902 toilet pictured in OHJ, June 1982, page 128, this unusual oak toilet, $699, is available from **Heads Up.** Their high-tank toilet with a plastic tank liner is only $299, not including a wood seat. For a free brochure, write Heads Up, 2980 E. Blue Star, Unit B, Dept. OHJ, Anaheim, CA 92806. (714) 630-5402.

**A-Ball's** high-tank toilet is $535, their low-tank toilet is $495; both have a fiberglass tank liner. The wash-down bowl pictured here is $60. Individual components which you can use as replacement parts, or to create your own old-fashioned fixture, are also found in their free catalog. A-Ball Plumbing Supply, 1703 W. Burnside, Dept. OHJ, Portland, OR 97209. (503) 228-0026.

**Sunrise Specialty's** high-tank toilet is $650. The price includes a copper liner, brass fittings and decorative brackets, and an oak seat. An oak low-tank toilet costs $550. A 25% direct-order discount applies to these and other items shown in their catalog, $1. Sunrise Specialty, 2210 San Pablo Avenue, Dept. COHJ, Berkeley, CA 94702. (415) 845-4751.

**Barclay** has a relatively inexpensive solution to creating a period-look toilet. The toilet tank cover, $150 (pictured here), fits over an existing tank. This and a high-tank toilet with a plastic tank liner, $635, are shown in a free color brochure. Barclay Products Co., PO Box 12257, Dept. OHJ, Chicago, IL 60612. (312) 243-1444.

*Stringer's Pill-Toilet*

**Stringer's E.R.D.** offers the *Pill Toilet* shown here. This c.1910 porcelain toilet costs $160 for the tank top and bowl. For a catalog, $2.50, write Stringer's Environmental Restoration & Design, 2140 San Pablo Avenue, Dept. OHJ, Berkeley, CA 94702. (415) 548-3967.

**Kohler's** *Vintage* is a high-tank toilet with an all-porcelain tank for ease of cleaning and the sanitary look which became popular about 1910. In polished chrome, without a seat, this toilet costs $465. For free information, specify the *Elegance* brochure. Kohler Co., Dept. OHJ, Kohler, WI 53044. (414) 457-4441.

## Seats

In addition to a full line of oak accessories, **DeWeese** makes oak toilet seats. These have brass hinges and are coated with a moisture-resistant lacquer in a light or dark finish. The standard size is $47.50, and the elongated is $51, delivered. For a free brochure, write DeWeese Woodworking Co., PO Box 576, Dept. OHJ, Philadelphia, MS 39350. (601) 656-4951.

# Opinion...
# Remuddling
## —Of The Month—

OUR REMUDDLING AWARD is normally reserved for insensitive alterations to houses. But this month's winner (a public building) is so breath-taking in its audacity that we had to share it with you. It's a brilliant negative example of Golden Rule #1 for sensitive rehabilitation: Thou shalt not destroy good old work! Here's what the OHJ subscriber who nominated this building has to say about it:

"THE ENGRAVING shows the Crawford County Court House in Robinson, Ill., as it looked when completed around 1895. It was a handsome brick and stone structure, with a tower having a Seth Thomas time-and-strike tower clock. Just after WWII, some bright souls decided that the tower was unsafe and that the building needed modern-izing. About 1948 a local contractor "improved" the building as shown below. Residents of the county have come to mourn the loss of character of this building. Old postcards and illustrations of the court house have appeared in local newspapers, with a general sense of regret. A few years ago there was talk of modernizing an equally handsome court house in a nearby county. But local citizens became enraged that their building might suffer the same fate as the one in Robinson, and the plan was dropped."

Submitted by: Chris H. Bailey, Managing Director, American Clock & Watch Museum, Bristol, Connecticut

At first glance, this structure looks like it might be a Moderne building from the 1930s. Only the semi-circular arches at the entrances provide a clue that the building once boasted . . .

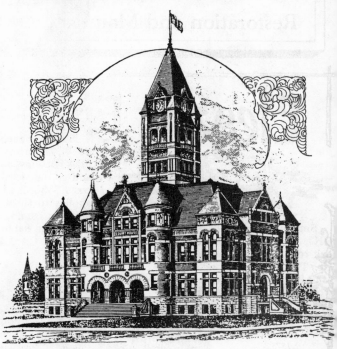

. . . a fanciful roofline with towers, finials, and cresting, along with round-headed windows and heavy transom bars that are the hallmarks of the robust Romanesque Revival style.

# The Old-House Journal®

69A Seventh Avenue,
Brooklyn, New York 11217

NO PAID ADVERTISING

Postmaster: Address Correction Requested

The
Old-House
Journal

Restoration and Maintenance Techniques For The Antique House

Vol. X No. 8        $2.00

# Elegant Embellishments
## American Gazebos of the 18th & 19th Centuries
by Ed Polk Douglas

*Binghamton, N.Y.
c.1875*

*A gazebo revival? Voices from the past tell us what we need to know about their history, usefulness, design, and placement in the garden.*

*Medford,
Mass.
c.1760*

IN OUR FINEST PLACES, or those country seats where much of the polish of pleasure ground or park scenery is kept up, one of the most striking defects is the want of 'union between the house and the grounds.'

SO WROTE American critic and tastemaker A.J. Downing (1815-1852) in his Theory and Practice of Landscape Gardening (1841). To remedy this deficiency, Downing recommends the addition of architectural embellishments and garden decorations to the grounds of both villas and cottages because of the "increased variety and richness imparted to the whole scene."

FOR DOWNING, the term "architectural embellishments" covered quite a large territory: terraces, sundials, balustrades, vases, fountains, rockwork, arbors, bridges, prospect towers, pavilions, open and covered seats. In this article,

I'll limit myself to "covered seats," or gazebos. These, according to Downing, are of two distinct types:

...one *architectural*, or formed after artist-like designs, of stone or wood, in Grecian, Gothic, or other forms; which may, if they are intended to produce an elegant effect, have vases or pedestals as accompaniments; the other, *rustic*, as they are called, which are formed out of trunks and branches of trees, roots, etc., in their natural forms.

THE WORD GAZEBO is odd and of uncertain origin. It is sometimes defined as a rooftop turret commanding an extensive view--20th century writers commonly use "cupola" or "belvedere" for this meaning. More often--and in this discussion--a gazebo is a man-made structure of

*cont'd on p. 166*

**The OHJ Staff** Here we are in Prospect Park with our new award.
*Back row:* Jean Baldwin, Ray Madera, Joan O'Reilly, and Barbara Bugg.
*Middle row:* Joni Monnich, Peggy Scaglione, and Cole Gagne.
*Front row:* Clem Labine, Patricia Poore, and Sally Goodman.

# The Old-House Journal®

*Editor*
**Clem Labine**

*Managing Editor*
**Patricia Poore**

*Assistant Editor*
**Cole Gagne**

*Editorial Assistant*
**Joni Monnich**

*Circulation Supervisor*
**Joan O'Reilly**

*Circulation Assistants*
**Margaret Scaglione**
**Barbara Bugg**
**Jean Baldwin**

*Office Manager*
**Sally Goodman**

*Office Assistant*
**Rafael Madera**

*Circulation Director*
**Paul T. McLoughlin**

*Technical Consultant*
**Alan D. Keiser**

*Architectural Consultant*
**Jonathan Poore**

*Contributing Editors*
**R. A. Labine, Sr.**
**John Mark Garrison**

Published by The Old-House Journal©
Corporation, 69A Seventh Avenue,
Brooklyn, New York 11217. Telephone
(212) 636-4514. Subscriptions $16 per
year in U.S. Not available elsewhere.
Published monthly. Contents are fully
protected by copyright and must not
be reproduced in any manner whatsoever without specific permission in
writing from the Editor.

We are happy to accept editorial contributions to The Old-House Journal.
Query letters that include an outline
of the proposed article are preferred.
All manuscripts will be reviewed, and
returned if unacceptable. However,
we cannot be responsible for non-
receipt or loss — please keep copies
of all materials sent.

**Printed at Photo Comp Press,**
New York City

*ISSN: 0094-0178*
**NO PAID ADVERTISING**

# It's Nice To Be Appreciated

**L**ET'S FACE IT: Staff and read-ers alike, The Journal family is pretty unusual. Being wrapped up in good work, an admiration of quality, and an ethic of conservation and preservation isn't exactly mainstream. But we cheerfully believe in what we publish, and we're having fun. Subscribers believe that time spent fixing up old houses is worthwhile--for lots of reasons. Judging from your letters, you're having fun, too.

BUT IT'S especially nice to be appreciated from outside the family. The OHJ was recently awarded a Certificate of Merit for "Creative Leadership in the field of Historic Preservation." This honor, our sixth award, was bestowed by the State of New York.

**P**EOPLE don't get recognition awards unless there's some tangible evidence of their con-tribution. Given that there are only ten of us here in the of-fice--and 65,000 of you out there working--it holds that it was the whole OHJ family who was recognized.

YOU'RE PART of that "creative leadership." Readers take an active creative role in The Journal, of course. (You really wrote the Dip-Strip piece on page 157.) And old-house people are blazing a trail.

**I**N AN OFFICE MEMO telling the staff about the award, I was downright proud: "This Certifi-cate is no empty honor. We didn't get it because we're new. (We've been around for al-most a decade.) We didn't get for being flashy. (Slick isn't our style!) We didn't get it because we're too big to ignore. (There are bigger magazines with more subscribers.)

"WE MUST have been noticed for a very special reason. We've been honored for consistent quality, integrity, and seed-sowing thoughtfulness."

THAT GOES for everybody associ-ated with our little newsletter. Preserving old houses isn't new, flashy, or big. But preserva-tion benefits neighborhoods; thus, we think, it lifts the spirit of the country.

*Patricia Poore*

Old-House Living...

# The House On Pleasant Street
## Restoring With Patience Instead Of Money

By Cole Gagne

RODNEY AND LYNN POLING looked at dozens of Massachusetts houses before they came upon the house on Pleasant Street. This lovely 1835 Victorian was exactly what they wanted: an untouched house with a lot of detail. It was also exactly what many other people wanted, and so the Polings had to submit a sealed bid along with over 300 other applicants. After a suspenseful waiting period, they made it to the semi-finals and from there, finally, to the house itself.

ONE REASON for the Polings' attraction to the house was that it had never suffered the heartbreak of remuddling. In the 1880s, it had passed into the hands of the Frost family, and two of the children, George and Mildred, lived in it until 1979. Mildred had made it a practice not to discard anything connected with the house. She would meticulously bundle, label, and store away everything in the barn.

THIS BARN, built in 1870, was part of the Polings' purchase, and with it they obtained a wealth of Frost family memorabilia, household items, woodwork, and more. Mildred's thoroughness proved invaluable when the Polings began to fix up the house. Among the rarities they discovered were lumber and shingles dating back to 1835, when the house was first built.

THERE WAS ANOTHER fringe benefit when the Polings bought the house; 15 tons of coal had

This photo shows most of the major features of the Polings' kitchen: the unglazed quarry tile floor, the island cabinet (lower left), the cabinets that Rod built, one of the two ceiling fixtures, and the tin ceiling.

been left in the cellar bin. But the house did come with something of a mixed blessing. George Frost had moved a wood-frame train station onto the property in the 1920s.

THE LITTLE STATION was totally falling apart by 1979, despite the fact that cement had been poured into its walls! (Ceramic blocks had been set into the plaster of its interior walls, and the cement was apparently someone's misguided attempt to stabilize the walls.) The station posed other problems as well. Not only did it obstruct the view of the house from the street, but it was also situated precisely where Rod and Lynn had to put their driveway. They decided to have the station torn down, making sure that the job was done as carefully as possible so they could salvage its woodwork, trim, and doors.

## Problems

THE BIGGEST PROBLEM with the house itself was the kitchen. It had a pantry and a back porch, which were both badly deteriorated (which is putting it mildly, seeing as how a tree was actually growing out of them). They had never been built with a real foundation, and so had always stood on nothing more than some bricks. After going over this termite-ridden mess, Rod and Lynn decided to gut and rip them out and then have them rebuilt with a foundation and a crawlspace.

THESE REPAIRS meant that the family had to live without a functional kitchen for months. Part of the time, the only water for the kitchen came from the backyard hose; the only food they could cook was whatever would fit into a microwave oven, which they kept in the dining room--along with the refrigerator.

ONCE THE KITCHEN was completed, Rod and Lynn went all out to fix it up. To eliminate the sags in the floor, they had a contractor put 2 x 8's under every other floorboard. This reinforcement was also required because the Polings then covered the floor with unglazed quarry tile, doing all the laying, grouting, and sealing themselves.

A LARGE ISLAND CABINET, salvaged from the old train station, was set up in the kitchen and topped with an elegant marble slab. The other cupboards for the kitchen were built by Rod himself, using salvaged door and cabinet fronts and old lumber. He designed the cupboards to match the island cabinet, and gave them marble tops as well. A tin ceiling from AA-Abbingdon of Brooklyn was installed. Two large brass chandeliers--purchased by Rod many years ago for only $5--were added as the perfect complement to the new ceiling.

ORIGINALLY, the dining room had a walk-in closet that was also a pass-through to the kitchen. When the kitchen was rebuilt, Lynn and Rod gave it a long, uninterrupted wall by reducing the dining room closet to shelf depth. They then decided to convert the closet into a china cabinet. They removed the door's wood panels, set a stained glass window into it, and added a light. However, if some future occupant of the house should want to restore the closet door, he or she will find the intact panels carefully stored away in the barn. "If Mildred could do it, I could do it," says Rod.

THE MOST STRIKING exterior feature of the house is its Gothic trim, which was added on to the house decades after it was built--probably at the same time the barn was constructed. The house has a tradition of accommodating the graceful additions of its inhabitants, and Rod had continued the tradition. He did all the stencilling in the hallways and downstairs bathroom and built a picket fence that runs some 50 feet along the property. Neither the stencilling nor the fence are precise reproductions of period work. Rather, they are Rod's original designs in Victorian styles that are consonant with the look of the house.

## Inevitabilities

The dining room closet was modified into a china cabinet by Rod and Lynn.

MOST OF THE INEVITABLE REPAIRS have been taken care of by now. Floors have been sanded and several rooms have been papered and painted. Of course, more work needs to be done. Two upstairs bedrooms have to be painted and stencilled. The front porch needs some work, siding has to be renailed, and the exterior is due for a polychrome paint job.

This triptych shows the fall and rise of a house. On the opposite page is a photo taken in 1880, the year the Frost family moved in. Above left is the sight that first greeted the Polings in 1979. The house is completely obscured by almost a century's growth of trees and by the train station. Above right is a recent photo of the house. The station is gone and a lot of trees have been cleared. Work remains to be done, but the house is definitely headed back to its original harmony with the landscape.

ALL THIS WORK will be done with the same basic approach Rod and Lynn have used all along. The entire restoration has been a matter of living with the house and getting a clear idea of precisely what was needed. Then they slowly and methodically could track down--or just luckily come across--exactly what they had envisioned. It required plenty of visits to auctions, junkyards, and salvage stores. It also took a lot of time. As Rod Poling says, "We have tried to use patience and a good eye to substitute for a large bankroll."

Right above: The elder Frosts, 1907. A lot of the Victoriana pictured, along with some of the children's clothes, are now in the Polings' possession. Right below: A detail from a portrait of the Frost family. George and Mildred are first and third from left. Above: The Polings' back parlor today. Note the portrait of George and Mildred.

# Tips From Readers
# Restorer's Notebook

### Lead Vs. Mildew

YOUR OCTOBER 1981 "ASK OHJ" recommends using penta to combat mildew on roof shingles. Penta will work, but it is rather short lived. It's also dangerous: Being oil based, it can lead to roof fires. And of course, it is extremely toxic. I suggest a different method. Put a strip of 4-lb. lead under the ridge coping. The "acid rain" seems to cause lead oxide to run down the shingles, and this material will kill moss and algae.

Andrew B. Buckner
Blackmore & Buckner Roofing, Inc.
Indianapolis, IN

### Removing Wallpaper Paste

FIGHTING TO GET OFF all the wallpaper paste on my 1906 house's ceiling was wearing out my arm. In desperation, I grabbed my Dobie pad from the kitchen. It worked perfectly! To clean it, I run it under the bathtub spouts.

Birdie Bates
Kellogg, IA

### More On Screw Heads

THE JANUARY 1982 "Restorer's Notebook" had an item on polishing screw heads. It reminded me of a quick and easy way of holding screws upright for painting, lacquering, etc. Simply take a bar of soap and jam the screws into it. No need to find a scrap of wood and drill holes into it for the screws. You can even get the paint or lacquer off the soap after a few washings.

Ted Lyon
Rochester, NY

### Repairing Scratched Glass

IN THE MAY 1982 "ASK OHJ," a reader asked what could be done to minimize scratches in her mirror glass. I recommend that she try rubbing the scratches very lightly with a common, mildly abrasive toothpaste. If the scratches are small enough and/or not too deep, this just might work. Rub in the toothpaste with a cotton-gloved fingertip or a small, soft pad. Polish it every so often to judge progress. (The glove and pad are suggested to save fingertips, not the mirror.)

C.A. "Bing" Perry IV
Dallas, TX

### Getting Old Glass

SALVAGED OLD GLASS is an inexpensive replacement for the broken window panes in your old house. Old glass with wavy surfaces and air bubbles can be obtained from building wrecking sites free or at a nominal cost. Another source is used building material yards, where a beat-up window sash--complete with glass--can be purchased more cheaply than the cost of the glass alone.

SEPARATING THE GLASS from the sash is hard work. You'll probably break it if you attempt to remove the old glazing putty. But you can cut the sash (and putty) away from the glass. Make a diagonal cut through the corner joint. Set the sash on the ground in a vertical position, with the severed joint at the top. Hold the horizontal sash member with your foot and carefully pull the sash away from the glass. Pull off any remaining putty with pliers.

Paul Schoenharl
Cincinnati, OH

### Researching Your House

I WANTED TO WRITE and share some of my research experience with other readers who may be having trouble finding information on their "new" old houses.

TO FIND OUT what was done before the remuddling, I went to the Minneapolis Bureau of Titles and Permits. They provided me with a photocopy of the original permit to build the house. It listed the original owner, the architect, and the contractor, as well as costs and dates.

WITH THIS INFORMATION, I took to the phone book to check for the same last names. I sent out letters to the 75 people in the area who had the same last name as the owner. My letters contained the information I already had, plus an explanation of why I was writing and not telephoning. (I felt phoning might be interpreted as a scam or an invasion of privacy.)

A RESPONSE came from the sister-in-law of the original owner. She had never been in the house but referred me to the only other living relative, the owner's granddaughter. I was so excited about this information that I couldn't wait to write her. I called her, saying I was referred by the sister-in-law. The granddaughter had lived in the house for 30 years and was delighted to help with old photographs and a personal visit, if I wished. These people get a good feeling knowing that their childhood home is on the return.

FROM THIS HELP, I am able to make intelligent moves toward restoration without the guessing of what was where and what should I do next. It saves a lot of money. . . .

Jonathan B. Webb
Minneapolis, MN

## The Fight Is Settled!

### Here Are Guidelines For Using...

# Dip-Stripping To Remove Paint

By Clem Labine

W E'VE ALL HEARD horror stories about using dip-stripping to remove paint: A valuable oak mantel comes back from the strip shop looking like a grey sponge. Yet there are others who've had great luck with commercial paint strippers and who'll never hand-strip again. To get the whole story, we asked OHJ readers (through a questionnaire in the March 1982 issue) for their experiences. We found that although the majority were satisfied, more than one out of every three customers were un-happy--some bitterly so.

| OHJ SUBSCRIBERS' EXPERIENCE WITH DIP-STRIPPING | |
|---|---|
| Satisfied | 54% |
| Dissatisfied | 38% |
| Mixed Feelings | 8% |

TO UNDERSTAND THIS DRAMATIC difference of opinion, we have to look more closely at the workings of the stripping business. Most large commercial strip shops have three tanks:

(1) A "cold tank" filled with a paint stripper based on methylene chloride and methanol.

(2) A "hot tank" containing a solution of lye or trisodium phosphate (TSP) in water. These tanks operate from 125 F. to 180 F.

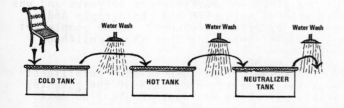

*Wood going through a strip shop is often treated in all three tanks, and is rinsed with pressurized water in between.*

(3) A bleach tank containing oxalic acid. This tank neutralizes the caustic from the hot tank, and bleaches out any darkening of the wood that occurred in previous steps.

BETWEEN DIPPINGS, there are usually pressure wash booths where dipping chemicals are rinsed off. In stripping a piece, one, two, or all three tanks may be used.

IN ADDITION to these total immersion methods, there's also a "cold tray" or "flow on" process that we'll describe later.

### Where Troubles Begin

T HE 38% WHO WERE UNHAPPY with dip-stripping reported raised and fuzzy grain, loosened joints, bubbling veneers, and drastic color changes. Most unhappy customers also reported that they did not know what stripping chemical had been used. And therein lies the problem.

SOME COMMERCIAL STRIPPERS resort to secrecy to hide the fact that they are dipping fine woods in harsh chemicals. They will assure customers that they have their own secret stripper that's guaranteed not to harm wood. WARNING: As soon as you hear "my own secret formula," head for the door!

MOST PROBLEMS OCCUR in the hot tank. Caustic strippers remove old finishes very effectively. But in the hands of a careless operator, caustic strippers will not only dissolve old glues, but will also attack the surface of the wood itself. And since it is a hot aqueous solution, it's almost impossible not to wind up with some raised grain.

COMMERCIAL STRIPPERS have a powerful economic incentive to do as much stripping as possible in the hot tank. Caustic stripper sells for about $50 per drum, while methylene chloride stripper runs around $275 per drum. So you can see why an unscrupulous operator might keep a cold tank around for show...and when no one is looking run all his work through the hot tank.

LET US EMPHASIZE that we are not condemning all use of the hot tank. Some fine, reputable shops have hot tanks. But it is important for the customer--as well as the strip shop operator--to recognize the difference between fine furniture and run-of-the-mill architectural woodwork. A run through the hot tank might be OK for paint-encrusted baseboards, but might

be a disaster for an oak dresser or walnut wainscotting.

THE FEDERAL GOVERNMENT, for example, takes a dim view of dip-stripping for furniture. The General Services Administration's specifications for refinishing the government's own wood furniture contains the following warning: "CAUTION: DIP-TYPE REMOVING OPERATIONS ARE NOT ACCEPTABLE FOR WOOD FURNITURE."

COLD TANKS are less harsh than hot tanks. They are called "cold" because they operate at room temperature. The stripper, a combination of methylene chloride and methanol, is similar to the liquid paint stripper you can buy at the hardware store.

THE COLD TANK avoids soaking wood in water; nonetheless, the wood is being immersed in a strong chemical. The wood will absorb some of the chemical; how much depends on how long it is soaked. So it is possible to get some swelling and grain raising through the combination of immersion plus water rinsing. Also, it's possible that not all of the methylene chloride will be washed out of the wood.

THE COLD TRAY or "flow on" method is the gentlest of all, since it is closest to hand stripping. It uses methylene chloride strippers that are similar to hardware store paint removers. To strip a paint-encrusted door by this method, for example, a semi-paste stripper would be sprayed on the door. After the paint softens, the bulk is removed with putty knives. Then liquid remover is pumped through a brush, which is worked back and forth over the door as it sits in a tray. The brush serves both to apply the stripper and to loosen the remaining finish. The remover collects in the bottom of the tray, and is pumped back through the brush.

MOST FLOW-ON stripping operators use a water spray to rinse off the paint remover. Really

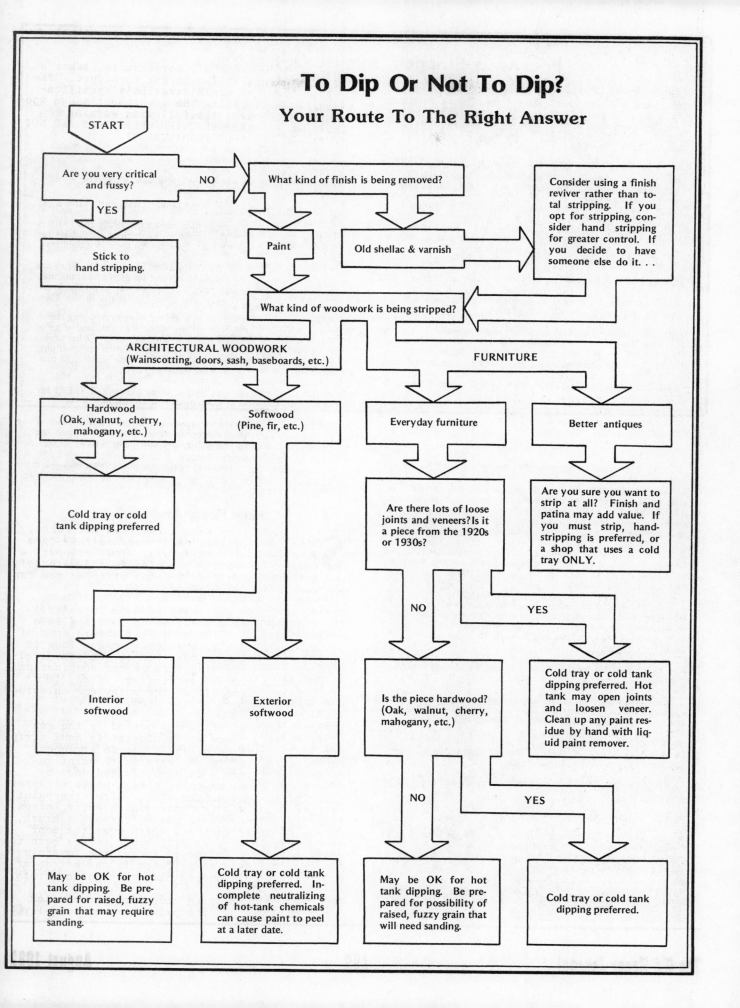

# To Dip Or Not To Dip?
## Your Route To The Right Answer

START

Are you very critical and fussy?

NO — What kind of finish is being removed?

YES

Stick to hand stripping.

Paint

Old shellac & varnish

Consider using a finish reviver rather than total stripping. If you opt for stripping, consider hand stripping for greater control. If you decide to have someone else do it. . .

What kind of woodwork is being stripped?

ARCHITECTURAL WOODWORK
(Wainscotting, doors, sash, baseboards, etc.)

FURNITURE

Hardwood
(Oak, walnut, cherry, mahogany, etc.)

Softwood
(Pine, fir, etc.)

Everyday furniture

Better antiques

Cold tray or cold tank dipping preferred

Are there lots of loose joints and veneers? Is it a piece from the 1920s or 1930s?

Are you sure you want to strip at all? Finish and patina may add value. If you must strip, hand-stripping is preferred, or a shop that uses a cold tray ONLY.

NO

YES

Interior softwood

Exterior softwood

Is the piece hardwood? (Oak, walnut, cherry, mahogany, etc.)

Cold tray or cold tank dipping preferred. Hot tank may open joints and loosen veneer. Clean up any paint residue by hand with liquid paint remover.

NO

YES

May be OK for hot tank dipping. Be prepared for raised, fuzzy grain that may require sanding.

Cold tray or cold tank dipping preferred. Incomplete neutralizing of hot-tank chemicals can cause paint to peel at a later date.

May be OK for hot tank dipping. Be prepared for possibility of raised, fuzzy grain that will need sanding.

Cold tray or cold tank dipping preferred.

# Peel-Away Stripper: Miracle Or Malarkey?

ADS HAVE BEEN APPEARING in countless magazines touting the virtues of a "peel away" paint stripper. The product sounds too good to be true: "Strips away up to 18 coats of paint with one 60-second application. . .no mess, no fuss, no odor. . .ends sanding, scraping FOREVER! Makes taking paint off even easier than putting it on!"

TO THE BEST of our knowledge, no publication has tested to see whether the stuff works as advertised. Since the OHJ does not have a zillion-dollar ad campaign at stake, we decided to evaluate the peel-away stripper. (This is one reason why we don't accept paid advertising.) We bought a "Homeowner Size" box of the stripper ($19.90, including postage) and set out to strip an oak chair and a piece of fir woodwork. Our conclusion: The peel-away process does work after a fashion, but is hardly the miracle the ads claim it to be. The stripper is an alkaline powder, similar to lye or TSP. It works as follows:

(1) You mix the powdered stripper in water to make a paste.

(2) You apply the creamy stripper paste to the surface with a spatula they provide, or with an old brush.

(3) The peel-away blanket is soaked in soapy water and is laid on over the stripper. The blanket keeps the stripper from drying out while it is working. The size of the blanket (about 4 ft. by 3 ft.) limits the amount of area you can strip at one time.

(4) Then you wait while the stripper does its work. This can be several hours. (You can catch up on your reading while waiting.)

(5) When the paint has softened all the way down to bare wood, you peel off the blanket. Theoretically, all the paint comes off with the blanket at this point.

(6) The wood surface then has to be neutralized by applying a solution of vinegar and water.

(7) In order to re-use the blanket, you have to wash it out in soapy water.

WE FOUND THAT, contrary to the picture in the ads, paint didn't come up out of the grooves; it had to be dug out with a scraping tool. And despite the claims of ending sanding forever, the stripper raised the grain on our test pieces, requiring sanding. The process of neutralizing the wood and washing out the blanket for re-use was decidedly messy.

BASED ON OUR TESTS to date, the Editors feel the product offers few advantages over conventional paint strippers. . .and certainly doesn't come close to living up to the ad hype. One possible use—which we didn't test—would be for stripping overhead; the stuff did seem viscous enough to stick to a ceiling. We continue to get questions about this product every day, so if you've had any experience with it—pro or con—we'd love to hear from you. Send your comments to: Refinishing Editor, Old-House Journal, 69A Seventh Ave., Brooklyn, NY 11217.

## TIPS ON REFINISHING STRIPPED WOOD

1. Any wood that's been exposed to moisture, either in the hot tank or in the rinsing booths, should be allowed to air-dry for AT LEAST three weeks before applying a new finish. (Allow more drying time in humid weather.) Don't try to speed the drying process with heat; you may cause warping and checking.

2. To clean up paint residue in grooves, apply paint stripper from a plastic squeeze bottle, such as the kind you put mustard in to take to a picnic. This allows you to put the stripper where you need it without waste.

3. When sanding fuzzy wood, apply the sealer (such as shellac) BEFORE sanding. The sealer stiffens the wood fibers and makes them easier to sand off. A few coats of shellac, with light sanding between coats, will smooth out most fuzzy raised grain.

4. Color will come back to most stripped wood after applying the finish. In some cases, stain will be required.

5. Best finish depends on the wood. The only safe course is to experiment on a small patch before proceeding. Oil finishes can turn some woods (e.g., redwood, walnut) dark.

6. Dresser drawers may not slide at first after stripping due to swelling. Wait two to three weeks for proper drying, then apply wax to drawer bottoms and sides.

7. Here are some finishing formulas that have worked for OHJ subscribers:

● Orange shellac returns color to redwood.

● To restore color to a variety of woods, coat with 1 part boiled linseed oil and 3 parts turpentine. Allow to dry. Apply a fruitwood stain (or other appropriate stain). After stain dries, coat with oil or varnish finish.

● To restore color to Honduras mahogany: Apply coating of boiled linseed oil and rub off excess with 0000 steel wool.

meticulous strippers, however, believe that water should never touch fine wood; they'll use alcohol or mineral spirits as the rinse. Obviously, this is a more expensive process.

## How Fussy Are You?

SELECTING A STRIPPING SHOP is like picking a mechanic for your car. There's a wide range of competence in the marketplace--and the consequences of a bad decision can be disastrous. Keep in mind that one person's "smooth" is another person's "raised fuzzy grain." If you are super-critical and fussy, there are probably few commercial stripping operations that will make you happy.

PRICES OF STRIPPING SERVICES can vary widely. Dipping alone doesn't remove paint from all the cracks and crevices; that has to be gotten out by hand. This is labor-intensive, and so you can expect that a shop that does a lot of meticulous hand cleanup is going to be more expensive than a shop that just boils your woodwork in a vat of lye. Whereas a typical price for stripping a door today might be around $30, expect to pay twice as much for a shop that uses only the flow-on method with a lot of hand clean-up.

THERE'S NO SUBSTITUTE for the judgement of a knowledgeable, conscientious strip shop operator. Through years of experience, he or she knows how your type of wood--with its accumulated finishes--should be handled. The trouble is that it's hard for the consumer to tell the difference between a conscientious operator and a fast-buck artist who's just an operator. With the tips from this article, we hope that you can tell the difference.

# Patching Brownstone

By Lynette Strangstad

OWNERS OF BROWNSTONE BUILDINGS often think that their problems are insolvable or else too complicated to be repaired economically. As a result, they resign themselves to deteriorating buildings. This article demonstrates practical, effective repair work that you can do yourself to extend the serviceable life of your brownstone building.

BROWNSTONE is a red-brown or dark chocolate brown sandstone, usually with a noticeable mica content. When it begins to deteriorate, water is inevitably the culprit. Look for crumbling pointing between blocks of brownstone. This leads to open joints, which allow water entry. Deteriorating details high on the building may also be channeling water in patterns that severely wear away the brownstone facade. Be sure to deal with any underlying water problems before or during your repair of the brownstone itself.

PERHAPS THE MOST FREQUENT water problem concerns the freeze-thaw cycle. Rain water enters the brownstone through cracks and gets trapped. When the temperature drops, the water freezes, expands, and further damages the stone. The ice thaws, revealing a bigger crack in which more water can be trapped--meaning more cracking, and so on. And on and on.

THE OTHER MAJOR PROBLEM is due to face bedding. Brownstone is a sedimentary rock, so it actually consists of sheets of stone layered one atop another. The illustration below shows a naturally-bedded stone and one that has been face-bedded. Water damages a face-bedded stone by flaking off entire sheets of brownstone. Some 19th-century builders would inadvertently face-bed a block of brownstone. But sometimes it would be done on purpose to expose a long surface of stone--which is why the problem is frequently seen around doorways.

HOMEOWNERS sometimes resort to methods of repair which are totally inadequate to the problem. Painting over deteriorated brownstone, for example, only hides the problem temporarily. Patching with cement always involves applying a brownstone paint to the whole facade, or else the patch will look like a patch. Such a paint job then has to be reapplied periodically if the patch is to remain hidden.

THE ONLY SENSIBLE, long-lasting solution is to prepare and apply a brownstone mix that will match the color and texture of the original brownstone. Such a patch, as it weathers, will come to look like the surrounding brownstone. This article is based on my experience in making and using brownstone mixes. If you experiment a little with the basic methods outlined below, you'll get something that will be just right for your particular situation.

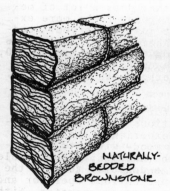 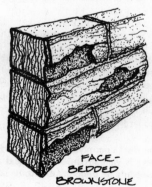

NATURALLY-BEDDED BROWNSTONE

FACE-BEDDED BROWNSTONE

Naturally bedded stones (left) suffer less damage from the weather than face-bedded stones (right).

## Preparing The Mix

PULVERIZED BROWNSTONE is a necessary component of the mix because other aggregates lack mica particles and so look "flat" next to the original brownstone. A possible source for brownstone is any salvage yard in your area. They are most likely to have brownstone that will closely resemble that of your building. Quarries or stone yards are the next best places to try. Don't worry if the brownstone they have isn't crushed; you can easily pulverize it yourself to obtain aggregate of the necessary size.

ALONG WITH CRUSHED BROWNSTONE, the mix will contain portland cement and dry mortar colors. When possible, you should also try to include sand as a component; it will reduce the amount of crushed brownstone required by the mix.

Sand will change the color and texture of the mix, so if it comes out wrong, change to sand of another color and/or grain size. (There's always a chance, however, that your particular brownstone's appearance won't enable you to use sand in the mix.)

BEGIN WITH a white portland cement, to avoid introducing unwanted color to the mix. (If you find you need a greyer hue, use a light grey portland.) Dry masonry colors permit you to vary the color of the mix. Many masonry supply stores stock several shades of red and brown. If you can't find these colors, or if they don't quite do the job, you may have to introduce blue or even yellow to the mix. A color wheel from an art supply store will make things easier if you do have to mix colors.

EXPERIMENT FIRST with the dry masonry colors alone, so you can see which colors are closest to what you need. Then introduce the cement, brownstone, and sand. Try to match the color of the original brownstone, not the weathered surface of the facade itself. When you undercut the patch area, you'll expose unweathered brownstone. This is the color your mix should match. This way, when the patch weathers, it will come to resemble the surrounding surface. (To speed up this weathering process, lightly wash ONLY the patch surface area with diluted muriatic acid after the patch has cured.)

AFTER SOME TRIAL AND ERROR, you'll get a satisfactory color for the brownstone mix. Texture plays a part in our perception of color, so once you're close to matching the color, use texturing techniques on your samples. Try sponging the still-damp surface of the mix with

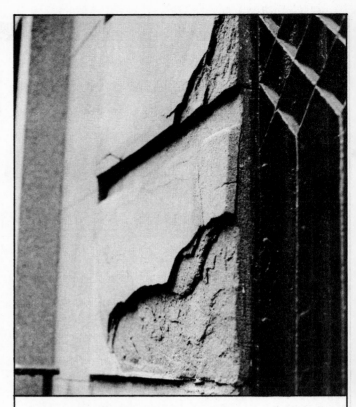

Although spalling doesn't pose an immediate structural problem, the exfoliation of bedded brownstone layers will only accelerate as water enters the rough, deteriorated surfaces.

# Brownstone-Mix Formulas

You'll have to test to find the proper mix for your brownstone repairs. Listed below are some mixes that I have used. There's no assurance that these exact formulas will work for your own building, but they are a good starting point.

Here are suggested ratios for the dry masonry colors:
A.   4 brown : 1 red
B.   8 brown : 1 red
C.  12 brown : 1 red

We followed a basic ratio of 1 part cement to 3 parts of the mixture of brownstone, dry masonry colors, and sand. Most actual formulations modify that ratio to some extent, but as long as you don't steer too far from it, your mix should be as strong and attractive as ours were. (Samples 4 and 5 were actually used on different parts of the same building.)

1)  15 T brownstone
    5 T white portland

2)  12 T brownstone
    4 T white portland
    1½ t mortar-color mix A

3)  12 T brownstone
    3 T white portland
    1 t mortar-color mix B

4)  12 T brownstone
    4 T white portland
    1 t mortar-color mix C

5)  6 T brownstone
    6 T sand
    4 T white portland
    5/8 t mortar-color mix A

Tablespoons (T) and teaspoons (t) are familiar and convenient measurements — small enough to use up a minimum of materials while still providing adequate samples for determining colors. If you keep the components in easy multiples of each other (3 teaspoons = 1 tablespoon), they translate well into larger quantities.

One final comment: Strive for perfection but don't expect it. There is virtually no such thing as an undetectable patch. But it needn't be undetectable to be unobtrusive — and effective.

Both of these previously unpainted brownstone buildings were spalling. Their owners hired contractors to do color-matched patches, so the headache of periodic maintenance painting could be avoided. Left: The contractor who worked on this job had an ex-cellent reputation. Right: This contractor had a spottier track record (pardon the pun), and the owner didn't insist on a test patch. Now it's either regular painting or permanent scars.

a fine-grained sponge or a piece of foam rubber from a cushion. This will expose the fine-grained aggregate and the mica.

SOME BROWNSTONE BLOCKS have streaks of an aggregate that differs in size and color from the main body of the stone. Select a sand that is matches the size and color of the aggregate and toss it into the patch while the patch is still wet. This will imitate the streaks in the surrounding brownstone. The next day, after the mix has begun to harden, prepare a solution of muriatic acid and water (1 part acid to 10 parts water). A light application of this solution will further expose the aggregate. (Take care not to overlap adjoining surfaces with the acid.)

PREPARE SEVERAL BATCHES of brownstone mix, each using a slightly different formulation, and let them cure outside for as long as possible, with two weeks as a minimum and three months none too long. Both this work and the actual patching should be done when the weather is warm. At a temperature below 40°F, the mix may not cure properly, and you'd lose a lot of your work.

## Applying The Mix

THE ACTUAL PROCEDURE for the repair of brownstone is similar to limestone-step repair (see the July 1982 OHJ). Using masonry hand tools, cut back the stone to a

solid subsurface. Undercut the perimeter of the patch to provide a key for the mix. If less than a full stone face is being resur-faced, you'll find that an irregularly shaped patch will be less noticeable than one that is squarely defined.

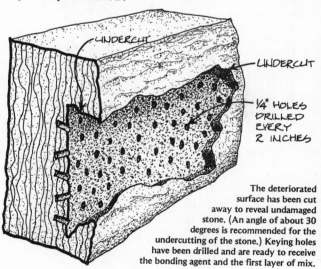

The deteriorated surface has been cut away to reveal undamaged stone. (An angle of about 30 degrees is recommended for the undercutting of the stone.) Keying holes have been drilled and are ready to receive the bonding agent and the first layer of mix.

ONCE THE DETERIORATED STONE has been removed, drill holes approximately 1/2 inch deep by 1/4 inch in diameter. The holes should be drilled at varying angles, about every 2 inches along the newly exposed surface. Remove stone dust from the patch area and lightly spray the area

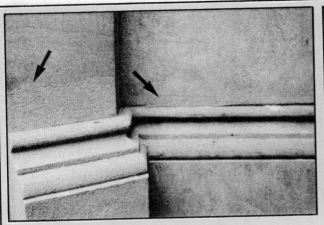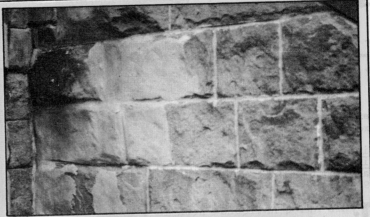

Left: You have to look hard to find the patch in the lower portion of this photo. Right: No arrow seemed necessary with this job.

with water. Then apply a bonding agent: a thin paste consisting of 1 part portland cement, 1/2 part lime, and 3 parts sand.

NOW APPLY THE BROWNSTONE MIX to fill the patch. The mix must be applied in layers that are not less than 3/4 inch or more than 3 inches in thickness. To provide keying, use a trowel to gouge many scratches into the surface of each layer. Be sure to apply each layer while the previous layer is still damp.

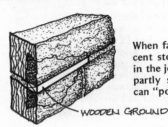

WOODEN GROUND

When facade deterioration spans adjacent stones, put a temporary ground in the joint. Remove it when mortar is partly set. After patch is cured, you can "point" the fake joint.

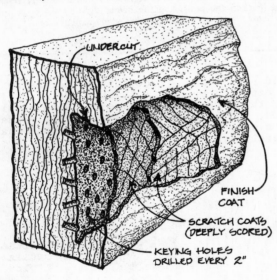

UNDERCUT

FINISH COAT

SCRATCH COATS (DEEPLY SCORED)

KEYING HOLES DRILLED EVERY 2"

IF YOU HAVE A DEEP PATCH, you can save on pulverized brownstone. Prepare a batch of mix that does not include any brownstone and use that as a scratch coat under the finish coat. Only the finish coat need contain brownstone dust. Once the finish coat has been applied and tooled to match the surrounding surface as closely as possible, you can use the texturing techniques discussed earlier to approximate the weathered texture of original brownstone.

TEFLON OR STAINLESS STEEL reinforcing rods may be required for stability if you have to rebuild architectural elements. Complex contours will require a wooden form that conforms to the negative profile of the element to be repaired. (See the July 1982 OHJ for more information on both procedures.)

BE MORE THAN FUSSY with your work. Today's "perfect patch" may look less than perfect tomorrow, so don't hesitate to remove a patch, even if it has almost cured. Patching brownstone is one of those tasks where care and patience really pay off. You can successfully return your crumbling brownstone facade to its former grandeur and physical integrity.

## SAFETY REMINDERS

Accessibility of the area to be repaired has to be considered. If the deterioration occurs in high, hard-to-reach areas such as architectural detailing near the roofline or upper window sills and lintels, scaffolding will be necessary. The additional safety considerations required by scaffolding will probably take the project out of the realm of the do-it-yourselfer.

There are standard safety measures that you must follow when working with lime and acid:

1. Avoid getting lime on your skin.
2. Always wear rubber gloves and safety glasses when working with acid.
3. Always pour acid into water — never the other way around.
4. Keep a pail of water handy to neutralize quickly any damage caused by spillage of acid.

LYNETTE STRANGSTAD worked with Structural Antiquities Unlimited on the restoration of the brownstone facade of the Theodore Roosevelt Birthplace in New York City.

# Helpful Publications

*Here are several books about furniture styles, and an excellent text on repairing antique furniture.*

## Nineteenth Century Furniture: Innovation, Revival and Reform
Mary Jean Madigan, Introduction
1982 (160 pp., profusely illustrated) Paper.

**T**HIS ART & ANTIQUES' BOOK is a collection of articles on furniture styles from 1820 to 1915. Written by curators and scholars, these articles are both authoritative and extremely helpful. The history and features of prominent furniture styles and manufacturers are thoroughly discussed and well illustrated-- Rococo Revival (Belter), Eastlake-influenced, Kimbel & Cabus, Hitchcock, and Stickley. There are also several sections on frequently overlooked furniture styles such as cast-iron, Egyptian Revival, and Adirondack Hickory. Color and black-and-white illustrations feature numerous museum pieces and period photographs.

To order, send $19.95 ppd. to:
Watson-Guptill Publications
1515 Broadway--Dept. CSAA-OHJ
New York, NY 10036
(212) 764-7300

*"Nineteenth Century Furniture" includes sections on frequently overlooked furniture.*

*A cast-iron garden bench.*

## American Country Furniture: 1780-1875
Ralph & Terry Kovel
1982 (256 pp., over 700 photographs) Paper.

**I**F YOU ARE TRYING to select antique, country furniture for moderate prices, this book will show you how to be sure of its authenticity and value. Another in a long list of books by the well-respected Kovels, it has over 700 black-and-white photographs showing furniture dating from 1780-1875, primarily from New England, although French Canada and other regions of the U.S. are occasionally illustrated. Many of the photos are keyed to the text to aid in identifying important furniture details. A large portion of the book is concerned with various styles and types of chairs; there is also special attention given to candlestands, painted furniture, and household accessories.

To order, send $10.45 ppd. to:
Crown Publishers, Inc.
34 Engelhard Ave.--Dept. OHJ
Avenel, NJ 07001
(201) 382-7600

## Three Centuries Of American Furniture
Oscar P. Fitzgerald
1982 (323 pp., profusely illustrated) Paper.

**A**FTER LOOKING AT NUMEROUS furniture style books, we feel this is the best overall survey book currently available. It covers the very broad period of the late 1600s to the turn of the twentieth century. There are only four pages of color plates, but the numerous black-and-white photographs more than make up for this, often with more photos than text. As a result, this book acts a handbook to teach the reader to recognize different styles from different time periods, and which is appropriate for your particular house. Another advantage is that the furnishings pictured are not all museum pieces; some are similar to a piece you might see in a quality antique store.

To order, send $18.95 ppd. to:
The Old-House Bookshop
69A Seventh Avenue
Brooklyn, NY 11217
(212) 636-4514

## The Encyclopedia of Furniture
Joseph Aronson
1965 (484 pp., profusely illustrated) Hardcover.

**W**E FELT THAT THIS OLD BOOK deserved renewed attention. It has over 2000 illustrations, many of which are style comparisons. In alphabetical, encyclopedic form, it serves as a handy reference guide for the furniture styles from the early 1700s to present day; the 19th century is highlighted.

To order, send $17.45 ppd. to:
Crown Publishers, Inc.
Attention: Retail Sales, Book #037351
Dept. OHJ
One Park Avenue
New York, NY 10016
(212) 532-9200

## Repairing And Restoring Antique Furniture
John Rodd
1981 (240 pp., illustrated--black & white) Paper.

**T**HIS IS NOT A BOOK for the novice furniture restorer. However, anyone with some carpentry and restoration skills will find that it's one of the best books on fine repair techniques. It often suggests various procedures for repairs and then discusses in detail the one which the author considers the best. Some of the selections are very specific ("a knob and ring handle for a Regency tea caddy"), while other procedures are more general ("drawer repair"). The text focuses on wood furniture repairs, but there are also sections on barometers, metal fittings, and mirrors and glass. Also included are several helpful formulas-- flour or rice paste, finishes to 'antique' new brass, etc.

To order, send $9.95 ppd. to:
Van Nostrand Reinhold Co.
7625 Empire Dr.--Dept. OHJ
Florence, KY 41042
(606) 525-6600

# Gazebos

*cont'd from p. 151*

any material or design erected
in a garden or park as a
resting place, the focal
point of a view, or a
place from which to con-
template the view.

GAZEBO is commonly explained as a somewhat humorous
form of the verb "gaze,"
(a play on the future tense
of a Latin verb such as videre,
"to see," videbo, "I shall
see"). But early usage suggests
that the term may possibly be
be a corruption of some
Oriental word. In W. and J.
Halfpenny's "New Designs for
Chinese Temples, Bridges, Doors,
Gates" (London, 1750), the authors mention the
"Elevation of a Chinese Tower or Gazebo."

*Columbia,
S.C. c.1870*

## History

TODAY'S common use of gazebo seems to date
from the early 19th century. "Pavilion"
and "summerhouse" were the preferred terms
in the 18th century; these words continue
to be used interchangeably. On the other hand,
"pergola" and "kiosque," Victorian in the origin of their popularity and certainly related
to gazebo, are often misused as synonyms.

THE ORIGIN of the form which gazebos have
come to symbolize is lost in time. Such
constructions are documented in most of
the Ancient World--Egypt, Mesopotamia,
Greece, Rome, the Orient. They received
renewed interest in Western Europe from
the time of the Renaissance on.

GAZEBOS and summerhouses could have
a variety of uses, according to architect Alexander F. Oakey. In
his Home Grounds (New York, 1881),
he enumerates them:

1st, to protect one from the sun while sitting
out of doors without hat or umbrella; 2d, to enable
one to enjoy whatever breeze may be stirring from any
quarter, not felt on the veranda owing to the position
of the house; 3d, to mark the most advantageous
points of view that gardens or the surrounding country
can be seen from; and, 4th, to embellish the grounds with
forms and colors unattainable in planting.

OUTDOOR STRUCTURES were important, albeit subservient, aspects of the formal French gardens
of the 17th and 18th centuries. They assumed a
more dominant role with the development of the
"natural" (or landscape) garden in England, c.
1730. The point here was picturesque informali-
ty--carefully planned.

SUCH DESIGNS were made famous and fashionable
by designers William Kent, Lancelot "Capability"
Brown, and others. Monuments, temples, towers,
cottages, grottoes, and fake ruins were focal
points of landscape schemes designed to evoke a

*Hudson, N.Y.
c.1880*

*Leroy,
N.Y. c.1855*

*Mecklenburg Co.,
Va. c.1795*

myriad of aesthetic associations--artistic, historic, and literary. One travelled through time as well as space while circumnavigating the garden.

ARCHITECTURE in the landscape garden was popularized in France and the rest of Europe as le jardin anglo-chinois, the emphasis not surprisingly placed on the chinois in France. Occasionally, landscape fantasies reached outlandish proportions in either design or expense. "Folly" (derived from the French word folie, "madness"), was first used in Britain to describe unfinished architectural embellishments, but soon came to describe anything built to satisfy a fanciful or whimsical taste. Now and then, "folly" and "gazebo" are mistakenly used to mean the same thing; a fancifully designed gazebo could be called a folly, but a folly might be anything from an obelisk to a triumphal arch.

## In America

GAZEBOS, it seems, are the humbler cousins of the temples and towers found in the English garden. The 19th century was the great era of the gazebo in America. There were many people who wanted and could af-

*Cutchogue,
L.I., N.Y.
c.1840*

*Vicksburg, Miss.
c.1855*

*Newnan,
Georgia c.1840*

*Watkinsville,
Georgia
c.1880*

Macon, Georgia
c.1860

Belfast,
Maine
c.1845

Demopolis,
Ala. c.1845

St. Francisville,
Louisiana
c.1840

Newburyport, Mass.
c.1830

ford the upkeep on some sort of garden, and fashion dictated ornaments be of more than just a floral nature, if at all possible. At first, Americans relied upon the advice of foreigners--British, French, and German--in gardening matters.

FOLLOWING the publication and great popularity of Downing's works (1841-1853), volumes by other Americans on similar topics mushroomed. Most had something to say about garden architecture. Reading some of these comments--even through the florid prose-- provides an excellent background for the 20th century restorer or re-creator.

ENGLISHMAN Shirley Hibberd, in Rustic Adornments for Homes of Taste (London, 1870), epitomizes the 19th century opinion that summerhouses are

> ...desirable, and indeed almost necessary features in gardens of all dimensions and styles. The grander the garden, the greater the need for places of retirement, for rest, shelter, conversation, and sometimes for that blessed change 'out of the house' which comes over every one of us at times when the air is balmy, the trees leafy, and the routine of domestic life a little tame or wearisome, as it will be on occasions in the best- regulated homesteads.

DOWNING, as we have seen, was of the same opin- ion, and was joined by other Americans such as Elias A. Long, who wrote in Ornamental Garden- ing for Americans (New York, 1884):

> Whatever the size or nature of a garden, there is al- most always need of some kind of architectural struc- tures besides the main buildings, for adding to its comfort, security, and interest.

## Placement

PLACEMENT of the gazebo in the garden merited thoughtful attention. Architect Oakey cautioned his readers:

> The design and the position of these structures are not to be arbitrarily determined, but are a part of of the scheme improvement, and are suggested by its conditions.

ANOTHER AMERICAN, G. M. Kern, had previously written in Practical Landscape Gardening (Cincinnati, 1855):

> It requires a correct and practical taste to superintend the distribution of...[summerhouses, temples, etc.] ...in a Garden, as however beautiful the objects may be in themselves, if placed in ungraceful positions, they will destroy the appearance of the whole scene. More discrimination is required in the adaptation of ornaments of this kind than in any other part of the gar- dener's duty. Too richly or highly ornamented, it will appear gaudy--too plain will argue poverty--and to be out of place will betray ignorance.

Newburyport, Mass. c.1825

*Nashville, Tenn. c.1860*

## Design

IN THE MATTER of gazebo design--probably the item of principal interest to modern read- ers--"appropriateness of style" (rather than style per se) was of major importance to our 19th century predecessors. Most writers on the subject felt that when such structures were within view of the house, they should be similar or at least complementary in style. In Downing's first work, he states:

> In the proximity of elegant and decorated buildings where all around has a polished air, it would evident- ly be doing violence to our own feeling and sense of propriety to admit many rustic seats and structures of any kind; but architectural definitions and archi- tectural seats are there correctly introduced.

ENGLISHMAN Edward Kemp, in How to Lay Out a Garden (London, 1850), echoes this sentiment by stating that:

> ...the employment of conspicuous grottoes, towers, summerhouses, or other buildings, within a short dis- tance, or in open view, from the house, when the style differs very widely from it, or is at all extravagant, cannot be defended on any known principle in landscape arrangement.

KEMP DOES concede that:

> If sparingly introduced, and of quiet appearance, and partially concealed, architectural objects, though not in the same style as the house, may be occasionally admissible.

> LATER in the work, he adds:

> A rustic arbour will not, however, be an unfit accompaniment to a building in the Swiss character, or even to some kinds of house Gothic, if its details be accommodated there-to. But it would be entirely inharmonious with a building in the Grecian or Italian manner, which demands more artistic and classical attendants.

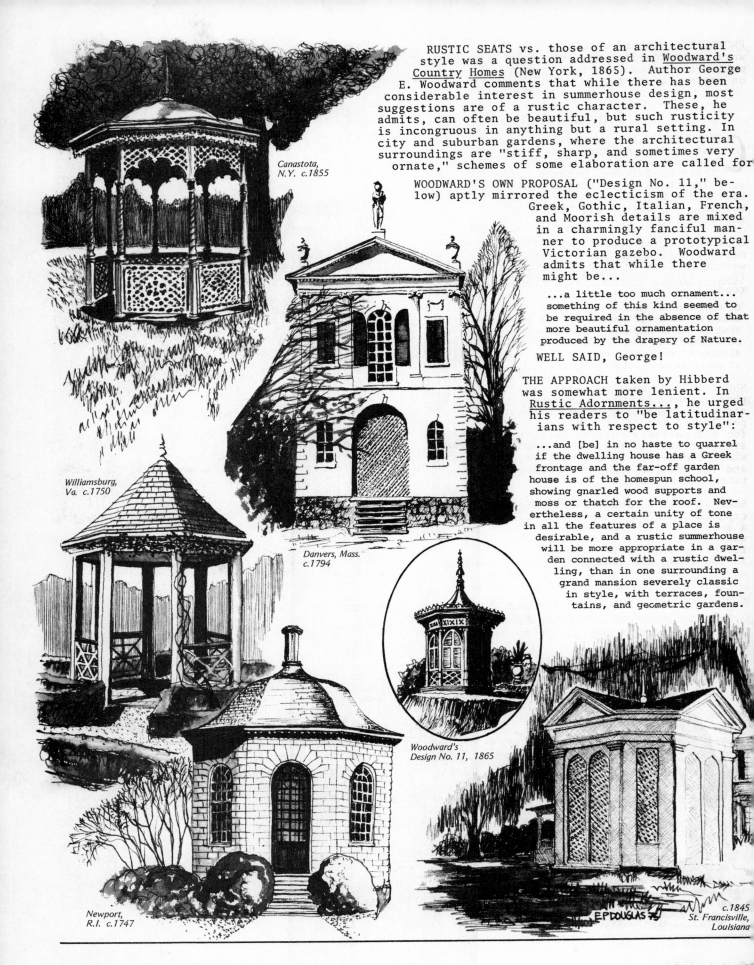

RUSTIC SEATS vs. those of an architectural style was a question addressed in Woodward's Country Homes (New York, 1865). Author George E. Woodward comments that while there has been considerable interest in summerhouse design, most suggestions are of a rustic character. These, he admits, can often be beautiful, but such rusticity is incongruous in anything but a rural setting. In city and suburban gardens, where the architectural surroundings are "stiff, sharp, and sometimes very ornate," schemes of some elaboration are called for.

WOODWARD'S OWN PROPOSAL ("Design No. 11," below) aptly mirrored the eclecticism of the era. Greek, Gothic, Italian, French, and Moorish details are mixed in a charmingly fanciful manner to produce a prototypical Victorian gazebo. Woodward admits that while there might be...

...a little too much ornament... something of this kind seemed to be required in the absence of that more beautiful ornamentation produced by the drapery of Nature.

WELL SAID, George!

THE APPROACH taken by Hibberd was somewhat more lenient. In Rustic Adornments..., he urged his readers to "be latitudinarians with respect to style":

...and [be] in no haste to quarrel if the dwelling house has a Greek frontage and the far-off garden house is of the homespun school, showing gnarled wood supports and moss or thatch for the roof. Nevertheless, a certain unity of tone in all the features of a place is desirable, and a rustic summerhouse will be more appropriate in a garden connected with a rustic dwelling, than in one surrounding a grand mansion severely classic in style, with terraces, fountains, and geometric gardens.

Canastota, N.Y. c.1855

Williamsburg, Va. c.1750

Danvers, Mass. c.1794

Woodward's Design No. 11, 1865

Newport, R.I. c.1747

E.P. DOUGLAS 75

c.1845 St. Francisville, Louisiana

PROPRIETY, Hibberd concludes, is "a question always worth considering; but not to the extent of making convenience subservient to extreme views on matters of taste."

## Practical Matters

CONSTRUCTION and comparative costs were of interest to 19th century gazebo builders, just as they are to us. Various materials differed in their usefulness; Hibberd discusses the topic at some length in order that the "summer-houses and arbours [not be] harbours for earwigs, cats and other vermin ... [instead of] tree bowers and trellis shelters...."

COST VARIED, of course, with the elaborateness of design and the availability of workmen. Even in 1870, Frank J. Scott (Beautifying Suburban Home Grounds), readily admits:

Of constructive garden ornaments...really tasteful and *durable* ornamentation of that kind is rather expensive, and therefore to be weighed well in the balance with expenditures of the same money for other modes of embellishment before ordering such work.

SURVIVING documentation--drawings, photographs, descriptions, and actual structures--happily indicates that many people did choose to satisfy the urge for a decorative outdoor retreat, an architectural or rustic "escape" for when "the air is balmy, the trees leafy, and the routine of domestic life a little tame or wearisome."

SOME WERE of an impermanent nature and have crumbled; others stand romantically in ruins; a very few have experienced the care that all would have liked. Time and money are the crucial factors necessary for a modern-day "gazebo revival"; is the trade worthwhile? I vote, "YES!"

*ED POLK DOUGLAS is an architectural historian and decorative arts consultant specializing in 18th and 19th century taste. A native of Mississippi, this 'gazebo watcher' is currently based in Rochester, N.Y.*

Thomsen, Georgia c.1890

Vicksburg, Miss. c.1860

Newburyport, Mass. c.1825

Sonoma, Calif. c.1858

EP DOUGLAS 76

## Gazebo Plans Today

You can't buy the historic gazebos pictured in this article. . .but you *can* buy a mail-order plan and build one to suit yourself.

*Top left*: Plans from A.S.L. include detailed drawings and a list of suggested materials. This is a six-sided gazebo of modest Victorian design (dia. 8', inside height 7' 4"). Send $10 (ppd) to A.S.L. Associates, PO Box 6296, Dept. OHJ, San Mateo, CA 94403. (415) 344-5044.

*Bottom*: Sun Designs' Study Plan Book shows 34 different gazebos ($6.55 ppd); they will also design and draw up your own idea. Construction plans for individual gazebos begin at $11.95 — for stock designs. Write to Sun Designs, PO Box 206, Dept. OHJ, Delafield, WI 53018. Tel. (414) 567-4255.

# Restoration Products News

## Bathroom Accessories

*Even if you can't afford to recreate an historical bathroom (or don't want to), you can add a period touch with brass, wood, and porcelain accessories. These accessories are often available in suites, sometimes with coordinating faucet sets, and include towel bars, soap dishes, toilet & tissue paper holders, etc. The list of companies that offer these products seems endless and many more than these are listed in the OHJ Catalog. Here we've highlighted just a couple of items that caught our eye or were hard to find.*

A towel warmer, originally just a metal rack placed in front of the fire, was a feature of the early, well-to-do bath. While they never lost popularity in Europe, it's only recently that we have seen them come back in the U.S. ARD imports two types of towel warmers, in a variety of sizes, from England. One model is heated through the domestic hot water supply or the heating system. The other requires no plumbing work since it's heated electrically (operating cost is claimed to be about that of a light bulb). Both types with polished chrome finishes are offered in wall- or floor-mounted styles. Prices begin at $145; orders under $300 are discounted 15%, and over $300 orders are discounted 20%. Specify the Myson Towel Warmers brochure, $.75, for information. ARD, 1 Fourth Place, Dept. OHJ, Brooklyn, NY 11231. (212) 624-5688.

Turn-of-the-century porcelain accessories, unlike wood and brass, are often not easy to obtain. This wall-mounted soap dish is $12.50 from Stringer's Environmental Restoration & Design, 2140 San Pablo Ave., Dept. OHJ, Berkeley, CA 94702. (415) 548-3967. Catalog, $2.50.

A-Ball Plumbing is another source for porcelain accessories, including switch plates ($4-$5) and a corner soap dish ($10.95). These and other accessories in brass and wood can be seen in their free catalog. A-Ball Plumbing Supply, 1703 W. Burnside, Dept. OHJ, Portland, OR 97209. (503) 228-0026.

*We aren't quite certain where people stored their 'necessities' in a turn-of-the-century bathroom, but featured here are several companies offering medicine cabinets and vanities. Although the vanities are not historical reproductions, their classic lines and similarity to other period cabinetwork make them appropriate for the old-house bathroom.*

Corner Legacy's solid oak corner medicine cabinet, pictured here, is $190 ppd. It's 17½-in. high, 15½-in. wide, and 10-in. deep. For a free brochure, write to Corner Legacy, 17 Hilton St., PO Box 102, Dept. OHJ, Eureka Springs, AR 72632. (501) 253-7416.

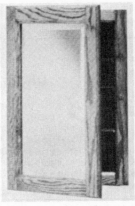

*Roe & Co.'s medicine cabinet, $136*

Most of us have had to live with one o[f] those ugly, metal medicine cabinets. Ro[e] & Co. frees us of them without sac[ri]ficing efficient use of space with thei[r] recessed medicine cabinets. (Also avail[-] able wall-mounted.) These and vanities[,] all made of solid oak, are pictured i[n] their catalog, $2. Roe & Co., 2971 Grac[e] Lane, Dept. OHJ, Costa Mesa, C[A] 92626. (714) 545-5723.

Sunrise Specialty sells a vanity in thre[e] sizes ($550-$850), with a choice of a[n] oak or marble top. The price includes [a] white china basin. Their color catalog [is] $1. Sunrise Specialty, 2210 San Pabl[o] Ave., Dept. COHJ, Berkeley, CA 9470[2.] (415) 845-4751.

Bathroom Machineries has just intro[-]duced this three-wing, solid oak scree[n.] Such a screen would have been used t[o] ward off drafts; today, it's a delightf[ul] way to enjoy a cozy bath or to create [a] change area in a large bathroom. So[ld] with removable fabric inserts, the scree[n] costs $195. A large selection of other oa[k] accessories, including towel bars and ti[s]sue box covers (about $18 each) can b[e] seen in their catalog, $2. Bathroo[m] Machineries, 495 Main St., PO Box 102[6,] Dept. OHJ, Murphys, CA 95247. (20[9]) 728-3860.

# Reproduction Bathroom Faucets

Artistic Brass' porcelain faucet set is available in solid white or floral patterns, $388.50 (sugg. retail); a similar centerset is $154.25 (sugg. retail).

Ideal for the Classic Revival bathroom, this P.E. Guerin faucet set begins at $525.

Watercolor's 'Edwardian Range' features this imported English brass faucet, $600 in brass, and $650 in polished chrome (both suggested retail).

Over twenty companies are listed in the 1982 Old-House Journal Catalog as sources for reproduction faucets. So choosing just a few wasn't easy. We've picked a representative sampling of manufacturers and suppliers. Most available reproductions are made of solid brass and offered in a variety of finishes, including 'antique brass' and polished chrome. Some of these companies will not sell direct, but they will be happy to put you in touch with a distributor in your area.

You might note that we haven't included any wooden faucet sets. We expect the finish would not hold up in the constant presence of water—and unprotected wood will deteriorate.

Artistic Brass, 4100 Ardmore Avenue, Dept. OHJ, South Gate, CA 90280. (213) 564-1100. Catalog, $5.

Broadway Collection, 601 W. 103rd St., Dept. OHJ, Kansas City, MO 64114. (800) 255-6365. Free brochure; catalog, $5. Will sell direct.

Chicago Faucet Co., 2100 S. Nuclear Dr., Dept. OHJ, Des Plaines, IL 60018. (312) 694-4400. Brochure, $.50.

P.E. Guerin, Inc., 23 Jane St., Dept. OHJ, New York, NY 10014. (212) 243-5270. Catalog, $5. Will sell direct.

S. Chris Rheinschild, 2220 Carlton Way, Dept. OHJ, Santa Barbara, CA 93109. (805) 962-8598. Catalog, $1.35. Will sell direct.

Watercolors, Dept. OHJ, Garrison-On-Hudson, NY 10524. (914) 424-3327. Free information sheets. Sold through architects and contractors.

Predecessor to the 'spoke' handle, these porcelain levers with chrome basin cocks are $116.25/pair (sugg. retail) from Chicago Faucet Co.

S. Chris Rheinschild manufactures this unusual and ornate late 1800s design cast-brass faucet, $64/pair.

A turn-of-the-century brass cross or 'spoke' handle faucet set, $299.95, from Broadway Collection.

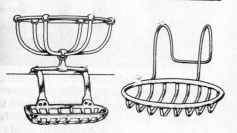

An unfortunate warning: It's been brought to our attention that this popular soap dish (left), is not very durable because of poor modern castings and an inherent design flaw. The soap dish on the right is not only a sturdier design, but at $15, it's also less expensive. Both of these models are available from A-Ball and other major bathroom supply companies.

Don't despair if the tile in your turn-of-the-century bathroom is missing or damaged. Those small, white hexagonal or glossy-black rectangular tiles are still available. Listed here are two sources for these and other period tiles.

Glossy and 'matte' glazed tiles in black, white, and a variety of colors are about $3/sq.ft. Sizes include 6- and 4-in. square, 8½-in. x 4½-in., and 2-in. hexagonal tiles. Products are sold through distributors nationwide, but free information is available from American Olean Tile Co., 1000 Cannon Ave., Dept. OHJ, Lansdale, PA 19446. (215) 855-1111, 855-1177.

A large selection of 1900-style tiles, including unglazed 1-in. and 2-in. white hexagonal tiles and glazed black trim tiles is offered by Tile Distributors. They will also supply or try to locate any pre-1940 ceramic tile. No literature. Tile Distributors, Inc., 7 Kings Highway, Dept. OHJ, New Rochelle, NY 10801. (914) 633-7200.

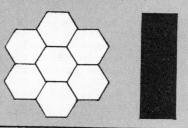

# Ask OHJ

## Rising Damp

MY VICTORIAN HOUSE was built in 1879. The brick partition walls in the basement were originally plastered. By now, nearly all the plaster is gone and the bricks are powdered and deteriorated. Is there anything that can be sprayed or brushed on these walls to prevent further deterioration?

--R.E. Moody  Rushville, NY

SOUNDS LIKE A CLASSIC CASE of "rising damp": Water enters the wall from the ground and leaves by evaporating from the surface of the wall. As it evaporates, the surface of the brick gradually deteriorates.

THERE ARE MANY masonry sealers on the market, but these almost always aggravate the problems caused by rising damp because they trap water inside the wall. Your first priority should be to reduce ground moisture: Are gutters leaking; does rainwater collect near the house instead of flowing away from it? If you can't reduce ground moisture, the only permanent solution is to install a damp-proof course at the bottom of the wall--a major undertaking. But many times the problem can be alleviated by parging the walls with a cement stucco, which "breathes" and helps hold intact the surface of the bricks.

## Let It Breathe

IS THERE ANY HARM in sealing the roof-top vents that lead to registers in the walls of our 1895 Victorian house? Squirrels have been entering through them and getting in the ceiling over the second floor. I have blocked the vents with steel mesh and am considering sealing them permanently.

--John Crossan  Chicago, IL

SEALING THE VENTS will prevent your house from breathing properly. Warm air can hold more water vapor than cold air. Because warm air rises, the attic is a trouble spot for condensation: Warm, humid air comes in contact with cold, uninsulated surfaces and releases water. If it is not properly ventilated, your attic can develop moisture problems such as damp ceiling insulation and even rotting wood. Your house has a system that lets air enter near the eaves and exit at or near the peak of the roof. You can cover the vents with a heavy screen to keep out squirrels or birds, but you mustn't interrupt the circulation of air in the house.

## Peeling Paint On Siding

A COMMON PROBLEM that I have often been confronted with is peeling paint on siding. I thoroughly scrape and then repaint with one or more coats, but a noticeable layered effect is left. How can I alleviate this? I've tried thinly applying patching plaster with a wide-blade knife. It makes the siding look smoother, but I'm worried that it might not hold up under the weather.

--Roy Neville  Schenectady, NY

THE BEST SOLUTION is to feather out the edges by lightly sanding the paint around the patch. A second choice is to apply a thin layer of exterior spackle around the edges of the scraped area, not over the whole surface. Let it dry and then prime and paint. DO NOT use any other puttying or patching compound that is not specifically designed for exterior woodwork. Plaster is sure to fail almost immediately.

## Cheaper To Reshingle

OUR HOUSE IS SIDED with cedar shingles covered with numerous coats of paint that is now all thick, alligatored, and cracked. The paint must be removed. Should we sandblast this type of siding? If not, what would you suggest?

--Harold Pier  Barneveld, NY

CEDAR SHINGLES are very porous, so you can't expect sandblasting to get out all of the paint. (A chemical stripper won't do a perfect job either, however.) Sandblasting also involves certain inevitable nuisances. For instance, your neighbors will not appreciate the mess. It might bother you too: Sand will get blasted into your house. You can expect to be discovering and cleaning out sand long after the sandblaster has left. Worst of all, sandblasted shingles will have to be treated afterward--every couple of years afterward. When you estimate the cost of sandblasting, include the cost of treating as well. You might find that, in the long run, residing your house doesn't represent such a dramatically greater expense.

# Opinion...
# Remuddling
## — Of The Month —

**I**T SOUNDS LIKE a preservation dream come true: A Savings & Loan company buys and renovates a run-down old house as a showcase project. And after the work is done, the S&L sells the house to a neighborhood group at less than cost so the group can resell it on the open market and use the profits to finance preservation.

AN S&L IN GEORGIA did all of the above. And we applaud them for trying to do the right thing. But the preposterous renovation earns them this month's Remuddling Award. Ironically, the company claims it wanted to do things in an authentic manner. A booklet of theirs states:

We did extensive research in the architectural library at Southern Technological Institute and consulted with Atlanta-area historical societies on period architecture.

GOOD INTENTIONS notwithstanding, all they ended up with is a very expensive remuddling. They bought a 1920s Craftsman Bungalow, and used it merely as a skeleton on which to drape a new exterior that they believe resembles an 1890s Victorian cottage. They basically rebuilt the house, inside and out.

IF THE COMPANY wanted a neo-Victorian house, it would have been easier and cheaper to build one from scratch. Instead, in the name of restoration, they destroyed an authentic Bungalow and replaced it with an ersatz Victorian whose clumsy handling shows that the designer had little fluency in the Victorian idiom.--C.L.

Submitted by: Elizabeth M. Gassel, Research & Construction Director, Historic Tampa/Hillsborough County Preservation Board, Tampa, Florida

This 1920s Craftsman Bungalow was rundown, but still had all of its basic features intact. Then it fell into the hands of a Savings & Loan Assn., which renovated the house as a demonstration project to show others how old houses should be rehabilitated. The "renovation"...

... involved, among other things, rebuilding the roof with a different pitch, and putting a completely new facade and porch on the house, all in an attempt to convert it into a "Victorian style gingerbread house." An honest Bungalow was remuddled into a caricature.

# The Old-House Journal®

**69A Seventh Avenue, Brooklyn, New York 11217**

NO PAID ADVERTISING

Postmaster: Address Correction Requested

Vol. X No. 9        $2.00

# The Old-House Journal

## Restoration and Maintenance Techniques For The Antique House

# Relining Your Chimney Flue

### By John Mark Garrison

*Whether you're reactivating a fireplace, buying a wood or coal stove, or adapting your heating system, you'll probably have to reline a flue or two. There are several different chimney-relining methods. Sorting out these options wasn't easy — we had to resolve conflicting information from manufacturers, installers, homeowners, fireplace specialists, and building codes — but now we've finally got it!*

THE DO-IT-YOURSELF SHELVES of most bookstores have a crowd of books about burning wood or coal. But, unfortunately, there's one area that's overlooked, sometimes with tragic results: the chimney. It seems people spend a lot of time learning how to make an intelligent stove purchase, but very little time thinking about chimney safety. This is alarming! Old chimneys have often been neglected or altered. And even a sound chimney may be unsuited to its new fuel or these new, super-efficient wood stoves.

YOU FACE additional problems if you have been thinking about adapting, reopening, or reactivating an <u>unused</u> chimney. Most heating systems in older buildings were converted once or more in the past. A flue pipe may have been cut into an old fireplace flue for a coal-burning stove; vents for basement oil or gas burners may have been run up the existing chimney stack. An entire fireplace could have been sealed up and then hidden behind a new wall.

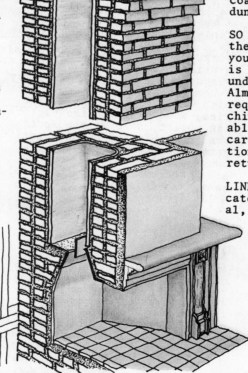

MOST OFTEN, you'll be required to install a liner in an old masonry chimney. A house built in the 20th century probably had a baked-clay flue liner as part of its original construction. But older chimneys, as they were being built, were parged on the inside with a special refractory mortar that was capable of withstanding high heat. And very early houses had chimneys that were either unlined or else coated with a mixture of cow dung and mortar.

SO IF YOU'RE about to change the fuel you burn or the way you burn it, and your chimney is old and unlined, it will undoubtedly need a new liner. Almost all building codes now require it. And even if your chimney already has an acceptable liner, please note that a careful, professional inspection should be made before you return an inactive flue to use.

LINERS fall into three basic categories: (1) the traditional, baked-clay liner; (2) a variety of metal liners; and (3) a poured-cement "liner" that hardens around a temporary, deflatable form inside the flue. All of these liners are UL approved and can be recommended for use under certain circumstances. This article will clarify precisely what those differing circumstances are.

*continued on page 188*

*A rustic gazebo, c. 1860, in Kingston, New Jersey.*

*Coincidentally, this first letter came to us while the August issue — with its articles on brownstone patching and gazebos — was still at the printer.*

WE'RE IN the midst of rehabilitating a mid-19th-century brownstone mansion in Kingston, N.J., so I've been following your summer articles on patching limestone (and brownstone). The house, Heathcote Farm, was originally designed by the firm of King & Kellum, of Orange and Fulton Sts. in Brooklyn, for use as a House of Refuge. King later designed the Brooklyn City Hall; Kellum designed the Tweed Courthouse in Manhattan. I'm interested in information any of your readers might have about this firm.

MY PRIMARY reason for this letter is to send you a photo of the summerhouse at Heathcote. It appears on the original landscape drawing when the building was converted to a private residence c.1860. The summerhouse resembles a rustic building illustrated in Andrew Jackson Downing's "Landscape Gardening & Rural Architecture."

WHILE LUNCHING in the summerhouse on a warm day, I discovered that the building really works! The open cupola acts as a flue which draws hot air through the roof, pulling a breeze through the walls. The gazebo is built of cedar and laurel root, and sits on top of a 22-foot-deep brownstone icehouse.

-- Clifford Zink
Princeton, N.J.

AS A previously intermittent reader (via my library's copies) and a recent subscriber (via your seductive Combination Package--which was meant to be bedtime reading for weeks, but was consumed very rapidly), may I compliment you on the success with which you have mixed articles, some aimed at the Victorian purist, some at the Southern log cabin set, others targeted nearer the vintage of my own house (±1910), but all of some interest to the thoughtful restorer of any period piece. Well done!

-- Colin F. Hasse
Berkeley, Calif.

I'D LIKE to congratulate you on one of the most unique and useful publications on the market. We were preparing to replace our double-hung Queen Anne windows with those newfangled vinyl ones at $280 a pop. Thank you for coming to their (and our!) rescue in the nick of time.

-- Phillip Garnes
Jersey City, N.J.

# The Old-House Journal®

*Editor*
**Clem Labine**

*Managing Editor*
**Patricia Poore**

*Assistant Editor*
**Cole Gagne**

*Editorial Assistant*
**Joni Monnich**

*Circulation Supervisor*
**Joan O'Reilly**

*Circulation Assistants*
**Margaret Scaglione**
**Barbara Bugg**
**Jean Baldwin**

*Office Manager*
**Sally Goodman**

*Office Assistant*
**Rafael Madera**

*Circulation Director*
**Paul T. McLoughlin**

*Technical Consultant*
**Alan D. Keiser**

*Architectural Consultant*
**Jonathan Poore**

*Contributing Editors*
**R. A. Labine, Sr.**
**John Mark Garrison**

*Published by The Old-House Journal© Corporation, 69A Seventh Avenue, Brooklyn, New York 11217. Telephone (212) 636-4514. Subscriptions $16 per year in U.S. Not available elsewhere. Published monthly. Contents are fully protected by copyright and must not be reproduced in any manner whatsoever without specific permission in writing from the Editor.*

*We are happy to accept editorial contributions to The Old-House Journal. Query letters that include an outline of the proposed article are preferred. All manuscripts will be reviewed, and returned if unacceptable. However, we cannot be responsible for non-receipt or loss — please keep copies of all materials sent.*

**Printed at Photo Comp Press, New York City**

*ISSN: 0094-0178*
**NO PAID ADVERTISING**

# unmuddling...
# Removing Formstone & Other Indignities

By Ron Pilling

WE KNOW that there are some purist preservationists who won't like this article. They'll say Formstone is part of the history of the building and therefore should not be disturbed. I'll admit we even found ourselves excitedly looking for the little bronze signature plaques proclaiming "good" Formstone jobs by the "original" Baltimore installer.

BUT FORMSTONE, Permastone, and other troweled, sprayed, nailed, or otherwise stuck-on sidings violate some preservationist rules too:

(1) They are not true to the style of the building, masking the architecture of the facade.

(2) The installers often removed ornamentation and architectural detail, destroying good old work as well as lessening the historic character of the building.

(3) Such coatings are subject to poor installation, mechanical damage, and weathering. Once their integrity is broken, water can and does enter. Substantial deterioration — of the coating and the building — is a reason why people want to remove the stuff today.

THIS ARTICLE proves it's not impossible to unmask your building. — P. Poore

ANYBODY BOTHERING to track down patent number 2,095,641 will find "a process by which artificial stone building surfaces can be applied to masonry, wood, etc." This patent, filed in 1937 by Albert Knight of the Lasting Products Company in Baltimore, protected his Formstone fortune. (In other cities, it went by the aliases "Permastone," "Fieldstone," "Dixie Stone," and "Stone of Ages.")

THE ADS FOR IT proclaimed that "Formstone makes your home the neighborhood showplace." They called it "beautiful," "long lasting," and "maintenance free." However, the ads failed to say one important thing: It's temporary. In city after city, homeowners have learned this particular lesson the hard way. Baltimore, by virtue of Knight's residence, is undoubtedly the Formstone capital of the United States. But this is changing: In recent years, the city has seen more of the gray, lifeless stuff come off than go on.

WHEN YOU remove Formstone, you'll find that you'll also have to repair the uncovered masonry surfaces. This is not a weekend job, but it is certainly within the realm of a serious and ambitious restorationist. And even if you decide to hire a contractor to strip away the Formstone, you should understand the procedure so you can protect yourself from a shoddy job. When done properly, there is minimal damage and the masonry beneath can be completely restored. Done wrong, it can create permanent damage.

Close to half the Formstone facade was removed in only 4 hours.

YOU CAN FIND FORMSTONE and its competitors on almost any surface that normally would have been painted. Bill Gasser, past Director of the Butcher's Hill restoration area in Baltimore, has commented that, "After the owner painted the front for the umpteenth time, he finally said, 'I've had it,' and on went the Formstone."

SOMETIMES, IT WAS PART of a major remodeling scheme. Examples abound where not only was the front Formstoned, but the windows and doors doors were reduced and replaced with aluminum sash. Often, the homeowner went crazy with modernization while he was about it. The result: Cornices and door surrounds removed, lintels taken off, and stone sills stoned over.

"FORMSTONE IS BASICALLY pretty easy to put on, and therefore easy to get off," says Gasser. First, a metal lath was nailed to the surface, ideally with galvanized nails. Then a scratch coat of mortar was troweled on and roughed up before it dried. Next, the skin coat went on, followed by the top coat. While still wet, the top coat was rolled with the stone pattern or cut with a trowel to imitate the joints between stones. "Natural stone colors," usually from bright pink to weak flesh in tone, were applied to some of the fake stones. Finally, tiny chips of mica or marble dust were sprayed onto the surface at high pressure. The whole veneer is usually about three quarters of an inch thick.

IN YOUR PRE-REMOVAL INSPECTION, study the facades of your non-Formstoned neighbors. If the house next door has some nifty terra-cotta ornamentation and your Formstoned facade is as flat as the sidewalk, you may be in for some sad surprises when the gray cement falls away. It isn't unusual to find that the Formstone contractors have chipped off terra-cotta decoration and corbelling to even the surface. They may have even chiselled away a belt course or hacked off the edges of the window sills to make the lathing easier.

MELVIN KNIGHT, of All American City Contractors in Baltimore, told me of a contractor who pulled off the Formstone only to find that large areas underneath had been filled with cement to even out a bulging wall. "The cement, put right on the brick, was pretty much on to stay." You can never be sure of what you'll find when you remove Formstone.

SEE IF THE DOORS AND WINDOWS seem to be the original size. When windows were shrunk to accommodate aluminum storm sash, the facades were not always bricked up very carefully. After all, the whole front was going to be covered up anyway, so why not fill in the window with cinder block, cement, or gravel and mortar? If you uncover such remuddling, you will have to chip it all out to restore the window to its correct size.

FORMSTONE CAN CONCEAL structural difficulties, covering up moisture damage, cracks, and insect infestation. But if the fake stone facade is cracked and bulging, it's usually the Formstone itself that's crumbling. A house settling over time will normally shift, eventually buckling the Formstone facade.

FORMSTONE CAN ALSO CAUSE structural damage. If the cornice has been removed and the gutters are faulty, water can seep between the Formstone and the wall. Gasser described this situation: "The cornice was on the house for a reason. Remove it and you're asking for water problems. If the contractor cut corners by using non-galvanized nails to hold the lath on, water will rust the nails when it gets under the Formstone. Eventually, the stuff gets loose and can cause real trouble if it's left on."

IT'S NOT HARD to spot these problems in advance. Look for water stains on interior plaster, especially under windows or where gutters are missing or rotted. Water can get in along any open edge, particularly at the top and around doors and windows.

It's most likely that, before Formstone, the house on the right had a cornice, windows, and terra-cotta ornamentation just like the painted house on the left.

WHEN YOU'RE PRETTY SURE you can handle whatever you're likely to uncover, you can begin the removal. Gasser reminds homeowners doing it themselves that "Getting it off is the easy part. What is hard is the cleaning, repair, and repointing that follows." The only tools you'll need are a pry bar, hammer, cold chisel, goggles, hardhat, and heavy work gloves. Gasser recommends working from a scaffold. "Formstone is pretty heavy stuff,"

Left:  Using a hammer and the short end of the pry bar, an opening is made at a raw edge of the Formstone.  Center:  Once the long edge of the pry bar is introduced under the facade, you can begin to pull the stuff back from the wall.  (If you have to strain to pull the bar toward you, try driving it further under the Formstone with the hammer.)  Right:  When a large section is loose, you can grab the Formstone and lift it away.

he says, "and it's best to be able to stand above your work while you're pulling it away."* Be sure to cordon off the work area so no passersby can be hit by falling debris.

FORMSTONE WENT ON IN BIG AREAS and can be pried away in equally large sheets, so don't waste time chipping at it with a hammer and chisel. Get your pry bar under the lath and then pull the lath, Formstone and all, away at one time. "Start at a window edge or a place where you can chisel an opening large enough to accommodate the end of your bar," counsels Knight. "Then begin working the bar behind the lath, pulling straight back to loosen the Formstone as you go.  Because of the weight, it will eventually break off and fall away."

FORMSTONE IS HEAVY and Gasser cautions against working with too big a sheet.  "When the sheet is heavy enough to fall back away from the wall, break it off by cutting through the lath. Then start prying off another section.  I always start at the top, and of course, never let anyone work above someone else."  He also advises not to pry too hard against the brick. "When a hunk is loose, grab it and pull straight back.  Too much hammering and prying on the brick wall can damage the masonry."

A CERTAIN AMOUNT OF DAMAGE is inevitable in even the best of circumstances.  Normally, the nails were driven into the mortar joints to secure the lath.  If the bricks were laid with thin joints, the edges of the bricks can get chipped, but that's about the worst you can expect.  It's a different matter, however, if nails were driven into the face of the brick. "We've had to chip out broken bricks from time to time," says Knight, "and then replace them with matching face bricks."

BRICKS WITH CHIPPED EDGES create little difficulty, but you should try to avoid chipping. Generally, edges are damaged when the nail is extracted.  You can't do much about nails that come out when the Formstone and lath are pulled away.  However, many nails will remain firmly in the mortar joints after all the Formstone's off.  "I pull those out as I'm raking the joints prior to repointing," says Knight.  A pry bar is handy here.  Use a small block of wood against which to lever the bar.  Pull in a direction parallel to the mortar joint, to avoid further chipping of the brick's edge.

Use a piece of wood when you pry out nails.

*Scaffolds are dangerous, so be aware of the restrictions on their use. Do you need a license or permit to use a scaffold in your city? Do you know a reputable rental company with well maintained equipment? Can the company advise you on the right kind of scaffolding for the job (probably tubular welded)? Will their people set it up and take it down? Are you calm about heights? If you can't meet all these requirements, better hire someone to do the job.

**P**OST-REMOVAL WORK is not unlike normal masonry restoration. The uncovered brick will have been painted and so must be chemically cleaned by the usual methods. "Paint seems to come off more easily if it has been Formstoned over," Knight points out. "For one thing, a lot of it comes off on the backside of the Formstone. For another, since the building was Formstoned, there aren't as many layers of paint." Removal of the paint that remains is generally carried out in the same fashion as removal when there was no Formstone.

REPLACEMENT OF BROKEN BRICK is usually limited to the edges of door and window openings. Bricks surrounding doorways are most subject to damage because the contractor often used a lot of nails there--perhaps suspecting harder wear at entrances. Large chips will be more evident here because every guest must pass through your front door. You may have to find some old, sound, face brick to replace bricks that were damaged during removal of the Formstone. When cutting back the mortar joints prior to repointing, you can remove the chipped bricks and set in the new ones.

THE CHIPS ON OTHER BRICKS are insignificant as long as the pointing is done carefully. If you use a buff-colored mortar, they seem to disappear. "Bright white or dark-colored mortar makes every chip stand out," warns Knight.

ALL THIS ASSUMES, of course, that you don't find shrunken windows, chiselled terra cotta, and missing wooden door surrounds. Damaged terra cotta is the most serious of these difficulties and will require trips to good salvage yards or consulting some brick dealers (especially those in the used brick business) in the OHJ Catalog. It is, naturally, easier to replace damaged terra cotta <u>before</u> repointing.

**F**ORMSTONE, Permastone, Silver Stone, or whatever is not the only affront to be sprayed, rolled, poured, or smeared over original exteriors. For instance, there was the "Merit Wall Method," marketed by Merit Enterprises in Baltimore. (Fortunately, it never caught on with the success of Formstone.) A thick, rubbery material was sprayed over everything but the window glass--cornices, gutters, and door frames were not exempted. Suspended in the goo was fine stone dust. The effect was that of a huge metalflake balloon having been stretched over the house and then cut out at the doors and windows. It comes off like paint, only a good deal more slowly and with a much bigger mess.

"THERE'S A HOUSE around the corner," Knight pointed out from his office in Baltimore's Ridgely's Delight neighborhood, "that has plain stucco put directly over the brick--no lath at all. The owner wanted me to take it off. I looked at it and then told him to paint it. Some jobs are doomed from the start, and without the lath, the stucco would be next to impossible to get off. You have to know your limits in this business."

RON PILLING, one of our original subscribers, is a frequent contributor to The Old-House Journal. A Baltimore resident, he also has a deep interest in hunting down and exorcising Formstone.

Above: The Formstone is off, the mortar joints have been cut back slightly, and the brick has been cleaned. If the job has been done properly, this is about as bad as the brick will look. Right: All three of these circa 1840 Federal rowhouses were once Formstoned. And unless you get really close, the bricks look fine, don't they?

# Helpful Publications

This month's books are related to home energy. The four devoted to solid fuel burning were chosen for their clear presentation of the basics. They give an essential education to anybody who's thinking about burning wood or coal.

*— Reviews by Jacqueline MacDonald*

## 1983 Woodstove Directory
Clifford Martel, Jr., publisher
1983 (264 pp., profusely illustrated) Paper

THIS CATALOG CONTAINS listings of woodstoves, coalstoves, fireplaces, chimney sweep training schools, furnaces, boilers, solar systems, and helpful accessories. (Up-to-date wood and coal stoves are shown in both antique and modern styles.) Each listing has a photograph, the manufacturer's description of the product, and the manufacturer's address. Retail outlets nationwide are indexed; for hard-to-find items, consumers can use the directory's free product locator service.

To order, send $2.95 plus $0.55 postage to:
Woodstove Directory
105 West Merrimack St.
P.O. Box 4474
Manchester, New Hampshire 03108
(603) 622-8206

## Coal Comfort: An Alternative Way to Heat Your House
Peter Hotton
1980 (167 pp., generously illustrated) Paper

THOSE WHO FIND MOST technical manuals cumbersome will enjoy Coal Comfort. Peter Hotton, home and garden editor for the Boston Globe, writes in a manner anyone can understand.

READING Coal Comfort is like shopping for a coal heating unit with a patient expert. Hotton explains what features to look for in an efficient coal burning stove, furnace, or boiler (like air vents and heat resistant lining). A complete list of questions to ask dealers gives the reader shopping guidelines. In addition, Coal Comfort features a catalog of coal stoves, furnaces, and boilers, with photos.

TIPS ON overseeing professional installations are also presented, along with information useful after you purchase and install your coal burner: how to build a coal fire, what to expect when burning coal in a new stove, how to dispose of coal ashes, and complete do-it-yourself directions for building a coal storage bin.

*Petit Godin*

To order, send $8.95 plus local sales tax to:
Little, Brown and Company
200 West Street
Waltham, MA 02154 (617) 227-0730

## Coalburning Stoves and Furnaces
James W. Morrison
1981 (172 pp., generously illustrated) Paper

THE INFORMATION IN THIS semi-technical manual overlaps that in Coal Comfort, but is more detailed. The book is scattered with tables such as "Figuring Comparative Costs of Various Fuels and Electric Energy to Supply One Therm of Usable Heat," and diagrams of chimneys, hot water systems, and coal heating systems.

THIS BOOK provides no catalog, but the author describes and recommends several coal stove, furnace, and boiler brands and tells where to shop for these items.

To order, send $6.95 plus $1.00 postage to:
Arco Publishing, Inc.
215 Park Avenue South
New York, New York 11003
(212) 777-6300

## Wood Heat Safety
Jay W. Shelton
1979 (165 pp., generously illustrated) Paper

HEATING WITH WOOD SAFELY "requires safe equipment, a safe installation, and safe operation and maintenance." These four topics are covered extensively for wood stoves and heating systems in this book. The book does not compare wood heating with other home heating methods, nor does it provide exact woodstove shopping guidelines, but deals entirely with safety. All safety factors are explained clearly with the aid of abundant diagrams and photographs. A mandatory reference for woodstove owners!

To order, send $9.95 plus $2.00 postage to:
Shelton Energy Research
P.O. Box 5235
Santa Fe, New Mexico 87502
(505) 983-9457

## Conserving Energy in Older Homes: A Do-It-Yourself Manual
Jeffrey M. Seisler
1982 (44 pp., profusely illustrated) Paper

THIS IS AN EASY-TO-FOLLOW manual written by an OHJ subscriber and preservationist. The manual starts with a simple, one-hour test that determines where energy conservation steps are necessary in the home. When energy gobbling areas are detected, you are referred to other sections of the book for further information. Price estimates for suggested energy saving conversions are also given.

THIS WAS to be the third book in the familiar HUD trilogy (In the Bank...or Up the Chimney?; The Energy-Wise Homebuyer)--but was published instead by the author when HUD's publications budget was cut.

To order, send $4.95 plus $0.65 postage to:
Analytech Suite C-30
915 King Street
Alexandria, VA 22314 (703) 836-7962

## Window Update:
# More About Double-Glazed Inserts

By Larry Jones, Salt Lake City, Utah

IN THE APRIL 1982 OHJ, there was a brief reference to a special way of retrofitting old window sash. This method involves replacing the glass with a sealed, double-glazed insert. I have found that this is an option worth serious consideration if you have 1-over-1 sash that is deep enough to rabbet for the new glazing unit.

THE UNITS ARE FABRICATED according to your window measurements and can be obtained fairly easily. In fact, locally fabricated, sealed, double-glazed window glass has become a big business. It's available from window dealers, glassworks, and some lumberyards. (Look at it this way: If we have it in Utah, everyone must have the stuff!)

SIMPLY ADDING a second layer of glass into existing sash will not offer the same energy efficiency as these units. They have a lasting edge seal made with a patented process (described in the sidebar on the next page). They also have an aluminum spacer filled with a dessicant that prevents condensation between the two sheets of glass.

THESE UNITS may be more expensive than storm windows, but they're also more effective. And they are certainly less expensive than new windows. They also come with good guarantees and follow-up support from the glass companies that produce them.

IN THIS ARTICLE, I'll be sharing with you some tips on how to handle, install, and maintain these units.* Frankly, I wish I'd had all this information prior to my own initial work with thermal glazing--some of the breakage would have been avoided.

---
\*Some of this information is based on an article by Irving Fenman which appeared in *Glass Digest* of March 15, 1982.

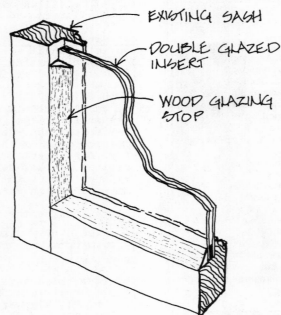

EXISTING SASH

DOUBLE GLAZED INSERT

WOOD GLAZING STOP

### Pre-Installation

THE WINDOW SASH itself should be square, tight, and capable of carrying the extra weight of thermal glass. (Any twisting or racking of the frame could break the glass.)

LAMINATED THERMAL GLASS shouldn't exceed 25 sq.ft. in area; if possible, it shouldn't be over 40 inches long in any one direction. The length-to-width ratio shouldn't be any greater than 2½:1.

AN AIRSPACE of 1/4 inch between the glass is considered to be the minimum; less would suggest questionable cost effectiveness and insulative value. The maximum functional airspace is generally thought to be 1 inch, with 5/8 inch considered ideal.

THE THERMAL GLAZING UNITS should be delivered to the job site in appropriate crates. Keep them that way until you're actually going to use them. Never lean the units on each other or against a wall; their weight can cause the upper light to shear the sealant, which in turn can result in misalignment or distortion of the shape of the window.

THE CORNERS of the thermal units are the weakest points. Never cartwheel them onto their corners.

### Installation

SHIMS are recommended around the top and sides of the glass at 18- to 24-inch intervals. (Fill the voids with glazing compound.) Neoprene setting blocks, 6 inches long and 1/8 inch wider than unit thickness, should be used. Along the bottom of the glass, these are placed at the two quarter points. (In other words, if the unit is 36 inches wide, the bottom blocks would be placed at two points, each 9 inches from the corners of the unit.)

■ INSUFFICIENT clearance for expansion due to temperature changes will result in broken units. (NEVER force fit them.) Leave an edge clearance of 1/4 inch between glass and frame for large windows; 1/8 inch for the smaller ones. For face clearance, leave 1/8 inch between the face of the glass and the wooden sash.

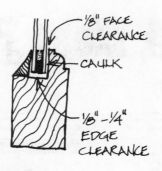

■ THE GLAZING COMPOUND or glazing stops, as well as the rabbet depth, must be sufficient to cover the metal spacer of the unit. Seal failures can result if the metal spacer is continuously exposed to solar ultra-violet rays.

■ GLAZING COMPOUNDS must be compatible with the edge sealants. Consult your source of units for appropriate types (such as DAP 33).

■ MANY SOURCES favor wood glazing stops to hold the glass in the sash. Such stops can even be routed to match the detail of your sash interior, or cut at a diagonal to resemble the glazing compound angle.

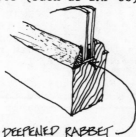

DEEPENED RABBET

■ USUALLY, THERMAL GLAZING will more than double the weight of the sash, so heavier sash weights will be required when the units are installed. Larger weights can be found at demolition sites or salvage yards. A welder can add on additional metal. If you have adequate clearance, large metal nuts can be used. Untie the sash cord, slip them on, and then reattach the cord. The nut rests on top of the sash weight. Additional weight can also be epoxied onto the bottom of the sash weight.

## Other Considerations

■ BE CERTAIN that water can't be trapped by the sash or sill. If the edges of glass and sealant are left standing in water, the sealant will rapidly deteriorate. Tight seals or caulking, the use of setting blocks, and good drainage are all essential.

■ THE THERMAL GLAZING described in this article is not recommended for insulated skylights or for use on any slope more than 15 degrees out of vertical. The glass can break if it cannot freely float. Also, rain, snow, and ice could deteriorate the sealant. Heat-strengthened glass could help alleviate some of the problem, but not all.

■ TRIPLE-GLAZING is also possible with the system. However, there is some question about the cost effectiveness of triple-glazing in all but the coldest climates.

The glass must be carefully test fitted to the sash--any binding or forcing of the glass will usually break it.

A LL OF THESE CAUTIONS might prompt you to wonder if insulating glass is really worth the trouble. Can it be used effectively in the average home? I think the answer is yes, most definitely. These precautions are simply guidelines to help homeowners and tradespeople get the best use possible out of double-glazed thermal units. 🏛

---

### HOW THEY MAKE IT

Two pieces of glass are cleaned with a solution that is compatible with the sealant to be used. An aluminum extrusion of a specified thickness serves as the spacer. When manufactured, this aluminum frame was filled with dessicant beads, and the side of the aluminum which faces into the airspace was perforated. These tiny holes allow the air trapped between the glazing to be dried by the beads. (You've definitely gotten a bad thermal window if the chemical has gotten loose and fallen into the airspace.)

The spacer is carefully inserted between the glazing. It is inset from the outside edge of the glass either 1/2 inch (residential glass) or 5/8 inch (commercial glass). The glazing is then sealed, either with butyl rubber or polysulfide. An extruder feeds molten butyl to an application gun that is hand operated. The gun forces the butyl into the channel formed by the spacer and the glazing. Once it has cooled, the material is trimmed and inspected for any gaps or defects. (Polysulfide works much like butyl, but must set up and cure before the glass can be put into service. The butyl system is ready for installation as soon as the sealer has cooled.)

---

LARRY JONES is Preservation Consultant to the Utah State Historical Society. With carpenter Jack Churchill, he was responsible for the reconditioning and thermal glazing of about forty windows last year and has been delighted by their performance. He extends a special thank you to Gib Groutage of Olympus Glass in Salt Lake City for his assistance in the researching of this article.

# How To Hide A Heat Pump

**Installing a heat pump in an old house can be quite disruptive because of the cumbersome ductwork. With its slender 3½-in. air supply pipes, the Space-Pak system allows you to conceal ducts inside partitions.**

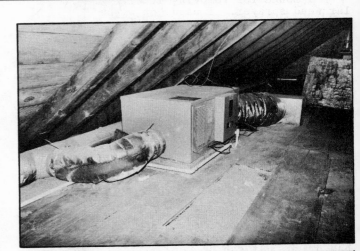

**H**EAT PUMPS have attracted a lot of attention in new construction because of their thermal and cost efficiency. A single unit can both heat a home in winter and cool it in summer. But for old houses, heat pumps have a major disadvantage: They can only be used on a circulating air heating/cooling system. And that means ductwork--which can be quite an eyesore if it is running through a beautiful plaster cornice.

ONE HEAT PUMP SYSTEM, though, avoids most of the ductwork problems. It's the Space-Pak system manufactured by Dunham-Bush. Several OHJ subscribers have installed the system in the past few years and have been very pleased with it.

THE BASIC DIFFERENCE between Space-Pak and other heat pump systems is the velocity of circulating air. Space-Pak uses high-velocity air, and thus can get by with much smaller ducts. The 3½-in. O.D. air supply tubing can usually be snaked through closets, partitions, attics, etc. As a result, all you see are the small circular terminator plates for each air duct, and one air return grille (about 14 in. by 26 in.).

**N**ORMALLY, THE OLD-HOUSE JOURNAL doesn't advocate replacing the entire central heating system in an old house. This is not cost-effective if you are just seeking to improve energy efficiency in your home. But if you're doing a top-to-bottom renovation--or if you have to replace your heating plant anyway-- then you should take a look at heat pumps. Air-to-air heat pumps are now cost-effective in much of the U.S. In colder climates you'll need a hybrid system--one with a fossil fuel backup system for very cold days. (See OHJ, Sept. 1981, p. 211.)

IF YOU'D LIKE more information about the Space-Pak heat pump, you can get free literature by contacting the Residential Div., Dunham-Bush, Harrisonburg, VA 22801. (703) 434-0711. 🏠

*PHOTOS: Top—Indoor coil/blower unit takes up little room in the attic. Behind blower is the plenum, from which individual 3½-in. air ducts branch out. Middle—In each room, the individual air ducts with their terminator plates are barely visible. Bottom—Biggest visual intrusion is the single return air grille, which here was placed in the ceiling of the top floor hall.*

---

# Restorer's Notebook

## A Vinegar Spray

**M**Y OLD HOUSE had layer after layer of old wallpaper. The best and least messy way I found for removing it was with a regular weed sprayer. I used hot water with vinegar and gave the wall a real fine spray by adjusting the nozzle. I waited a bit and then scraped it off with a wide putty knife. This method worked wonderfully--and it was a lot easier on my arms and neck. It's less messy and certainly cheaper than renting a steamer. It works well on ceiling paper too.

Claire Ashling
Dawson, MN

## Furniture In Bondage

**A**LL OLD-HOUSE OWNERS seem to have rickety old chairs that need to be reglued or drawers that are falling apart because the old glue has dried. It can be very difficult to clamp together the many odd-sized pieces that need to be glued. Sometimes extensive and expensive clamping systems seem to be needed.

MY SOLUTION is a length of sash cord or similar rope. It can conform to any shape, inexpensively clamp large pieces, evenly distribute the required pressure, and it will not mar the surface. First do a dry run. Make sure all pieces fit together well and then tie them together with the rope to insure proper fit and alignment. Then take the pieces apart again and apply the glue. To take up the slack in the rope and increase the clamping pressure, use a dowel or stick, tourniquet style. Tighten until the rope is taut, but don't overtighten.

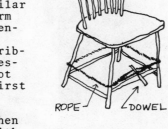

ROPE — DOWEL

John Kornbluh
Cincinnati, OH

## The Joy Of Oil-Dry

**B**EING INSPIRED by Daniel Mehn's article, "Floor Finishing--A Radical Alternative" (August 1977 OHJ), we searched for someone to help us strip our floors. Finally, we found Charles McKee of McKee Chemical & Supply

Company, Stamford, Conn. Charles used a water-soluble paint stripper on 4 ft. by 4 ft. squares, let it work, and scrubbed a bit to loosen the varnish. Then he sprinkled on some oil-dry, a claylike substance that looks like sawdust. It's usually used by garage mechanics to absorb oil spills. (Common brand names include Dri-Zorb and Safety-Dri.) He brushed off the oil-dry with a push broom and revealed beautiful bare wood. After being cleaned with paint thinner and receiving two coats of Watco Oil, the floor looked so terrific that we just buffed it and left it unwaxed.

THIS METHOD is quick and surprisingly free of mess. Three men were able to strip and oil our 1000-sq.ft. living room and dining room in one day; late the next day, they returned to buff it and replace the furniture. The oil-dry eliminated the scraping up, the rags--all the mess that usually accompanies paint stripper. It is amazingly quick, and results in a floor with a deep, soft lustre and the rich, warm patina of age.

Kathy Richards
Old Greenwich, CT

## Stripping Wood

**H**ERE'S A WOOD-STRIPPING METHOD used by a lot of people in my area. It's quite good on the cedar millwork, fireplaces, doors, panelling, and so on, in Victorian houses of British Columbia.

FIRST, USE A HEAT GUN to remove as much paint as you can without scorching the wood. Then brush water-soluble stripper on the panelling--leave it on for at least 20 minutes. Then take a tough scrub brush and wash it off with a solution of 1 cup TSP for each gallon of boiling water. (Don't be afraid to use a lot!) The secret is the heat--the hotter the water, the better it'll work.

THE PAINT AND VARNISH practically explode off the wood. The few bits left are soft and easy to remove. There is much less damage to the soft cedar panelling than would happen if you were to pick and scrape at all the grooves. I also suggest wearing a mask when you do this; fumes arise when the hot water goes on. It's a messy job, but it's good, successful, and probably the quickest way to do it.

Lucy Chambers
New Westminster, BC

**Tips To Share?** Do you have any hints or short cuts that might help other old-house owners? We'll pay $15 for any short how-to items that are used in this "Restorer's Notebook" column. Write to Notebook Editor, The Old-House Journal, 69A Seventh Avenue, Brooklyn, NY 11217.

# flues  *continued from page 177*

## Clay Liners

CLAY (TILE) LINERS have long been the approved method for new construction, so they have a known track record and could therefore be considered the most reliable. They are also readily available from a local building-materials yard or your installer, and come in a variety of round or rectangular sizes. (Round liners create a better draft, as smoke spirals as it travels upward; the corners in the rectangular tiles impede the flow. On the other hand, round tiles may reduce the functional size of the flue. See sidebar on p. 190.) Most contractors prefer to use the rectangular liner because it's easier to store and install. Liners come in thicknesses from 5/8 inch up to 1½ inches; 5/8 inch is sufficient for most residential use.

THE PRIMARY DISADVANTAGE of this method is that, in all cases, it requires partial demolition of the existing chimney. The installation is therefore messy and time consuming. The exact extent of demolition depends on specific conditions: If the chimney is relatively straight, it's possible simply to remove a section of bricks at each floor level and slide the liner up and down inside the flue.

IF THERE ARE BENDS OR OFFSETS in the chimney, these sections will have to be dismantled as well in order to cut and fit the liner. The whole operation requires a knowledgeable and skilled contractor who can make sure that the joints fit tightly and are well mortared, and that the sections of liner align with one another to provide a smooth, unobstructed surface. A botched job, with gaps in the mortar or badly fitting joints, means a chimney that is still dangerous.

IF YOUR EXISTING CHIMNEY needs partial rebuilding anyway, this method won't involve much extra demolition. On the other hand, you'll want to consider adjacent building materials. Installing a clay liner may require breaking through sections of plaster walls or wood panelling.

THE INSULATION FACTOR is not a crucial one with this method. A clay liner increases the insulating capacity of a chimney slightly, by the amount equivalent to the additional thickness of masonry. It does, of course, leave an insulating airspace between liner and existing stack walls.

## Metal Liners

INSERTING A METAL LINER is usually simpler and cheaper. If the chimney is a straight run from top to bottom, the installation is easy. If there are bends or offsets, however, these will have to be handled in the same way as with clay liner . . . by removing a section of brick at each bend. Angle sections of pipe are available for this purpose.

Above: This section of clay liner has been buttered with refractory mortar. It will be lowered onto another, similarly coated section, and will have another section lowered onto it. Below: In this photo, you can see that the chimney stack has four flues, only one of which is being lined.

THE MOST COMMON VARIETY of metal pipe is stainless steel sections from 6 to 36 in. in length, and from 5 to 10 in. in diameter. These fit together with small sheet-metal screws. Starting from the top of the chimney, one section is lowered down at a time, the next section is screwed to it, and so on to the bottom of the chimney. Rain caps and other fittings are available to complete the installation.

A NEW, FLEXIBLE, stainless steel liner overcomes the difficulties of installing metal pipe in curved or offset chimneys. (Word isn't in yet on how easy it is to clean.) This corrugated metal tube, in diameters from 5 to 8 inches, is sold by the linear foot. (see page 192) A rope is first lowered down the chimney. The liner is fastened to it at the top using a special bracket. The liner is then fed down the chimney and guided with the rope from below. (For a stove, the pipe itself is simply led through a hole in the side of the chimney, eliminating the need for a thimble to the appliance.) A metal cap is installed, same as for rigid pipe.

SINGLE-WALL STEEL LINERS don't provide any additional insulation for the flue, and in fact probably decrease the insulating capacity of the chimney somewhat, due to the tendency of metal to transmit heat to the outside. This disadvantage may be partially overcome if you fill the space between the liner and the masonry with an insulating material such as mica chips or vermiculite. Do not use fiberglass, as moisture will render it useless. ABSOLUTELY avoid the use of any flammable material, such as styrofoam.

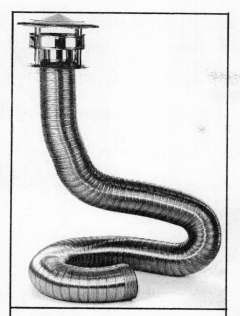

This is the new Z-Flex flexible stainless steel liner for chimneys with offsets.

THE DOUBLE- AND TRIPLE-WALL, "self-insulating" steel flue pipes are designed to be used as unenclosed stove pipe. Double-wall pipes have the space between the steel walls filled with asbestos or mineral wool. The triple-wall pipes use air space to insulate and are actually less insulative because the air is allowed to circulate between the inner and outer chamber. These have little application for relining an existing masonry chimney.

ONLY STAINLESS STEEL should be used for flue lining. Simple stove pipe will not stand up to the high temperatures and prolonged exposure to tars and acids. Stainless steel is classed by Underwriter's Laboratories as "Class A, All Fuel" pipe. Nevertheless, because of recent evidence, The OHJ goes on record as recommending that NO metal liner of any sort be used with coal, due to the metal's inability to resist attack by sulfuric and nitric acid. An attempt has been made to overcome this problem by using a different steel alloy in installations for use with coal stoves. Molybdenum steel, resistant to chemical attack, is available--but this is too new and unpredictable, and also too expensive for most residential purposes.

A MORE TRIED-AND-TRUE ANSWER to the problem of metal's vulnerability is the enamel-coated steel liner, which is similar to single-wall steel pipe but has a baked-on coating that's resistant to chemical attack. See page 192 for more information on this product.

## Poured-Cement Liners

Your THIRD CHOICE is new in the States, although it's been used in England since the 1960s. There, extensive use of coal made metal liners impractical, and an alternative to the relatively destructive installation of a clay liner was sought. In outline, the process is simple: A new cement lining is pumped into the chimney around a flexible, inflatable form, which is removed after the cement has cured. In practice, of course, the procedure is a little more complicated.

IN THIS COUNTRY, the system is marketed by at least four operations. The two with widest distribution are National SUPA-FLU Systems, Inc., and the BPF or British Poured Flueliner system, available through Chimney Relining, Inc. (see p. 192 for listings). Both of these companies market the system through certified dealers only, so availability is limited in some parts of the country.

AFTER A DETAILED inspection and repairs, a rubber "former" (which before inflation resembles a fire hose) is dropped down the chimney from the top, extending all the way down and out through the fireplace or furnace opening. The installer places a wooden form around the bottom of the hose, bracing it to prevent mortar from escaping at the bottom. Any secondary fireplaces or openings are similarly sealed. The rubber former is inflated to the desired flue size (usually 6 to 8 in. in diameter). Spacers hold the rubber former away from the chimney's walls and center it in the opening.

IN CHIMNEYS WITH OFFSETS, as with the other liner types, it's usually necessary to cut a hole in the side of the chimney in order to position the former properly. A special cement mortar in a slurry consistency is mixed on the

Rain Cap

90° elbow

These are some components of stainless steel liner pipe.

ground and pumped by hose to the top of the chimney, then down around the form. This mix, a proprietary formula, is basically a cementitious, refractory mortar with admixtures to decrease its weight and increase its insulating capacity, as well as aid its workability, durability, and fire retardancy. Properly applied, the mixture also seals cracks and increases the stability of the chimney.

AFTER THE MIX HAS CURED (10 to 12 hours), the former is deflated and removed, along with the other formwork. Any finish work is done now. Barring major repair work to the chimney, the whole process can be completed in two days.

THE MORTAR MIXTURE can withstand temperatures in excess of 2000° F., while clay or metal liners both start to melt at about 1700°. Temperatures over 1700° would be encountered only during a chimney fire. Still, it's nice to know that a cement-lined chimney could survive such a fire . . . IF, that is, the installation was done right.

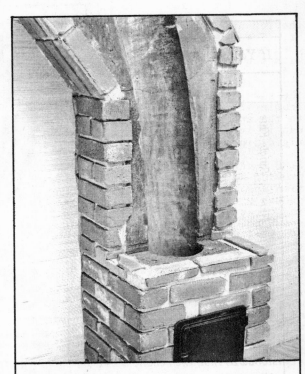

In this demonstration photo of PermaFlu, supplied by Chimney Relining, Inc., you can see the round flue formed by the cementitious refractory mortar. Supaflu is the trademark name of a similar process.

## The Bottom Line

A COMPARISON OF THE COSTS of these different systems is nearly impossible on paper. You can, of course, get estimates locally for each type of lining permitted by code. Cost factors include chimney size and condition, number and acuteness of angles, local regulations, and finish work. Materials vary in cost, too, but that cost is negligible in comparison to labor costs.

CLAY LINERS come in two-foot sections and sell for about $4 apiece for a per-foot price of $2. That doesn't include mortar or labor.

A THREE-FOOT LENGTH of standard, stainless steel, single-wall pipe, 6-in. diameter, is about $23, or about $7.50 per foot. Shorter sections and angles are higher. Labor costs for this system, however, should be considerably lower. Also, a straight-forward installation isn't beyond the abilities of a handy do-it-yourselfer.

FLEXIBLE STEEL LINER is more expensive, with 6-in. diameter selling for about $10 per linear foot. Here again, speed and ease of installation probably justify the added material cost.

THE FORM-AND-CEMENT METHOD COSTS vary with the nature of the chimney, but a standard installation in a two-storey house runs between $700 and $800. This is comparable to the cost of a clay-tile installation in an internal chimney—where the installer has to break through interior walls.

## Basics Of Chimney Construction

Chimney design varies, but basic principles of good construction are the same for all chimneys. The chimney has three functions: (1) to conduct waste gases out of the building; (2) to keep the gases hot while in the flue; and (3) to protect the other building materials from this heat. Good building practice and code regulations reflect these three objectives. If your chimney doesn't stack up to these basics, maybe you should think twice about reactivating unused flues.

• Think of the smoke leaving your stove or fireplace as a stream of water. Any sharp corners or turns, or any projections or roughness on the inside surface, will impede the flow. At no point should the chimney bend more than 30 degrees away from the vertical.

• In buildings where there is more than one flue in a single chimney stack, each flue should be completely separated by at least 4½ inches — the width of one brick. Holes or gaps in the masonry separating one flue from another will interfere with the draft of each. This is especially dangerous when one flue services a fireplace or woodstove and the other vents an oil- or gas-burning furnace. In such a case, the draft from the fireplace could cause back-puffing in the furnace flue, forcing flammable exhaust gases back into the furnace, creating an explosion. (This is also the reason why two heating appliances should not be vented through the same flue; in some areas, building codes specifically forbid it.)

• When a chimney runs along the outside of a building, the wall facing the outside should be 9 inches (the width of two bricks) in thickness, to adequately in-

sulate the flue from the colder outside air during the winter. This, unfortunately, is a rule that's ignored in all but the best construction. In an extremely cold climate, an air space is sometimes built into the chimney on the outside wall to insulate even more.

• There should be no wood touching the chimney in any place. The usual clearances are 2 inches for all framing members and ¾ inch for flooring and sub-floors. A firestop or spacing member in the framing should be installed at every floor level.

• The flue should extend one to two feet above the highest point on the building to prevent eddying air currents from causing back-puffing. On flat roofs, three feet is recommended. If two flues run in the same chimney, the tops should be set at different heights to aid the draft in each. A variety of chimney caps is available to keep rain out of the flue and still provide adequate draft (see p. 192).

• As to the size of the flue: For a fireplace, the flue area should be 1/10 the size of the area of the fireplace opening for a chimney over 15 feet tall. For a shorter chimney, this should be increased slightly.

• There are standard practices for safe and efficient stovepipe installation and stove hookup. You should, of course, become absolutely familiar with these before burning solid fuel.

| If Your Chimney Is... | And Your Heating System Is... | | | |
|---|---|---|---|---|
| | | Coal-Burning | Woodstove/Insert | Wood Fireplace | Gas/Oil Furnace |

| | | Coal-Burning | Woodstove/Insert | Wood Fireplace | Gas/Oil Furnace |
|---|---|---|---|---|---|
| *Single Flue* | Straight | cement; clay | cement; clay | stainless; cement; clay | stainless; cement; clay |
| | Slightly Offset | cement; clay | cement; clay | flexible | flexible |
| | Moderately Offset | cement | clay; cement | flexible | flexible |
| *Multi-Flue* | Straight | clay; enam. | stainless | stainless; clay | stainless |
| | Slightly Offset | clay | clay | flexible | flexible |
| | Moderately Offset | clay | clay | flexible | flexible |
| A Do-It-Yourself Job (straight flues only) | | *don't* | *don't* | stainless; flexible | stainless; flexible |

cement = poured cementitious refractory mortar; clay = clay tiles; enam. = enamelled steel; stainless = stainless steel liner pipe; flexible = flexible stainless steel. *We've based these guidelines for choosing a liner on conservative safety standards first, then economy. It should not override the recommendations of a competent installer or building codes.*

## Some Conclusions

WE CAN'T DISMISS any of the three basic relining systems, nor can we pick out one as "best." We've never before seen a clear discussion of these options, never found a logical list of dos and don'ts. So the OHJ editors and I have come up with a set of conservative guidelines to help you make a choice. We welcome any further experience or expert commentary from any of our readers.

● The single, most important factor is that you you trust your installer. If one mason or fireplace specialist comes highly recommended, buy that person's time AND expertise. If she or he has been installing clay tile for 30 years with the approval of the building inspector, for heaven's sake don't insist on an explanation of how many pennies you'd save by using metal.

● Don't trust someone who's never done it before to install clay tile in a chimney with offset angles. It takes special skill to mitre the clay tiles and mortar them in the bends. (Be sure refractory cement is used.)

● Unless your circumstances are unusual, metal isn't cost-effective for wood-burning stoves. It lasts from 4 to 10 years. Clay tile lasts upwards of 50 years, as does a poured liner.

● You can get away with a metal liner for exhausting a little-used fireplace. Just be sure to have it cleaned every year or so.

● We have doubts about the flexible steel liner for use with wood, because of the difficulty of cleaning creosote from the corrugations. In a few years, sweeps will know more about it. But it sounds like a great answer for any masonry chimney, straight or not, that is just used to

vent exhaust from a gas or oil furnace.

● DO NOT use metal liner if you're burning coal. Enamelled metal may be okay, but won't last as long as clay or poured lining. It makes sense only if you'd save a lot on labor costs for a straight chimney. (Installing enamelled metal in an offset chimney costs as much as clay.)

● The ONLY method we consider do-it-yourself is steel liner--and then only if the chimney is straight and sound, you're not burning coal, and the job is inspected by a fire marshal, qualified chimney sweep, professional installer, or code officer before its first use.

● Poured linings have the advantage of no seams--important for chimneys with offsets, because there's no seam or shelf for creosote to collect on. But it will cost as much or more than clay liner, because the installer will have to break the masonry, just as with clay.

● Dealers of the poured linings themselves expressed doubts about its use in multi-flue chimney stacks. It's virtually impossible to be sure of the condition of the brick partition between the flues. If there were any structural weakness in that partition, the added weight of Supaflu or Permaflu might cause it to give way. Also, any cracks would allow the slurrylike cement mixture to flow through into the other flue.

● Now for the requisite mention of reversibility: A clay liner or a metal liner can be removed--not easily, but it's possible. A poured lining, bonded to the original masonry chimney, cannot. This isn't a serious consideration for most old houses, with one exception: If the installation job is botched, you've got a real mess. We're back to the importance of finding a competent installer.

# Chimneys...

*In collaboration with this month's cover article, we have listed some national sources for flue liners or dealer information. Products like stainless steel or clay liners are generally available through your installer. Material costs do vary, but your most significant cost will be installation. Labor costs vary depending on your chimney and your location. So for local prices, consult your yellow pages under "Fireplaces" and "Chimney Builders and Repairers" for a dealer or installer.*

Almost identical to *Supaflu, Permaflu* is also a poured masonry reliner. The cost is comparable. For free information and the location of an installer in your area, write Chimney Relining Inc., 105 W. Merrimack St., PO Box 4035, Dept. OHJ, Manchester, NH 03108. (603) 668-5195.

*The temporary rubber former in place for a poured masonry chimney liner.*

(Photo courtesy of Chimney Relining, Inc.)

*Supaflu*, recently introduced in this country, has been used for many years in England and Europe. The process, described on page 190, involves inflating a stiff, tube-like former in the chimney, and pouring a patented refractory cement around it. After the cement sets, the rubber former is removed. Although it's no less expensive than traditional methods at $700-$800 for a direct chimney, and there isn't a proven track record in this country, *Supaflu* does provide an alternative for offset angles. Dealers/installers are in many areas of the U.S.; free literature. National Supaflu Systems, Inc., Rt. 30A, PO Box 289, Dept. OHJ, Central Bridge, NY 12035. (518) 868-4585.

Superior Clay makes these pretty chimney tops, as well as clay liners.

Best known for their handmade clay chimney tops, **Superior Clay** is also a manufacturer of traditional clay chimney lining. Available in a variety of sizes —7½ in. x 7½ in. to 24 in. x 24 in. (outside diameter), and 6 in. to 36 in. round (inside diameter)—clay liners can even be used in chimneys with wood frames. However, the manufacturer doesn't recommend use of this product in chimneys with severe offset angles. (Refractory cement only should be used to connect clay sections together.) Maintained properly, clay liners can last a lifetime. Write for a free brochure to Superior Clay Corp., PO Box 352, Dept. OHJ, Uhrichsville, OH 44683. (614) 922-4122.

*Z-Flex* is an air-tight, flexible, stainless steel liner that resembles a giant Slinky toy. Once installed, the liner is surrounded by Vermiculite, a loose-fill mineral insulation. Its advantages are in its seamless construction and uncom-

plicated installation. Available in 3- to 22-inch diameters, the liner is recommended for use only in masonry chimneys. The average installed cost is $400-$700, depending on the work involved, and the liner is said to last at least 4-5 years. Sold through distributors or direct; free literature is offered by Energy House, 105 W. Merrimack St., PO Box 4035, Dept. OHJ, Manchester, NH 03108. (603) 668-5195.

If you are considering a solid, stainless steel liner (an economical and practical choice for venting furnace gases), then you should know that no. 304, 24 gauge stainless is most often recommended as having the best performance at a residential cost. Mirror Stove Pipe Co., a long-time manufacturer of stove pipes, offers this product in a variety of sizes. A 6 in. diameter, 36 in. long stainless steel section is about $30; a direct 30 ft. liner would cost about $350-$400, installed. This product should only be used for relining a masonry chimney; it's approved for use with wood, but we wouldn't recommend it for use with coal. No literature is offered, but they will put you in contact with a distributor in your area. Mirror Stove Pipe Co., *Mirror Stainless Flue*, Box A, Dept. OHJ, Bloomfield, CT 06002. (203) 243-8358.

Europeans have used enamel-coated steel chimney liners for many years. Unlike uncoated steel, these can be used when burning coal. Heat-Fab's liner is enamelled inside and out; the cost is $10/ft. — about the same as stainless steel liners. These liners, as well as a #304, 24 gauge stainless-steel liner, are sold through distributors. Free information. Heat-Fab, Inc., 38 Haywood St., Dept. OHJ, Greenfield, MA 01301. (413) 774-2356.

## Stamps

For the Victorian buff who has everything: A unique collection of rubber stamps with designs dating from 1885 to the turn of the century! These aren't exactly a necessity for the old house, but we couldn't resist bringing them to your attention. The deeply etched rubber stamp is mounted on a wooden block; a turned wooden handle is a nice finishing touch. About 300 different designs — many of which are authentic copies of Victorian patterns — are yours to play with for $1.95 to $12 each. Gift certificates are also offered. Send $1 to see all the delightful designs and letter samples. Good Impressions, 1126 Avery St., Dept. OHJ, Parkersburg, WV 26101. (304) 422-1147.

## Solar/Conservation Products Catalog

If you are confused by the endless number of ads you see for solar components, then a catalog compiled annually by the Solar Components Corp. could help. It lets you see many different solar/energy products all at once, with write-ups that point out their various functions and specifications. Because energy conservation is an important adjunct to solar power, energy-saving products such as insulation (movable and fixed), window shades, and heat reflectors are described as well. Products listed are geared toward the do-it-yourselfer. Dozens of manufacturers are represented, but you can buy all the products from this single source. In addition, an extensive selection of books for beginners and experts is listed. The 82-page catalog is $3 from Solar Components Corp., PO Box 237, Dept. OHJ, Manchester, NH 03105. (603) 668-8186.

## Wood Mantels

*This imported English mantel is one of Readybuilt's top of the line.*

Wood fireplace mantels in Classical, Colonial and Colonial Revival, and Louis XV styles are offered by Readybuilt. Two reproductions of early 18th-century English mantels have recently been added to their line. Imported from England, these mantels are hand-carved from pine, have a wax finish, and are designed to fit American fireplaces. The mantel shown here is $1800; their other mantels begin at $200. (Custom models are also available.) Send $2 for their catalog to Readybuilt Products Co., Box 4425, 1701 McHenry St., Dept. OHJ, Baltimore, MD 21223. (301) 233-5833.

## Paint Stripping

As we mentioned in our August issue, we have been flooded with inquiries about *Peel Away* and other wonder products, all promoted as solutions for the most hated restoration task — stripping paint. So to be honest, when we heard about *QRB* our reaction was "so, another chemical paint stripper." But after a demonstration by Ronald Hack, the manufacturer of the product, we were quite impressed. *QRB* can be used without immediately burning your skin, and has only a bare trace of obnoxious fumes. It's applied in the usual liquid stripper fashion; you have to be sure to keep the surface moist, and wait until the stripper penetrates through all the paint layers (about the same length of time as any quality stripper).

On our oak sample, *QRB* barely raised the grain of the wood; we'd expect that only minimal sanding would ever be required. Also, the chemical doesn't need to be neutralized. But the feature we liked the best was clean-up: The terry-cloth rag the stripper was applied with was used again, like a shoe-shine rag, to remove the loosened paint. This was especially effective on spindles and carved details. Excess stripper can be wrung out and saved for reuse. Then, with a gentle shake of the rag, the paint chips are removed from the cloth (unlike most chemical strippers where the cost of paper towels seems to equal the cost of the stripper).

Drawbacks? The stripper is a soup of petroleum products and thus is highly flammable. The price is $15.98/gal. not including U.P.S. shipping. For free information and order forms write QRB Industries, 3139 U.S. 31 N., Dept. OHJ, Niles, MI 49120. (616) 683-7908 or 471-3887.

## Shades Of The Past

Elegant, flamboyant, vibrant...Victorian and turn-of-the-century lamp shades we thought we'd never see again are

now available, custom-made by Tracy Holcomb of Shades of the Past. One of these shades, hand-sewn of velvet, silk, and imported trimmings, will not only act as a centerpiece of a period room today, but is sure to become a family heirloom. Nine styles can be covered in your choice of color and trim; beads carry an extra charge. Shade prices run from $199 to $499. The company also stocks antique-finish, brass-plated floor- and table-lamp bases with prices beginning at $49. Send $2 for a color brochure, and feel free to call with questions or special requirements. Shades of the Past, Box 502, Dept. OHJ, Corte Madera, CA 94925. (415) 459-6999.

OHJ subscriber Clinton Kenneth Lokey of Princess Anne, Maryland, told us he's tried many different tools to aid in the stripping of exterior paint. He reports that the Red Devil #3005 tungsten-carbide scraper is the most helpful. Our experts agree that it's one of the best scrapers on the market. It costs about $30, and is so durable that it doesn't need frequent sharpening.

The OHJ staff recently learned of another great tool for paint strippers: A tapered, polypropylene, automotive-parts cleaner brush. Ask for ¾ in. or 1 in. size at most automotive stores; cost is about $4. These durable, stiff brushes are ideal for use with chemical stripper (which doesn't eat away at it) to get the paint out of details and carvings without damaging the wood.

# Opinion... Remuddling
## —Of The Month—

BEHIND THAT CUBIST facade (look hard!) are two handsome 19th century row-houses. We know they are owned by an educational institution, but we don't know the history of this unfortunate addition. However, just by looking at the new facade--which is nearly devoid of function--we can construct the probable scenario.

CAN'T YOU ALMOST hear the school's Dean of External Appearances declare: "Let's do something to update those dowdy old buildings!" So the school architect is unleashed and told to create a bold contemporary statement.

A BOLD CONTEMPORARY statement is fine...on a bold contemporary building. But to so blatantly destroy the integrity and character of someone else's work is self-indulgent--and a cultural crime.

IN 100 YEARS (if the new wall lasts that long), architectural historians will find this clash of styles fascinating. But for those of us who mourn the loss of still two more 19th century buildings, this misguided improvement is merely another tiresome example of remuddling.--C.L.

Submitted by: James W. Rhodes, AIA
New York, N.Y.

## The Old-House Journal®

69A Seventh Avenue,
Brooklyn, New York 11217

BULK RATE
U.S. Postage
PAID
New York, N.Y.
Permit No. 6964

Vol. X No. 10                                    $2.00

## The Old-House Journal

**Restoration and Maintenance Techniques For The Antique House**

# Exterior Wood Columns
## Practical Repairs For Do-It-Yourselfers

### By John Leeke

HOUSES WITH COLUMNED PORCHES and facades have been built in this country for over 150 years. These Classical and Colonial Revival homes are still popular today. But the quiet dignity of such houses is ruined when a rotting column threatens to let the porch roof collapse. This article explains methods for repairing columns, so your house can maintain its composure and serenity.

EXTERIOR COLUMNS are made of components that work together to provide massive visual and structural support for the entablature and roof framework. The main shaft is supported by a round base and square plinth. The capital visually terminates the column and serves to spread the load from the span above.

### Inspection

BEFORE YOU BEGIN working on your columns, you should carefully inspect your porch.
● What is the condition of the porch foundations?
● Do the joists and other structural floor members provide adequate support for the deck?
● Does the floor have weak or loose boards?
● Does the structural span above the columns sag between them? (If there is evidence of water trickling out between the soffit and architrave or fascia, remove these boards and inspect the timbers beneath.)

IF STRUCTURAL MEMBERS have been damaged, have an engineer or architect make a more complete assessment. Of course, you may not be able to proceed immediately with major repairs of the porch structure. Nevertheless, the condition of your columns should be stabilized or improved right away.

ROT CAN PROGRESS to such a point that you'll have to remove the column to work on it. (Rot can damage a column so severely that it's no longer supporting anything.) Removing a column isn't a complicated job. Use a system of wedges and heavy timbers to provide temporary shoring. Make sure that the load is being transferred to the ground. Place wooden plates at the top and bottom of the timbers to spread the load. Then remove the base of the column and drop down the shaft. If you're going to work on the porch before repairing the column, store it in a cool, dry place.

SPRUNG STAVES, large cracks, and chunks of rotten wood that have fallen away are the obvious indications that your columns need repair. But there are more subtle clues as well, such as the condition of the paint. If the paint is peeling, there's probably a lot of moisture in the wood. This moisture can also deteriorate the glue in the joints.

A HIGH MOISTURE CONTENT in the wood can cause expansion, stressing the struc-

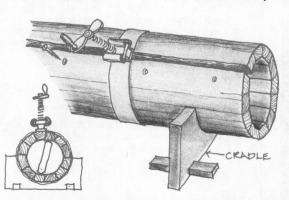

CRADLE

*continued on page 212*

![The Old-House Journal logo]

# The Old-House Journal®

*Editor*
**Clem Labine**

*Managing Editor*
**Patricia Poore**

*Assistant Editor*
**Cole Gagne**

*Assistant Editor/Products*
**Joni Monnich**

*Circulation Supervisor*
**Joan O'Reilly**

*Circulation Assistants*
**Peggy Scaglione**
**Barbara Bugg**
**Jeanne Baldwin**

*Office Assistant*
**Rafael Madera**

*Circulation Director*
**Paul T. McLoughlin**

*Technical Consultant*
**Alan D. Keiser**

*Architectural Consultant*
**Jonathan Poore**

*Contributing Editors*
**R. A. Labine, Sr.**
**John Mark Garrison**

*Published by The Old-House Journal
Corporation, 69A Seventh Avenue,
Brooklyn, New York 11217. Telephone
(212) 636-4514. Subscriptions $16 per
year in U.S. Not available elsewhere.
Published ten times per year. Contents
are fully protected by copyright and
must not be reproduced in any manner
whatsoever without specific permission
in writing from the Editor.*

*We are happy to accept editorial contri-
butions to The Old-House Journal.
Query letters that include an outline
of the proposed article are preferred.
All manuscripts will be reviewed, and
returned if unacceptable. However,
we cannot be responsible for non-
receipt or loss — please keep copies
of all materials sent.*

Printed at Photo Comp Press,
New York City

ISSN: 0094-0178
**NO PAID ADVERTISING**

Opinion...
# remuddling

*...continued from the back page*

**B**EFORE the solarizing portion of this remodeling took place, the owner had already taken all of the sensible steps we have advocated in OHJ (and more). The house had been caulked, windows were rebuilt and weatherstripped, counter-weights removed, exterior walls insulated and stuccoed (hmmm), roof insulated with both fiber-glass and rigid board, roofing material and color changed, an air-lock entry installed, all exterior gaps closed, convert-ed-from-coal furnace replaced with a super-efficient, tank-less gas boiler, and baseboard convectors had taken the place of old cast-iron radiators.

**A**FTER all these energy-conser-vation measures, the solar demonstration wall was added, with financing from the Depart-ment of Energy, to the tune of $10,000 to $17,000 additional.

UNDOUBTEDLY, the house is more energy efficient than it was. But how much more energy effi-cient did it become after the addition of the solar wall to an already much-improved house? Most individuals would not be able to justify the additional cost and payback time of adding solar after making all the con-servation improvements listed above.

THEN THERE are the not-insigni-ficant historical and aesthetic considerations...about which our readers have commented passionately on the following page.

*Patricia Poore*

## United States Department of the Interior

NATIONAL PARK SERVICE
WASHINGTON, D.C. 20240

The Old-House Journal
69A Seventh Avenue
Brooklyn, NY 11217

Dear Ms. Poore:

I can assure you that the rehabilitation of the 19th century residence shown in the Rodale brochure does not meet the Secretary of the Interior's "Standards for Rehabilitation." It clearly would be denied certification for tax purposes. The guidelines for applying the Standards call for "installing necessary mechanical systems in areas and spaces that will require the least possible alteration to the structural integrity and physical appearance of the building." The alterations to the roof lines, walls, windows, and porches have effectively destroyed the character of this historic building.

You may wish to call to the attention of your readers our recent publication, "Energy Conservation and Solar Energy for Historic Buildings: Guidelines for Appropriate Designs." Published in 1981, copies are available for $6.95 apiece from: The National Center for Architecture and Urbanism, 1927 S Street, N.W., Suite 300, Washington, DC 20009.

Sincerely,

*Ward Jandl*

Ward Jandl
Chief, Technical Preservation Services Branch
Preservation Assistance Division
National Park Service

Attached is a nomination for the Remuddled section, except this seems to be a re-remuddle.

I love Rodale Press and their publications. But, bless their collective hearts, I don't consider these pictures to be good advertising.

— Judith Abbott, Denton, Texas

I don't know if I will be the first of thousands of submissions you should get for Rodale Press as your Remuddling of the Month winner.

Granting the overwhelming need to use renewable energy sources, and granting that not every Victorian house must be saved in pristine purity; nevertheless, defacing an old house needn't be displayed to the public as the ideal path to the future.

The sin which most offends me with its needlessness is the corrugated roofing.

Many of your remuddling winners are quiet, simple houses in residential neighborhoods, whose only crime may be to offend the taste and sensibility of a few hundred people. With this example, Rodale has the capability to ruin innumerable houses and offend even millions of people.

— Verne Windham, Spokane, Wash.

This advertising came in the mail a few weeks ago. As the owner of a building about [the same] size, I vote for being cold and broke rather than doing something like this.

— Ed Bergo, Green Bay, Wisc.

Normally I don't write letters to editors but this was too much. The article* attached almost made me sick. It was such a screw-up, I felt you must know about it.

This poor house was destroyed. . . . I'd love to see this example exposed by OHJ.

— Rich Schaufert, Glendale, Missouri

*The article appeared in Home Improvement Contractor magazine. Their title for the article? "It May Not Look Like Much, But It's Certainly Energy Efficient!"
— ed.

Enclosed is a photo candidate for the remuddling of the year! The material is a promotion piece from our (usual) friends at Rodale. I buy many of their books but wouldn't buy this one, out of disgust for their poor taste.

— L. Roush, Philadelphia

Inside this brochure is a picture of the remuddling of the decade. Actually, as you can see, it is a re-remuddling of a Queen Anne. The back of the brochure, under the big '5,' claims the designs are 'aesthetically pleasing,' and that 'it is difficult to spot a retrofit.' The card we are to use to order the book wears a picture of a beautiful old house — just waiting, I suppose, for some solar retrofitting so it can look like the other house.

What is even more devastating to me is that Rodale Press is the company doing this. I'd have expected more respect from them. I suggest the OHJ write Rodale in protest and give them some valuable information on the subject of old houses.

— Judee Reel, Red Hook, N.Y.

Here's a grotesque remuddling that one normally tasteful publisher actually found commendable. If a compromise between historical integrity and energy efficiency had to be made (as it often does),increasing the exterior wall thickness on the inside and adding more insulation, or placing solar collectors on the roof where they'd be less obtrusive, would have been a gentler solution. As it is now, the house looks like an architectural skeleton.

Rodale Press usually keeps a tasteful eye open toward aesthetics in its New Shelter magazine, but this time someone fell asleep.

— Donald Smith-Weiss, Westbrook, Maine

Before solar, the house was by no means untouched — that's "stonecoating." But it did have its original window openings, massing, and slate roof. And when it looked like this, of course, nobody was displaying it as the path to the future.

As you can guess, I was quite disgusted by the cruel costume this proud old house is being forced to wear, but at the same time amused that anyone could call such a weird-looking place home.

The saddest part is that the owner could've achieved the same high fuel efficiency with proper storm windows, blown-in insulation,and good quality weatherstripping. I shudder to think how many people received this piece of trash, and who are thinking now of making a bad mistake. I don't know where this place is, and it's a good thing because I don't think I could stomach seeing it every day.

— David M. Doody, Wilmington, Del.

Rodale's books and magazines are excellent sources on solar energy, but in Solarizing Your Present Home, a happy marriage between renovation/restoration and solar energy does not exist.

— Bob Steigerwaldt, Tomahawk, Wisc.

I didn't have to look far for this example; it came in the mail. Also, look at 'Solar Myth No. 5' on the back. Doesn't quite jive with the photo!

— Bo Curtis, Curtis & Litzinger Bldrs., Long Beach, Cal.

I cannot believe that Rodale is pushing this!
— Mr. Schlesinger, Libertyville, Ill.

Enclosed is a brochure. . .it shows 'before solar' and 'after solar' pictures of a home which exemplify technology at its worst. At first, I thought the second picture was a photographic hoax, but I am now convinced that author Joe Carter and Rodale Press believe that the house [as shown] in the second photo is a substantial improvement. . . . They may be right, but only in one sense: the energy efficiency of the house.

— Wayne E. Stiefvater, San Francisco

From the book's author. . .

I recently received a letter from Ms. Judith Abbott in which she decried the appearance of the solar retrofit I did on my house. Her main contention seemed to be that the beauty of the building was destroyed by the passive solar space-heating system I built.

My essential response is that all old houses do not merit preservation as much as they very much need energy conservation improvements. The solar project at my house was funded by the U.S. Dept. of Energy as a demonstration to the public and to the building trades of just what is possible for using solar space heating on existing houses. The solar wall, as I call it, includes a Trombe-type wall, a greenhouse, a solar porch, and an air-heating collector (non-mass), along with the direct-gain dormer and skylights that heat and light the attic, which is being converted to living space.

Ms. Abbott stated that she was sending a photo of my house, which was used in a promotional piece for my book on solar retrofitting, to you for consideration in your remuddle of the month column. I'm rather surprised at the woman's temerity in this, and I trust you all will have the good sense not to run the picture. In any event, I also refuse permission for the use of my house to be represented in any negative way. The house is not a remuddle by any means, but a carefully planned series of energy and aesthetic improvements. Thank you.

— Joe Carter, Assoc. Editor, Book Div.
Rodale Books, Emmaus, Penn.

5  "I DON'T WANT MY HOUSE TO LOOK WEIRD." Neither does anyone else. All of the designs in SOLARIZING YOUR PRESENT HOME are aesthetically pleasing as well as super-efficient. In many cases, it's difficult to spot a retrofit. You'll find designs and examples that will blend well with your home's present style.

Rodale blasts "Solar Myth No. 5."

## Post-Victorian Domestic Architecture

# The Spanish Colonial Revival Style

By Alan Gowans

IT COULD WELL BE that more single-family houses were built between 1890 and 1930 than during all the preceding years of America's existence. A sizable minority of these belong to what is most commonly called the "Spanish Colonial Revival."

AT FIRST, this style was usually called Mission; by the 1920s, it was being called Mediterranean in California, Venetian in Florida, or (by the more erudite) Andalusian. A variant of it was called Pueblo, especially in New Mexico. But most consistently, it has been called Spanish Colonial.

THE BULK of Spanish Colonial buildings, especially the kind of small and medium-sized houses that most concern OHJ readers, generally have some or all of the following features:

● TILES are orangey-red or reddish-brown (sometimes terra cotta, sometimes painted metal) and cover all or at least the visible parts of roofs. This is perhaps Spanish Colonial's most distinctive characteristic. (Magazines of the period often call American Foursquares "Spanish" simply because they have such tiled roofs.) Most of these houses were built in areas having little rainfall or snow, and so the typical Spanish Colonial roof is low pitched.

● WALLS are white--sometimes painted concrete, more often stuccoed.

● ORNAMENT, if any, consists of terra-cotta patches set into both interior and exterior walls. Occasionally, these were made of painted, moulded concrete. Patterns are vegetal and/or abstract; sometimes, they're borrowed from Islamic as well as Spanish patterns.

● EXPOSED WOOD (in verandah posts or ceilings, for example) is stained and otherwise darkened.

● WROUGHT IRON GRILLEWORK is thin and often appears at windows or archways.

● OPENINGS (at least one, sometimes all) are round-headed.

● FORMS OF PEDIMENTS OR WALLS, especially in more elaborate buildings, tend to be slightly rounded. Gable-ends are scalloped, with vaguely parapet-like terminations.

THESE ARE, OF COURSE, only the most general characteristics of the style. But they identify as "Spanish Colonial" those rows and rows of box-bungalows lining streets in suburbs and small towns of California and Florida (and, more sparsely, in Texas and on through the more northerly states). Or rather, they identify vernacular, speculator Spanish Colonial for the lower and lower-middle classes. Spanish Colonial, as handled by professional architects for upper and upper-middle class clients, had additional characteristics that identify four or five distinct variants. In due course these details, too, came to be incoporated in speculatively built suburban houses.

BROADLY SPEAKING, each of these Spanish Colonial substyles was dominant over a particular period of time: Mission, from the mid-1880s to c. 1910; Mediterranean, from c. 1910 to 1930 (and within that, Andalusian, during the 1920s). And there were substyles that run across the whole period, such as the Pueblo.

## Mission Houses

THE MISSION REVIVAL got its name from a romantic interest in the missions built between the 1780s and the 1820s by Spanish missionary padres from Mexico.* Built in a string reaching from southern California to north of San Francisco, they were mostly fallen into ruin and abandoned after the Mexican Revolution of the 1820s, which nationalized and secularized them. They began to recover in the 1880s, and by the turn of the 20th century became objects of romantic pilgrimages (and often, unfortunately, romantic restoration) for the American population of California.

THE MISSIONS gave California a special romantic character. They made it seem as though it had long been settled--a quality that appealed to its 20th-century American population. The Mission substyle of Spanish Colonial, while featuring generally "Spanish" characteristics, is identifiable by elements copied or adapted or supposedly derived from mission churches. Among these elements:

This house is a full-blown and unmistakable example of the Mission substyle, with its full mission church facade, verandah in the shape of an atrium, scalloped chimneys, and side gables. It would be nice to report that such a splendid specimen was found on its native sod (or scrub, better) somewhere in central or southern California. Alas for logical expectations — this one was built on the Windsor side of the Detroit River, a block or two from the Ambassador Bridge! But it does show how far the magic of Hollywood glamour could carry a style.

● FACADES resemble mission-church facades, with prominently scalloped outlines and clearly recognizable parapets. They sometimes have towers on one end; occasionally on both.

● ARCADES are used to form an entranceway or side porch.

● BELL-TOWERS are seen most frequently on public buildings like railroad stations and city halls, but occasionally they appear on pretentious mansions. These have tiled roofs covering a series of diminishing squares, capped with a round or elliptical cupola.

● CLASSICAL DETAILS are extremely simplified, such as pilasters and tapering columns.

*It had nothing to do with the "Craftsman mission" furniture produced by Gustav Stickley. He called his populist version of Arts-and-Crafts "mission" because he felt a mission to refine and restore to good taste American design. Whatever Stickley's designs were, they weren't Spanish Colonial.

● CEILINGS are treated to resemble the open-timberwork ceilings of missions. In practice, this means beams (or boards imitating the effect of beams) are dark (usually stained) and exposed.

USING CHURCHES as primary models for houses or hotels or public buildings posed some obvious problems. In many cases, bell-towers were inappropriate and arcades impractical. Churches provided no models for interior plans. Similarly, California's missions didn't offer much in the way of ornament. This was at a time when most people still felt that a house without ornament definitely lacked something. So interior plans and ornament in the Mission style were, in general, borrowed:

● INTERIOR PLANS of mansions and public buildings in Spanish Colonial Mission tend to be along the same lines as those in other styles (e.g., Georgian or Tudor Revival). For small houses, Gustav Stickley's typical, simple boxlike rooms were characteristic from around 1910 on. Insofar as Spanish Mission had a distinctive character, it was represented by a greater emphasis on arches leading from room to room (although most styles of the 1890-1930 period had this feature to some degree).

● ORNAMENT, when there is any (and there usually is some), is of simple floral or abstract form, derived from churrigueresque churches or church interior furnishings of Mexico. (In general, Mexican churches were more lavish, bigger, and above all older than the Californian missions. They still had the tradition of patches of lavish ornament associated with the Churriguera family-- sculptor-architects active in Barcelona from the 1680s through the 1730s. Their "churrigueresque" effects could be easily simplified and replicated in plaster, iron, or cement.)

## Mediterranean Houses

BORROWING FROM MODELS other than California mission churches became an accepted practice, and so it was a short step to borrowing elements that looked more or less Spanish, wherever they came from. Acceptable models included the domestic buildings of adobe brick, which were built in California from the late 18th through the early 19th centuries; after that, the domestic buildings of Spain itself; then Spanish churches; Italian architecture; and details from Islamic North Africa.

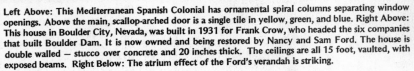

Left Above: This Mediterranean Spanish Colonial has ornamental spiral columns separating window openings. Above the main, scallop-arched door is a single tile in yellow, green, and blue. Right Above: This house in Boulder City, Nevada, was built in 1931 for Frank Crow, who headed the six companies that built Boulder Dam. It is now owned and being restored by Nancy and Sam Ford. The house is double walled — stucco over concrete and 20 inches thick. The ceilings are all 15 foot, vaulted, with exposed beams. Right Below: The atrium effect of the Ford's verandah is striking.

HENCE, the term "Mediterranean" seemed appropriate, because California's coastal climate is one of only five areas on earth classified as Mediterranean. (The others are southwest Africa, southwest Australia, and coastal Chile.) High style architects, as usual, led the way. But details and concepts from famous mansions like "The Breakers" at Newport (R.M. Hunt, mid-1890s) or the Gillespie house in Montecito (Bertram Goodhue, 1903) or Goodhue's churrigueresque extravaganzas for the San Diego Panama California International Exposition (1915) soon began filtering down into ordinary speculative building. These are some of the resultant characteristics:

● WALLS, exterior and (especially) interior, are plastered to simulate adobe: rough, lumpy texture; white or earth-hue colors.

● TRIM is scarlet, orange, azure blue, and other "Mediterranean" colors.

● CASEMENT WINDOWS are used, often framed with iron grilles.

● VERANDAHS are treated like an arcade, atrium, or cloister typical of Mediterranean domestic building.

● WALKS and driveways are paved with random flat stones, often painted a variety of colors to match the trim.

● ONE WALL is extended to make an entrance (usually a round-headed arch) into the backyard or the garage--an obvious attempt, like the verandah treatment, to suggest the effect of an internal atrium typical of Spanish domestic architecture.

● ARCHES are featured in a rather sophisticated manner, outside and in. Round-headed, Mission-type arches persist, but pointed, flattened, or scalloped Moslem-type arches also appear.

Interior arches often repeat exterior forms, both in walls separating rooms and in recessed niches flanking fireplaces.

● ROOF TILES tend to be red and semi-cylindrical, in imitation of Spanish peasant and vernacular building; an uneven effect is thereby produced. Sometimes, these tiles are real terra cotta, but often the effect is reproduced in metal.

● FIREPLACES set into walls are common, often with ceramic tiles of Spanish or Moorish design in addition to or instead of niches.

THESE FEATURES also characterize the "Venetian" of Florida--a term meant especially to publicize Miami and Coral Gables, where Merrick and other developers simulated canals and lagoons of Venice, and provided bridges, islands, and other exotica.

BY 1930, EVEN SMALL Spanish Colonial houses were quite sophisticated, part of a general trend toward academic correctness, which set in all across the country by the turn of the century. Every style, not just Spanish Colonial, was used more self-consciously than before. The idea of houses with each room in a different style was generally condemned by 1930 as absurdly bad taste.

YET THIS GREATER AWARENESS of correctness did not mean inflexibility. High Style Spanish Colonial (such as the work of George Washington Smith and James Osborn Craig of Santa Barbara or Wallace Neff of Pasadena) as well as ordinary middle-class homes showed enormous variety and inventiveness. These qualities appear particularly in the Pueblo and proto-Modern varieties (or substyles) of Spanish Colonial.

IT IS OUTSIDE of our focus here to have a detailed discussion of how architects such as Bernard Maybeck of San Francisco, Irving Gill

The Spanish Colonial Revival style is typified by the features of this house: tiled, low-pitched roof; white walls; round-headed windows and doors.

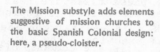

The Mission substyle adds elements suggestive of mission churches to the basic Spanish Colonial design: here, a pseudo-cloister.

The Mediterranean substyle brings new qualities to Spanish Colonial: an extended wall forming an archway into the backyard; the verandah with tower, reminiscent of Italian architecture.

of Pasadena, Gregory Ain, or (to a lesser degree) Julia Morgan used Spanish Colonial as a vehicle for personal expression. Nor can we more than mention such proto-Modern Spanish Colonial buildings on the popular level as you find in the "Art Deco Historic District" of Miami. However, the Pueblo substyle, or Santa Fe Revival as it is sometimes called, deserves more extended mention.

## Pueblo Houses

CENTERED IN NEW MEXICO, Pueblo is, in one sense, not part of the Spanish Colonial Revival, because its forms derived not so much from Spanish buildings as from pueblos (villages) built by Native Americans of the region that became New Mexico. (The old pueblo outside Taos is perhaps the most famous of them.) These forms were adopted by the Spaniards more by necessity than choice, because virtually the only labor force available was Native American. The Governor's Palace at Santa Fe, originally built in 1609-10, is the best known Pueblo model. The Pueblo Revival style has several distinguishing features:

● BEAM ENDS project at the tops of walls. These are the beams that carry ceilings; normally, they would be sawn off level with the top sill of the wall framing. But in the original manner of building they weren't sawn off because adobe walls decayed faster than wood in this arid climate, and the same beams could be used in another building that might be bigger (and so require longer beams). Of course, in modern versions, the beam ends are sometimes artificial.

● WALLS are treated as a moulded, sculptural unit (properly rounded, but in mass-produced houses, sharp-angled). This is a distinct contrast with the thin, flat plane of Spanish Colonial proper.

● WINDOWS are recessed and squarish, rather than round-headed. In Pueblo buildings proper, there were no arches, vaults, or domes.

IN MORE ELABORATE BUILDINGS--shopping centers, theaters, and the like--other features appear:

● TOWERS are squarish and tapering, with open "belfries." Sometimes, they have a grillework of metal or wood in the openings.

● COLUMNS consist of posts with simple cross-pieces for capitals. (A version of these also appears in Spanish Colonial proper; a famous example is Maybeck's Packard Showroom in San Francisco.)

A FEW PUEBLO STYLE EXAMPLES had already appeared in New Mexico in the 1890s; a hotel had been built in California in this style by 1893. Like other Spanish Colonial substyles, Pueblo flourished mightily in the 1920s and on into the 1930s. Unlike them, it is still very much alive today.

DRIVING WEST OUT OF TEXAS, you're struck by the appearance of Pueblo rather than Spanish Colonial proper as soon as you cross the New Mexico border. Native New Mexicans will tell you that Texas tried to annex the much poorer territory of New Mexico several times, but were resisted because New Mexico was a free state and Texas a slave state. Hence, New Mexicans have always felt a need to distinguish themselves from their richer, aggressive, and more powerful neighbor. Be that as it may, this style does indeed mark the border, giving New Mexico a distinct regional character. This may well be why Pueblo continues to flourish: Architecture whose social function is still vital never really goes out of date.

With this Pueblo house in Las Cruces, New Mexico, you can clearly see the exposed beam ends and square windows typical of the style. (Note the matching garage at right.)

## The Hollywood Halo

WHICH BRINGS US to a general consideration of social function. Why should Americans have built in Spanish Colonial at all? In 1898, Americans were engaged in a war against Spain, undertaken to rescue Spanish colonials from a corrupt and decadent regime. Less than 30 years later, they were putting up courthouses (Santa Barbara's is the famous example) in pure Spanish style--"most appropriate to the traditions of California" and (from the Santa Barbara guidebook) "an example of government service to coming generations."

TRULY, THE APPEAL of exotic, tropical Spain, its dances and romances, overwhelmed all reservations. Combine that with glamourous movie stars living in Spanish Colonial mansions, and one can understand how Spanish Colonial mansions might be built in the fogs of Seattle, the snows of Ottawa, and the freezing winters of Minnesota. But that is another, book-length, story.

DR. ALAN GOWANS is a Fellow at the Center for Advanced Study in the Visual Arts at the National Gallery of Art in Washington, D.C. He is also a Professor of History in Art at the University of Victoria in British Columbia and the author of numerous articles and books. Currently, Dr. Gowans is writing a book about post-Victorian architecture, to be published by The Old-House Journal.

# Lincrusta-Walton

## Can The Democratic Wallcovering Be Revived?

By Bruce Bradbury

IN 1877, LINCRUSTA-WALTON was patented by Frederick Walton, the Englishman who had previously scored an international success with his revolutionary floor covering 'linoleum'. (See OHJ, Jan. & Feb. 1982.) Basically a thin and beautifully embossed version of linoleum mounted on either canvas or water-proof paper, Lincrusta-Walton was the first durable embossed wallcovering to be machine-made and mass marketed. It's still found in many American houses, most commonly as a wainscotting, or as a wallcovering in dining areas. If unpainted, it may be in excellent condition, but more frequently its delicate relief has been obscured by successive layers of paint.

AMERICAN MANUFACTURE of lincrusta was started in 1883 by Fr. Beck & Co. of Stamford, Connecticut, under license from the original English firm. The restrained and 'artistic' patterns of England were soon joined by an avalanche of new designs intended to feed the American public's insatiable appetite for novelty. By 1885, Beck & Co. was offering 150 different patterns in Egyptian, Greek, Persian, Mooresque, Japanesque, Medieval, Renaissance, Louis XVI, and Eastlake styles.

SPECIAL PATTERNS were produced for dados, dado rails, wall fillings, mantels, book bindings, splash plates for washstands, table mats, and fingerplates. In the American West, where fine wood for wainscotting was extremely expensive, lincrusta became the logical and ubiquitous substitute.

LINCRUSTA'S immediate success on both sides of the Atlantic was partially due to its own intrinsic merit, and partially due to its embodiment of specific virtues held in high esteem by the Victorians.

**Frederick Walton**
A 19th-century entrepreneur.

IT WAS INHERENTLY IMITATIVE. The Victorian middle class took keen delight in machine-manufactured items that imitated materials previously available only to the wealthy. A shrewd businessman as well as an inventor, Walton produced a series of patterns in close imitation of expensive, hand-tooled Cordovan leather, which since the Renaissance period has been a hallmark of wealth and conspicuous consumption.

LINCRUSTA'S delicate relief and ability to take a broad variety of finishes enabled not only the imitation of leather, but also fine plasterwork, carved wood, repoussé metalwork, and carved ivory. The intrinsic beauty of the material was recognized by leading architects and decorators of the period, who frequently specified its use either in its plain state (with a protective coating of varnish), or given a simple glaze to highlight the relief pattern.

IT WAS "SANITARY." Great strides in hygiene were made in the Victorian era, and by 1877 a strong interest had developed in "sanitary" or washable wall surfaces to replace calcimine paint and water soluble pigments in wall-paper. Lincrusta was, as a linoleum derivative, impervious to water and could easily be scrubbed without damage. So wholesome was its reputation that it was even recommended as a hygienic decoration for hospital wards.

IT WAS DURABLE. Enthusiastically touted as the "indestructible wallcovering," lincrusta lived up to its reputation. Period advertisements claimed that it could be trodden, beaten, struck with the sharp end of

Here is a small sampling of the many patterns Lincrusta-Walton was embossed in. Besides numerous decorative patterns, imitation leather and "oak panelling" were popular. Perhaps the most common use of lincrusta was as a dado or wainscot in stairhalls, but it was also used in panels on a wall, or as a frieze. By 1885, an American manufacturer offered 150 patterns. The material was usually finished in place with an endless variety of glazing techniques.

a hammer, immersed in water, exposed to weather, and otherwise abused without any signs of deterioration. It did not warp or rot, and could not be eaten by worms or white ants, which encouraged its use in tropical areas. An immediate and popular use of the product was as wainscotting in stairway halls. This allowed the moving of heavy furnishings up and down stairs without damage to the walls. Its uses spread outside the home to include public buildings, ships, railway carriages, early motor cars, and shopfronts.

🜨 IT WAS DEMOCRATIC. The bulk of lincrusta was sold in its raw state, ready to be finished in place. Lavishly decorated in imitation of leather, it was found to be suitable to adorn the walls of the mansions of Rockefeller and Carnegie. The same material treated with a simple glaze could be found in middle class houses and workingman's cottages from Maine to California. Although comparatively more expensive than wallpaper, its extreme durability made it a cost effective wall treatment for all classes.

## Linoleum For The Wall

HE MANUFACTURING PROCESS was similar to that of linoleum, but cork was removed from the formula to allow for greater embossed detail and a finer texture. Oxidized linseed oil, gum, resin, wood fiber, paraffin wax, and pigment were mixed together and then spread on a canvas backing. The canvas and mixture was then run, under great pressure, through two rollers set close together on a parallel axis. One of the cylinders was engraved with the desired pattern, which was then transferred to the lincrusta mixture.

ONCE EMBOSSED, the material was hung to dry in heated sheds for two weeks, after which it was ready for shipping. In 1887, the canvas backing was replaced by a waterproof paper. When lincrusta is damaged or pulled away from a wall, it's this paper backing that separates and gives rise to the erroneous impression that lincrusta is some sort of paper or cardboard composite.

ROLLS OF LINCRUSTA are 22 in. wide, 11 yards long, from 2 to 7 millimeters thick, and can weigh up to 28 lbs. depending on the design. Lincrusta is as pliable as a stiff cloth, and when warmed can easily bend to cover a curved or uneven surface. It was pigmented in the manufacturing process, the most popular shades being bone and a pale brick color. These tints were generally intended to serve as suitable backgrounds for more elaborate finishes applied by the purchaser, although some ready-finished patterns were made available by 1885.

## Reviving Your Lincrusta

OT SURPRISINGLY, lincrusta has often been obscured by layers of paint in an old house. There is no reliable way to strip paint from lincrusta, because chemicals eat away at it, heat makes it pliable and easily damaged, a flame will set it on fire, and it's an uneven, unscrapable surface.

ANDY LADYGO, Workshop Director for The Society for the Preservation of New England Antiquities in Boston, has been experimenting with lincrusta stripping. He's been generous enough to reveal his current experimental method -- but warns that it doesn't always work, and doesn't remove all the paint: Carefully warm the embossed

(Left) Bruce Bradbury was a consultant in the re-creation of the "lincrusta" panels for the California State Capitol. Cast in gypsum, the moulds required a skilled artist to carve the fine details.

(Right) Lincrusta in the reception hall of the Pettigrew House, Sioux Falls, South Dakota (1886), is a moss green with gilded highlights.

(painted) surface with a heat plate or heat gun, being careful not to hold it in one place for too long. When the paint becomes just barely soft (before it bubbles), apply non-hardening modeling clay (such as plasteline), putty, or softened paraffin to the surface. Gently press the clay into the embossed material, then carefully pull it away. If you are lucky some of the softened paint will come with it. After the surface dries completely (and hardens) you can try to remove the remaining paint with patience and controlled chipping with a scalpel.

WITH THIS METHOD, or any other, be sure to try a test patch in an obscure corner of the room. A note of caution: Lincrusta is a flammable material. Under no circumstances should it be exposed to an open flame.

LINCRUSTA IS A LINSEED OIL COMPOUND and thus absorbs into itself a portion of any oil-based glaze applied to it. Transparent glazes were much preferred for finishing as they built up rich variations of tone in the crevices and valleys of the pattern. The following traditional glaze can be adapted to reglaze your lincrusta:

1) BEGIN BY CHOOSING YOUR COLOR. Mix a glaze consisting of colors-in-oil (finely ground color pigments in linseed oil),[1] and a small amount of Japan drier. Thin this mixture with turpentine to the consistency of a stiff paste. The mixture should be able to stay on a board without running. (It might be tricky to match an existing glaze, so take your time and test the color in an inconspicuous place.)

2) TAKE A STIFF BRUSH, such as a stencilling brush, and "rub in" the color across the surface. "Rubbing in" doesn't require that the entire area be covered with a uniform layer of color, only that the entire surface be covered. Slight variations in tone enrich the final appearance. When half a wall is covered (the time needed for the penetration of the color), go back over the surface with a rag to wipe off the excess glaze and highlight chosen details, such as the rib of a leaf.

3) WHEN DRY, coat with gloss varnish and then add a second coat of flat varnish (flat, satin, and gloss varnishes were all used --- flat and satin were preferred for the finish coats).

LIGHTER SHADES OF COLORING can be had by mixing the colors in oil with a commercial glazing liquid. More elaborate treatments could include the laying of gold leaf, Dutch metal, or bronzing powder on areas of the pattern; painting various elements in oil colors straight from the tube; and the sprinkling of gold dust or bronzing powder on a nearly dry varnish coat and then polishing the surface with a chamois cloth. (The decorating trade of the period soon realized that the simplest treatments were often the most effective. Elaborate painting and gilding tended to obscure the beauty of the finely detailed embossing--something that is still true today.)

---

(1) Raw sienna, burnt sienna, raw umber, burnt umber, and their various admixtures were the colors most commonly used. If you can't locate colors-in-oil in a local paint store they can be mail ordered from Wolf Paints and Wallpapers, 771 Ninth Avenue, Dept. OHJ, New York, NY 10019. (212) 245-7777.

## Lincrusta Today

LINCRUSTA-WALTON IS STILL BEING MANUFACTURED in England today, using the original machinery and only slight variations in formula. It's a very inexpensive wallcovering, readily available in English hardware stores. Unfortunately, no designs dating before 1950 are being produced at present and the patterns available (fake brick, stucco, barnboard, and some quasi-psychedelic geometrics) could not satisfy even the most desperate historic-house renovator.

FOUR ORIGINAL ROLLERS have been located at the mill, including an Eastlake dado and a Renaissance damask wall pattern. These rollers sit unused for several reasons. (1) Lincrusta machines were made for mass production and cannot be economically employed for runs of under 1000 rolls.

*Around 1900 Lincrusta was produced to imitate oak paneling.*

(2) The British public, with a conveniently long decorative arts history, is not as imbued with enthusiasm for the Victorian era as their American counterparts, who have little else to choose from. No domestic English market for Victorian lincrusta is thought to exist by the company. (3) The linseed oil base that gives lincrusta many of its desirable qualities makes it unable to meet current fire codes for new construction and major rehabilitation jobs, such as hotels, from which a manufacturer would derive a considerable percentage of sales.

DESPITE THESE DRAWBACKS, company officials have indicated a willingness to produce some of the old designs, should a suitable market be proven to exist. If you would care to write a letter of encouragement, the address is:

> Gordon Fearnley
> Crown Decorative Products, Ltd.
> Paint Division
> PO Box No. 37  Crown House
> Hollins Road
> Darwen
> Lancashire, England

IN THE MEANTIME, another of the great embossed wallcoverings, Anaglypta, is being test-marketed by Crown in Canada. Its invention, uses, and current availability will be discussed in another article, coming soon.

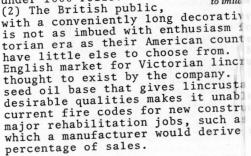

Bruce Bradbury fell in love with the history of Lincrusta during his years spent researching English design of the 1800s. He's a noted wallpaper historian as well as a maker of fine, hand-printed wallpapers in the style of leaders of the late 19th century, such as Morris, Pugin, and Dresser (his papers are affordable!) To get in touch with Bruce: Bradbury and Bradbury Wallpapers, PO Box 155, Dept. OHJ, CA 94510. (707) 746-1900.

Many of the photos in this article were taken by Bruce, an architectural historian, and associate of Bradbury.

# Don't Despair...Bondo's Here

## How To Patch Your Lincrusta

*There are numerous techniques currently being used by preservationists to reproduce/recreate lincrusta and other embossed papers (or to mould patches for existing sections). However, all of these methods have one or more of the following drawbacks: They're expensive; you might have to handle potentially dangerous chemicals; some require an artist/sculptor to carve fine details; and the casting materials are usually not pliable.*

*But don't despair...When repairing a damaged dado for rock star Graham Nash, Jerry Goss, a California sculptor, developed a simple and inexpensive process that is practical for the average homeowner. This process enables you to create a patch where only a small area has been damaged—much better than ripping it all off because of a small hole!*

**INGREDIENTS (and where to find them):**
- *Micro-crystalline wax (art supply store)
- *Silicone lubricant spray (3-M Spray-Mate Dry Lubricant or equivalent—hardware store)
- *Auto body putty (Bondo or equivalent—hardware store or auto supply shop)
- *Aluminum window screening (hardware store)
- *Contact cement (building supply store)
- *Fiberglass primer (marine supply)

**TOOLS:**
- *Pencil and sheet of paper
- *Pan of hot water
- *Shallow baking pan or heavy canvas
- *Small sculptor's modelling tool
- *Tin snips                    *Matte knife

**PROCESS:**
1. Begin by creating a tablet of wax about ¼-in. thick and a little larger in area than the projected patch. Melt some micro-crystalline wax (be sure to use indirect heat such as a double-boiler—it's flammable), and pour it into a shallow baking pan that has been sprayed with silicone lubricant. You can improvise a 'pan' by using damp canvas or heavy cloth placed on a flat surface with the edges propped up to prevent the wax from spilling. It's advisable to make a few wax tablets in case your first attempt at mould-making is unsatisfactory. Once the tablets are made, set them aside and proceed with the following steps:

2. Cut out the damaged section(s). A jigsaw-shaped patch will generally be less noticeable than a geometric one.

3. Tape a sheet of paper over the cut-out area and, with a pencil, make a rubbing of the edges of the area to be patched and the surrounding lincrusta pattern (as if making a brass rubbing).

4. Remove the paper from the wall and carefully cut away the central area that's to be patched with a matte knife, creating a paper template.

5. Take the paper template and tape it over a section of lincrusta that is in good condition, matching it to the same repeating elements as marked by the "rubbing" on the template.

6. Spray the lincrusta that's exposed, through the hole in the template, with silicone lubricant.

7. Soften the wax tablet by soaking it in a pan of hot water. Remove from water, wipe dry, and press against the template. With your fingers, work the wax gently into the lincrusta to achieve an accurate impression.

8. Remove paper template and wax together from wall and check the quality of the impression. This is now your mould for the lincrusta patch.

9. Spray the wax mould with silicone lubricant.

10. Mix up some Bondo or other auto body putty according to the directions on the label. With a small palette knife, gently work the putty into the wax mould until the thickness of the putty approximates the thickness of the lincrusta on the wall.

11. Take a piece of aluminum window screening, slightly larger than the intended patch, and press it gently down into the Bondo to provide a stable backing for the patch.

12. When the Bondo has set, remove it from the mould with the paper template attached to the Bondo. Turn it over and cut the finished patch (Bondo plus screening) as marked by the paper template, using tin snips.

13. Use contact cement to stick patch to wall. Fresh Bondo applied with a modelling tool can be used to patch the seam between the patch and the original lincrusta. Coat the patch with fiberglass primer and it's ready to be painted or glazed.

*(Note) The Bondo continues to harden with time, so it can be glued to a wall when still pliable — a great asset in older houses with uneven wall surfaces.*

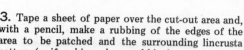

# How To Clean And Polish MARBLE

By Lynette Strangstad

IF YOUR OLD HOUSE has marble mantels, no doubt you consider yourself quite lucky. A marble mantel lends grace and elegance to any room. But a marble mantel can also pose quite a restoration challenge if it's covered with paint--or else so badly stained that you almost wish it were painted! No need to despair, however: Restoring marble mantels is a task that you can undertake yourself. The secret lies in first carefully analyzing what needs to be done, and then proceeding slowly until you've had a chance to thoroughly test the treatment method you've chosen.

## Dirt & Grime

THE MOST COMMON AILMENT that afflicts marble mantels is simply a layer of dirt and grime that obscures the beauty of the stone. This film can usually be removed with water and a non-ionic detergent (e.g., Ivory Liquid), applied with a medium-stiff natural-bristle brush. A tampico masonry brush will also work, as will a plastic-bristled brush. Avoid wire brushes and steel wool, as the metal can scratch the marble and possibly create rust stains. A toothbrush is handy for cleaning carvings.

ANY DIRT remaining after the initial washing calls for a stronger cleaning agent. Try household ammonia diluted with water, or full-strength ammonia if necessary. Some stains will respond better to hydrogen peroxide and water. If you prefer, a commercial alkaline masonry/marble cleaner may be used as well.

TWO OTHER POSSIBILITIES--not particularly recommended--for evening out the color of unevenly cleaned marble are: (1) Washing with oxalic acid (available in crystal form in drugstores) diluted with water; or (2) Washing with dilute household bleach. Oxalic acid and bleach are both weak acids, and so will react chemically with marble. Even fairly weak solutions may cause etching and removal of the highly polished marble surface.

DO NOT, under any circumstances, use bleach an ammonia together. Laundry bleach and ammonia produce toxic chloramine gases. Severe irrita tion of the respiratory system can result afte prolonged exposure or in sensitive individuals Don't mix bleach and oxalic acid, either.

## Paint

PAINT, the second likeliest camouflage of your marble's beauty, can be removed with standard chemical paint strippers used according to manufacturers' directions. Since marble can be easily gouged with a single misguided stroke of a metallic scraper, remove paint sludge with a wooden scraper with rounded corners. You can also use Teflon or wooden spatulas of the type used with Teflon-coated frying pans.

TO REMOVE THE LAST TRACES of paint, re-apply the paint remover and let it soak. If you are using a methylene chloride stripper, at this point you could use water, alcohol, or liquid paint remover to wash the surface, scrubbing with a natural bristle brush. (DO NOT use steel wool!) If you're using a solvent-type, liquid paint remover such as QRB (see OHJ, Sept. 1982 p. 193), you should be able to just brush the softened paint off with a poly propylene-bristle parts cleaning brush.

## Poultice For Stains

STAINS ARE TROUBLESOME because in most cases the discoloration is down in the pores of the stone. Commercially available poultices can deal with most marble stains, but if you want to try your hand at making your own poultice, the process is outlined below.

A FEW STAINS can be removed by washing with solvent alone. In using this procedure, however, i is important to pre-wet the marbl surrounding the stain with water t

## Poultice Solvents For Removing Marble Stains

| | |
|---|---|
| **SMOKE STAINS** | Absorbent + powdered alkaline cleaner and water (baking soda is a good choice) |
| **OIL STAINS**<br>Butter, wax, crayon,<br>magic marker, etc. | Absorbent + acetone, or naphtha, or mineral spirits |
| **ORGANIC STAINS**<br>Coffee, fruit juice,<br>fabric dyes, etc. | Absorbent + full-strength household ammonia or 20% hydrogen peroxide |
| **RUST STAINS** | Rust is one of the most difficult stains to remove. The commercial "Italian Crafts-man" poultice will take out some rust stains. More difficult rust spots require a two-step process: first wetting with a sodium hydrosulfate solution, then treating with sodium citrate crystals and a water-wet poultice. Professional help may be needed. |

The poultice absorbent can be any absorbent white material, such as whiting (powdered chalk), marble dust, talc, Fuller's earth, tin oxide, white blotting paper, white facial tissue, white paper towels, etc. There are also commercial poultices, such as the "Italian Craftsman" brand. The thicker the poultice layer, the better it will draw; minimum thickness is about ¼ inch.

*(1) Test fragment of marble had surface grime cleaned off by scrubbing with a soft brush and detergent solution. An unidentified stain remains in the marble. (2) A poultice of Fuller's earth and mineral spirits was applied. In photo, the poultice is almost dry. (3) After dried poultice powder was removed, some of the stain is gone—indicating that some of the components of the stain were oil-based, since they dissolved in the mineral spirits. (4) Test fragment is completely clean after a second poultice of Fuller's earth and ammonia was applied. Successful use of the ammonia solvent indicates that some of the stain was organic.*

*The result of a successful cleaning project.*

avoid spreading the stain to a larger area. After pre-wetting, apply the proper solvent, allow it to set, then soak it up with paper towels. In most cases, however, a poultice will provide better results than a solvent alone.

A POULTICE IS MADE by combining a highly absorbent white material with either water or a solvent to form a creamy paste. This mixture is then troweled on and allowed to dry. Upon initial application, the dry stone will pull in the solvent, which will in turn dissolve the stain. As the poultice starts to dry out through evaporation, the solvent in the stone migrates back into the poultice, carrying the stain with it. For greatest ef-

fectiveness, the poultice should be applied in a thick layer--at least ¼-inch. The thicker the poultice layer, the more solvent that can come into contact with the stain.

TO ALLOW MAXIMUM working time for the poultice cover the treated area with Saran Wrap or othe plastic for up to 48 hours. Then remove the plastic and allow the poultice to become thoroughly dry. Once dry, it can be carefully scraped (that wooden scraper is again a good idea), brushed or vacuumed off the marble. In stubborn cases, you may have to apply a poultice two or three times to get complete removal.

THE POULTICE MATERIAL can be Fuller's earth (available in many drugstores) or tin oxide (available through lapidary supply stores). You can also use whiting (powdered chalk), or even shredded white facial tissue, or white

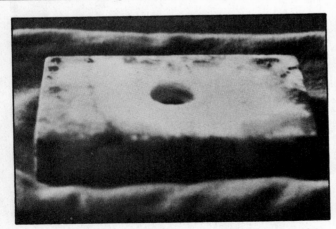

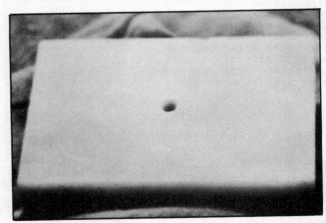

*The small marble base in photo at left was badly streaked by smoke and soot. The piece was allowed to soak for a week in a* commercial marble cleaner. *The result, shown in photo at the right, was almost complete removal of the stains.*

paper towels, or white blotting paper. For appropriate solvents, see page 209.

RUST STAINS are among the most difficult to remove. Beware of commercial rust removers; most are acidic and will etch the surface of the marble. Commercial poultices will remove some rust stains--but not all. Difficult rust stains call for a two-step process: First, make a soaking solution from 1 qt. of water and ¼-lb. of sodium hydrosulfate crystals. Apply this solution to the stain with a wet cloth, and leave the cloth on the stain for at least 15 min. Then, place about ¼-in. of sodium citrate crystals over the damp stain, and cover the sodium citrate with a thick poultice made from water and a powdered absorbent such as whiting or talc. Cover the poultice with Saran Wrap, and keep it in contact with the stain for at least 48 hours. Then remove the plastic and allow the poultice to dry. Since the chemicals are not readily available, you might prefer to leave this to a professional marble refinisher. (Look in the Yellow Pages under "Marble" to see if any of the installers offer refinishing services.)

WHEN WORKING ON VERTICAL surfaces, the poultice has to be extra thick to have the proper adhesion. On black or other dark marbles, don't use the white powder poultices because you may not be able to get all the white powder out of the pores. The white blotting paper type poultices should be satisfactory, however.

## Sticky Spots & Fungi

FOR REMOVING adhesives, such as tar or gum, try chilling with dry ice. The intense cold will make the adhesive brittle, and fairly easy to pop off. If dry ice is unavailable, a carbon dioxide fire extinguisher--or even ice cubes--will sometimes work. When using dry ice, be sure the marble is completely dry; if there's any moisture in the stone it could turn to ice and crack the marble.

IF THE CHILLING METHOD doesn't work, try acetone solvent.

IF THE HOUSE has been damp and empty for a long period of time, there could even be lichen or other fungal growths on the marble. These can sometimes be removed with detergent and water plus a natural-fiber scrub brush. If necessary, add a little household bleach to the scrubbing solution. Or, if the growth appears particularly tenacious, nearly any commercial herbicide, cautiously applied, will force these plants to release their grip.

## Commercial Cleaners

COMMERCIAL CLEANERS are available that will handle most of these cleaning problems. While they may be more expensive, they'll do the job as well--and often better--than your own homemade formulations. However, beware of using commercial masonry and brick cleaners on marble. These are acidic, and will speedily dissolve the surface of your

### HOW TO REPOLISH MARBLE

AFTER YOU'VE CLEANED your marble, you may find that it is so scratched and pitted that it needs refinishing as well. To produce a fine-honed finish, begin by using a wet-dry finishing paper such as is used in auto body shops. If the marble is rough, begin with an 80-grit paper. If your finish is in relatively good shape, start with a somewhat finer paper. The finer paper, of course, will not cut so deeply nor work so quickly as the coarser grades. A series of papers of 80-grit, 120, 320 and 400 is generally adequate. A dark marble will require continuing to a 600-grit paper for its final finish. Be sure to keep the surface wet, and frequently wipe off the grit produced.

FOLLOW UP with a buffing powder. Tin oxide is a good buffing powder, but may be difficult to obtain. Aluminum oxide may also be used. (See list of mail-order sources.) The buffing powder is used with water and a hand rubbing pad or a buffing wheel.

A FINAL FINISH is obtained by using a good polish formulated specifically for marble. These polishes are easy to apply, provide some protection for the marble, and add lustre as well.

ONE LAST NOTE: It's possible that your marble may need no more than the final polishing step. Since a good fine-honed finish is quite time-consuming and sometimes difficult to produce, you have nothing to lose by applying the marble polish first. If the results aren't satisfactory, you can always go back and start with the wet-dry abrasive papers.

mantel. Make sure the cleaner is formulated specifically for marble.

COMMERCIAL MARBLE CLEANERS may be hard to find locally. We've listed some mail-order sources in the accompanying box. You might also check your local Yellow Pages for companies that fabricate and install either marble or ceramic tile.

MARBLE that has been cracked or chipped can often be repaired successfully. Procedures include gluing and clamping of cracked marble, as well as repair of chipped marble by applying a mortar of marble dust, white portland cement, and lime. See OHJ, July 1982, for step-by-step details on this process.

MISCELLANEOUS STAIN REMOVAL ADVICE: If an epoxy-based material is spilled on your marble, you may be able to remove it with ethylene dichloride solvent.

REMEMBER that marble is a natural material and that no two pieces will behave exactly alike. To clean and restore your particular piece, you may have to do some careful experimentation.

**Lynette Strangstad** is a restoration contractor in Mineral Point, Wisconsin. Among the more interesting marble restoration projects she's handled was a study for gravestone preservation at the Circular Congregational Church in Charleston, S.C., which included the cleaning and restoration of a sample marble crypt. Lynette is a graduate of the Restoration Workshop in Tarrytown, N.Y., which is run by the National Trust for Historic Preservation.

**Special thanks to**. . .Mr. Joe Donatelli of Eastern Marble Supply for his technical assistance, and to The Marble Institute of America for their cooperation.

# Columns *continued from page 195*

ture of the column and resulting in loosened joints and sprung staves. Extremes of wet and dry can cause solid and hollow-bored columns to check severely. Continuous high moisture is one of the main conditions leading to fungus rot. (See the May 1981 OHJ for methods of detecting and defeating decay.)

IN A STAVE-BUILT COLUMN, a sprung stave will have a raised surface that stands out from the surfaces of the staves next to it. More than one sprung stave in a row can indicate that the column is being unevenly loaded from above or that the support below is shifting position or failing through decay. If this is the case, you have more than just column problems--get a structural engineer to examine the situation.

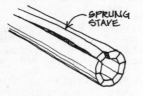

SPRUNG STAVE

AFTER INSPECTION, you'll have to decide whether to repair and reuse the existing columns or to replace them. Columns often cost less to repair than replace, but in some cases repair costs can be higher. Saving some original materials at a higher cost is justified if the structure has historical significance or the Department of the Interior's Standards for Rehabilitation are being followed for National Register or Tax Act purposes.

A NEW, 13-INCH DIAMETER by nine-foot high column can cost between $350 and $600; a lot of restoration can be done before replacement would be cheaper. Even if you hire a professional woodworker, the completely decayed end of a shaft can be restored, or a stave or two replaced, for less than the cost of a new shaft. Replacing a base and plinth or regluing open joints and sprung staves are jobs that can be done by any homeowner with experience in practical matters--and that's what this article is all about!

## Defenses

IT IS CRUCIAL to keep water from entering the wooden parts of a column. The first line of defense is a sound, continuous film of paint that covers all surfaces. Caulk should be used to seal joints between various parts. Water can enter even through hairline cracks in the paint. Once it soaks in, it can cause the paint to peel down to bare wood. This peeling occurs near breaks in the film at opened joints of wood, or where the film has been scraped or scratched.

PEELING CAN ALSO OCCUR over large areas because there is too much moisture in the whole column. In that case, the only way water vapor can escape is to push paint off the wood. This peeling also happens if the paint film is not permeable enough. A too-thick film of paint (more than .015 inch--about the thickness of four pages of the OHJ) could be too resistant to the passing of moisture.

IN EITHER CASE, strip all the paint and recoat the columns. Bare wood, whether stripped or new, should be treated with a clear, paintable

Left: Here's an extreme example of how uneven loading can split a sound shaft. Center: Paint peeling near checks and joints allows water to soak in. This column will deteriorate rapidly if it isn't repaired. Right: Water from a leak in the roof entered this column through the unflashed capital. That's all that was needed for rot to cause this extensive damage.

# ANATOMY OF A COLUMN

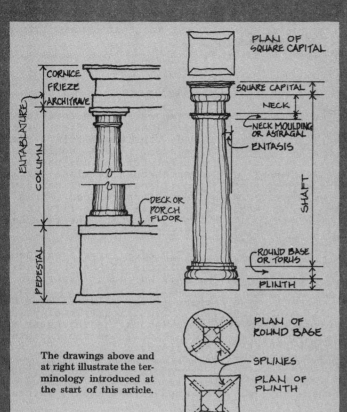

*The drawings above and at right illustrate the terminology introduced at the start of this article.*

The capital in this photograph is an example of the care and forethought that must go into a column part if it is to last. The endgrain of this plank-cut piece is covered with a mitred-in piece of sidegrained wood. Notice that the joint is caulked prior to assembly. It will be nailed on, which will allow for some expansion in the main piece (indicated by the arrows).

## Types Of Columns

In the past, blanks were made from the trunk of a tree, with the heart of the tree down the center of the finished column. This type of column almost always develops large cracks, or checks, because it shrinks as it dries.

If the tree was large enough, a solid blank would be cut "beside the heart" of a log. Such wood is less likely to check.

With a hollow-bored shaft, the center of the blank has been bored out. This allows the wood to shrink without the stress that causes checks.

Shafts are also made by gluing up common lumber into a blank. After the rough blank is made, it is mounted between the centers of a lathe and the outer surface is turned down to the proper size and shape. These shafts can carry heavier weights. They usually fail by delamination, coming apart at their "seams."

In a hollow, stave-constructed column, the individual stave is shaped with the correct bevel on its edges and a taper along its length. A set of staves is then assembled into a blank. These columns are more stable dimensionally than other types. However, they are subject to glue failure and stave separation.

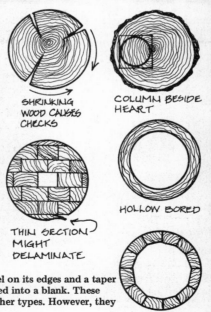

## Types Of Joints Used In Stave-Built Shafts

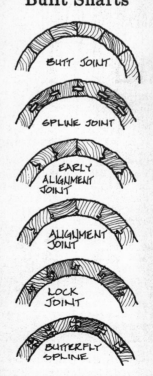

wood preservative such as Cuprinol #20. After two or three good dry days, a linseed oil or alkyd primer should be used, followed by two coats of exterior latex paint, which is more permeable than oil/alkyd paint. If the old paint is oil or alkyd paint and in good shape, use an alkyd primer and a latex or alkyd finish coat.

HOLLOW COLUMNS should be vented top and bottom. If yours are not, it's a design flaw that you should correct now. Even without removing the old columns, you can probably drill or cut inconspicuous holes in them.

SOMETIMES IT'S POSSIBLE to vent through the soffit above the capital. If not, drill the vent holes through the face of the capital on the non-weathering side. The vents should be located to keep out rainwater but to allow air to circulate into the column and to allow water vapor to exit. (Use screened vents if you have a problem keeping birds, insects, and so on, out of the column.)

AT THE BOTTOM, cut weep holes or slots to allow water drainage out of the column interior. You may be able simply to cut through floor decking under the hollow column.

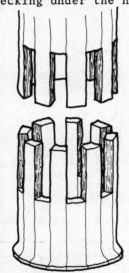

THE DAMAGE caused by decay may force you to make replacements in your column. In this situation, the column should probably be removed so all of its parts can be inspected thoroughly. The replacement of shaft ends is a job for a professional woodworker who has had experience with columns. Careful attention should be paid to matching the species of wood as well as the direction of the grain. Also, the original method of construction for the blank should be used.

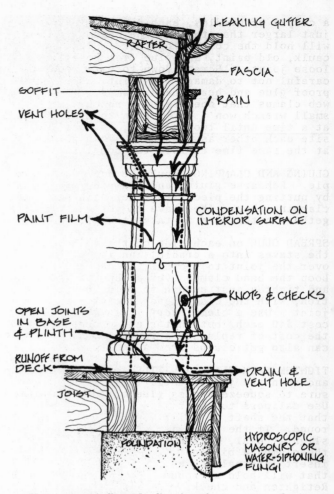

Heavy arrows indicate the direction of water entry and exit.

## Repairing Checks

SOME CHECKS CAN BE REPAIRED with the shaft in place. Minor checks (1/8 inch or less) on solid and hollow-bored shafts can just be caulked. But larger checks demand special consideration. They should be filled with a long slat of soft pine, tapered very slightly in cross section and wider than the crack on its widest edge. (Have

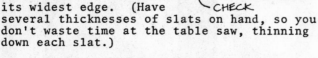

several thicknesses of slats on hand, so you don't waste time at the table saw, thinning down each slat.)

FIRST CLEAN ANY OLD PAINT OR PUTTY out of the check. Select a slat that is about the right width for the crack at hand. With checks that taper to nothing at each end, start at the middle and work towards each end with a separate

slat. Apply a resorcinol resin glue (such as Elmer's Weatherproof) to only one side of the slat. To the other side, apply a thin layer of caulk. Drive the slat into the check with light taps from a hammer. Enough of the slat should be down in the check to make good contact with the sides of the check.

LEAVE SOME OF THE SLAT standing above the surface. After the glue has set, trim off the excess glue and slat. The caulk will seal the check but allow it to open up again without stress. Use this method only near the end of the wet season in your area; that's when the checks are narrowest. If you do this in the dry season, when the checks are wide, the wood of the shaft will expand later, build pressure on the slat, and possibly cause the shaft to crack elsewhere. This long-lasting solution is especially useful for checks wider than 1/4 inch. Never try to close a check by clamping. A solid shaft can't be clamped. A hollow-bore column will probably just crack somewhere else if you clamp it.

## Staved-Column Repair

THE FOLLOWING METHOD is used to repair a staved column with joints that have become unglued. Work with the column laid across a couple of sawhorses. If more than one joint is open and the column is falling apart, make a couple of cradles, each with an inside radius just larger than that of the column. These will hold the column together. Clean off all caulk, old paint, and glue from both sides of loose joints. Scrape down to bare wood but be careful not to damage the joint. Use weather-proof glue and heavy band clamps. (Lightweight web clamps that operate on a ratchet with a small wrench won't do.) Plan to glue one joint at a time until two are left, as nearly opposite each other as possible. Then glue both at the same time to form the complete shaft.

GLUING AND CLAMPING should be done by two people. Rehearse gluing and clamping procedures by putting the pieces together without glue and clamping them. (You have to get everything together in the time it takes the glue to dry.)

SPREAD GLUE on each side of the joint, assemble the staves into a cradle, and lay wax paper over the joint to protect the canvas bands. Loop the band clamps over an end of the shaft and tighten just enough to hold them in position, with the clamp heads directly over the joint. Use a clamp every 12 inches. (Clamps cost $40 each, but that's cheap compared with the cost of replacing a few columns. And you can also get clamps from a tool-rental store.)

TIGHTEN EACH CLAMP A LITTLE, in succession up and down the joint, until there is enough pressure to squeeze excess glue out of the joint. Use calipers to check that the shaft is still round. If the shaft is slightly oval, loosen the clamps a bit and insert internal braces that will hold it round. Retighten and check again for roundness. Allow one or two days for a full-strength cure, because the joint will be put under heavy stress when the next joint is glued up. When taking the clamps off, loosen each one a little at a time.

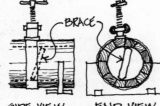

SIDE VIEW    END VIEW

WHEN GLUING only one joint, be certain that there is enough flexibility in the shaft to allow the joint to close without breaking another joint or splitting a stave. If the joint can be completely closed by hand, it is flexible enough. (If it doesn't have sufficient flexibility, insert a wooden slat, using the procedure described earlier.) If the surfaces beside the joint don't line up, use the following method instead.

MAKE A "SCREW-STICK" out of an old broom handle. Cut off the head of a #12 or #14 steel

wood screw. Use pliers to twist it into a pre-drilled hole in the broom handle. (Be careful not to mash up the threads too much.) Lock the screw into position by drilling a hole through both the stick and the screw and driving in a thin finish nail.

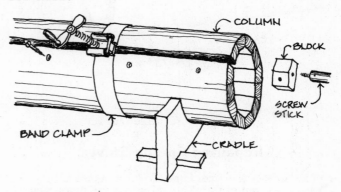

CUT SOME BLOCKS that have two surfaces that are the same angle as that of the flat inside surfaces of the staves. Clean the joint in preparation for gluing. Drill 3/16-inch countersunk holes, about 7/8 inch from the edge of the joint in the higher stave. Use a #10, rust-resistant (hot-dipped galvanized or better) screw. Starting with a block near the middle of the joint, hold it in position behind

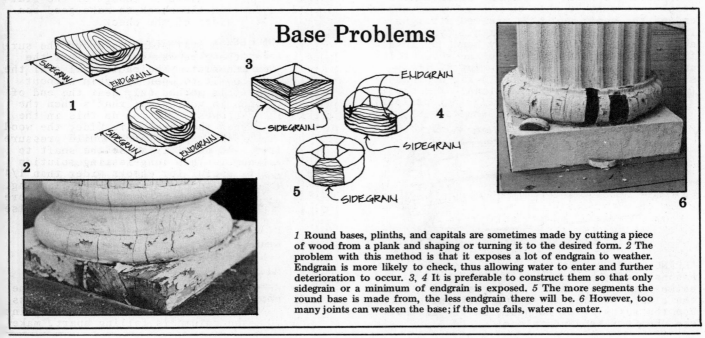

# Base Problems

1 Round bases, plinths, and capitals are sometimes made by cutting a piece of wood from a plank and shaping or turning it to the desired form. 2 The problem with this method is that it exposes a lot of endgrain to weather. Endgrain is more likely to check, thus allowing water to enter and further deterioration to occur. 3, 4 It is preferable to construct them so that only sidegrain or a minimum of endgrain is exposed. 5 The more segments the round base is made from, the less endgrain there will be. 6 However, too many joints can weaken the base; if the glue fails, water can enter.

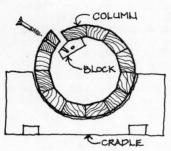

COLUMN

BLOCK

CRADLE

the joint with the screw-stick. As it is screwed to the higher stave, the lower stave will be brought up level to it. Unscrew the screw-stick and fasten it in the next block. When all blocks are in place, the surface of the staves should be even; you can then proceed to glue the joint, using band clamps.

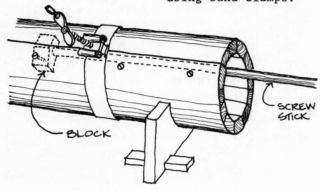

BLOCK

SCREW STICK

## Repairing Sprung Staves

SPRUNG STAVES are repaired in a somewhat similar manner. The plan is to push the stave back down and realign it with the surface of the adjacent staves. Use caulk instead of glue to seal the joint, if you find that you can't work fast enough to complete the procedure before the glue sets.

BEGIN BY supporting the ends of the sprung stave with a block cut precisely to fit the inside of the staves. Screw the block to the neighboring staves, not to the sprung stave itself; it must be able to slide out to the end of the shaft as it is pressed straight. If the stave is thin and flexible, you may be able to push it into place by hand, while a friend positions a block with the screw-stick and you screw it into place. But if it is stubborn, use one of the following approaches (which can be done working alone).

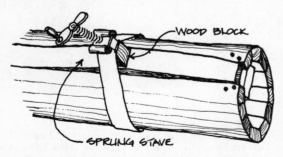

WOOD BLOCK

SPRUNG STAVE

ARRANGE ONE OR TWO band clamps over the highest part of the stave, with a block of wood between the clamp head and the stave. Tighten the clamp, pushing the stave back into place. Use the screw-stick to position blocks that are then screwed into place.

IF THE BAND CLAMPS aren't powerful enough (or if you don't have any), get a blacksmith or welding shop to make a hoop of 3/8-inch mild-steel barstock, with an inside diameter just larger than that of the shaft plus the height of the sprung stave. Explain how you plan to use it so it can be made strong enough. (A hoop like this should cost much less than a band clamp.)

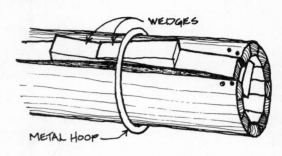

WEDGES

METAL HOOP

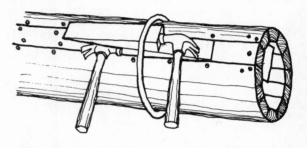

PROTECT THE OPPOSITE SIDE of the column by placing a 1/4-inch-thick slip of hardwood between it and the hoop. Arrange the wedges and drive them together with two hammers, forcing the stave down. Fasten it with blocks as before. Fill the countersunk holes with a good exterior filler, such as Woodepox-I.

JOHN LEEKE does historic-house restoration and architectural woodworking in the southern Maine and New Hampshire area. Readers who wish to contact his company can write to John Leeke, Woodworker, RR 1, Box 847, Sanford, ME 04073, or call (207) 324-9597.

A CONTRIBUTOR to *Fine Woodworking*, Mr. Leeke is also a member of the APT and does consulting on column restoration and installation. He wishes to thank Paul Morse of Saco Manufacturing Company and Virgil I. Pitstick for their help in the preparation of this article.

IN AN UPCOMING ISSUE, we'll be featuring another article by Mr. Leeke. This one will deal with how to install new columns. In the meantime, please see Restoration Products News — pages 218 and 219 — for a list of sources for replacement columns.

## Replacement Columns

*The cover article of this issue features detailed instructions for the repair of wood columns — but sometimes the wood is beyond repair. So we have listed sources for replacement columns...in wood, aluminum, and stone. Unless otherwise stated, these columns are all load-bearing, and have entasis (the almost imperceptible convex swelling in the shaft of a column). All of the companies offer a large selection of sizes and styles including Tuscan, Doric, Ionic, Corinthian, and Square — fluted and plain. Simple capitals, e.g., Doric, are usually made of the same material as the column; detailed capitals, e.g., Corinthian, are usually composition.*

### Wood

American Wood Column can custom produce any column to your specifications. You can request any type of wood, and they will ship nationwide. For a price quote and a free brochure, contact American Wood Column, 913 Grand St., Dept. OHJ, Brooklyn, NY 11211. (212) 782-3163.

For 80-plus-years Hartmann-Sanders has been manufacturing columns in rot-resistant, clear, heart redwood. All of their columns are custom-made to meet your requirements, primed, and feature *Koll's lock-joint* (pictured here) for strong, interlocking construction. Sizes range from 8 to 36 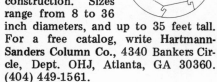 inch diameters, and up to 35 feet tall. For a free catalog, write Hartmann-Sanders Column Co., 4340 Bankers Circle, Dept. OHJ, Atlanta, GA 30360. (404) 449-1561.

Manufacturers of wood columns since 1860, Schwerd offers an extensive selection of stock columns; they will also do custom work. Constructed of seasoned northeastern white pine, these columns are primed before shipping. The sizes range from 4 to 50 inches in diameter, and up to 40 feet in height. For free information, specify the *Column Brochure*. A.F. Schwerd Manufacturing Co., 3215 McClure Ave., Dept. OHJ, Pittsburgh, PA 15212. (412) 766-6322.

Columns, made from Ponderosa pine or Douglas fir, are stocked in 6 to 12 inch diameters; 8 to 12 feet in height. Custom sizes range from 12 to 30 inches in diameter, and 12 to 30 feet in height. Each column is treated with a wood preservative (penta), and shipped unprimed. These columns are sold through distributors in the South, Southeast, Midwest, and Mid-Atlantic; the company will be happy to send you a free *Wood Column Brochure* and the location of your nearest distributor. Henderson, Black, and Greene, Inc., PO Box 589, Dept. OHJ, Troy, AL 36081. (205) 566-5000.

In addition to northeastern white pine, Somerset's columns can be ordered in redwood and a variety of other woods. Two coats of primer are applied to the exterior, and the interior is sealed with asphalt. Stock columns are available in the no. 100 series with diameters up to 12 inches, and heights up to 9 feet; an 8-ft. high, 8-in. diameter column in this series is $100. Numerous other made-to-order columns ranging from 6 to 40 inches in diameter, and up to 40 feet tall are shown in their free *Column Brochure*. Somerset Door & Column Co., PO Box 328, Dept. OHJ, Somerset, PA 15501. (814) 445-9608.

### Aluminum

Moultrie recently introduced aluminum columns that snap together. They are inexpensive, light-weight, can support up to 11 tons, and are easy to install. (According to the company president all you need is, "A husband/wife, 1 can elbow grease, two cokes, and a Saturday morning.") The columns are

(From left to right) Henderson, Black, & Greene's Square Fluted Column; The No. 100 Column From Somerset; Fluted Column With Erechtheum Capital From Hartmann-Sanders; Schwerd's Plain Column With Corinthian Capital; and Ionic Column From Campbellsville Industries.

*Assembling a Moultrie Column.*

straight (without entasis), and range in size from 6 to 24 inches in diameter, and from 8 to 30 feet tall. Prices begin at $44 for an 8-ft. high, 6-inch diameter column, with a choice of baked-enamel or primed finish, and an aluminum base and capital. *While the manufacturer states that the column can be constructed around an existing column, we would advise against it; you could be covering up an old problem and creating a worse one.* You can call, toll free, for free literature and a price list. Moultrie Manufacturing Co., PO Drawer 1179, Dept. OHJ, Moultrie, GA 31768. (800) 841-8674.

Campbellsville Industries is best known for their exterior metal ornament in aluminum (steeples, cupolas, cornices, etc.). They also make aluminum columns (without entasis), from 6 to 24 inches in diameter, and up to 24 feet tall, with a white-baked enamel or primed finish. An 8-ft. high, 8-in. diameter column with aluminum capital and base is about $70. The company pays shipping charges on orders over 300 pounds. Reproduction orders for historic buildings are welcomed. In addition to their free brochure, a free (and helpful) consultation service is offered. Mr. Jerry Bennett, Campbellsville Industries, Inc., PO Box 278, Dept. OHJ, Campbellsville, KY 42718. (502) 465-8135.

## Stone

Architectural sculptors Albert Lachin & Assoc. specialize in ornamental plaster, cement, and cast-stone (a marble dust aggregate) work. Generally all their work is custom, but they do stock a line of Tuscan columns, in cast-stone or cement, ranging from 14 to 24 inch diameters, with heights of 5 to 22 feet. An 8- to 9-ft. column (about 16-in. dia.) costs $480 in concrete, and $580 in cast-stone. When writing for free information, specify the *Cast-Stone Brochure.* Albert Lachin & Associates, Inc., 618 Piety St., Dept. OHJ, New Orleans, LA 70117. (504) 948-3533.

## Fretwork

Nothing quite compares with the graceful and often fanciful fretwork patterns found in Victorian and early turn-of-the-century houses. If you would like to restore, recreate, or add this characteristic to your house—Cumberland can help. They have an extensive selection of wooden exterior and interior millwork, offering endless design possibilities with brackets, corbels, spandrels, and grilles. Some of these patterns are period inspired; others are reproductions of originals. A new addition is the two-panel fretwork screen pictured here. Each solid oak panel is 96 in. high x 24 in. wide. The cost, $695, includes shipping but not a center insert (an ideal spot for etched, stained, or bevelled glass, or a fabric insert). A 24-page color catalog is $3.50. Cumberland Woodcraft Co., Inc., 2500 Walnut Bottom Rd., Dept. OHJ, Carlisle, PA 17013. (717) 243-0063.

# Registers & Grilles

*The floor register pictured here enables a functional device to also be an attractive decorative feature of your old house. Registers with movable louvers allow you to regulate the heat flow (a real plus in a big, old house); floor or ceiling grilles have no movable parts. Both Renovator's Supply and Reggio Register manufacture these products from turn-of-the-century patterns, in cast iron...or solid brass for an extravagant touch.*

Reggio has registers and grilles in the following overall dimensions — 9 in. x 13 in., 12 in. x 14 in., 16 in. x 20 in., and 32 in. square. Floor grilles have cutoff dimensions (for duct sizes) of 2¼ in. x 10 in., 2¼ in. x 12 in., 4 in. x 10 in., 4 in. x 12 in., and 4 in. x 14 in. Register prices begin at $18.50; grilles range from

$9-$11 (prices don't include shipping). They can also provide some types of custom-made grilles (not registers), but bear in mind that prices for these will not be competitive with stock items. For a brochure, $1, write Reggio Register Co., PO Box 511, Dept. OHJ, Ayer, MA 01432. (617) 772-3493.

Renovator's cast-iron register, 11-1/2 in. x 9-5/8 in., is $30.50 ppd.; $63.50 in solid brass. A cast-iron grille with the same dimensions is $11 ppd., and $44 ppd. in brass. A round, cast-iron, 10 in. register is $21.50 ppd. (All measurements are overall dimensions.) A color catalog showing these and hundreds of other restoration products is $2, refundable with purchase. Renovator's Supply, 710 Northfield Rd., Dept. OHJ, Millers Falls, MA 01349. (413) 659-3542.

*Two of Reggio Register's cast-iron grilles.*

*Cast-iron register from Renovator's Supply.*

# Opinion...
# Remuddling
## — Of The Month —

## Solar Salvation . . . or Technological Trashing ?
## Rodale Press Makes It a Public Issue

The house in the photo above is not the unhappy result of changing fashion or a fast-talking remodeling contractor. Instead, it looks this way on purpose — the result of a carefully planned and executed solar demonstration project. The worst part is that the house is now being presented as state-of-the-art retrofitting in an influential book and mail-order brochure.

YOU MAY ALREADY have seen this house. Rodale Press used it to illustrate their new "solarizing" book in a sales brochure that was mailed by the thousands. It has managed to turn off even moderate preservationists. Unfortunately for Rodale, they have probably turned off energy-conscious homeowners as well: Nobody wants to live in a house that looks like the inside of an air conditioner.

BY MAILING this brochure, author Joe Carter and Rodale have made public their opinion that (1) this house is a commendable example of solar remodeling, and (2) the solar apparatus was a necessary component of its energy retrofit.

THE OLD-HOUSE JOURNAL has an obligation to publish a contrary opinion, despite our fondness and respect for Rodale Press. This opinion is shared by people all over the country, including the Technical Preservation Services Branch of the U.S. Department of the Interior (see p. 196). The response we got from our readers was astonishing!

IN OUR OPINION, too, saving energy is sensible and moral. But draping expensive solar hardware all over an old building--irreversibly changing its architecture--is, we think, neither sensible, nor moral, nor necessary.

*We couldn't say it all on one page this month. Please turn to pages 196 and 197 for more.*

# The Old-House Journal®

69A Seventh Avenue,
Brooklyn, New York 11217

NO PAID ADVERTISING

Postmaster: Address Correction Requested

BULK RATE
U.S. Postage
PAID
New York, N.Y.
Permit No. 6964

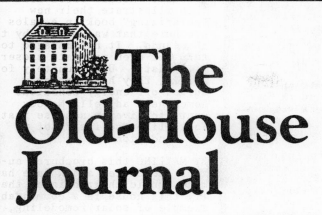

# The Old-House Journal

### Restoration and Maintenance Techniques For The Antique House

Vol. X No. 11      $2.00

## November 1982

# RESTORING CLEAR FINISHES

## Reviving Is Easier And Cheaper Than Total Stripping

By Clem Labine

MANY AMERICANS are converts to the new Stripping Religion. The basic belief of this new religion is that any old finish on woodwork or furniture has to be completely stripped and a fresh new finish applied. The prophets of this new religion are the makers of chemical strippers and the new finishes. And the high priests are the authors of the dozens of wood refinishing manuals.

THE CHIEF EVIL of the new religion is dark woodwork. Whether it's the wainscotting in an old-house hallway, or the finish on a Morris chair, the injunction is always the same: "Strip the old and apply the new." But I tell you, brothers and sisters, 'taint necessarily so!

AS AN ADHERENT of the old-time religion, I'd like to convince you that the Strippers are worshipping false idols. Listen to them and you'll often spend more money and expend more effort than you have to. We believers in the old-time religion say that when it

comes to clear finishes, there is no single universal truth. The path to enlightenment requires a lot of personal discovery.

THERE ARE FOUR basic reasons why a clear finish may look dark or worn out. The remedy in each of these cases is quite different:

1. The finish may be covered with layers of dirt, grime, and old wax.

2. The finish itself may contain some coloring agents that were used originally to disguise cheap wood.

3. The finish itself may have darkened. The darkening may be (a) concentrated in the top surface, or (b) go completely through the finish.

4. The finish may have cracked due to aging.

COMPLETE STRIPPING is appropriate only in cases (3b) and (4). If the finish is merely dirty, simple cleaning

*continued on page 238*

# Letters

*Our product stories are more useful to some people than to others, it seems. They're offered as helpful news . . . not as advertising. So we welcome your letters on good sources for old-house products yet undiscovered by us.*

To the Editors:

AS A SUBSCRIBER for five years, I thoroughly enjoy your publication. But I feel compelled to ask you to treat advertising as advertising--not as news. I specifically refer to the "Restoration Products News" section. We all know that magazines survive on advertising, not subscriptions--so be it! Let's not pretend ads for specific companies are simply helpful information provided gratis.

THE SEPT. 1982 issue is a perfect example. You describe a hand-made Victorian lampshade manufacturer in California who produces shades starting at $199. I have no problem with that presented as advertising. But I'm appalled by those prices in an ad disguised as "news."

WE JUST had a custom shade done for us on the West Coast for under $100, including shipping.

IF THE "Restoration Products News" section is indeed researched, you're not doing your homework. I'll send you more information on our lampshade company if you're really interested.

I WANT OHJ to survive, but I also want you to be upfront where advertising is concerned. Capitalism isn't all that bad.

-- *Kay Hawkins*
*Morgantown, West Virginia*

Dear Readers:

IT SEEMS we're too good to be true! Restoration Products News isn't advertising--honest! Each month, Joni Monnich picks products; personally contacts each company; then writes the items herself. They aren't paid-for ads, or even rehashed press releases.

WE CAN think of only two consumer magazines in this country that survive on subs instead of ads: OHJ and MAD magazine. We attribute it to our editorial efficiency (the editors wear a lot of hats) and perhaps to modest financial expectations. And there's no expensive four-color printing.

OHJ friend and contributor Bruce Bradbury told us about those marvelous silk shades. We got excited about their novelty, and thought readers would want to know about them.

WE COULDN'T, of course, guess the existence of another company making Victorian lampshades. We follow up all leads --but we count on reader tips.

IF WE EVER decide to accept advertising, we promise that we'll be upfront about it... and that advertisers won't dictate what appears in the editorial pages.

-- *P. Poore*

(The lampshade company Ms. Hawkins refers to is YESTERSHADES, 3534 SW Hawthorne, Dept. OHJ, Portland, OR 97214. Tel. 503-238-5755. Free brochure shows reproduction shades from c. 1890-1920s.

The lampshade manufacturer featured in the September issue was SHADES OF THE PAST, Box 502, Dept. OHJ, Corte Madera, CA 94925. Tel. 415-459-6999. Brochure $2.)

To the Editors:

IN AN ISSUE of OHJ sometime last spring, I came across an article on roofing materials which mentioned SupraSlate by Supradur. I was restoring an 1870 house that originally had a fine hexagonal slate roof, and I was disappointed in the roofing materials available today. Real slate was too expensive, but anything else looked all wrong for the house. I contacted Supradur, and they sent me a sample--just what we needed.

WE'VE CUT the SupraSlate to match the original hexagonal shingles. It is spectacular. The material resembles slate in texture and color, and behaves like slate in its application. Our roofers, who had never seen it, were surprised and pleased.

THANK YOU, Old-House Journal, for bringing this material to our attention; I would never have discovered it otherwise.

-- *Nancy O'Neil*
*Hartford, Conn.*

(Supradur Manufacturing Corp., 122 E. 42nd St., New York, NY 10168. 212-697-1160. Free literature.)

# The Old-House Journal®

*Editor*
**Clem Labine**

*Managing Editor*
**Patricia Poore**

*Assistant Editor*
**Cole Gagne**

*Assistant Editor/Products*
**Joni Monnich**

*Circulation Supervisor*
**Joan O'Reilly**

*Circulation Assistants*
**Peggy Scaglione**
**Barbara Bugg**
**Jeanne Baldwin**

*Office Assistant*
**Rafael Madera**

*Circulation Director*
**Paul T. McLoughlin**

*Technical Consultant*
**Alan D. Keiser**

*Architectural Consultant*
**Jonathan Poore**

*Contributing Editors*
**R. A. Labine, Sr.**
**John Mark Garrison**

*Published by The Old-House Journal Corporation, 69A Seventh Avenue, Brooklyn, New York 11217. Telephone (212) 636-4514. Subscriptions $16 per year in U.S. Not available elsewhere. Published ten times per year. Contents are fully protected by copyright and must not be reproduced in any manner whatsoever without specific permission in writing from the Editor.*

*We are happy to accept editorial contributions to The Old-House Journal. Query letters that include an outline of the proposed article are preferred. All manuscripts will be reviewed, and returned if unacceptable. However, we cannot be responsible for non-receipt or loss — please keep copies of all materials sent.*

Printed at Photo Comp Press, New York City

ISSN: 0094-0178
**NO PAID ADVERTISING**

# Old-House Living In Central Texas

### By Susan M. Ridgway, Coupland, Texas

MOST OLD HOUSE PROJECTS start with the house. Ours started with the land--our family farm is the remaining parcel of an 1830s land grant from the Republic of Texas to my husband's great-great-grandfather. My husband M.B. Garry, Jr., our daughter Madeleine, and I loved old houses. And we were faced with a dilemma: We had our historic site ... but no old house. Our solution? For $6000, a nearby farmer sold us a house that had been in his family since it was built in 1905. He was building a new house and wanted the old one out of the way.

RECENTLY, our house has become something of a celebrity. It starred in a national television commercial and was considered for a major motion picture. But when we first visited it in 1976, the house wouldn't have rated a second glance from the casual observer. It was hidden behind overgrown shrubs, and the front of its hipped roof, where dormers should have been, was only a flat plane. We later learned that the three front dormers had been hacked off in a 1920s remuddling.

PRELIMINARY WORK included consulting a restoration architect--John Klein of Austin, Texas--to determine if the house was sound enough to warrant the required blood, sweat, and tears. In addition to checking the house, the architect also referred us to an experienced and dedicated housemover, Earl Bradford of Austin. His expertise included not just physically moving the house, but securing the proper permits and coordination from the utility companies and the Texas Department of Highways.

EARL'S $8000 ESTIMATE included "laying down" the peak of the roof and cutting the house in two. These pieces would be low enough to pass under some power lines and small enough to move along the roads. Before cutting, the house measured a square 50 feet by 50 feet, excluding the verandah.

GENERALLY, it's a good idea to get more than one estimate. After we moved into the house, we received a visit from a family who, unbeknownst to us, also had wanted to move the house. They'd given up after another housemover had proposed moving the house in <u>four</u> pieces at a cost of $25,000!

PRIOR TO THE MOVE, it was necessary to carefully dismantle the wrap-around verandah and attached gazebo. Pieces were numbered, photos taken, and diagrams drawn. Many pieces, including pillars, railings, and ceiling beaded boards, were stacked inside the house for the move. We moved the salvageable plaster Corinthian capitals separately in an old cotton trailer. All the masonry work was also removed--three brick chimneys, flues, and fireboxes. (So far, we've replaced only one; replacing the other two is our next major project.)

EARL THEN LITERALLY SAWED THE HOUSE in half, from the front door to the back door, cutting through all layers--siding, floors, joists,

Left: No, this isn't a damaged photograph. The line you see is part of the great bifurcation performed by housemover Earl Bradford. The section of stairway was removed before the house was cut. Above: Here's half the house moving down the street. Notice the timbers propped up to support the house.

double ship-lap walls, beams, and rafters. Inside, near the cut edges, timbers were propped vertically between floors and ceilings to support the structure and prevent sagging. Huge steel beams were placed under the house. They were supported by wooden cribbings that were replaced by wheels just prior to the move.

## Getting Rolling

THE MOVING ROUTE covered 12 miles--farm-to-market road, state highway, and the narrow country road to our farm. Unfortunately, just when the house was ready to go, the autumn rains began. The highway department had specified that the house would have to be pulled off the road onto the dirt shoulders to allow traffic to pass. Therefore, officials wouldn't give the go-ahead until the shoulders were dry enough to support the house without being damaged.

PROBABLY DUE TO some corollary of Murphy's Law, every time the shoulders were almost dry, it would rain again ... not only onto the shoulders, but also into our bisected house. Following each rain, we would go to the house and mop out the water.

BY THE END OF THE YEAR, the rains let up and the highway department issued the permit. The house rolled on December 29, spending the night by the side of the road. On December 30, it reached our farm. Along the route, overhead power and phone lines were either held higher for the house to pass under, or lowered to the ground for the house to roll over. The house was accompanied by crews from Texas Power & Light and from various phone companies. (We passed through three different phone territories within the space of 12 miles.) Leading the procession was a highway crew--moving roadside signs and trimming overhanging tree branches.

## Hassles

WE FIGURED THAT once we reached our farm, all our moving problems would be over. However, when our house turned off the country road and into the front field, it promptly got stuck in the blackland mud. Earl hitched up two trucks to one-half of the house; it wouldn't budge. Then he tried three trucks; still nothing.

The house prepares to make a turn on its 12-mile journey to its new site.

LUCKILY, we were able to find a bulldozer operator who was nice enough to bring his machine out--and this was on a New Year's Eve that was also the coldest morning of that winter: 18°F. By simultaneously lifting and pushing, he was able to free the house. Then the trucks moved it the remaining half mile to our site--a hill overlooking the Brushy Creek bottom.

THE HOUSE was positioned over the foundation, which had been prepared in advance. Designed by an engineer, the reinforced concrete "ring" foundation floats in the land, which is a viscous clay hill sitting on the blackland prairie, with no bedrock. So when the land shifts, the house and foundation can move as a unit without cracking.

THE MOVER positioned the east half of the house over the foundation, and then pulled the west half alongside. During the next several days, the west half was pulled snug against the east with metal cables and winches. The joists and beams that had been cut were "scabbed" together--the cut ends placed together and the joints reinforced by new beams and joists nailed alongside the cut ones. Brick piers were built up from the foundation to the house.

FORTUNATELY, two relatives of the previous owner had given us photos taken when the house was new. Our contractor, Curtis Martin of Taylor, Texas, reassembled the verandah utilizing the numbered pieces, photos, and diagrams. By following the two photos and observing the remaining structural clues, Martin was able to

Three cherry-pickers work in the air at one time to get the house through this intersection.

reconstruct the balcony and the missing dormers (thus restoring to the house its original total of seven). On the exterior, cut marks were covered by reworking the clapboard siding where necessary and by the presence of the new cedar shingle roof. Inside, they're being hidden gradually as we finish the rooms.

## Extra Considerations

EXTRA EXPENSES ARE INVOLVED in moving a house to a relatively isolated location. We were responsible for putting in a septic tank, as well as over one-half-mile each of gravel driveway, water line, and electric line (with poles). We went without a phone for a couple of years; when we had a phone line brought in, it cost almost $2000.

EXTRA PROBLEMS occur with old-farm-house living. In addition to the birds and bats upstairs (experienced by many old-house owners), we have field mice everywhere. A six-foot-long bullsnake (nonpoisonous) shed its skin in the front hall and curled up for a snooze in the unfinished parlor fireplace. Before I could shoot a rattlesnake (poisonous) that was in the front yard, I had to flip it away from the house with a hoe, lest the shotgun blast damage our new latticework.

ALTHOUGH THE EXTERIOR is not completely finished, it looks finished enough to have gained some notoriety. Our house was considered for the title role

Half the house is stuck in the mud. It took more than these two trucks to budge it.

Left: The house — seen from the back — gets ready to pull itself together. Above: Once it was back in one piece, the real work on the house began. Here you see the reassembling of the verandah and the reconstruction of the dormers and balcony. Below: Does this house look familiar when seen from a distance? Picture a young woman in an old jalopy. She gets up, takes off her hat, and calls out to the man on the porch, "Travis, you're a year too late." (Incidentally, nobody who made the commercial knows what that line means either.)

in The Best Little Whorehouse In Texas. Ultimately, it was rejected in favor of a wooded location. However, for a television commercial, Levi-Strauss wanted a solitary house silhouetted on a hill--a stark look reminiscent of the George Stevens film Giant. We looked just right, and the commercial was filmed at our house in the fall of 1981. Our house is now being seen on television screens, billboards, and in print advertising all over the country.

WE'RE STILL WORKING on such tasks as stripping the paint from the East Texas pine woodwork. The approximately 4500 square feet provide plenty of living space, as well as ample room for a home office, where I conduct my writing and public relations business. In addition, inspired by our old-house experience, a newsletter focusing on the historic homes and antiques of Texas is in the planning stage.

WE MUST LOVE OUR OLD HOUSE; otherwise, we'd never have survived the day the upstairs pipes broke and rained through the kitchen ceiling. Or the night the stovepipe fell. And then there was the time I climbed up into the built-in china cabinet to strip the beaded board panelling; the door broke and fell, trapping me inside ... but that's another story.

SUSAN M. RIDGWAY is a long-time OHJ subscriber. Her articles have appeared in Austin Homes & Gardens, Texas Homes, and Austin. In addition to her writing career, she has her own public relations firm. Readers interested in the newsletter Ms. Ridgway describes in her article can send inquiries to her at Rt. 1, Box 213, Coupland, TX 78615.

## Tips From Readers
# Restorer's Notebook

### Removing Putty

I HAVE FOUND an easy way to remove hardened glazing compound without damaging the window. Get a coarse-cut, carbide burr--a $14 item that will save you a lot of time. Place the tool in a variable speed, 1/4-inch electric drill. This will allow you to remove the putty, regardless of how old or hard it is. It'll also work on the glazing points without damaging the wood frame or the window sash. I have done this several times and found it to be unmatched by any other means of putty removal. (You can probably buy the burr at a local tool shop; mine came from SJ Industrial Supply, 7600 Boone Ave. North, Minneapolis, MN 55428. Telephone (612) 424-3113.)

Jack B. Curtis
Minneapolis, MN

### Homemade Waterproofer

DO-IT-YOURSELFERS should be interested in this: I make my own waterproofer for con-crete-block walls. I make a thick paste using rubberized latex paint blended with port-land cement. Make sure it leaves no gaps or air pockets when you brush it on. One coat, carefully applied, will last several years.

Bernis Copeland
Long Beach, CA

### Homemade Refinisher

ANYONE REFINISHING FURNITURE will appreciate this tip. Mix equal parts of denatured alcohol and lacquer thinner. You can use this solution just as you'd use a brand-name product: Dampen some 00 steel wool with the mixture and work it into the surface of the wood. When the old finish is softened, wipe it away with a cloth or paper towel. (Work a small area at a time--the mixture evaporates.) Once you've evenly cleaned off the old finish, go over the wood with clean mixture, using the steel wool to lift the finish and a clean cloth to remove it. No sanding is needed because the steel wool smoothes the surface. Now you can apply stain, varnish, or tung oil.

THIS MIXTURE will cost about $10 per gallon-- about half the price of prepared furniture refinishers. One more thing: Pour small quan-tities of the mixture into a covered jar and keep it covered when not in use. Work in a well ventilated area, and always wear lined rubber gloves whenever working with chemicals.

Jan Zenner
Dubuque, IA

### Wrap It

HERE'S A PAINT-STRIPPING METHOD that I've used successfully for years. After I ap-ply stripper to about two feet of wood-work, I immediately cover it with plastic wrap (Saran Wrap or another similar product from the grocery store). The wrap sticks to the wet remover and prevents it from drying before it soaks in and lifts the paint. If you work in sections, you can move along pretty quickly. I find that, with this method, just two appli-cations can remove six or seven layers of paint down to the bare wood.

Joseph Trapani
Baldwin, NY

### Graining Tools

WHEN I READ a book about wood graining, I was flabbergasted by the huge list of tools and materials suggested for doing the work. But it challenged my imagination. On a hunch, I ransacked my kitchen drawers as well as the sale stand at a neighborhood hard-ware store. As a result, I found several gad-gets that are useful as graining tools. My best discovery? Wire whisks, any size. Great for mixing colors with various thinners. They are especially useful for dissolving thick lumps of color, and they're easy to clean for later re-use.

Linda E. Liebelt
San Francisco, CA

### Bronze Wool

FOLLOWING FAITHFULLY the instructions on the side of my first gallon of stripper, I used steel wool and water wash to clean up the final coat. What the nice folks didn't say is that splinters of steel wool inevitably remain on the wood. Eventually, they rust and transfer a rust stain to the wood. After many hours of sanding the stains away, I started looking around for a better way.

A BOAT RENOVATOR suggested bronze wool, and I am happy to report that it is a winner. Not only are there no rust stains, but it also lasts longer and is less prone to splintering than steel wool. (Bronze wool is available at marine supply stores.)

John Kuoni
Brooklyn, NY

**Tips To Share?** Do you have any hints or short cuts that might help other old-house owners? We'll pay $15 for any short how-to items that are used in this "Restorer's Note-book" column. Write to Notebook Editor, The Old-House Journal, 69A Seventh Avenue, Brooklyn, NY 11217.

# A Glimpse Of An
# Old-Fashioned Christmas

By Joni Monnich

IT'S ALWAYS A PLEASURE for the OHJ staff to see someone putting an article of ours to work. We thought it would be fun to share one such example with other readers. These photographs show the results of an annual workshop given by The 1890 House, "How To Celebrate A Victorian Christmas." The Christmas articles featured in The Old-House Journal Nov. 1979, Nov. 1980, and Nov. 1981 served as guidelines for their authentic Christmas projects. A book, The Gift of Christmas Past by Sunny O'Neil,* was also consulted.

THE 1890 HOUSE is a house museum and educational center in Cortland, New York, with both public and private funding. This year the museum will hold its workshop series on Saturday, December 4, from 10AM to 1PM.

A variety of paper fan, cornucopia, and *tussie mussie* tree ornaments.

Classes include decorating your house with greenery, decoration for your Victorian Christmas tree, and recipes and serving methods for a traditional Christmas dinner. If you want to take a class -- or for friendly advice on how you can set up a similar workshop -- contact Cathy Canfield, Curator of Education at The 1890 House, 37 Tompkins Street, Cortland, NY 13045. (607) 756-5872.

*✻ "The Gift of Christmas Past" is available from AASLH, Dept. OHJ, 708 Berry Rd., Nashville, TN 37204. (615) 383-5991. $12.95/copy, $10 for AASLH members (prepaid). Add $1.25 for rush handling.*

*(Left)* A scrawny but authentic and lovingly decorated snow tree. *(Above)* The east parlor at The 1890 House, all decked out with greenery, Victorian ornaments, and candles.

# What To Do In Case Of
# A CHIMNEY FIRE

By Cole Gagne

PICTURE A COZY SCENE: It's a cold night of early winter, and you build a nice, warm fire. You haven't had one in a while, so why not make this one good and hot? Of course, the chimney hasn't been cleaned in a couple of years, but there's plenty of time to have that done. So you throw in some newspaper, toss on an extra log or two, and curl up in front of that big, hot fire.

AT FIRST, things smell a little odd, and you hear some peculiar noises. But that happens with fires, doesn't it ... sometimes? Nothing to worry about. If you're using a stove, you notice that the stovepipe is shuddering and rattling. Now it's definitely time to start worrying. And when you hear a noise that sounds like a rocket blasting off inside your chimney, you really hit the panic button.

AND WHAT HAPPENS while you run around like a decapitated chicken? The noise roars on and on; the mortar between the bricks melts and spills into the fire; and from a distance, it looks like someone is celebrating the Fourth of July, as sparks and fireballs--and vicious flames--shoot out of that faraway chimney and light up the sky.

UNFORTUNATELY, this ugly scenario doesn't always end here. Sometimes the fire will burn itself out inside the chimney and damage nothing (except your nerves). Other times, it will lead inexorably to an inferno that consumes the house. The recipe for this catastrophe is very simple: Burn a hot fire in a dirty chimney. The deposits of creosote and soot ignite, and the fire quickly rages throughout the entire length of your chimney; maybe throughout your home too.

## Inspection Now

THE FIRST THING you have to do now, before you're confronted with an emergency, is inspect your heating system. Certain defects in it can make a chimney fire impossible to control. Perhaps the most serious--and invisible--defect is insufficient clearance.

WITH THIS KIND OF FIRE, the heat inside the chimney can soar above 2000°F. This intense heat will communicate through the chimney and stovepipe and ignite adjacent surfaces. Examine the chimney where it intersects the floors and roof. There should be no point of contact between wood--or any combustible material--and your chimney. A two-inch clearance is adequate. (A gypsum-board or sheet-metal ceiling that actually touches the chimney is recommended as an effective firestop.) Be sure you don't have any wood panelling too close to the chimney.

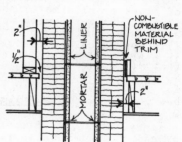

SECTION THROUGH CHIMNEY

BE ON THE ALERT for other defects. Does your chimney leak? During a fire, flames and chunks of burning creosote can escape from the cracks. Has any creosote seeped out of your chimney or stovepipe? A fire can ignite it and thus spread a blaze that otherwise could have been contained. If you have a stove, check the joints of the stovepipe. If they aren't fastened by sheet metal screws, the vibrations of the fire can cause them to separate and release the flames.

BUT YOU DON'T have to have any defects to suffer a devastating fire. Certain complications are simply unavoidable. As the fire burns, flames, sparks, and burning creosote shoots out of the top of the chimney. All this stuff spills out onto your roof, porch, trees, and lawn, and the fire can spread uncontrollably. There's a similar hazard if you have other appliances connected to the same flue. (You shouldn't!) A fire can travel through any pipes connecting the chimney to your oil furnace or gas water heater or stove.

## Fire Fighting

ALL RIGHT--chimney fires are dangerous. The question remains, what should you do in the event of such a fire? The standard advice that you get about any kind of fire is "Get out!" That's excellent advice. Your first move should be to evacuate the house and have someone call the Fire Department from outside the house.

BUT KEEP IN MIND that a chimney fire is somewhat different from other fires in that it's contained--initially, at least. Most wood-fire-safety books recommend certain steps you can follow to help extinguish a chimney fire early. If you keep your head during the first crucial moments, you can make a big difference.

THE FIRST THING to do inside the house is shut any doors and air inlet dampers on the appliance. (This takes only a few seconds.) In this way, you can cut off most of the fire's air supply and help put it out. (If you have other appliances connected to the same flue, however, this won't completely cut off the air. Worse, an oil or gas appliance could go on when its chimney connector is thus detached or blocked.)

IF YOUR FIREPLACE has doors, closing them will help somewhat. If there are no doors, a board of asbestos or a metal sheet can be used. A blanket saturated with water can also be very effective, but the suction from the chimney fire can make it difficult to keep the blanket in place. If the fireplace has a flue damper, shut it slowly once you've gotten the flames in the fireplace under control.

HOW DO YOU GET those flames under control? Not with water. Dumping a lot of water on the chimney, stove, or fireplace can cause serious cracking. You'll also generate a lot of steam inside the house, which won't help matters any. Rock salt, sand, or sodium bicarbonate will be more effective in extinguishing the flames in the stove or fireplace. But even if you put out those flames, the fire will continue to burn inside the chimney.

STANDARD HOUSEHOLD fire extinguishers will be of limited effectiveness. If the fire is really raging, you'll have a tough time getting the spray into the chimney. Even if you do get to the fire and are able to extinguish it, there's always the chance that it can re-ignite from intense heat still in the chimney.

THERE IS A SPECIAL chimney-fire extinguishing flare called Chimfex. It's available from Standard Railway Fuse Corp., Signal Flare Division, P.O. Box 178, Boonton, NJ 07005, (201) 334-0535. It works by discharging huge amounts of smoke and suffocating the fire. You may need more than one during a fire, so keep several on hand. Be sure to follow carefully all instructions concerning their storage and use.

AFTER THE FIRE is under control, check the house at all points of contact with the chimney. If you find any smoke or smoldering, douse the danger areas with water. Pay particular attention to the chimney's upper portions, where the fire will be the hottest. Go up the stairs and check the attic and any upstairs bedrooms. Even if you don't see or smell any hints of fire, feel the walls; soak anything that feels intensely hot, and move away any furniture that's too close to the heat.

MOST OF THESE firefighting methods are rather limited in the face of a serious blaze. The best way to fight a chimney fire is to make sure one doesn't start. Keep the flue clean of creosote build-ups. If your fireplace does a lot of work, have it cleaned out once a year; for an active stove, clean the flue every six months. Do-it-yourselfers can refer to the August 1978 OHJ for information on sweeping their chimneys. If you want this messy job done by a professional, they're listed in the Yellow Pages under "Chimney Cleaning."

This article is based on material from Jay W. Shelton's *Wood Heat Safety* — a clearly written, well illustrated book that examines virtually every aspect of how to heat your home with wood safely. If you're using a wood stove, this is one book you have to own. It's available for $9.95 plus $2.00 postage from Shelton Energy Research, Dept. OHJ, P.O. Box 5235, Santa Fe, NM 87502. (505) 983-9457.

# All About Combustion

*Chimney fires are caused by the ignition of creosote deposits in the chimney stack. Below, you'll find an explanation of how that stuff builds up.*

Both wood and coal are organic hydrocarbons, composed of carbon, hydrogen, and oxygen. Combustion is the combination of these elements with oxygen under heat. Hydrogen and oxygen have the strongest affinity for each other, combining first to form gaseous water. (Moisture still in the wood is driven out in this stage.) During this process, a number of other flammable gases form, all compounds of carbon and hydrogen. As these gases further combine with oxygen, they raise the temperature to a point between 1100 and 2000° F.

If this process were to complete itself, the only waste products would be water vapor, carbon dioxide, a small amount of carbon monoxide, and a little ash. In reality, however, combustion this complete (for wood) requires temperatures above 3000°, with a forced-air draft. Such a fire happens only in the laboratory.

Most wood burning in the home, even in a good stove, is about 40 to 60% efficient. In addition to the gases mentioned above, many of which go up the chimney only partially combusted, a variety of liquid tars are created. Creosote is only one of them, although they all are generally lumped together under the name "creosote." Some acids are also formed in the process.

These chemicals spell destruction for your chimney. The gases leaving a fireplace or wood stove vary from 100° or less up to a maximum of about 1600°, with the normal range for stoves being from 200 to 700°. As these gases cool down to below 250° inside the chimney, the tars and acids reach their "dew point" and condense out onto the walls of their chimney. Pieces of ash and unburned carbon stick to them, and a sooty build-up forms inside the chimney. If the temperature inside the chimney should ever rise sufficiently, these tars can reignite, causing a further rise in temperature inside the flue, increasing the draft, and so on, in a vicious cycle. Under the worst conditions, heat can reach a point where the mortar in the joints melts, and small molten particles can be lifted out of the chimney on the rushing updraft to land on your roof.

With coal, the process of combustion is further complicated by impurities in the coal. These vary a lot, depending on the grade and type of coal, but the most prevalent are nitrogen and sulfur. During the middle stages of combustion, these produce nitric and sulfuric acids, which are much more powerful acids than any of those found in wood. They rapidly attack metal liners, even stainless steel, and so metal liners can't be recommended for use with coal. (For more information on liners, see "Relining Your Chimney Flue" in the September 1982 OHJ.)

— *John Mark Garrison*

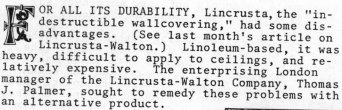

# Anaglypta & Other Embossed Wallcoverings

## Their History & Their Use Today

### By Bruce Bradbury

FOR ALL ITS DURABILITY, Lincrusta, the "indestructible wallcovering," had some disadvantages. (See last month's article on Lincrusta-Walton.) Linoleum-based, it was heavy, difficult to apply to ceilings, and relatively expensive. The enterprising London manager of the Lincrusta-Walton Company, Thomas J. Palmer, sought to remedy these problems with an alternative product.

BEFORE PALMER'S successful experiments, machine-embossed wallpapers could not rival Lincrusta for a few simple reasons. First, a flat sheet of paper run through an embossing machine, and then subjected to the stress of being wetted and pressed against a wall, tends to lose some of its relief as it seeks to revert to a flat sheet. Second, the depth of relief in embossed paper is strictly limited in order that the paper not tear.

PALMER CLEVERLY CIRCUMVENTED both of these technical problems by introducing an embossing cylinder directly into the paper-making process, pressing the embossment into a cotton paper while it was still in the pulp stage. Two remarkable advantages were achieved: (1) Having no flat "memory," the material kept its relief under stress. (2) Due to the plasticity of the pulp, a deep relief rivaling or surpassing that of Lincrusta-Walton was possible. Palmer called his new product Anaglypta, from the Greek "ana" meaning raised and "glypta" meaning cameo.

## Tough Times

PALMER'S UNBOUNDED enthusiasm for his new invention was not seconded by his employer, Frederick Walton, who foresaw the dangers

of a product that shared many of the virtues of his own Lincrusta-Walton, and few of its faults. Confronted with technical problems and his employer's apathy, Palmer labored several years before he was able to take out patents for his product in 1887. When production began a year later in Lancaster, England, Anaglypta was greeted with acclaim by the decorating trade and general public.

THOUGH GENERALLY REGARDED as less desirable than Lincrusta for wainscots (Lincrusta being more durable), Anaglypta was viewed as a decoration for friezes and ceilings, where it handily and inexpensively mocked the most expensive plasterwork. Playing on this advantage, elaborate ceiling combinations were produced by the firm in the Adamesque and Louis XV styles. (The cylinders for producing the Adam ceiling are still in existence in England, but the patterns are no longer in production.)

ANAGLYPTA CAN BE DISTINGUISHED from Lincrusta by its hollow relief. Lincrusta is a solid material; you can press your fingernail into Anaglypta. When varnished Anaglypta is pressed, it sometimes produces a small popping sound, like popping seaweed pods on a beach. This activity was reportedly a favorite entertainment for naughty children left alone in a grand Victorian parlor.

IN THE UNITED STATES, the use of Anaglypta declined by the 1920s, and it eventually ceased to be imported. Luckily it was revived in San Francisco in the 1970s. Anaglypta fared much better in England, where it has been in (more or less) uninterrupted production since the 19th century. It's commonly used, commonly priced, and sold off the shelf in the English equivalent of K-Mart stores. So Anaglypta survives, but beware: its name has been stolen.

THE FIRST THING that any prospective purchaser of Anaglypta needs to know is that anything which says "Anaglypta" on the label isn't really the original cotton-fiber wallcovering invented by Mr. Palmer. Some unsung hero of corporate marketing in England decided in 1966 that less expensive, laminated wood-pulp papers would sell more successfully if ennobled with the title Anaglypta, and robbed Palmer's product of its name.

PALMER'S ORIGINAL ANAGLYPTA was then renamed "Supaglypta," the label under which it's available today. The so-called "Anaglypta" currently produced by the Crown Co., and Schumacher's "High Relief," are relatively inexpensive and certainly usable, but they have neither the depth of relief nor the durability of true Anagylpta (now Supaglytpa). Get it?

*Thomas J. Palmer*

## Finishing Techniques

I FOUND THE SIMPLEST but least effective way to finish Anaglypta (or any embossed wall-covering) is to apply a coat of latex paint, as recommended by the manufacturer. Semi-gloss is preferred as it gives a little more detail to the relief. This simple technique is especially satisfactory for areas--such as ceilings--where Anaglypta is intended to imitate plasterwork.

AN EXCELLENT METHOD for imitating the rich color effects in the 19th-century manner is to work with oil glazes or stains. The Anaglypta should first be sealed with a coat of alkyd-base, semi-gloss enamel, which will provide a suitable surface for working with oil-base products. The variety of finishing effects that can be achieved is limited only by the imagination of the practitioner -- staining, glazing, gilding or bronzing, in-painting with artists' oils, etc. As with Lincrusta, however, the most effective treatment is often a simple glaze which relies on the inherent beauty of the embossed pattern for its effect.

FOR THOSE OF YOU who have experimented with wood-graining, the same shades of undercoats and glazes can be used to great effect on Anaglypta. The only difference is that the glaze coat is simply wiped with a soft rag to create highlights; no special graining tools are used. Commercial glazing liquid, used tinted either with artists' oil colors or universal tints, will make a rich glaze. A drawback to traditional oil glazing is the drying time, which in a humid climate can extend over a period of weeks.

TO CIRCUMVENT THE PROBLEM of drying time, and to try to avoid the use of exotic materials, I went to my local paint store, Ray's Paints of Walnut Creek, California. I showed a traditional 19th-century lincrusta finishing formula to owner Mike Michaels, and together we came up with a simple, quick-drying method for finishing Anaglypta. Our method uses only readily available materials. My desire was to recreate the rich carved wood effect of a Lincrusta wainscot, but you can adapt the material and methods in lighter shades for full wall treatments.

HERE'S THE FORMULA we came up with for an ersatz mahogany finish. The main points of the process are shown in the photographs below:

(1) PAINT THE ANAGLYPTA with an orange-toned, alkyd-base, semi-gloss enamel. I used Martin Seynour "Free Spirit" Nut Brown color (#M-42-015). Allow to dry overnight.

(2) TAKE A CAN of commonly available mahogany wood stain (I used Flecto Varathane #805 Mahogany), and paint over the enamel base coat. Let the stain sit for a few minutes, and then wipe lightly with a soft cloth. The result when dry will look drab, but the following varnish coats add lustre.

(3) PAINT ON A COAT of gloss varnish. When this is dry, finish with a coat of flat or satin varnish to cut the sheen as you prefer. NOTE: The last coat of varnish should be painted over the gloss coat as

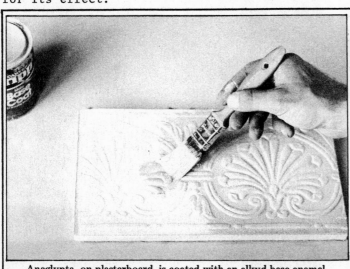

Anaglypta, on plasterboard, is coated with an alkyd-base enamel.

Wood stain being brushed on.

soon as the gloss has dried. If you wait for weeks between coats you may have an adhesion problem between layers.

THIS SAME COMBINATION of semi-gloss enamel and wood stain can be used to achieve a broad variety of wood effects. I had particular success using Zar Beverlee's brand wood stains which come in a variety of colors, and are thick-bodied for use in wood graining. If you want to imitate a specific wood finish, pick out the lightest color visible in the grain, and match your enamel base coat to that color. Remember that your base coat should be lighter and brighter than the desired end effect, as stains and glazes will darken and tone down the original base color. Always test your colors and stains on a practice piece before you tackle an entire wall. Be sure to paint and wipe the wall in sections, so that the stain can be wiped before it dries.

(Photo by Stacy Geiken)

An eye-catching Anaglypta pattern on the entrance hall ceiling of the Kearney Mansion in Fresno, California.

coat will dissolve the Chromotone. If you have problems with the Chromotone dissolving, seal the Chromotone with a coat of spray varnish. Then you can proceed with staining or glazing. Richness of effect in this method depends on a meticulous rubbing technique, so work on small sections of the wall at a time.

## Today...

A COLLECTION of Anaglypta and Supaglypta is currently being introduced to the United States by Crown Ltd. of England (successor to the original Lincrusta-Walton and Anaglypta companies). Distribution is nationwide and the pattern selection includes 19th-century and contemporary designs. There are also three embossed Victorian-style wallpapers in Schumacher's Victorian Collection. See the Restoration Products News section on page 242 for further details about these and other embossed wallcoverings.

*Samples of Anaglypta and other types of embossed wallcoverings can be seen on the following page.*

## Gilding The Lily

Y OU CAN ACHIEVE THE LOOK of gilded leather by first sealing the Anaglypta with a semi-gloss, alkyd enamel. When dry, overpaint with a solid coat of Chromotone brand stabilized Roman Gold. On top of this, lay a full-bodied Mahogany stain (such as Varathane #805 Mahogany), and wipe carefully with a rag. Chosen highlights are rubbed nearly back to pure gold. Finish with a single coat of satin Varathane, which will restore the lustre to the gold.

AGAIN, IT'S ESSENTIAL to try a practice run of this method: You must determine which of the highlights you wish to emphasize in gold. You will also want to know if the stain or glaze

Bruce Bradbury is a remarkable person and a dear friend of The Journal. It's been a pleasure to watch Bradbury & Bradbury Wallpapers grow from his idea to a respected and influential manufacturer of historic wallpapers. Besides a line of stock patterns, dating from 1860 to 1901, he occasionally runs a custom historic reproduction. If you have not seen Bruce's high-quality papers, a brochure illustrating the patterns is $1. Bradbury & Bradbury Wallpapers, PO Box 155, Dept. OHJ, Benicia, CA 94510. (707) 746-1900.

Gloss varnish tinted with artists' color is highlighted.

A final coat of semi-gloss varnish is applied.

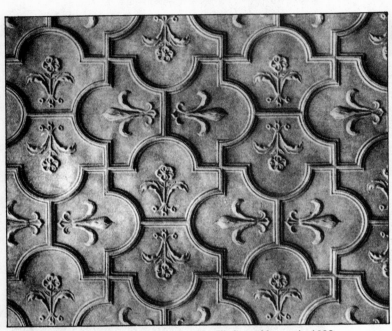

*TYNECASTLE — "Fleur-de-lis" designed by W. Scott Morton in 1892.*

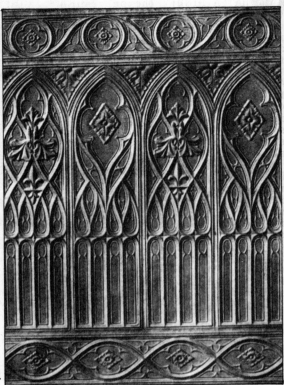

*LIGNOMUR — designed by Ellingham and produced in 1912.*

*CORDELOVA*
*The "Tournament"*
*Frieze, produced in 1902.*

# Ersatz Lincrusta

With their usual exuberance and love of detail, the Victorians introduced what seems like an endlesss variety of embossed wallcoverings (all of which have since faded into obscurity). So if your embossed wallcovering doesn't appear to be Lincrusta or Anaglypta, you may have:

**Japan Paper:** One of Japan's earliest export drives began in the 1860s by combining traditional Japanese paper making skills and low labor costs to create a hand-made paper imitation of leather wallhangings for Western tastes.

Made of embossed mulberry paper, individual sheets were skillfully joined together to make rolls which were then luxuriously finished with gilding, colors, and varnish.

**Subercorium:** Produced in 1881 in imitation of Lincrusta; cork and rubber were its components.

**Calcorian:** Another rubber and cork combination with the mixture affixed to a paper backing.

**Lignomur:** First produced in the U.S. in 1880, using a wood fiber pulp. Wood was later replaced by a fine rag pulp.

**Cortecine:** Produced in 1880 by a former Lincrusta-Walton employee, it shared a similar manufacturing technique, but used different base materials.

**Cordelova:** This 1890s embossed paper consisted of pressed paper beaten into the recesses of cast-iron plates.

**Salamander:** Originating in 1895, it featured high relief achieved by pressing asbestos pulp into cast-iron plates.

**Tynecastle Tapestry:** First produced in 1874, it consisted of a fine canvas that had been hand-pressed into moulds.

**Cameoid:** A low-relief paper produced by the Lincrusta-Walton Company in 1898.

*An excellent source for further information on obscure, 19th-century embossed wallcoverings is "A History of English Wallpaper," by Sugden and Edmondson, 1925.*

# Helpful Publications

*—Reviews by Jacqueline MacDonald*

### Victorian Lighting: The Dietz Catalogue of 1860
Ulysses G. Dietz
1982 (128 pp., profusely illustrated)
Paper

**W**HAT A FIND! The only surviving copy of Dietz and Company's illustrated lighting catalog was discovered by a descendant...and that's how this facsimile edition came to be.

ANYONE INTERESTED in Victorian lighting will be delighted by the 41 oversize plates (six in color) in this rare catalog. Lamps, sconces, girandoles, chandeliers, shades, and other c. 1860 lighting accessories are shown.

DIETZ AND COMPANY was the "first to manufacture lamp goods by steam power in quantities, in this country." The history of Dietz and Company's thriving New York-based business is described in the introduction by descendant Ulysses G. Dietz, Curator of Decorative Arts at the Newark Museum. There's also a brief discussion of lighting terminology, and a categoric discussion of various lighting fixture designs, with photographs of original Dietz fixtures.

No 43. 18½ in.

To order, send $29.50, postage paid, to:
American Life Foundation
Box 349
Watkins Glen, New York 14891
(607) 535-4737

### Wallpapers: An International History and Illustrated Survey
Charles C. Oman and Jean Hamilton
1982 (485 pp., profusely illustrated) Cloth

**A**T $75, THIS BOOK MAY interest only serious students of wallpaper history. The volume contains a complete catalog of the wallpapers assembled in London's Victoria and Albert Museum. Black-and-white and a few color photographs of most wallpapers from the museum are shown, with a limited description of each paper. Papers not pictured are also listed.

THE CATALOG is divided into three sections: "Anonymous Wallapers and Wallpaper Designs," "Pattern Books," and "Designers." An extensive sub-section on William Morris is included. Thorough histories of wallpaper origins are given in the two introductions, by Oman and Hamilton.

To order, send $75.00 plus $3.00 postage to:
Harry N. Abrams, Inc.
110 East 59th Street
New York, New York 10022
(212) 758-8600

### The Kit Furniture Book
Lynda Graham-Barber
1982 (159 pp., profusely illustrated) Paper

**"K**ITS ARE CONTAGIOUS." Lynda Graham-Barber feels anyone can furnish a home for half the store-bought price by using kits. This new manual tells how.

IT CONTAINS a catalog of over 50 kit furniture companies personally researched by the author. The catalog is divided into categories: Colonial, Queen Anne, Shaker, turn-of-the-century, and contemporary furnishings; clocks and musical instruments; and houses. Each listing is accompanied by a black-and-white photograph and pertinent information such as assembly time, price, and wood type. There's also a color section showing ways to decorate with kits; a step-by-step guide to the assembly of three kits; as well as tips on gluing, sanding, staining, and waxing.

To order, send $9.95 plus $1.00 postage to:
Random House, Inc.
400 Hahn Road
West Minster, Maryland 21157
(800) 638-6460

### Victorians at Home
Susan Lasdun
1981 (160 pp., profusely illustrated) Cloth

**T**HROUGH NUMEROUS PICTURES and short essays, *Victorians at Home* shows the variety of English lifestyles that existed during the life of Queen Victoria. The book offers glimpses into the lives of, among others, an artist and his family in the countryside, a wealthy banking family, a bachelor and professional man, a minister, and even Queen Victoria herself. A chapter is devoted to the activities and cottages of the Victorian working class, as well. Once you've read this pictorial, you'll realize that Victorians were as diverse as contemporary people are.

ILLUSTRATIONS in the book are drawings and watercolors by inhabitants (including children) of homes shown, with some photographs, too. Much information in the essays is from diaries and letters written by these Victorians.

YOU NEEDN'T be an architectural historian to be fascinated by *Victorians at Home*.

To order, send $20.00 plus $1.00 postage to:
The Viking Press
Attn: Direct Mail Order
299 Murray Hill Pkwy.
East Rutherford, NJ 07073
(201) 933-1460

# Ask OHJ

## Instant Old Age

**O**NE ROOM in our house will be refloored with random-width, yellow pine flooring. What can we use on the floor to give it a used look? We are hoping to have the patina of an old floor immediately, rather than wait for the lumber to age naturally.

--Kathryn W. Twetten  Boyds, MD

**H**OW TO DEAL with your floor depends on what you intend to use for a final finish. Try various choices on small pieces until you arrive at a color and finish that satisfy you and blend with the other floors of your house. You may want to tone down the floor color with a light stain before the final finish to prevent "the shock of the new." But beware of going too far. Almost all finishes, especially on floors, darken with age and use. You may soon find your new floor standing out dark and dingy against the old. We recommend against any attempt to fake or artificially "distress" elements of houses. Be patient, and let time and use do the work for you.

## Rolled Roofing

**I**S THERE A WAY to install a deck or duckboards on top of a flat roof without damaging the roofing paper? Several of our block association members have installed new roofs, and the contractors have been negative about having duckboards on them--or even walking on them. Yet everywhere you read about roof gardens on top of brownstones. Any suggestions?

--Judith Mortenson  New York, NY

**R**OLLED ASPHALT ROOFING is not designed to take traffic. Even under the best conditions, it becomes brittle in a few years and cracks easily. This becomes a problem only when it is subjected to sudden movements or loads. So tread lightly when you're up on the roof, and use boards to spread the weight as much as possible.

IF YOU'RE SERIOUS ABOUT a deck on your roof, then you might investigate a built-up roofing system that consists of layers of tar and gravel (although a good one is bound to be more expensive than rolled roofing). Your deck should still be designed to spread the load on as wide an area as possible. Remember that unless it's well insulated, a built-up roof can develop cracks and leaks due to thermal expansion and contraction. Have a reliable engineer assess the structural condition of your roof before adding the additional weight of a built-up roof. After all, it was never designed to be a floor.

## All That Jazz (Finish)

**T**HERE WAS A WALL FINISH used in the 1920s and '30s called a "Jazz" or "Tiffany" finish. Can you give me any information on what this process involves?

--D. Fuhs  Evanston, IL

**W**E COULDN'T LEARN VERY MUCH on this subject, but here's what we found out. It is a glaze finish that requires three or more coats to produce the effect. The glazing colors are mixed separately, using raw sienna, raw umber, rose pink, and cobalt blue. A coat of flatting oil is applied to an ivory-colored background, working on a two-yard square at a time. While the oil is still wet, the colors are applied here and there. With a wad of cheesecloth, the colors are blended into one another with a circular motion. Then the work is stippled, taking care not to smear the colors. Highlights are wiped out here and there to permit the ground colors to show through. A rich blend is the result, with none of the colors predominating.

THIS IS NOT A JOB FOR AMATEURS, unless they're willing to experiment on their walls. There aren't any books in print (that we know of) which offer hard information on this process; this makes it even more difficult for the do-it-yourselfer. If you're near a well stocked library, you can look in Painting & Paper Hanging for the Home Owner by Charles Moore or Painting and Decorating by D. Joseph DiBernardo for more details.

*(We would be interested to hear from our readers about any further information or experience they might have to share regarding this subject.--The Editors)*

## Cracks In The House

**I**N THE PAST FEW MONTHS, cracks and crazing have been occurring on the walls and ceiling of our 1936 house. They look dry, although we are in a humid area. We are running a small dehumidifier in the basement (only during the summer) and have insulated the attic, but we don't think we have made the house "too tight" with these measures. We would appreciate your help.

--Jan Jennings  Ames, IA

**S**MALL SCATTERED CRACKS across the surface of the wall and ceiling are probably due to too much drying and heating, as opposed to too much moisture. It sounds as if you have recently made a lot of changes in the temperature and humidity cycle of your building. If conditions aren't uncomfortable and you have no basement flooding, try doing without the dehumidifier. Beyond that, it may be just a question of allowing the house to "settle in" to its new heating cycle.

## A Cistern Situation

THE TURN-OF-THE-CENTURY that I purchased has had very little modernization and therefore, no remuddling. In fact, it doesn't even have 20th-century plumbing! The only source of water in the house comes from an open concrete cistern located in the basement, which is an earth cellar. The cistern collects rainwater from two outside leader pipes; a hand pump in the kitchen pumps water up to the sink.

MY PROBLEM concerns the dampness caused by the cistern. I go to the house only on weekends, and on several freezing weekends this winter, there was frost on the exposed wooden beams and concrete walls of the cellar. When I got the house warmed, the frost melted, and the beams and walls got all wet. Months later, in June, the earth floor is still quite damp. The concrete on parts of the cellar walls is crumbling off. Anything left down there gets all mildewed and rusty. I plan to run plumbing from an outside well within the next few years, but what can I do to alleviate this dampness in the meantime?

--Barbara Gentile   New York, NY

YOUR BEST BET is to keep the cellar unheated and well ventilated. There's probably no effective way to prevent the cistern's moisture from entering the basement. All you can do is allow it to dissipate as fast as possible: Keep plenty of air moving through. (In winter, this means keeping the basement cold.) You have no indoor plumbing, so freezing pipes won't be a problem. You may want to install additional insulation between the basement and the living area, just for your own comfort. When you install plumbing, you'll need to heat the basement, so you might then consider putting in a cellar floor over a vapor barrier and insulation. In the meantime, a plastic vapor barrier over the dirt should help cut down on ground moisture.

## Hoosier Hints

MY HOOSIER was built in 1920 and is still complete. Unfortunately, the metal of the flour bin has been painted over. The paint is now flaking and peeling, but the metal is generally clear and bright. How can I remove the paint and not darken or scratch the metal?

--Arthur T. Roberts
Elizabethton, TN

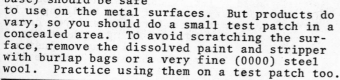

A SEMI-PASTE chemical paint remover (such as one with a methylene-chloride base) should be safe to use on the metal surfaces. But products do vary, so you should do a small test patch in a concealed area. To avoid scratching the surface, remove the dissolved paint and stripper with burlap bags or a very fine (0000) steel wool. Practice using them on a test patch too.

## Sandblasted Slate

LAST SPRING, we had a roofer take the slate shingles off our leaky roof. We re-roofed, salvaging some of the original slate from our house and some from another building. Before laying any of the salvaged slate, the roofer sandblasted each piece to clean it. Does sandblasting damage the slate or cause it to become water-permeable in the future? What is your opinion of this procedure?

--Stephen P. Parkhurst  Portland, ME

WE HAVE NEVER heard of this specific procedure, but lightly sandblasting slate should not present the same problems that occur when sandblasting brick, which is relatively soft and porous. The process will cut down the thickness of the shingles by removing the outer layers of stone, but this is not damaging. Good quality, well applied slate is one of the longest-lasting roofing materials.

## Spackle Your Troubles Away

HOW CAN I ELIMINATE the small pits and holes in my plaster wall, now that the wallpaper has been scraped off? I don't want to repaper or hire a plasterer to put a skim coat over the whole thing.

--Stewart McDermet  Boston, MA

A SPACKLING COMPOUND is the standard answer to cracks and small holes. It comes in either a powdered form or, more frequently, ready-mixed in a can. It can be applied with a putty knife, dries quickly, and sands easily. It has a tendency to shrink as it cures, however, and so you may have to make a second application. For larger holes, rake out the edges to provide a "key" for the new material, then fill with a plaster mix intended specifically for patching. Pure plaster of paris will dry too quickly for this use.

## Don't Fill Those Grooves

THE WALLS AND CEILINGS in two rooms of our 1870 farmhouse are beaded tongue and groove siding. There are gaps of 1/16 inch between many of the boards where they have dried out. What would you suggest using as a filler, and how should we apply it?

--Martha Fraser  Houston, TX

IF THE GAPS are only around 1/16 inch, the best thing to do is leave them alone. The tongue below should still more than cover the joint. There's a bead at the edge of every board, designed to highlight the joint, so it doesn't seem like the gap should be noticeable. Siding of this kind should be laid up with a slight spacing between the boards, to allow for expansion and contraction with the seasons.

# Route To The Best Method For Restoring Clear Finishes

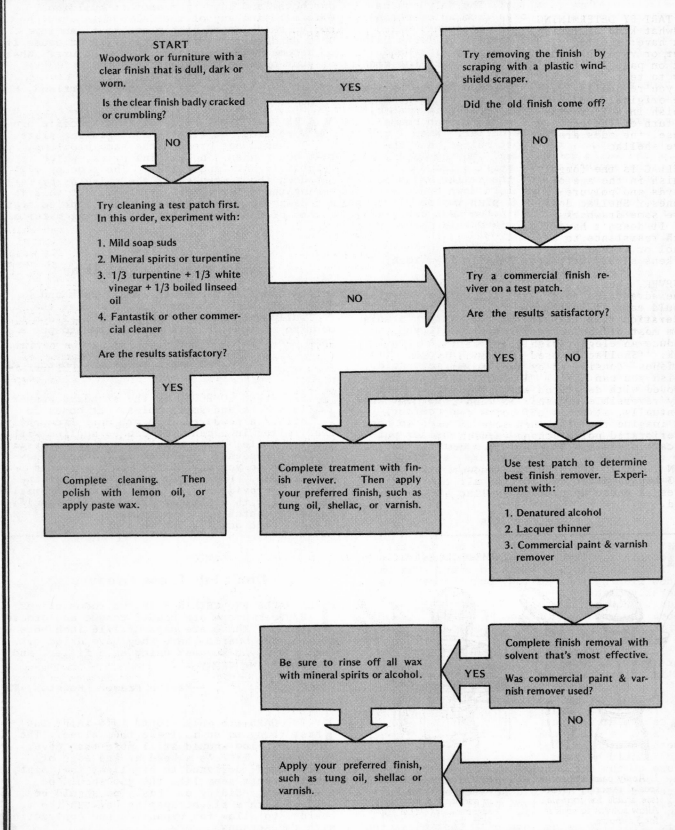

**START**
Woodwork or furniture with a clear finish that is dull, dark or worn.

Is the clear finish badly cracked or crumbling?

Try removing the finish by scraping with a plastic windshield scraper.

Did the old finish come off?

Try cleaning a test patch first. In this order, experiment with:

1. Mild soap suds
2. Mineral spirits or turpentine
3. 1/3 turpentine + 1/3 white vinegar + 1/3 boiled linseed oil
4. Fantastik or other commercial cleaner

Are the results satisfactory?

Try a commercial finish reviver on a test patch.

Are the results satisfactory?

Complete cleaning. Then polish with lemon oil, or apply paste wax.

Complete treatment with finish reviver. Then apply your preferred finish, such as tung oil, shellac, or varnish.

Use test patch to determine best finish remover. Experiment with:

1. Denatured alcohol
2. Lacquer thinner
3. Commercial paint & varnish remover

Be sure to rinse off all wax with mineral spirits or alcohol.

Complete finish removal with solvent that's most effective.

Was commercial paint & varnish remover used?

Apply your preferred finish, such as tung oil, shellac or varnish.

YES   NO

will renew it quickly and economically. And if the finish has deteriorated, finish revivers are usually preferred to strippers.

START BY DETERMINING what kind of finish you have: shellac, lacquer, or varnish. The box on page 240 tells how to test for each. If you're dealing with the original woodwork finish in a Victorian or turn-of-the-century house, the odds are you have shellac.

SHELLAC is the forgotten finish in the age of alkyds and polyurethanes. Shellac does have some drawbacks: (1) It doesn't have much resistance to alcohol or water; (2) It darkens slowly with age.

HOWEVER, shellac has some advantages that should earn it more consideration than it gets from most old-house restorers. Shellac can produce an elegant high gloss without a plastic look. (Shellac is used in French polish finishes--considered by many to be the finest finish you can have.) And shellac is easily removed with denatured alcohol--making it a very reversible finish. So when it darkens eventually, it comes off quite readily. Can you imagine the mess when someone has to strip deteriorated polyurethane varnish out of intricate mouldings 50 years from now?

WHEN I HAD TO REFINISH the woodwork in my 1883 house, after considering all the alternatives, I ended up putting shellac back on the wood.

THE GENERAL IDEA in restoring a clear finish --as in so much other restoration work--is to start with the gentlest procedure and gradually work up to the more drastic ones. The secret is to START SMALL. Use a small, inconspicuous area to test various procedures. Only when you've found a method that you know works should you tackle the entire job.

## Consider Cleaning

IF THERE IS only a small accumulation of dirt and grime on the finish, cleaning with mild soap suds will do:

● Put a tablespoon of Ivory Liquid in a quart of warm water and whip it to create a lot of suds. Dip an old wash cloth or piece of terrycloth toweling into the suds (NOT into the water). Rub the test area vigorously, then wipe with a dry towel to absorb any dampness. This procedure will remove surface grime without harming the patina. (It's recommended for the annual cleaning of fine wood furniture.) However, it will not remove any wax build-up. If cleaning with soap suds still leaves a dark residue, try this method:

● Brush some mineral spirits (paint thinner) onto the test patch. Allow the mineral spirits to soak in for 3 minutes. Then take a pad of fine steel wool (#0000) and gently rub the surface in the direction of the grain. (If it's a high gloss finish, use a terrycloth rag instead. Steel wool will dull the gloss.) On carved detail, scrub out softened wax and dirt

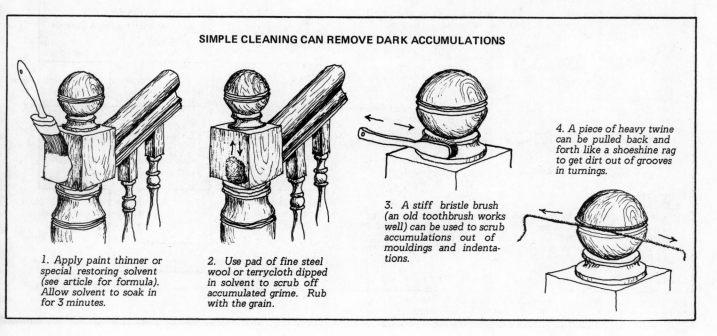

## SIMPLE CLEANING CAN REMOVE DARK ACCUMULATIONS

*1. Apply paint thinner or special restoring solvent (see article for formula). Allow solvent to soak in for 3 minutes.*

*2. Use pad of fine steel wool or terrycloth dipped in solvent to scrub off accumulated grime. Rub with the grain.*

*3. A stiff bristle brush (an old toothbrush works well) can be used to scrub accumulations out of mouldings and indentations.*

*4. A piece of heavy twine can be pulled back and forth like a shoeshine rag to get dirt out of grooves in turnings.*

with an old toothbrush. On turnings, you can remove the loosened dirt by using a piece of heavy twine and pulling it back and forth in the turnings like a shoeshine rag.

WIPE UP any excess mineral spirits with a paper towel, then let the test patch dry for an hour. At this point, it will look quite dull. Apply a bit of lemon oil or paste wax to the test patch and see if you like the result. (NOTE: Never apply lemon oil over paste wax, or vice versa. Lemon oil will dissolve wax, and you'll wind up with a gummy mess.)

● An alternative to cleaning with mineral spirits is this old-time recipe for a cleaner-restorer. I have used this recipe in restoring an 1885 mantel, and the results were gratifying.

TO MAKE the cleaner-restorer, mix 1 cup boiled linseed oil, 1 cup white vinegar, and 1 cup turpentine. Before using, shake vigorously to mix the ingredients. Apply to the surface with an old paint brush, and allow to soak for 3 minutes. Then dip a pad of fine steel wool (#0000) in the restorer and gently scrub off the loosened grime. Again, if it's a high-gloss finish, you'll want to scrub with terry-cloth, rather than steel wool.

WIPE OFF any excess restorer with paper towels or rags. (The rags contain linseed oil, so there's the danger of spontaneous combustion. Get them outside IMMEDIATELY, and either burn them, or store in a water-filled metal can.)

LET THE RESTORED PATCH dry for 24 hours. A little paste wax gives you the final result. If you like the look, repeat the process on the entire surface. If you're not happy, then it's on to stronger cleaners...

● Proprietary cleaners such as Fantastik or Spic 'n Span will clean...as well as remove some of the finish. So testing gingerly on a SMALL area is in order. You can also make your own strong cleaner by dissolving 1 lb. of washing soda in 1 gallon of hot water. Wearing rubber gloves, rub down the surface with your cleaner and fine steel wool. Work with the steel wool damp, rather than dripping, and wipe up any water immediately with paper towels to avoid water spotting.

THESE CLEANERS will definitely leave the surface dull. Polish with lemon oil or paste wax to get the final effect.

## Finish Revivers

IF SIMPLE CLEANING didn't do the job, then you've got to remove some more of the old finish. There are a number of commercial finish revivers (or 'refinishers'). A finish reviver is a solvent soup, containing such chemicals as toluene and methyl alcohol. You can also experiment with your own formulas. Start with "A" and work down the list:

A. 15% by volume lacquer thinner in mineral spirits

B. 50/50 lacquer thinner and denatured alcohol

C. Pure denatured alcohol

D. Pure lacquer thinner

THE PROCEDURE for using these finish revivers is the same, whether you're working with a commercial product, or your own concoction:

PUT THE REVIVER in a wide-mouth jar, and keep covered. (The solvents are highly volatile and evaporate rapidly.) Dip a small piece of fine steel wool (#0000) in the reviver, and

### SHELLAC, LACQUER, OR VARNISH?

When restoring a clear finish, it's helpful to know what kind of finish you're dealing with. Here's a brief guide to the chemical properties and history of the three major types of clear finishes.

Shellac is made from a resin derived from the lac beetle that is native to the Far East. The solid resin, dissolved in denatured alcohol, is shellac. This formulation has been used from the 18th century to the present. The clear finish on much of the furniture and woodwork of the 19th century is shellac. Shellac was preferred for commercial work because it dried fast and didn't hold up production. Just to confuse matters, much of the 19th century literature refers to shellac as 'varnish' (as opposed to oil finishes or wax). Today's varnish is a very different animal (see below).

Lacquer today is a totally synthetic finish, dating back to the introduction of nitrocellulose in the 1920s. It dries rapidly, making it a highly desirable finish for production furniture. Because it dries so fast, lacquer can be successfully applied only with power spray equipment. More terminology confusion: In the 19th century, shellac was sometimes called lacquer. Also, the Japanese lacquer used for centuries on Oriental woodwork is derived from a tree resin, and is more closely related to what we would call 'varnish.'

Varnish is a solution of resins in a drying oil. The resins can be based on natural materials (e.g., tung oil, linseed oil) or else totally synthetic (e.g., alkyd, polyurethane). Varnish as we know it was introduced commercially in the 1860s. More resistant to water and chemicals than shellac, varnish has the drawback of being slower drying, and harder to renew or remove.

Shellac and lacquer are sometimes referred to as 'spirit varnishes.' This means that they cure by the evaporation of their 'spirits' or solvent. Shellac and lacquer finishes can be dissolved by the application of their solvents—alcohol or lacquer thinner.

Today's varnishes (e.g., spar varnish, floor varnish, polyurethane varnish) are classified as 'oil varnishes' because they cure chemically by combining with oxygen in the air. Once cured, only a powerful solvent like methylene chloride can dissolve an oil varnish.

#### How To Tell The Difference

To test whether a clear finish is shellac, lacquer, or varnish, you need some denatured alcohol, lacquer thinner, and a soft rag. First, wet the rag with alcohol. Rub a small area of the finish in an inconspicuous spot. If the finish starts to dissolve, it's shellac. Denatured alcohol won't dissolve lacquer or varnish.

If the finish resists alcohol, take the rag and wet it with lacquer thinner. Rub briskly on a test spot. If the finish starts to dissolve, it's lacquer. Note: Lacquer thinner may cause some varnish finishes to wrinkle, but they won't dissolve.

If the finish won't dissolve in either alcohol or lacquer thinner, it's varnish.

squeeze out any excess. Gently rub a small area (about 1 sq. ft. at a time). The pad will start picking up the old finish, so either rinse frequently in your reviver solution, or discard the pad and start fresh. Remove finish until you get a color you like, or until all tackiness disappears.

ALLOW THE TEST PATCH to dry, then apply a coat of finish; tung oil is the usual choice. Tung oil can be applied with the hand, or with a lint-free rag. Apply a thin coat, rubbing with the grain, and wipe off all excess. One coat gives a satin lustre; two or more coats gives a higher gloss. (Beware of spontaneous combustion in any rags or paper towels containing tung oil!)

IF THE TEST PATCH is satisfactory, go over the whole surface with finish reviver, doing about one square foot at a time. You may have to go over the entire surface a second time with a dampened steel wool pad to remove any lap marks between sections.

BUT IF THE TEST shows the finish is too far gone for reviving, you've no choice but to strip.

## Take It All Off

PICKING A STRIPPER for a clear finish isn't critical; all the commercial brands will cut shellac, lacquer, and varnish without much trouble. You can also remove shellac with denatured alcohol, and lacquer with lacquer thinner.

A SEMI-PASTE REMOVER is probably the best choice--especially if vertical surfaces are involved. Apply the stripper with a soft old paint brush. (It's best to use a natural bristle brush; some plastic bristles dissolve in paint remover.) Allow the stripper to sit

on the surface for 15 minutes, then probe with a putty knife. The finish should be softened down to bare wood.

IF THE FINISH didn't soften completely in 15 minutes, let the stripper sit a while longer. If it starts to dry out, dab some fresh stripper right on top of the old. Don't disturb the sludge until you can get down to bare wood.

ONCE THE FINISH is loose, here's the best way to get the sludge off: Remove as much as you can using a scraper such as a putty knife. (Round its corners with a file so you don't gouge the wood.) Remove the rest of the sludge by washing with pads of fine steel wool or terrycloth saturated with mineral spirits. Although it's an extra expense, by using mineral spirits instead of water, you won't raise the grain or lift veneers. And you'll also remove any possible waxy residue from the stripper.

### WATCH OUT FOR WAX

Some commercial paint and varnish removers (especially the cheaper brands) contain wax, which retards evaporation of the stripping solvents. The wax, however, can interfere with the adhesion of the new finish, unless the wax has been thoroughly removed by washing.

The best quality semi-paste strippers are thickened with methyl cellulose, rather than wax, which eliminates a potential source of problems with your finish. If you can't tell from the label what the thickener is (and you usually can't), here are a couple of tests:

1. Heft the cans in the store. A gallon of semi-paste stripper thickened with methyl cellulose weighs about 11 lb., while a wax-containing stripper will be noticeably lighter—about 8 lb.

2. If you have a can of semi-paste stripper at home and you don't know if it contains wax, chill it to 40 degrees in your refrigerator. If the stripper contains wax, it will get very thick and just about unpourable. A stripper with methyl cellulose, however, will flow at 40 degrees almost as well as it does at room temperature.

If you are using a wax-containing stripper and you are worried about your finish, the safest course is to wash the wood with a rag soaked in mineral spirits after the stripping is complete.

### SAFETY HINTS
— or —
### PLEASE DON'T EAT THE CHEMICALS

Paint strippers and finish revivers are a powerful witch's brew of noxious chemicals. Liquid and semi-paste strippers and revivers contain one or more of the following solvents:

| | | |
|---|---|---|
| Acetone | Benzol | Methanol |
| Propylene dichloride | Methylene chloride | Toluene |
| Methyl ethyl ketone | Isopropyl alcohol | Xylenes |

Some of these solvents are flammable. All are toxic to varying degrees, and some can enter the body through the skin as well as by being inhaled. ALWAYS have plenty of ventilation when your're using paint strippers or revivers. To be safe, that means more than just having a window open; you should have fans blowing, too.

Flammable paint strippers and revivers (the liquid types) should never be used in a closed space, such as a basement workshop, where collecting vapors could be ignited by a pilot light or an electric motor. Be especially careful using flammable removers and steel wool around electrical outlets. OHJ knows of several fires that started when steel wool brushed by an electrical outlet, causing a spark that ignited panelling soaked in flammable paint remover.

# Restoration Products News

## Anaglypta
## And Other Embossed Wallcoverings

*Last month's article on Lincrusta-Walton, and the article about Anaglypta in this issue, may have piqued your interest in embossed wallcoverings. We've made a careful search for current sources of Anaglypta, Supaglypta, and other facsimiles.*

Eagle & Lion is the sole U.S. importer of *Crown's* embossed wallcoverings. The manufacture of these wallcoverings has been continuous in England, though the number and styles of patterns have changed with passing fads. The selection currently includes some Victorian patterns in Supaglypta and Anaglypta, numerous inappropriate contemporary designs, and the notorious Lincrusta barnboard.

Today you can choose from 103 Anaglypta, 34 Supaglypta, 19 Lincrusta, and 19 Vynaglypta patterns. (Vynaglypta is a shiny, vinyl embossed wallcovering introduced in the early '70s.) All the patterns are sold in rolls about 22 in. wide and 33 ft. long — enough to cover approximately 57 sq.ft. The wallcovering should be hung with a good vinyl or heavy-duty wallpaper paste. It comes ready for finishing; some techniques are described on page 232.

Their suggested retail for Anaglypta is $30/roll, Supaglypta $38/roll, Vynaglypta $42/roll, and Lincrusta $98/roll. Although they won't sell direct, you can contact Eagle & Lion for a dealer in your area who retails all or part of the collection. They also offer a brochure, $2, which describes the various patterns. Eagle & Lion, Inc., 11362-K Amalgam Way, Dept. OHJ, Rancho Cordova, CA 95670. (916) 635-0141.

*Floral Crown Border (7-7/8 in. wide)*

Antique, embossed borders are offered by San Francisco Victoriana, in addition to their selection of *Crown* patterns. These eight borders, manufactured in Germany c.1890-1915, are pre-finished in period colors. (Colors and gilding were air-brushed by hand to produce fine detailing.) After the borders are hung, they should be covered with a clear sealer or satin urethane to enhance the colors and prevent fading. The borders range in width from 3 in. to 14¼ in., and in price from $6 to $25 per yard.

This past year, Schumacher introduced *The Victorian Collection*: reproductions and adaptations of actual historic fabrics and wallpapers. The collection, officially endorsed by The Victorian Society in America, includes three embossed papers, in addition to the large selection of period-inspired Victorian wallpapers. The embossed papers are called *High Relief* — something of an exaggeration, as you'll have to be careful not to obscure some of the relief when finishing the paper. But they're relatively inexpensive, and the patterns are appropriate. The papers are sold in double roll packages (about 33 ft.) for $9.95/roll. They can be seen in sample books at wallpaper dealers nationwide. Schumacher, 939 3rd Ave., Dept OHJ, New York, NY 10022. (212) 644-5943.

Another source for embossed wallcoverings is Kingsway . They offer three embossed, low-relief patterns imported from England (not from *Crown*). The patterns are $21.98 or $27.94 for a double roll. You can call or write for free samples; a catalog showing their other restoration products (mostly millwork) is $3. Kingsway, 4723 Chromium Dr., Dept. OHJ, Colorado Springs, CO 80918. (303) 599-4512.

SFV sells the *Crown* patterns (11 Anaglypta and 2 Supaglypta) they've found to be the most popular and appropriate for decorating Victorian houses. Their Anaglypta is $30/roll; the Supaglypta $38/roll. A border sampler is $16 ppd., and a sampler of *Crown* patterns is $15 ppd. Send $3 for a catalog with information about these and other products. San Francisco Victoriana, 2245 Palou Ave., Dept. OHJ, San Francisco, CA 94124. (415) 648-0313.

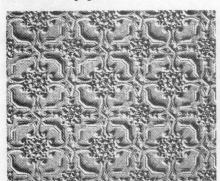

**Crown Patterns** — *Three Anaglypta patterns (from left to right) Celestine, Kenilworth, and Acanthus.*

Dovetail, famous for their exquisite plaster ornament, is now retailing the reproduction lincrusta patterns they manufactured for the restoration of the California State Capitol. Long hours and immense creative energy were spent duplicating the three finely detailed panels and two friezes. The *Scroll panel* is 58¼ in. x 18 in. ($65/panel); *Ascending Foliated panel* is 36½ in. x 18-5/8 in. ($45/panel); and the *Crest panel* is 31-1/8 in. x 19-1/8 in. ($45/panel). They all have a 1/8-inch relief. (Discounts are available on more than five panels.) The two friezes are 4¼ or 5 inches wide, and $8.70/ft. or $9.50/ft. (respectively) with a ¼-inch relief. Made of gypsum reinforced with fiberglass, these relief patterns can be installed with panel adhesive or contact cement, and standard finishing techniques applied. Their $2 catalog shows both relief patterns and plaster ornaments. Dovetail, Inc., PO Box 1569, Dept. OHJ, Lowell, MA 01853. (617) 454-2944.

*The Crest Panel from Dovetail*

*Wall Sculpture* is a selection of embossed papers manufactured by *Worley* in England. Most of the patterns have names like *Cracked Ice* and are modern in design. But they offer one pattern, *Grandeur*, which is appropriate for 19th-century houses. It sells for $12/roll (plus $1.50 for postage and handling); a roll is 21 in. wide and 11 yds. long, approximately 57.75 sq.ft. No literature, but they will send free samples. Decor International Wallcovering, Inc., 37-39 Crescent St., Dept. OHJ, Long Island City, NY 11101. (212) 392-4990; outside NY, (800) 221-0444.

*Alhambra—One of Crown's Supaglyptas*

## Other Mail-Order Sources

*The following are other mail-order sources for embossed wallcoverings:*

Rejuvenation House Parts Co., 901 N. Skidmore St., Dept. OHJ, Portland, OR 97217. (503) 249-0774. *Crown* patterns: 10 Anaglypta, $25/roll; 2 Supaglypta, $38/roll. Catalog, $2, includes small samples; 9 in. x 12 in. samples are $2 each.

Remodelers' & Renovators', 611 E. 44th St., No. 5, Dept. OHJ, Boise, ID 83704. (208) 377-5465. They sell *Schumacher's High Relief*, $20/double roll. A catalog, showing these and other restoration products, is $2, refundable upon purchase.

Restoration Hardware, 438 Second St., Dept. OHJ, Eureka, CA 95501. (707) 443-3152. *Crown* patterns: 11 Anaglypta, $27.95/roll; 2 Supaglypta, $35/roll. A 10% discount is given on 10 or more rolls. The Anaglypta/Supaglypta catalog includes some samples and is $1.50, refundable upon purchase. The owner of this restoration supply store, who used Anaglypta in his own house, recommends DAP putty as an excellent way to seal the corner seams.

Wolf Paints and Wallpapers, 771 Ninth Ave., Dept. OHJ, New York, NY 10019. (212) 245-7777. In addition to carrying everything you need to expertly finish your embossed wallcovering, they stock the complete selection of *Crown* embossed wallcoverings. Anaglypta is $60/double roll; Supaglypta is $68/double roll. Each roll is 22 in. wide and 7 yds. long; the price includes delivery.

## Deck The Tree

*Looking for old-fashioned Christmas ornaments? Here are two mail-order sources we've come across recently.*

Amazon Drygoods has everything you need to create a period Christmas. It would be impossible to list all the 19th-century reproduction decorations they offer, so we've chosen a brief sampling:

*Large brass ornaments*

🔔 Double clip candleholders, for real candles, with a Victorian embossed design on pewter colored metal. (Off-season they can be fastened to the tops of hoops for a candlelit game of croquet!) A set of 12, with white candles, is $7.75. Also, color-lithographed metal candleholders depicting Santas, trees, children, and toys. A set of 6, including candles, is $6.75. 🔔 Electric candles, 10 for $9.95. 🔔 Hand-tattered white cotton snowflakes, $1 each or 6 for $15. 🔔 A variety of stamped brass ornaments (cherubs, wreaths, and reindeer), about 4½—5½ inches, and ranging in price from $1.50 to $4. Also, 2-in. brass ornaments $2 each, or 2½-in. size at $3 each. 🔔 Glass icicles, 8 for $15. 🔔 And last, but not least...embossed and glazed cardboard cornucopias, to be filled with gifts or treats, $1.50 each or 6 for $8.

Books about Victorian Christmas and old-fashioned toys are also offered in this potpourri of 19th-century items. Send $1 for a 40-page catalog and special Christmas catalog. Amazon Drygoods, 2218 East 11th St., Dept. OHJ, Davenport, IA 52803. (319) 322-6800, days; (309) 786-3504, evenings.

An appropriate crowning touch for your Victorian Christmas tree could be a hand-painted china doll head, surrounded with satin and lace. This tree-topper is 8 in. high and sells for $37.50. A smaller, matching version costs $15.95. These ornaments can be seen in a free color catalog, along with other Christmas decorations and traditional American reproductions. Sturbridge Yankee Workshop, Blueberry Road, Dept. OHJ, Westbrook, ME 04092. (800) 343-1144.

# Opinion... Remuddling
## —Of The Month—

"I'VE SEEN quite a few bad remodeling jobs, but few as completely bad as this. The owner of the house on the left retained nothing except the third-storey window hoods."

-- *name withheld on request*
*Washington, D.C.*

YOU'D THINK phoney-colonializing was a thing of the past, and buildings victimized thus were a legacy of the time when "Victorian" was synonymous with "the ugly junk Aunt Gertrude left in the attic." But no, there are still great numbers of products that sell instant early-Americana, and lots of people who still buy it.

THE POOR HOUSE shown here got the full treatment. Gone are the fancy-cut roofing slates, the romantic 2-over-2 Italianate window sash and their characteristic hoods, the well proportioned front door and hood, and the graceful iron balcony.

IS THE OWNER really hoping to turn a mansard-roofed row house into a Colonial building? This example, unhappily, is practically a classic. You can tell by the broken-pediment doorway and the neo-Colonial lantern.

ALL THAT MONEY spent, and we're left with an expressionless building of no vintage wrapped in short-lived garbage. The perpetrator destroyed good old work, was not true to the style of the house, and sought to create an impossibly early look for a building that had a clear pedigree. What a shame.

-- *P. Poore*

# The Old-House Journal®

69A Seventh Avenue,
Brooklyn, New York 11217

NO PAID ADVERTISING

Postmaster: Address Correction Requested

![The Old-House Journal logo]

Vol. X No. 12                    $2.00

# The Old-House Journal

## Restoration and Maintenance Techniques For The Antique House

# ALL ABOUT ADOBE

*Far from being ancient history, adobe has been and still is a major building material in parts of the United States. With this article, we explain methods of making, repairing, and maintaining adobe. There's also an overview of the different American architectural styles peculiar to this historic material.*

ADOBE is the original old-house building material. The world's first towns--Ur, Jericho, Babylon, Nineveh--were built primarily of sun-dried mud brick, which is just another way of saying "adobe." The very word is redolent with history. It originated in the American Southwest, deriving from the Spanish adobar, "to plaster," and it reflects the influence of Spanish colonists from Mexico, who brought their own brick-making techniques with them when they settled in New Mexico at the end of the 16th century. The Spanish word, in turn, has been traced (via the Arabic at-tob) all the way back to the Egyptian hieroglyphic t'b, meaning "brick." So it's plain to see that, as far as building traditions go, adobe is the most vital and long-lasting of them all.

*continued on page 256*

# Our Post-Victorian Year

**W**E DIDN'T make any money this year, but we sure had fun! Our series on post-Victorian houses, especially, was recognized as an editorial triumph--by us editors and readers alike. The most recent sign came when Clem and I were invited to give a slide lecture on the subject at the National Trust meeting in Louisville.

THERE'S more coming: the Prairie style, Bungalows, the Colonial and English Revivals. We'll be breaking new ground in 1983 with a series on the interiors of early 20th-century houses.

OF COURSE, the OHJ is primarily about fixing up old houses. Crumbling plaster, rotting wood, sagging stairs, and unsympathetic contractors pose the same problems and solutions no matter if your house is vintage 1799 or 1927. Style articles give the 'why' behind the 'how to'; we think they're what make OHJ different from a mere technical journal.

A SUBSCRIBER tells me she gave the February article about the American Foursquare to a friend who owns one. This friend had previously shown no interest in her own house ... never mind in preservation.

NOW THIS new reader is researching her house's history and looking for information on authentic furnishings! Until she saw in print that hers had a special style called the American Foursquare, she'd thought it was "just an old house."

THAT'S THE SPIRIT! The story illustrates why we're so excited about houses like the ones on this page. More houses were built in the U.S. between 1890 and 1930 than in all our previous history. Yet they've been unfairly ignored in architectural stylebooks. Sadly, owners of these solid, comfortable houses often apologize for them with "my house isn't really a Victorian." Worse, with nowhere to turn for good information, owners have sometimes Victorianized these houses in an effort to legitimize them-- much as Victorian houses were once made to look Colonial.

A HOUSE with a style name and a history gets respect. And that is why The Old-House Journal is devoting pages to the subject of early 20th-century buildings. It's about time these fine and abundant old houses were appreciated and treated sensitively.

*Patricia Poore*

*Please note we're going the way of most 'monthly' magazines, and will be mailing ten issues per year from now on. The January/February 1983 issue coming up will reach you about one week later than the January issue normally would have arrived. We'll be adding extra pages to the two double issues — so you won't get fewer pages per year. The whole point is to reduce our annual number of big post office bills from 12 to 10. Our mailing costs continue to skyrocket.*

# The Old-House Journal®

*Editor*
**Clem Labine**

*Managing Editor*
**Patricia Poore**

*Assistant Editor*
**Cole Gagne**

*Assistant Editor/Products*
**Joni Monnich**

*Circulation Supervisor*
**Joan O'Reilly**

*Circulation Assistants*
**Peggy Scaglione**
**Barbara Bugg**
**Jeanne Baldwin**

*Office Assistant*
**Rafael Madera**

*Circulation Director*
**Paul T. McLoughlin**

*Technical Consultant*
**Alan D. Keiser**

*Architectural Consultant*
**Jonathan Poore**

*Contributing Editors*
**R. A. Labine, Sr.**
**John Mark Garrison**

Published by The Old-House Journal Corporation, 69A Seventh Avenue, Brooklyn, New York 11217. Telephone (212) 636-4514. Subscriptions $16 per year in U.S. Not available elsewhere. Published ten times per year. Contents are fully protected by copyright and must not be reproduced in any manner whatsoever without specific permission in writing from the Editor.

We are happy to accept editorial contributions to The Old-House Journal. Query letters that include an outline of the proposed article are preferred. All manuscripts will be reviewed, and returned if unacceptable. However, we cannot be responsible for non-receipt or loss — please keep copies of all materials sent.

Printed at Photo Comp Press, New York City

ISSN: 0094-0178
**NO PAID ADVERTISING**

# STRIPPING PAINT

## Sometimes it's not worth the trouble.
## And when it is, no single method does it all.

By The Old-House Journal Technical Staff

IN THE POPULAR MIND, there are two hallmarks of a "restored" house: (1) The plaster has been removed from all the brick walls; (2) The paint has been stripped from all the woodwork. We have pointed out the error of "the bare brick mistake" in past issues. In this article, we'd like to demolish the assumption that all old paint has to be stripped.

PAINT STRIPPING is one of the most messy, time-consuming, and aggravating of all old-house projects. It is also one of the most dangerous. So it's not something to automatically rush into. Rather, assume that all old paint should be left in place <u>unless</u> you can make a strong case for its removal.

### Why Strip?

THERE ARE THREE major reasons for removing paint from a wood surface: (1) To reveal the color and grain of beautiful wood; (2) To remove cracked or peeling layers prior to repainting; (3) To remove excessive layers that obscure architectural detail prior to repainting.

IN A TIME in which reverence for "the natural beauty of wood" has been elevated to cult status, many people assume that ALL woodwork should be stripped of paint and given a clear finish. This assumption can not only cause a lot of unnecessary work, but can also result in woodwork that looks downright messy.

MOST WOODWORK in the late 18th and early 19th centuries was painted originally. And so was the woodwork in many post-Victorian homes. There are a number of reasons for not "going natural" with wood that was originally painted. First, the wood is usually softwood (e.g., fir, pine) and doesn't have a particularly beautiful color or grain. Second, the original paint usually soaked into the pores of the wood to an extent that makes complete removal impossible. So you wind up with wood that has paint "freckles." Third, a natural finish is not historically appropriate in these instances. So you'll have done a lot of work to get woodwork that's not very good-looking and is not authentic.

THE ONLY TIME you should consider stripping woodwork that was originally painted is when the paint layers are so thick that they are hiding moulding details, or when the paint is cracked or peeling in a way that prevents a new paint layer from bonding properly. In both these cases, the stripping is merely a prelude to repainting.

### The Strip/No Strip Decision

THE FLOW CHART on the following page will help guide you to an appropriate when-to-strip decision. The chart is designed with interior woodwork in mind. The decision factors, and the methods to be used, are somewhat different for exterior stripping.

AS WITH most other refinishing projects, a small test patch is in order to determine what's under all the paint. You could use a bit of paint remover in an inconspicuous corner. Many prefer, however, to scrape away the layers with a razor blade or scalpel. Removing the layers mechanically often makes it easier to tell if the bottom layer is shellac or varnish.

THE PRESENCE OF SHELLAC or varnish under the paint indicates the wood probably had a clear finish in the beginning. Thus, the wood is a good candidate for stripping; someone in the past felt that the wood was good-looking enough to warrant a clear finish. The presence of varnish also makes it easier to get the paint off. The first layer of varnish sealed the wood so the paint isn't down in the pores.

### The Grained Finish

VARNISH was also used to seal a layer of graining--a painted finish meant to look like wood. If you encounter a grained finish at the bottom of your layers of paint, pause before stripping. It usually means that the underlying wood is a cheap softwood. If in doubt, test-strip a small patch.

IT IS TECHNICALLY POSSIBLE to remove paint layers from graining if there is an intervening layer of varnish. But it calls for more patience than most of us have. One satisfactory solution is to add a fresh graining layer on top of the existing paint. That way, you have a finish that closely approximates the original ...and it is much less work than complete stripping. Also, you haven't disturbed any of the original finishes for succeeding generations of paint detectives. Creating a grained finish is about the work-equivalent of applying two coats of paint plus a protective layer of varnish. For more details about graining, see OHJ's Dec. 1978 and Jan. 1979 issues.

# Architectural Woodwork:
# TO STRIP OR NOT TO STRIP?

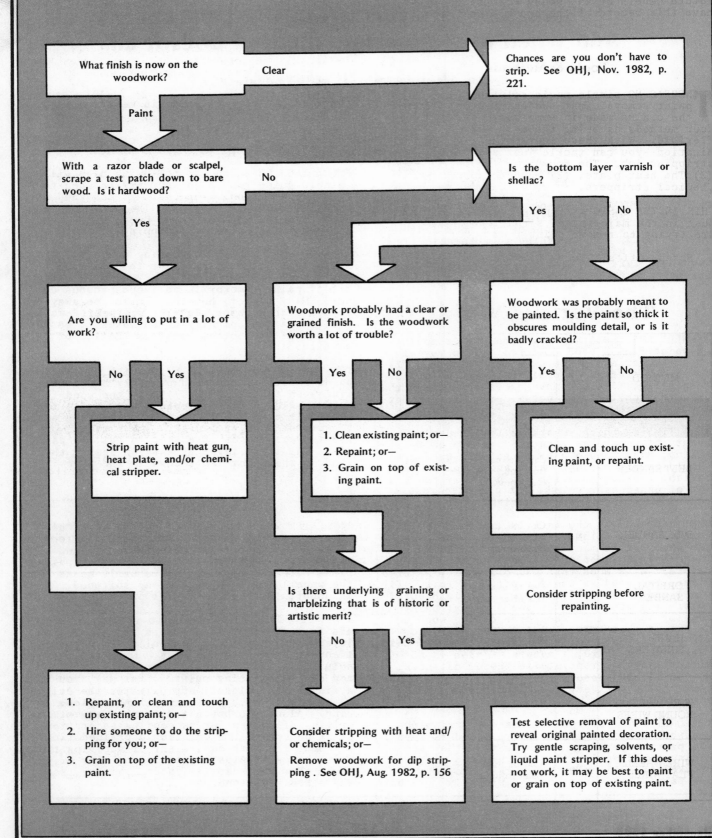

**What finish is now on the woodwork?**

— Clear → Chances are you don't have to strip. See OHJ, Nov. 1982, p. 221.

— Paint ↓

**With a razor blade or scalpel, scrape a test patch down to bare wood. Is it hardwood?**

— No → **Is the bottom layer varnish or shellac?**

— Yes ↓

### Is it hardwood? → Yes

**Are you willing to put in a lot of work?**

— No
— Yes → **Strip paint with heat gun, heat plate, and/or chemical stripper.**

No →
1. Repaint, or clean and touch up existing paint; or—
2. Hire someone to do the stripping for you; or—
3. Grain on top of the existing paint.

### Is the bottom layer varnish or shellac? → Yes

**Woodwork probably had a clear or grained finish. Is the woodwork worth a lot of trouble?**

— Yes
— No → 
1. Clean existing paint; or—
2. Repaint; or—
3. Grain on top of existing paint.

**Is there underlying graining or marbleizing that is of historic or artistic merit?**

— No → Consider stripping with heat and/or chemicals; or—

Remove woodwork for dip stripping . See OHJ, Aug. 1982, p. 156

— Yes

### Is the bottom layer varnish or shellac? → No

**Woodwork was probably meant to be painted. Is the paint so thick it obscures moulding detail, or is it badly cracked?**

— Yes
— No → Clean and touch up existing paint, or repaint.

**Consider stripping before repainting.**

Test selective removal of paint to reveal original painted decoration. Try gentle scraping, solvents, or liquid paint stripper. If this does not work, it may be best to paint or grain on top of existing paint.

ONE FURTHER CONSIDERATION when you opt for total stripping: Realize that you're removing a big part of your home's interior history. Those paint layers tell a story of changing tastes through the decades. So if at all possible, leave a square foot unstripped in some inconspicuous corner. It can become a great conversation piece...and as time passes, you and future owners of the house will be happy to have this record of the house's past history.

## Tools & Methods

THERE'S NO single magic solution that makes paint removal fast and easy--notwithstanding the claims made in some ads. We've selected four methods as being the most effective and flexible. With these four--singly or in combination--you can tackle just about any paint stripping job. The four are: (1) The heat gun; (2) The heat plate; (3) Hand scrapers; (4) Chemical strippers.

THIS IS THE BASIC stripping sequence that works best in the majority of situations where you are trying to remove paint from wood:

1. Scrape off all loose paint.

2. Use heat to remove everything that comes off easily without scorching the surface. (The heat gun and heat plate work best on thick layers of paint. If there are only one or two layers, go straight to step #3.)

3. Use a semi-paste chemical stripper to soften any paint remaining from step #2. Allow the stripper plenty of time to work; don't attempt to lift the sludge until all the paint is loose down to bare wood.

4. Rinse with alcohol or mineral spirits. (While many strippers are water-rinsable, water will raise the grain on some woods.)

5. If you plan to apply a clear finish, you may need to pick out paint residue from cracks and carvings with dental picks, pointed dowels, sharpened screwdrivers, etc.

6. Fill and sand as needed.

7. Apply paint or clear finish, as appropriate.

THERE ARE MANY ADDITIONAL tricks of the trade in using these paint removal procedures most effectively. We'll be dealing with these in upcoming articles--along with more details on health hazards and the stripping of masonry and metals.

# The Various Ways To Remove Paint From Wood

| METHOD | RECOMMENDED? | GOOD FOR | LIMITATIONS | SAFETY CONSIDERATIONS |
|---|---|---|---|---|
| ABRASIVE METHODS | | | | |
| BELT SANDER | No | Can be used to remove paint from large flat surfaces, such as clapboards. | Heavy and awkward to use; needs electrical cord; hard to control; can't reach into corners; creates a lot of dust. | Dust mask is essential to avoid inhaling or swallowing lead-containing dust. |
| DISC SANDER | No | Can be used to remove paint from large flat surfaces, such as clapboards. | Very light touch needed; otherwise you get circular marks in wood. Hard to control; can't reach into corners; needs electrical cord; creates a lot of dust. | Dust mask is essential to avoid inhaling or swallowing lead-containing dust. |
| ORBITAL SANDER | No | Can be used for smoothing a surface after paint removal. | Very slow; electrical cord needed; some dust created. | Dust mask is required. |
| HAND SCRAPERS | Yes | Can be used to remove paint that is not tightly bonded to wood; very versatile; requires no electrical cord. | Lots of elbow grease required. Must keep scrapers sharp; careful work essential to avoid gouging the wood. | Dust mask is recommended. |
| WIRE WHEELS: ROUND WIRES | No | Never use on wood. | Tends to gouge wood, especially where there are mouldings. | Eye protection required to guard against flying paint chips and broken wires. Dust mask is required. |
| WIRE WHEELS: FLAT WIRES | No | Can be used for removing loose paint from flat surfaces. | Electrical cord is needed; less control than hand scrapers. Very slow if paint isn't loose already. | Eye protection required to guard against flying paint chips and broken wires. Dust mask is required. |

*continued on next page*

| METHOD | RECOMMENDED? | GOOD FOR | LIMITATIONS | SAFETY CONSIDERATIONS |
|---|---|---|---|---|
| SANDBLASTING | No | Never use on wood. | Causes pitting and marring of wood. Hard to control; requires masking of adjacent surfaces. Creates a dust nuisance. Requires special equipment. | Requires appropriate respirator and eye protection. |

## HEAT METHODS

| METHOD | RECOMMENDED? | GOOD FOR | LIMITATIONS | SAFETY CONSIDERATIONS |
|---|---|---|---|---|
| HEAT PLATE | Yes | Can be used to remove paint from clapboards and other flat surfaces. | Not effective on mouldings and carved work. Needs electrical cord; not effective on varnish. Can scorch wood if left too long in one place. Don't use near glass. | Wear gloves to avoid burns. Eye protection and dust mask recommended. |
| HEAT GUN | Yes | Can be used to remove paint from mouldings and solid decorative elements, newels, balusters, capitals, doors, wainscotting, door and window frames, etc. | Too slow for stripping exterior clapboards. Needs electrical cord; don't use near glass; can scorch wood if left too long in one spot. | Tool could ignite dust inside hollow partitions such as cornices. Dust mask for micro-particulate lead recommended. |
| HEAT LAMP | No | Can be used to strip some flat work. | Difficult to control; needs electric cord; can scorch wood if left too long in one spot. | Eye hazard—special dark glasses required. Can ignite paint. Dust mask recommended. |
| INFRARED TORCH | No | Stripping vertical surfaces. | Bulky to handle. | Possible fire hazard when held in non-vertical position. Dust mask recommended. |
| PROPANE TORCH or BLOWTORCH | No | Don't use! | Will scorch wood; don't use near glass. | Great lead poisoning hazard from micro-particulate lead. Vapor-type mask essential. Highest risk of fire. |

## CHEMICAL METHODS

| METHOD | RECOMMENDED? | GOOD FOR | LIMITATIONS | SAFETY CONSIDERATIONS |
|---|---|---|---|---|
| ORGANIC SOLVENTS (e.g. Methylene Chloride strippers) | Yes | Stripping fine furniture; large-scale production stripping; window muntins; cleanup after heat tools. | Expensive; not good for start-and-stop projects. Very messy; difficult cleanup and disposal. | Need plenty of ventilation. Eye and skin protection required. |
| LYE | No | Removes large amount of paint at low cost. | Raises grain; may also change color of the wood. Prolonged soaking may damage wood. | Eye and skin protection required. |
| CANNED POWDER STRIPPERS | OK | Can be especially useful in removing old casein and milk paints. | Messy; may raise the grain. | Eye and skin protection required. |
| PEEL-AWAY BLANKET | No | Can be used to strip paint from softwood woodwork. | Messy; slow-acting; raises the grain; blanket must be washed to be re-used. Wood must be neutralized with vinegar. | Eye and skin protection required. |

**GENERAL SAFETY NOTES:**

1. Assume that any house built before 1950 has one or more layers of lead-containing paint. The scrapings, dust, and sludge from a paint-removal operation should be treated as a poisonous material. Local environmental regulations may dictate how to safely dispose of lead-containing paint scrapings.

2. When using any heat tool, such as an electric heat plate or electric heat gun, be sure to keep a fire extinguisher handy.

# Ask OHJ

## The Raccoon Invasion

**W**E HAVE BEEN INVADED BY RACCOONS! Last winter, they persisted in tearing holes in our cedar-shingle roof; in the spring, we caught a female and three kits in their nest in our attic. After that, there was no trouble through the entire summer. But one night this fall we heard a racket upstairs, and found out to our dismay that the raccoons were back for the winter. We've spoken to exterminators and conservationists, but nobody knows a way to keep these pests out of our attic. We've set Hav-a-Hart traps, leg traps, scents, but nothing seems to work. We don't mind the raccoons--what we mind are the holes in our roof. Can anyone help us?

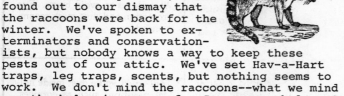

--Heather Dina  Wading River, NY

**U**NFORTUNATELY--as you've found out--it's very difficult to keep raccoons out of the house. They're strong, smart, and very determined. The best thing to do is get a roofer to go over your shingles--they have to be somewhat loose for the raccoons to pry them up. A roofer could make sure they're down firmly. Another possibility is to put some kind of heavy wire mesh over the attic ceiling. Then, even if the raccoons pry up the shingles, they won't be able to get into the attic.

YOU SHOULD ALSO see what you can do to keep them from getting onto your roof in the first place. Chop away any tree branches that overhang your roof. If the raccoons are climbing up a drainpipe or some utility wires, perhaps you can figure out a way to screen them so that they are tough to climb. If the raccoons really can't get at your roof, perhaps they'll spread the word that your raccoon motel is permanently closed.

## Varnish Troubles?

**I** RECENTLY BOUGHT YOUR HEAT GUN and read the instructions carefully. But when I use it, all the layers of paint come off except for the last. What am I doing wrong?

--D. Stachowiak  Rock Falls, IL

**A** LAYER OF VARNISH could be covering this last, immovable coat--and heat methods aren't very effective on varnish. You'll have to use a chemical paint stripper. But it could be that the last layer of paint is an old formulation such as milk paint or whitewash. Try ammonia; then consider mechanical stripping techniques such as sanding or scraping.

## Canvas Vs. Humidity

**M**Y EIGHT-ROOM VICTORIAN HOUSE was built in 1907. Four of the eight rooms have canvas on the ceilings. We heat with a combination oil/coal hot-air system with a built-in humidifier. During the winter, the dryness caused shrinking and cracking in our furniture. I would like to install another humidifier upstairs, but I am worried about the effect it might have on the canvas ceilings.

--J.R. Phelps  Newington, CT

**H**UMIDITY FROM THE AIR should not affect your ceilings, but you are wise to be concerned about levels of humidity. Excessive humidity can cause condensation problems and damage your home. A relative humidity level between 20 and 30% should be a happy compromise that will keep you, your house, and your furniture all comfortable.

## Stretching Wallpaper

**R**ECENTLY, we took wallpaper off our dining room wall and repapered. A fireplace and chimney go across one corner of the room. Now, in the corner above the mantel, the wallpaper is stretching and may eventually tear. We slightly overlapped the paper in these corners. What we want to know is: (1) The house was built in 1918--is it still settling? (2) How do we 'undo' the wallpaper at the corners and repaste the edges?

--O. Stauffer  Portsmouth, VA

**T**HOSE CORNERS where the wallpaper is stretched are between two different materials: the masonry chimney and the wood-framed plaster walls. You're probably seeing cyclical differential movement. The masonry is fairly stable, but the walls shrink and swell with changes in temperature and humidity. Unless you continue to see major shifting of the chimney, don't worry about it.

THE WALLPAPER can be gently pried up and re-glued (if it's vinyl or "strippable"), or steamed away from the corner (if it's unstrippable paper). The best solution, however, is to remove the paper at the troublesome corners and put up two new panels that butt right in the corner--don't overlap at all.

# Recipe For Old~Fashioned Gingerbread

How to make new gingerbread . . . the kind of sawn-wood ornament that might have been stripped off your old house in the past. We'll have to leave it up to each individual to find a pattern appropriate in period and design. What's shown here is not pattern layout, but rather the *best* procedure for fabricating and installing the pieces. Even cooks who are new to the woodshop can handle this recipe.

## ingredients

- pattern or piece to copy
- oaktag or cardboard
- Masonite or ¼" plywood
- dimensional lumber
- carpenter's wood glue or better
- polyurethane or butyl caulk
- exterior wood primer (same brand as finish paint)
- liquid wood preservative
- galvanized nails or screws
- exterior trim paint

- What about equipment? Whether this is an easy job or a hard one depends on the quality and versatility of your tool collection. If you intend to create multiple pieces, you may want to invest in a few good tools; a minimal number are required for this project. Here's a list: pencil; saber/jigsaw or bandsaw; clamps; various rasps, planes, or a spokeshave; sandpaper and sanding block; electric or hand drill; dipping tray; caulk gun; paintbrush.

## the recipe

### Step 1: MAKE THE TEMPLATE

- Draw the pattern actual size and cut it out of cardboard, oaktag, or other heavy paper.
- Trace this pattern onto Masonite or ¼-inch plywood. Plywood is better if you're making multiples and accuracy of the final pieces is important — it's more dimensionally stable than Masonite.
- This becomes your master template. *Accuracy is important.* Cut with a saber/jigsaw, or a bandsaw as shown here. File or plane the edges smooth.

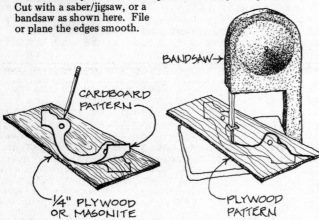

CARDBOARD PATTERN

BANDSAW

¼" PLYWOOD OR MASONITE

PLYWOOD PATTERN

**Restoration Design File #11**

### Step 2: CHOOSE THE LUMBER

- Poplar or clear pine are suitable. You must use *clear* pine because knots will weaken thin sections of sawn ornament.
- Oak is stronger and more durable than softwood. This is important if the designs have inherently weak, thin sections. However, oak is a bit more difficult to work than most other common woods.
- Redwood is most insect- and rot-proof. But it's soft, so it won't hold fasteners as well as oak. Keep this in mind during installation of redwood pieces.

### Step 3: GLUE UP STOCK

- If necessary, glue up stock to the required thickness.
- Grain of glued pieces should run in approximately the same direction.
- Use carpenter's wood glue or better, such as a waterproof glue for exterior use. Clamp tightly and allow to set.

### Step 4: TRANSFER THE PATTERN

- Trace the pattern carefully onto the wood. For maximum strength in the finished piece, be sure that the pattern follows the long grain as much as possible. The drawing illustrates the inherent weakness of thin sections that cross the grain.

*pattern with the long grain*

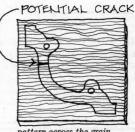

POTENTIAL CRACK

- Also, minimize waste by thinking ahead. Fit several patterns or pieces together on the wood like a jigsaw puzzle.

*pattern across the grain*

### Step 5: CUT IT OUT

- Cut out the pattern with a saber/jigsaw or a bandsaw.
- Clean up the edges with cutting and smoothing tools such as rasps or planes.

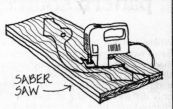

SABER SAW

*By Patricia Poore
Illustrations by Jonathan Poore*

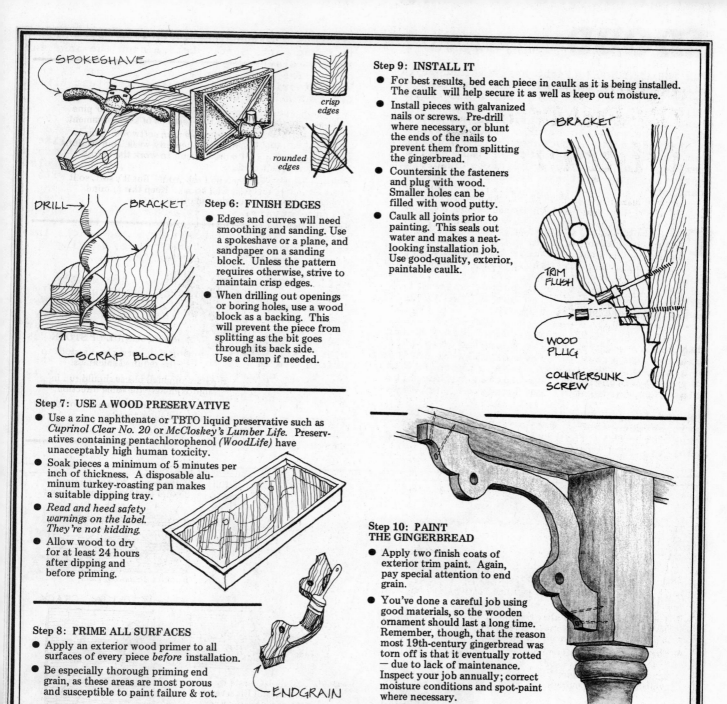

**Step 6: FINISH EDGES**

- Edges and curves will need smoothing and sanding. Use a spokeshave or a plane, and sandpaper on a sanding block. Unless the pattern requires otherwise, strive to maintain crisp edges.

- When drilling out openings or boring holes, use a wood block as a backing. This will prevent the piece from splitting as the bit goes through its back side. Use a clamp if needed.

SPOKESHAVE

crisp edges

rounded edges

DRILL → ← BRACKET

SCRAP BLOCK

**Step 9: INSTALL IT**

- For best results, bed each piece in caulk as it is being installed. The caulk will help secure it as well as keep out moisture.

- Install pieces with galvanized nails or screws. Pre-drill where necessary, or blunt the ends of the nails to prevent them from splitting the gingerbread.

- Countersink the fasteners and plug with wood. Smaller holes can be filled with wood putty.

- Caulk all joints prior to painting. This seals out water and makes a neat-looking installation job. Use good-quality, exterior, paintable caulk.

BRACKET

TRIM FLUSH

WOOD PLUG

COUNTERSUNK SCREW

**Step 7: USE A WOOD PRESERVATIVE**

- Use a zinc naphthenate or TBTO liquid preservative such as *Cuprinol Clear No. 20* or *McCloskey's Lumber Life*. Preservatives containing pentachlorophenol *(WoodLife)* have unacceptably high human toxicity.

- Soak pieces a minimum of 5 minutes per inch of thickness. A disposable aluminum turkey-roasting pan makes a suitable dipping tray.

- *Read and heed safety warnings on the label. They're not kidding.*

- Allow wood to dry for at least 24 hours after dipping and before priming.

**Step 8: PRIME ALL SURFACES**

- Apply an exterior wood primer to all surfaces of every piece *before* installation.

- Be especially thorough priming end grain, as these areas are most porous and susceptible to paint failure & rot.

ENDGRAIN

**Step 10: PAINT THE GINGERBREAD**

- Apply two finish coats of exterior trim paint. Again, pay special attention to end grain.

- You've done a careful job using good materials, so the wooden ornament should last a long time. Remember, though, that the reason most 19th-century gingerbread was torn off is that it eventually rotted — due to lack of maintenance. Inspect your job annually; correct moisture conditions and spot-paint where necessary.

# pattern sources

Where do ideas for patterns come from? Sawn-wood ornament was produced in as many shapes as there are imaginations . . . although each neighborhood, city, and region had its most popular patterns. Designs not only differed with the style of the house, but changed over time, too. The most popular patterns in 1870 are in some places quite unlike those common in 1900.

Your first sources for pattern designs should be local. Do any period photos of your house still exist? Are there similar houses in town with their gingerbread intact? If historical accuracy is paramount, a little investigation through the paint layers of your own building might reveal ghosts of the original ornament.

Next come pattern books of the period. Some are available in reprint editions; a few give details of the pieces besides showing them in place on the facade.

We've recently come across a source for *knee* or bracket patterns. This is a package of nine stencils from a turn-of-the-century wood-working mill in New England. They represent some of the most common designs from New England and elsewhere, and are suitable for porches, eaves, and gables. The nine paper stencils range in size from 6 in. x 10 in. to 18 in. x 30 in. All nine cost $6.20 postpaid from **Marsh Stream Enterprises, RFD 2, Box 490, Dept. OHJ, Brooks, Maine 04921.**

# ADOBE

*continued from page 247*

OVER THE CENTURIES, adobe has remained an excellent building material. The basic ingredient is dirt, which is both common and cheap ("dirt cheap," so to speak). It requires no great skill to turn the dirt into mud and then to form the mud into bricks. And, if properly maintained, adobe structures last a long time. When the Spanish came to New Mexico, Native Americans had been living in adobe pueblos for centuries; many of these structures are still standing.

THE TECHNIQUES for making sun-dried bricks have remained much the same over the millennia. In the American Southwest, bricks have been produced in many sizes, ranging from about 10 x 14 x 4 inches to 12 x 18 x 5 inches and weighing some 50 to 60 pounds apiece. (Extra-large bricks, up to one or two yards in length, are called "adobines.")

THE BRICKS ARE MADE from sand and clay, mixed with water. Gravel may be added to provide texture, and straw or grass usually is included as a binder. The binder doesn't increase the long-term strength of the bricks; rather, it helps them shrink more uniformly as they dry.

THE KEY TO THE DURABILITY of the bricks is the ratio between sand and clay. Too much sand makes for bricks that "melt" under a moderate rain; too much clay causes shrinking and cracks. A common formula is five parts clay to seven parts sand. Determining the inherent sand-to-clay ratio of local soil may be difficult. The best formula for a good mix is to have experience--and to make a few test bricks before the real work begins.

AFTER THE SOIL IS SELECTED and sifted to remove lumps and rocks, it is mixed with sand and water until it has a plastic, fudge-like consistency. The mud is shoveled into bottomless wooden molds, and then tamped and leveled. Then the mold is turned over and lifted with a gentle, back-and-forth, side-to-side motion. The bricks are emptied out onto a dry, level surface covered with straw or grass (so the new, damp bricks won't stick where they're placed). The adobe maker lays the bricks in rows, usually about 30 feet long, leaving enough room to walk between them.

AFTER SEVERAL DAYS, the bricks are gently raised on edge so they can cure more quickly and be carefully cleaned. The bricks may be left to dry right where they are or they may be "racked" in specially formed piles that are covered on top. In either case, curing takes about four weeks. The way to tell if the bricks are dry is to break one open. If the center is darker than the edges, the brick is not yet dry. A uniform color means that it is ready for building.

BECAUSE THE BRICKS have not been kiln hardened, they are inherently unstable--perhaps only slightly stronger than the soil of which they

These two men are mixing the mud from which adobe bricks will be made.

are composed. According to their water content, the bricks will continue to shrink or swell, as will walls and other structures made from them. These fluctuations of course affect their strength: The wetter the bricks, the weaker they are. Given too much moisture, the adobe will be soft as putty. When fully saturated, adobe walls will flow like liquid.

DEPENDING ON RAINFALL, exposed adobe in the American Southwest weathers about one inch every ten years. In ancient Mesopotamia, the average house stood for about 75 years before it collapsed and another was built on top of it. Here, the Acoma Indians, with their 600-year-old pueblo, have done a lot better. The secret is maintenance.

A CYCLICAL MAINTENANCE PROGRAM should be established for every adobe building. Deterioration can be deterred if buildings are monitored continually for subtle changes and if repairs are regularly made. Properly maintained, an adobe structure can remain relatively stable despite the ravages of wind, rain, and time.

ADOBE BUILDINGS are subject to many forms of natural deterioration. High winds--sandstorms, especially--will erode them. Seeds can germinate in roofs and walls, while the roots of nearby shrubs and trees can grow into the adobe, conducting excess moisture into it and otherwise physically weakening the structure. Small animals can burrow into the adobe; termites can tunnel through it, just as they would go through soil, to reach lintels, floors, shutters, and other delectable wooden portions of the building.

WATER IS the principal enemy of adobe. Rainwater can create furrows, cracks, and fissures in roofs and walls. The splash of raindrops near the base of a wall can gradually gouge it out--a condition called "coving." (Coving can also be caused by the spalling, or splintering, of adobe during freeze-thaw cycles.) Groundwater--from a spring, say, or from too much plant watering--can rise through capillary action in a wall and cause it to erode, bulge, and cove. Groundwater can also bring with it dissolved salts or minerals from the soil. When deposited in sufficient concentrations on or near the surface, these can cause the adobe to crack and crumble as it dries.

THE SOLUTIONS to structural problems are as diverse as the problems themselves. To reduce wind damage, the planting of trees may be indicated. On the other hand, if shrubs and trees are growing too close to the building, they may have to be removed--not always an easy job when the roots have become an integral part of the structure. For excess moisture, common solutions include regrading so that the ground

slopes away from the building, and digging drainage trenches (about 2 to 2½ feet wide and several feet deep) around the sides of the structure. (See "Wet Basements" in the August 1981 OHJ for more details.)

ONCE THE UNDERLYING SOURCE of a problem has been found and fixed, repairs can be made with some confidence. Leaning or bulging walls can be realigned or buttressed, rotted door or window lintels can be replaced, and areas where walls have begun to cove or deteriorate can be patched with new bricks, adobe mud, and whitewash.

CRACKS IN ADOBE WALLS are repaired in much the same way as cracks in masonry. Clean out the crack to a depth of double or triple the width of the new mortar joint. This will give you a good mechanical bond, or key, between the mortar and the brick. Of course, adobe mud mortar should be used. It consists of approximately equal parts of clay and sand--almost the same recipe used in making the bricks themselves. Lightly spray water on the area around the crack to improve the bond; mortar can then be applied with a large grout gun.

MODERATELY ERODED AREAS usually can be filled in with adobe mud plaster (same formula as for the mortar). Brush and clean the surface to remove loose particles of adobe. Then wet the area to ensure a good bond. The plaster tends to crack if put on in layers more than 3/8 of an inch thick, so apply it in coats until the eroded area has been brought up to grade. Scratch the intermediate coats and allow each coat time to dry before applying the next one.

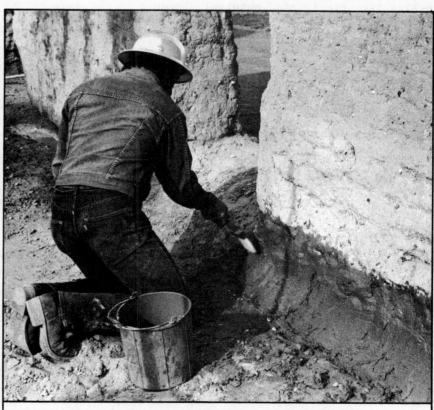

Adobe plaster is being applied to the base of this eroded wall.

New Mexico's Fort Selden was built in 1865 and permanently abandoned by the Army in 1891. In 1963 it was declared a State Park, and restoration work began in the early 1970s. This photograph shows the west side of the post Hospital after stabilization was completed. A berm was placed against the entire west exterior of the Hospital, to the same level as the existing floors. It was then saturated with water and compacted. This fill covered the exposed stone foundation and the eroded areas near the base of the wall. Unfortunately, as the text below details, other aspects of the restoration proved to be less successful: For a few years, the Hospital walls were capped with stabilized bricks that wound up doing more harm than good for Fort Selden.

IF AN ENTIRE BRICK has partially disintegrated, a patch can be made by scraping out the deteriorated material and filling in the hole with adobe mud. In the past, the mud for the patch was made by mixing the scrapings with water. Now, doubts have grown about the wisdom of reusing the deteriorated material, because it often contains high concentrations of salts.

WHERE SEVERE DETERIORATION extends over a larger area, it probably will be necessary to put in new bricks. You can make these yourself, or buy ready-made bricks and half-bricks. Just be sure you don't use bricks that have been "stabilized." Some commercial makers of adobe bricks add cement, asphalt, silicones, and bituminous or other materials to their mix to make the bricks more durable and water resistant than traditional sun-dried bricks.

STABILIZED BRICKS can change both the appearance and the fabric of a traditional adobe structure. The restorers of New Mexico's Fort Selden (see the photo above) tried to preserve the hundred-year-old adobe walls by capping them with stabilized bricks. These bricks formed a moisture barrier that caused the old adobe underneath them to deteriorate at an even faster rate. On the walls that hadn't been tampered with, weathering had produced a rounded top section that prevented the formation of rivulets on wall surfaces. In effect, the original walls had stabilized themselves. (The stabilized bricks have since been removed.)

SALVAGE IS A GOOD ALTERNATIVE if you have to replace bricks. If you're lucky enough to hear of someone razing an adobe house in the neighborhood, go buy some old bricks. Weathered bricks with rounded corners will probably blend in with the undamaged part of your wall better than any bricks you can make yourself. And they're likely to be just as strong, too.

WHEN DOING LARGER REPAIRS, it may be necessary to cut into undeteriorated portions of a wall to make a flush fit for the replacement bricks. Lay these in line with the existing bricks and spray the area with water. (Always be careful not to soak the area--wet bricks expand!) Be sure to use traditional mud mortar.

REMUDDLING IS A CURSE that has befallen even adobe. Often the most complex problems posed by an adobe structure are the "renovations" of its former owners. In the early 20th century, cement stucco became a popular coating. The material doesn't bond to adobe bricks, so it was applied to a wire mesh that was nailed to the adobe surface. This Formstone-progenitor is even more problematic than its notorious descendants.

ADOBE BRICKS SHRINK AND SWELL according to their water content. Even the longest nails can rust, and so the result is some not very firm stucco surfaces. And then there are the traditional headaches created by such additions: The stucco surface can trap moisture and prevent the wall from drying. It can also conceal a serious problem, such as rising damp, until it reaches crisis proportions.

ANOTHER COMMON MISTAKE of early renovators was their assumption that the best mortar is the hardest mortar. Thus, when making repairs, they used lime mortar or portland cement mortar instead of the original adobe mud mortar. Unfortunately, these harder mortars don't contract and expand at the same rate as the adobe bricks. Result: The harder mortar gradually cracks and crumbles the (comparatively) weaker bricks. Eventually, nothing is left but a honeycomb of mortar joints! In this way, small repair jobs can blossom into major operations.

THE MORAL OF ALL THESE HORROR STORIES is that materials generally should be replaced with like materials and with original construction techniques. Adobe bricks should not be re-pointed with portland cement. Wooden lintels should not be replaced with steel ones, as was commonly done until recently. Steel is too rigid and will force walls to twist as they expand. Plastic and latex sealers should not be used in lieu of whitewash; they keep the surface from expanding along with the rest of the brick, with the result that portions of the wall could simply break off. (Whitewash has been used on adobe buildings since practically the beginning of time, so get used to the idea of having it and renewing it annually.)

THIS RULE about using compatible materials extends to non-traditional ones. Some adobe houses were originally built with portland cement mortar, and so it is inadvisable to replace this material with adobe mud mortar. Most likely, the adobe bricks would be ruined in getting the cement out. By the same token, complete removal of a stucco coating can prove more destructive to the underlying brick than would natural deterioration. You should try to get expert advice for your particular situation. But the general rule about patching like with like still holds--and it's a good one to follow no matter what material your house is made of.

# ADOBE HOUSE STYLES

**A**DOBE HOUSES come in two basic styles: the original Pueblo or Santa Fe Style, and the later Territorial Style. The first is a single-storey, boxlike building with few openings for doors and windows. It has rounded corners within and without, and a flat, slightly sloping roof with a low parapet around it. Essentially a Spanish form, it was strongly influenced by the Native American pueblo.

SANTA FE STYLE ADOBES are as simple inside as out. The fireplace--a gently rounded, cone-shaped mass bulging from a corner of the main room--has always been a focal point of adobe interiors. Some old houses still have a "sheepherders" fireplace: an adobe platform, large enough to sleep on, over the hearth. On the ceilings, the _vigas_, or crossbeams, are left exposed, as is the roof decking above them. Floors, at least originally, were of hard-packed adobe, often coated with a mixture of animal blood and ashes to increase hardness and water resistance.

THE WALLS, two or more feet thick, were plastered with adobe mud on the interior as well as the exterior, and then sealed with a surface coating of whitewash. The interior walls might also be painted a light color, perhaps with a darker, harmonizing color at the bases, around doors and windows, and at the intersections of ceilings and walls. (See "The Spanish Colonial Revival Style" in the Oct. 1982 OHJ for more information about the Pueblo Style.)

THE TERRITORIAL STYLE evolved in the 19th century, as the Territory itself became more settled. Newcomers tried to imitate in adobe the housing fashions of the "civilized" world from which they had come. The result was a style similar to the American Army posts, which were more like military villages than actual forts that could be defended.

Top: The rounded corners, flat roof, and protruding _vigas_ are all standard characteristics of the Pueblo Style. Bottom: This Territorial Style house is distinguished by the multipane windows and the brick copings added to the roof.

HALLMARKS of the Territorial Style include the brick copings that were added to roofs and the large windows set on the outside walls with early American (i.e., Greek Revival) exterior shutters and trim. Roof decks used tongue-and-groove lumber. Porches were supported with slender wooden pilasters instead of fat, round columns. Walls were made thinner and "modernized" inside and out with a coating of lime

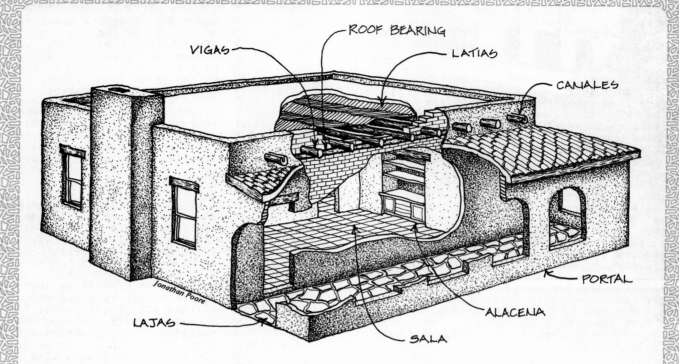

Labels on illustration: ROOF BEARING, VIGAS, LATIAS, CANALES, PORTAL, ALACENA, SALA, LAJAS

*Jonathan Poore*

# ADOBE TALK

**ALACENAS** — Cupboards and shelves built into the thick adobe house walls.

**CANALES (or GARGOLAS)** — Drains for carrying rainwater away from the walls and foundations. They're made by hollowing out the ends of the crossbeams, or VIGAS, that support the roof.

**CEDROS** — Handsplit cedar planks, laid lengthwise or in a herringbone pattern on top of the VIGAS; an alternative to LATIAS. The planks, in turn, support layers of twigs, earth (6 to 24 inches of it), and adobe mud that form the roof proper. Cypress planks are called *savinos*. Cactus, or *saguaro*, ribs also have been used in the Tucson area.

**LAJAS** — Flagstones that are used for flooring in some adobe buildings. Alternatives include adobe brick, fired brick, tile, and wooden floors.

**LATIAS (also LATILLAS)** — Peeled poles, often juniper or willow, about two inches in diameter, which are laid on top of the VIGAS and used instead of planking (see CEDROS). The LATIAS might be placed lengthwise across the VIGAS or arranged in a pleasing herringbone pattern. Split pine logs, called *rajas*, also serve the same function.

**PORTAL** — The porch, which often runs around all four sides of an adobe building, shielding the walls from rain.

**ROOF BEARINGS** — Supports for the VIGAS which are used to take the weight of the roof. If the VIGAS were set directly onto the adobe bricks, the bricks would eventually crumble from the vibrations of the roof caused by wind. Bricks, cement blocks, projecting wooden corbels, and long wooden beams have been built into adobe walls to support the VIGAS.

**SALA** — The main drawing room of an adobe house. Traditionally, rooms tended to be 13 to 15 feet wide, depending on the length of the VIGAS available. To make a large room, therefore, one had to make a long room. A SALA for formal occasions might be as much as 40 feet in length.

**VIGAS** — The crossbeams for supporting the roof. The VIGAS are set two to three feet apart and rest on the ROOF BEARINGS. They often protrude through the facades of the side walls — a construction detail that has come to typify adobe architecture in the minds of many. Traditionally, the VIGAS were of aspen, mesquite, cedar, or whatever else was available in a wood-short countryside. Whether they were shaped and squared or left as roughly dressed logs, VIGAS were cut with diminishing size; this gave the roof enough pitch to stimulate drainage. The ends of some VIGAS were hollowed out to make drains, or CANALES.

**ZAGUAN** — The large door or entryway to an inner courtyard. To assure strong walls and to keep out light and heat, adobe builders were very careful about the spacing of the doors and windows. A rule of thumb was that all openings had to be placed further from the corner of a building than the width of the opening itself. A large ZAGUAN allowed wagons, livestock, etc., to be driven inside for protection against bad weather or enemy attack.

plaster (which is harder than the original mud plaster but doesn't bond as well to the adobe). Everything about the Territorial Style seems more "finished": Houses often boast wooden mantelpieces, wide pegged floors, and doors that have been dressed up with moulding, or even carved.

MORE MODIFICATIONS appeared as time went on. The coming of the railroads made new roofing materials available: wooden shingles, terra-cotta tiles (especially popular in southern California), and sheet metal (widely used in New Mexico). Old, flat roofs were "upgraded" into gable roofs, hip roofs, gambrels, and even mansards (producing what technically could be called "French Academic Pueblos").

BUILDERS also began to use bricks that were fired or stabilized with the addition of asphalt, cement, or some other material. They coated walls with cement stucco. Some early Santa Fe Style houses also had large, Classical windows punched through their thick walls, giving rise to what has been called, with tongue in cheek, Rio Grande Greek.

IN THE EARLY 20th century, about the time that Gustav Stickley was popularizing the rustic "Craftsman" house, people began rediscovering the virtues of the original Santa Fe Style. Today, both forms are being built. And not only as houses--if you are ever in Taos and want some fast food (and have a strong stomach for architecture as well), you can run down to the local Kentucky Fried Chicken, which is housed in Pueblo Style splendor.

The primary material for this article was written by Web Wilson, of Frederick, Maryland. Thomas J. Caperton, who worked on the stabilization of Fort Selden, contributed the photos as well as his expertise. The article was edited by Hugh Rawson, a freelance writer and editor who is a long-time fan of OHJ.

Readers interested in learning more on adobe should consult Preservation Brief No. 5, "Preservation of Historic Adobe Buildings," (1978). It's available free of charge from the Technical Preservation Services Branch, U.S. Department of the Interior, National Park Service, 440 G St. NW, Washington, DC 20240.

Top: Yes, that's an adobe house, one built in New Mexico in the early 1880s. The two adobe storeys were topped with an elegant mansard roof, and there's no feeling of incongruity in the result. Center: This 1890 adobe structure features Classical window and porch treatment and a hipped, standing-seam tin roof. Bottom: Dating back to the early 1800s, this Pueblo Style house has the requisite flat roof and protruding *vigas*. It's the windows and door that pull it into that special sub-genre affectionately dubbed Rio Grande Greek.

# Letters

## Linseed Oil Paint

IN MY ORIGINAL MANUSCRIPT of "Exterior Wood Columns" (October 1982 OHJ), I recommended a linseed oil paint as a top coat for painting a column. When the article was edited for publication, the text was changed to a recommendation for exterior latex paint. I realize this change was made because linseed oil paint is almost impossible to find. I'm now happy to report that, after some investigation, I've found a source:

> Mr. Timothy Bragdon
> c/o Paints 'N' Papers
> Dept. OHJ
> 107 Brook Street
> Sanford, ME 04073
> (207) 324-9705

THE FOLLOWING PRODUCTS are available from them by phone or mail order, at a cost of $21.50 per gallon, plus shipping:
1. #100 Linseed Oil House Paint Primer--It has a small amount of alkyd resin, but it's suitable for columns.
2. #200 Pure Linseed Oil House Paint--This has no alkyd resins. It comes in white and colors, and there are paint chips available.

ALSO, Dutch Boy Paint's #100 Linseed Oil Paint is a new offering by that company. I haven't had any personal experience with it, but it might be a good second choice.

MY RECOMMENDATION of linseed oil paint is based on both my own observations and a study done by the Forest Products Laboratory in Madison. Most columns are hollow, and an alkyd resin primer and top coat can make the column surface impermeable, causing paint peeling and column damage. A latex top coat-- although normally recommended for exterior painting--is in my opinion so water permeable that it can actually permit the entrance of moisture into the column. Therefore, I argue that a linseed oil paint is most effective for good adhesion and as a compromise regarding permeability.

--John Leeke
Sanford, Maine

## Window Repairs

THE APRIL 1982 ISSUE devoted to windows was one of the most informative you have put out. We've been able to repair many of the windows in our 85-year-old house by using the techniques you showed. I thought you'd be interested in some things that seem to work for us:

1) WHEN REPLACING the sill or sub-sill, we use treated lumber to prevent rot.

2) "QUAKER" BRAND window channels do more than any one thing to solve the problem of air infiltration around the sash. (The paint must be stripped from the sash to make a good airtight seal.) These strips allow the removal of the window weights and the insulation of the weight boxes.

3) AFTER STRIPPING THE PAINT from the exterior portions of the window, we apply several coats of the 50-50 mix of boiled linseed oil and paint thinner, followed by several coats of wood preservative. After letting it dry for at least two weeks, we apply one or two coats of "Val-Oil" (made by Valspar). This puts a tough water-shedding surface under the paint. After all this, the exterior is painted in a normal manner.

USING THESE TECHNIQUES, we have had up to five years exposure on some of the repaired windows with no signs of deterioration. Keep up the good work!

--Tod I. Myers
Baltimore, Maryland

## Storm Window Latches

A BELATED AGREEMENT with your evaluation on the spring latch on storm windows ("Storm Windows," April 1982 OHJ). After buying "top of the line," dark bronze finish, triple-track storm windows to mount inside, I too found the spring latch seldom works. Nearly lost all the fingers on both hands when the gigantic upper glass insert came crashing down! The windows are over seven feet tall, so you can imagine my horror when seeing them come crashing down, waiting for glass shards to finish my restoration career.

I NOW RESORT to Coke cans and (occasionally) bricks to hold up the storm sash. I especially recommend broom handles. They fit nicely into the track areas and are almost invisible, especially when you paint them a "dark bronze finish." Lord save me from modern conveniences and high-powered salesmen!

--Judith Johnson
St. Louis, Missouri

## More On Flue Liners

YOUR INFORMATIVE ARTICLE, "Relining Your Chimney Flue" (September 1982 OHJ), discussed the pros and cons of stainless steel vs. enamel-coated liners. One of your conclusions was not to use a stainless steel liner for a coal-burning stove. I agree that an enamel-coated liner may be used for a coal-burning stove, but I've learned that a chimney fire will burn at a temperature greater than the heat used to apply enamel to steel. Such a fire would thus melt an enamel-coated liner. Therefore, I would conclude that an enamel-coated liner should not be used for a wood-burning stove.

--Sandra Eskin
Iowa City, Iowa

# Helpful Publications

*Four milestones in publishing have come to our attention recently — below are our reactions to these important books.*

## American Decorative Arts
Robert Bishop & Patricia Coblentz
1982 (394 pp., profusely illustrated) Cloth

**I**S IT IMPRACTICAL to try to cover 360 years' worth of all the decorative arts in America in one book? Yes ... but this 400-page extravaganza is visually stimulating (how could it not be?) and a whirlwind introduction to the subject. In this book, you'll get a hurried tour across the whole spectrum: furniture, ceramics, glass, paintings, clocks, and textiles. A majority of the 443 illustrations show interior decorative accessories from the country's best museums. The book would be a beautiful, expensive gift for a newcomer to America's decorative arts history.

To order, send $44.75 ppd. (regularly $65, but there's a 35% discount for prepaid orders) to
    Harry N. Abrams, Inc.
    Attention: Cash Sales, Dept. OHJ
    110 East 59th Street
    New York, NY 10022
    (212) 758-8600

## Great Camps Of The Adirondacks
Harvey H. Kaiser
1982 (240 pp., profusely illustrated) Cloth

**F**ROM 1870 TO 1930, New York's Adirondacks had its Gilded Age. During these years, America's millionaire families built elaborate, imaginative retreats deep among the forests. Constructed primarily of wood and stone, these fabulous structures are both rustic and sophisticated--treasures of the past unique in American architecture.

THE GREAT CAMPS have finally received their long overdue appreciation in Harvey Kaiser's definitive book. The range of the research is breathtaking--from the history and geography of the Adirondacks to the stories of the wealthy (and eccentric) families who sojourned there. Sumptuously illustrated with Kaiser's own discerning photos, this oversized book is also a thoughtful architectural study.

MOST IMPORTANTLY, the book is a courageous stand in defense of the camps, which are now threatened with demolition under the "forever wild" mandate of the New York State Constitution. We hope that the deserved success of this landmark book will help rally support for the Great Camps.

To order, send $45 ($60 after December 31, 1982), plus $2 postage, to:
    David R. Godine Publishers
    306 Dartmouth Street
    Boston, MA 02116
    (617) 536-0761

## Renovation, A Complete Guide
Michael Litchfield
1982 (587 pp., illustrated) Cloth

**T**HIS 587-PAGE TOME has the heft and dryness of an engineering manual, but lacks the narrowness of focus that would make it an effective one. (It reads as though Mr. Litchfield wrote down everything he knows.) Don't look for romance here, or even qualitative judgements. The first page of Chapter 1 starts off, "A house, whatever its age, reveals much to those who look closely." That's it for flowery prose. We're immediately launched into a terse discussion of dead and live loads, and then mercilessly pressed on through the renovation process, for 19 long chapters and 9 appendices.

THE BOOK might have been better if the author had ignored preservation and historicism entirely; as it is, he comes across as awkwardly uninitiated. For example, after a chapter devoted to every nuance of drywall taping and panelling installation, he passingly mentions that old plaster might be saved in unusual circumstances. To those few who care about such things, he makes the quaint suggestion that they contact "a local branch of the National Historic Trust [sic]," because restoration specialists know of techniques for plaster repair.

STILL, THIS BOOK is more worthy as a technical document than most books on home repair and remodeling. And a big, all-the-facts-in-one-place encyclopedia is nice to have around. We have this book in the OHJ library; architects, contractors, engineers, and everyone else concerned with building renovation probably should, too.

To order, send $29.95 ($34.95 after December 31, 1982) ppd., plus applicable sales tax, to
    John Wiley & Sons
    605 Third Avenue
    New York, NY 10158
    (212) 850-6336

## The Complete Concrete, Masonry, & Brick Handbook
J.T. Adams
1979 (1130 pp., well illustrated) Cloth

**A**T 1130 PAGES, this book certainly lives up to the description on its jacket; it is the longest and most complete book available on the subject. Or rather, subjects--it covers virtually every aspect of working with concrete, masonry, and brick. There's only one disadvantage: The emphasis is squarely on construction, not repair. You won't find a detailed explanation of repointing techniques. Nevertheless, this book is a significant addition to anyone's home-improvement library. Especially if you plan to do any stuccoing--the whole job, from start to finish, is explained with exceptional clarity. This book is also a must for masons, contractors, architects, and engineers.

To order, send $24.95, plus $1 postage, to
    Arco Publishing, Inc.
    215 Park Avenue South
    New York, NY 10003
    (212) 777-6300

# Restoration Products News

Winter may be long and cold, but all your old-house projects needn't wait. It is a perfect time to get involved in an indoor project...making something traditional or giving new life to an ignored treasure. This month we've listed parts and pieces for old-house projects: repair and restoration materials, kits, and tools.

## Winter Glow

You can bring Victorian elegance to your house with one of the three Tiffany-style reproduction lampshade kits from **Whittemore-Durgin.** The 26 in. *Grape Trellis* shade is $136; the *Tulip* and *Dogwood* are 16 in. shades selling for $55.95. Kits include everything you need except the tools of the trade and solder. Eleven lampshade kits designed for novice stained glass workers range in price from $33.95 to $47.95.

For the more advanced craftsperson, there are over 75 stained glass window and lampshade patterns to choose from. The patterns range in price from $.35 to $2.25. Reusable styrene lampshade forms, $13.95 to $15.95, in a variety of sizes and shapes are helpful in assembling simple and complicated designs. To see the complete selection of stained glass kits and patterns, send $1 for a catalog. **Whittemore-Durgin Glass Co.,** PO Box 2065OH, Hanover, MA 02339. (617) 871-1743.

*The Dogwood Lampshade*

## Time Passage

We can't all be lucky enough to own an authentic, period clock, so you might consider building your own. **Viking Clocks** offers this *Teardrop Clock*, a late 1800s design with a solid black walnut case that stands 23¼ inches high. In kit form, with an eight-day key-wound movement, the clock is $198; it can also be purchased finished for $258. A $25 factory rebate is in effect until December 31st. For a free color catalog, write **Viking Clocks,** Viking Building, Industrial Park, Box 490, Dept. OHJ, Foley, AL 36536. (205) 943-5081.

*The Teardrop Clock*

With the help of **Selva-Borel**, there is no excuse not to get your mantel, wall, or floor clock in working order. They have a seemingly endless selection of replacement parts such as movements, dials, pendulums, clock hands and numbers, and ornaments. If you would like to really immerse yourself in clock repair, note the eight pages of tools, cleaners, and lubricants in their catalog. Then you'll also need a good basic guidebook — *Practical Clock Repair* by Donald DeCarle. The book is presently on sale for $13.50 (reg. $16.50). For full details, send $2 for their color catalog. **Selva-Borel,** PO Box 796, Dept. OHJ, Oakland, CA 94604. (415) 832-0356.

## Sitting Around

You can still buy honest-to-goodness leather replacement chair seats. Pressed-fiber seats (in imitation of leather patterns) are readily available, but **Furniture Revival** also carries the real thing. They are authentic reproductions with deeply embossed patterns in oak-tanned leather that won't *sit-out*. The four patterns — two round, one bell-shaped, and one rectangular — are available in 12 in. ($22.50), 14 in. ($24.50), and 16 in. ($34) sizes. Custom-size seats begin at $42. Brass tacks and a tack strip can be ordered to secure the seat to the chair frame. For a catalog, $2, write **Furniture Revival & Co.,** PO Box 994, Dept. OHJ, Corvallis, OR 97339. (503) 754-6323.

Recaning old chairs is a productive winter activity. **Cane & Basket Supply** offers complete hand-caning kits which include weaving and binding cane, caning pegs and awl, and an instruction book. The kits, in your choice of cane, ranging from *carriage* (extra, extra fine) to *common* are $6.25 for 250 ft.; this is enough material to weave a 12 in. x 12 in. area. (The size of the cane needed for your particular project is determined by the diameter of the drilled holes, and the distance between these holes, center to center.)

Caning, fibre rush, genuine rush, and splint can also be purchased in a variety of sizes and lengths. If you're not a purist, you can buy pre-woven cane webbing for $3.25 per linear ft., in traditional and modern patterns. A helpful, illustrated catalog is $1. **Cane & Basket Supply Co.,** 1283 S. Cochran Ave., Dept. OHJ, Los Angeles, CA 90019. (213) 939-9644.

# Victoriana Stencils

Although traditional and Early American stencils have been available for years, Victoriana enthusiasts generally have had to make their own designs and patterns. Adele Bishop has come to the rescue by introducing three Victorian border stencil kits. The stencils are reproductions of designs found on the second floor of the Mark Twain House in Hartford, Connecticut. They are on pre-cut Mylar, with pre-printed register

*(above) Arrow-head and Tassels (left) Little Bells*

marks to permit the correct positioning of each stencil. *Little Bells* is 3¼ inches wide and costs $5.95; *Tassels*, 6 inches wide, and *Arrowhead*, 5 inches wide, are $6.95 each.

Together with the stencils, six new Victorian colors were added to her selection of Japan paints. A 4oz. can is $3.95. Information about these and other stencils — as well as stencilling supplies — can be found in a color catalog, $2. Adele Bishop, Inc., Box 557, Dept. OHJ, Manchester, VT 05254. (802) 362-3537.

# Summer Dreams

*Victorian Porch Swing*

Assembling a porch swing lets you dream of those warm, relaxing summer evenings only a few months away. The 4 ft. long, clear pine porch swing pictured here is sold by Renovation Products. It's shipped unfinished and partially assembled, with a metal chain for hanging. The cost is $199 (plus 7% handling charge). This swing and other wooden architectural embellishments can be seen in their catalog, $2. Renovation Products, 5302 Junius, Dept. OHJ, Dallas, TX 75214. (214) 827-5111.

# Finishing Touch

Woodcraft Supply is one of the best known suppliers of woodworking tools. Their catalog shows supplies for other kinds of projects, too, including a gilding kit. The kit costs $16.25 ppd. and contains everything you need to apply a gilded finish: twenty-five 5½ in. x 5½ in. sheets of imitation gold leaf, a magnet to handle the leaf, and complete instruc-

tions. Another hard-to-find item in their mail-order catalog is shellac flakes, a component of the traditional French Polish. If you'd like to learn more about this museum-quality, painstaking finish, order *The French Polisher's Manual* ($4.50 ppd.). These products are shown in the *Tool Catalog*, $2.50; a *Kit Catalog* is free. Woodcraft Supply Corp., 41 Atlantic Ave., PO Box 4000, Dept. OHJ, Woburn, MA 01888. (617) 935-5860.

# Traditional Handcrafts

Handmade hooked or braided rugs create a cozy period touch in any house. Braid-Aid features a complete selection of tools, materials, kits, and instruction books for these and other handcrafts. You can start small with a 2 ft. x 3 ft. braided rug kit, or for the more advanced craftsperson there's a 6 ft. x 9 ft. rug kit. Kits sold with 100% wool strips begin at $69; with remnant woolens, prices begin at $38.50.

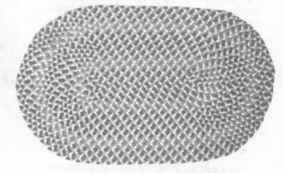

You'll be hard-pressed not to find something you like in the over 200 rug-hooking patterns, many of which are available in kit form. Patterns begin at about $4, kits begin at $16. Their catalog also features weaving looms ($546 to $770) and necessary accessories. For a catalog describing these and other items in detail, send $2 to Braid-Aid, 466 Washington St., Dept. OHJ, Pembroke, MA 02359. (617) 826-6091.

A source for unusual and hard-to-find items needed in traditional crafts is S. & C. Huber. With their help, you can step

back into the past by spinning and dyeing your own wool, making candles, soap, and paper. (They will also custom make these and other items, such as bedcoverings and curtains, to your specifications.) Of special interest is their selection of instruction manuals and history books covering traditional crafts including those already mentioned, weaving, and herbal gardening. For additional training, classes are offered. Send $.25 for a schedule. All this and current prices can be found in their catalog, $.75. S. & C. Huber — Accoutrements, 82 Plants Dam Rd., Dept. OHJ, East Lyme, CT 06333. (203) 739-0772.

# Opinion...
# Remuddling
## — Of The Month —

WE ORDINARILY don't feature public buildings in this column. But there was simply no way we could ignore the National Bank of Ypsilanti, Michigan.

THE PHOTO AT UPPER RIGHT was taken in 1909. In those days, the bank must have been one of the neighborhood's architectural highlights. Today, it's still attracting attention. Mr. Donald Randazzo, who submitted the photographs, explains:

"... pigeons have come home to roost behind the aluminum 'cheese grater' facade. They are a problem for pedestrians. The marble slabs require frequent attention; some have separated from the building and have had to be reset."

A LOT of time, energy, and money was spent transforming something handsome and useful into something that soils both Ypsilanti and pedestrians.

"THE IMAGE that was supposed to have solved problems has caused others," remarks Mr. Randazzo. The overhaul has proven to be such an annoying fiasco that the bank's board of directors now have to consider another remodeling. Unfortunately, the proposed designs that we've seen look like a cross between the Parthenon and a MacDonald's. No one seems to have learned the lesson that's staring everyone in the face: A real building is screaming for help under all that aluminum.

--Cole Gagne

# The Old-House Journal®

69A Seventh Avenue,
Brooklyn, New York 11217

NO PAID ADVERTISING

Postmaster: Address Correction Requested

# Don't Believe Anyone Who Says, "They Don't Make That Anymore."

By now, you've probably learned that it's hard to find appropriate and authentic products for your old house. You've undoubtedly encountered sales clerks who've said, "They don't make that anymore!" Well, they do still make the products and provide the services you need to restore, maintain, and decorate your old house. But many of these companies are relatively small and are scattered across the country — you just can't find their products in hardware stores or building-supply centers. A lot of them will sell to you through a dealer or by mail, but how do you track them down in the first place?

THE 1983 OLD-HOUSE JOURNAL CATALOG is the most complete buyer's guide to products and services for old houses. We have personally contacted and evaluated over 1200 companies throughout the United States. You have almost 10,000 products and services to choose from! Every entry in THE 1983 OLD-HOUSE JOURNAL CATALOG has detailed, up-to-date information: current prices, addresses, phone numbers, even information on brochures. And the CATALOG is extensively cross-referenced; you won't go crazy looking for "Chimney Collars" when that information is listed under "Stove Pipe & Fittings."

The 196 pages of THE 1983 OLD-HOUSE JOURNAL CATALOG are crammed with information you can't find anywhere else. Does your property cry out for special garden ornaments or a gazebo? Are you hunting for good tools, historic paint colors, or unusual roofing tiles? Do you want to decorate with antique or reproduction furniture, period bathroom fittings, or hand-printed wallpaper? Do you need the help of special restoration services? Whatever you want, you'll find it in THE 1983 OLD-HOUSE JOURNAL CATALOG. And practically every entry lists several different companies, so you can pick the source that's just right for you!

But we've saved the best news for last. As a member of the OHJ Network, you save $2 on each copy of THE 1983 OLD-HOUSE JOURNAL CATALOG. The non-subscriber price is $9.95, plus $2 postage and handling. Current OHJ subscribers pay only $7.95, plus $2 postage and handling. To order your copy of THE 1983 OLD-HOUSE JOURNAL CATALOG via fast UPS shipping, just use the Order Form in this Yearbook, or send your check to

The Old-House Journal
69A Seventh Avenue, Brooklyn, NY 11217

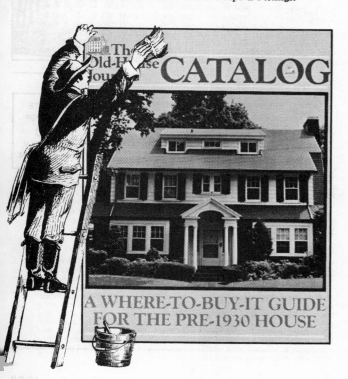

CATALOG

A WHERE-TO-BUY-IT GUIDE
FOR THE PRE-1930 HOUSE

Here are just a few of the products you'll find in
THE 1983 OLD-HOUSE JOURNAL CATALOG:

Mouldings & Gingerbread Trim
Architectural Millwork
Old-Style Roofing & Siding
Ornamental Ironwork
Reproduction Doors & Windows
Flooring
Fretwork
Staircases & Parts
Tin Ceilings
Wainscotting
Ornamental Plaster
Furniture & Furnishings
Columns & Capitals
Replacement Balusters
Glass — Stained, Etched, Bevelled
Mantels
Period Fabrics & Wallpapers
Hinges, Knobs, & Other Hardware
Period Plumbing & Fixtures
Lighting Fixtures & Parts
Authentic Paints & Finishes
Tools & Supplies
Antique & Recycled House Parts
Ceiling Medallions & Centerpieces

*And much, much more!*

# The Only Restoration Encyclopedia: A Full Set Of OHJ Yearbooks

THE OLD-HOUSE JOURNAL YEARBOOK series is our answer to subscribers who have asked us for bound volumes. Now you can get softcover books of seven full years of OHJ know-how, covering 1976 through 1982.

These seven information-packed YEARBOOKS are an instant old-house library that you will read and refer to again and again.

With today's tools and materials, and these unique reference books, you can become your own old-house craftsperson. In this mass-produced, fast-food world, you can have the satisfaction of producing high-quality work for your home . . . with your own two hands.

The new OLD-HOUSE JOURNAL YEARBOOKS feature:
♦ a total of 513 articles
♦ 1,396 pages in seven volumes
♦ quality softcover binding
♦ every volume fully indexed
♦ tables of contents

THE OLD-HOUSE JOURNAL YEARBOOK series is the most complete source of old-house know-how available anywhere. Each YEARBOOK can be ordered individually at the prices given below. But you can get the full set for only $59.95 — a saving of $28! Just use the box on the Order Form in this Yearbook, or send your check to

**1976** Repairing Window Sash * Taking An Architectural Inventory * Co-existing With Old Pipes * Gothic Decoration * Adding A Fireplace Damper * Tips On Storm Windows * Preserving Exterior Woodwork * Early American Kitchens * American Folk Decoration * Restoring Porch Spindles * Installing New Joists And Beams * Creating A Victorian Hallway * Reconstructing A Log House * Heating The Early American House * Cutting And Using Wall Stencils * Dating The Old House * Caulking Wood Cracks * Lighting The Colonial House * Restoration Health Hazards * Decorating With Wallpaper * Fixing Double-Hung Windows * Mouldings Made By Hand * Reproduction Wallpaper * Fixing Sagging Shutters * Reshaping An Old Fireplace * Lighting The Old House * and much more! ($10)

**1977** The Queen Anne Style * Sticky Problems Of Linoleum Paste * Landscaping The Pre-1840 House * Repairing Old Chimneys * Restoring Picture Frames * The Co-Insurance Trap * Keeping High Tank Toilets Working * Tudor Houses * Basic Timber Framing * Some Tips On Old Glass * Dealing With Old Sinks And Tubs * Removing Stains From Masonry * Victorian Fountains And Urns * Refinishing Wood Floors * Roofing With Wood Shingles * Portieres * The Bungalow Style * Restoring Marble Sinks * Late 19th Century Decoration * A Simple Damper * Patching Cracks In Plaster * Victorian Landscaping * Unsticking A Balky Sliding Door * Etched And Cut Glass * Simulating Lincrusta * Using Wood Stoves Safely * Preserving Wooden Columns * Removing Paint From Fireplaces * and much more! ($10)

**1978** The Colonial Revival House * Applying Wood Preservatives * Overcoming Musty Odors * The Art Of Graining * Old Storefronts, 1870-1920 * Bracing Up An Old Building * Building An Old-Fashioned Garden * Glass Glossary * Gluing Chairs * Alligatoring Paint * The Victorian Christmas Tree And Garden * Chimney Sweeping * Installing A Hot-Air Heating System * An Inexpensive Wainscot * The American Farmhouse * Etched And Brilliant Cut Glass * Solar Heater For An Old House * Protecting Exterior Doors * Planting A Knot Garden * Patching Cast Iron Pipe * Dangers Of Linseed Oil * Re-anchoring A Plaster Wall * Victorian Window Gardens * Removing Woodwork For Paint Stripping * Kitchen Cabinets For The Old House * Sprucing Up Old Radiators * Fancy Bevelled Glass * and much more! ($12)

**1979** Coupling Terra Cotta To PVC Pipe * Restoring Damaged Plaster * The Craftsman House * Making A Flue Liner * Fly-By-Night Contractors * Mid-19th Century Wallpaper * Sand Paint * The Mysterious Roof Leak * Glossary Of Old-House Parts * Cooling The Natural Way * Disconnecting Hot-Water Radiators * The Interpretive Restoration * Fireplace Safety * Fences * Coping With A Small Bathroom * Sealing Fence Posts * Painting Galvanized Metal * Maintenance Of Gutters * Gilding With Gold Leaf * Removing Exterior Paint * Repairing Stucco * Cleaning Marble Mantels * Metal Ceilings * Removing Painted Wallpaper * Masonry Repointing * Battling Brass Tarnish With Tung Oil * Finding Faults In Electric Bell Systems * Peeling Problems On Shutters * and much more! ($12)

**1980** The Federal House * Technological Trashing * Screen-Door Patterns * The Case Against Substitute Siding * A Fancy Picket Fence * Pattern-Book Architecture * Repairing A Golden Oak Door * Creating A Victorian Kitchen * Weatherstripping * Taking Down A Ceiling Medallion * Your House And The National Register * Setting Tiles In Concrete * Cat Odors * Rotten Window Sills * Cast Iron * Adding A Pantry * Victorian Drapery * Insulating Hints * How To Save That Old Ceiling * Sanding A Parquet Floor * Slate Roofs * House-Framing Systems * Colonial Floor Reproduction * Brick Walks * Ice Dams * Stacking Wood To Dry * Hot-Water Heating System * Turkish Corners * De-rating An Oil Burner * Beware Of Lead Paint * Front Gardens In The City * Cosy Corners And Inglenooks * and much more! ($12)

**1981** The Curse of Sandblasting * The Italian Style * Tinplate And Terneplate Roofing * Old-House Security * The Bare Brick Mistake * Window-Box Gardening * Insects That Eat Houses * The Joy Of Arc Welding * Is The Old House Ready For Solar? * In Praise Of Porches * Make Your Own Ornamental Wood Screens * The Crack Detective * Energy Audits, Consultants, And Contractors * Wet Basements * Picking A Floor Finish * Moving A House * Dumb-Waiters * Painting The American House * Twining Vines * Radiator Covers * Tuning Up A Steam Heating System * Restoring Crumbling Porches * Italian Style Decoration * Wooden Staircases * Defeating Decay * Indoor Air Quality * Solutions To The Pigeon Problem * Historic Paint Research * Refinishing Floors * Repairing Stairs * and much more! ($16)

**1982** The Comfortable House * How To Install Weatherstripping * Linoleum Care And Repair * American Gazebos * Repairing A Stair * The Dutch Colonial Revival Style * Relining Your Chimney Flue * Seeing Through Bad Stained Glass * Croquet And Roque * Bathrooms With Character * Patching Brownstone * Storm Windows * Demystifying Epoxy * Electrical Capacity * The Princess Anne House * How To Clean And Polish Marble * Lincrusta-Walton * Replacing Old Windows * Decorative Cast Iron * Recovering An Old Silk Lampshade * Movable Insulation * Exterior Wood Columns * Rack On A High-Pitched Roof * Anaglypta And Other Embossed Wallcoverings * All About Adobe * Patching Limestone And Marble * Restoring Clear Finishes * Fixing Our Balustrade * Stripping Paint * and much more! ($16)

# Why would over 9,000 OHJ subscribers buy The Master Heavy-Duty Heat Gun?

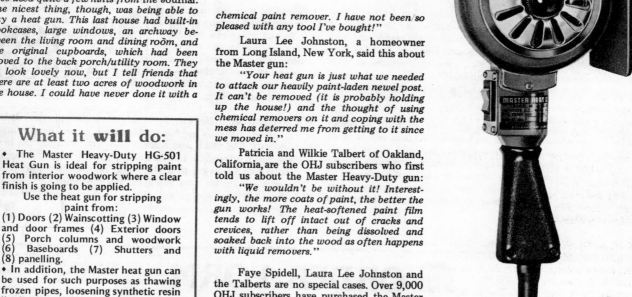

Faye Spidell of Eugene, Oregon, restores old houses in her spare time. Here's what she said in an *unsolicited* letter about the Master Heavy-Duty Heat Gun:

*"I read each issue very carefully and have used quite a few hints from the Journal. The nicest thing, though, was being able to buy a heat gun. This last house had built-in bookcases, large windows, an archway between the living room and dining room, and the original cupboards, which had been moved to the back porch/utility room. They all look lovely now, but I tell friends that there are at least two acres of woodwork in the house. I could have never done it with a* chemical paint remover. I have not been so pleased with any tool I've bought!"

Laura Lee Johnston, a homeowner from Long Island, New York, said this about the Master gun:

*"Your heat gun is just what we needed to attack our heavily paint-laden newel post. It can't be removed (it is probably holding up the house!) and the thought of using chemical removers on it and coping with the mess has deterred me from getting to it since we moved in."*

Patricia and Wilkie Talbert of Oakland, California, are the OHJ subscribers who first told us about the Master Heavy-Duty gun:

*"We wouldn't be without it! Interestingly, the more coats of paint, the better the gun works! The heat-softened paint film tends to lift off intact out of cracks and crevices, rather than being dissolved and soaked back into the wood as often happens with liquid removers."*

Faye Spidell, Laura Lee Johnston and the Talberts are no special cases. Over 9,000 OHJ subscribers have purchased the Master Heavy-Duty Heat Gun. And the raves keep coming in.

We sell this heat gun because it's the best one money can buy. It makes your job a lot easier . . . and minimizes inhalation of dangerous methylene chloride vapors, given off by most chemical removers.

The electric-powered heat gun softens paint in a uniform way so it can be scraped off with a knife. A small amount of chemical remover is suggested for clean-up and tight crevices, but the heat gun takes care of almost all the work.

In addition to minimizing chemical use, another important safety feature is a lower operating temperature than a propane torch or blowtorch. Thus the danger of vaporizing lead is eliminated, and fire danger is greatly reduced, too.

(Precautions should be taken when handling scrapings from lead-based paint and caution should be observed with wall partitions that contain dust.)

The HG-501 is an industrial-gauge tool. That means it isn't cheaply-made or cheaply-priced. But paint remover is going for $12 to $20 per gallon . . . so if you use the Master Heat Gun just a few times, it pays for itself.

When it comes to stripping paint, there are no magic wands — but we think this is the best method and best gun for the job.

*$72.95 postpaid, shipping via UPS*

To order your Master Heat Gun, just use the Order Form in this Yearbook, or send your check to The Old-House Journal, 69A Seventh Ave., Brooklyn, NY 11217.

## What it **will** do:

◆ The Master Heavy-Duty HG-501 Heat Gun is ideal for stripping paint from interior woodwork where a clear finish is going to be applied.

Use the heat gun for stripping paint from:
(1) Doors (2) Wainscotting (3) Window and door frames (4) Exterior doors (5) Porch columns and woodwork (6) Baseboards (7) Shutters and (8) panelling.

◆ In addition, the Master heat gun can be used for such purposes as thawing frozen pipes, loosening synthetic resin linoleum pastes, and softening old putty when replacing window glass.

## What it **won't** do:

The heat gun is **not** recommended for:
(1) Removing shellac and varnish; (2) Stripping paint on window mullions (the glass might crack from the heat); (3) Stripping the entire exterior of a house (too slow); (4) Stripping Early American milk paint (only ammonia will do that); (6) Stripping exterior cornices (could ignite dust or animal nests inside).

## Note these outstanding features:

◆ Heavy-duty industrial construction for long life

◆ Pistol-grip handle; 3-position finger-tip switch

◆ Rubber-backed stand keeps floors from scorching; stand swivels 90°; has keyhole for hanging and storage

◆ Adjustable air intake regulates temperature between 500°F & 750°F.

◆ Rugged die-cast aluminum body — no plastics

◆ 8'-long 3-wire cord, grounded, with molded plug

◆ No asbestos used in construction

◆ Double-jacketed heater

◆ Rated at 120 v. and 15 amps

◆ Approved by Underwriters Laboratories

**The Old-House Journal Guarantee:** If your heat gun should malfunction for any reason within two months of purchase, return it to The Old-House Journal and we'll replace it.

# What Is The Old-House Journal

The Old-House Journal is the only national publication devoted exclusively to the sensitive rehabilitation, maintenance, and decoration of old houses. For ten years, our newsletter has brought readers the best how-to articles, written in plain, down-to-earth language. And The Old-House Journal offers more: case histories, house-style articles, an overview of restoration products, readers' questions and tips, book reviews, free classified ads for our subscribers — all for the person who loves old houses.

This Yearbook is a compilation of one full year's worth of Old-House Journal issues. No editorial content has been deleted from any of those issues; all the solid, practical information we've prepared, all the contributions from both homeowners and professional restorationists, is here between these two covers. And it's only one in a series of Yearbooks. If you're a newcomer to The Old-House Journal, this series can give you the most complete and thorough library of home-restoration techniques available anywhere.

The Old-House Journal also publishes an indispensable Buyer's Guide to products and services for the pre-1930 house. Local stores will tell you, "No one makes that anymore," but our Catalog lists over 1200 companies nationwide who will supply just what your old house needs. We've personally contacted and carefully screened every company and craftsperson in The Old-House Journal Buyer's Guide Catalog; it's the most complete and accurate Buyer's Guide available, listing almost 10,000 products and services.

If you love old houses . . . the beauty of restored interiors and facades . . . quality materials and fine craftsmanship . . . and have an urge to do it yourself, The Old-House Journal is for you. You can use the Order Form below to send for the Yearbooks, Buyer's Guide Catalog, and our popular paint-stripping Heat Gun. You can even place gift orders for someone special. We hope you'll also use the Order Form to subscribe to The Old-House Journal newsletter . . . and become part of the OHJ Network.

# ORDER FORM

## Subscription To The Old-House Journal

☐ New Subscription    ☐ Renewal (Enclose Current Mailing Label)

☐ 1 Year — $16    ☐ 2 Years — $28    ☐ 3 Years — $36

## Heat Gun

☐ MASTER APPLIANCE HG-501 HEAT GUN — $72.95
11   The Master Heavy-Duty Heat Gun operates at 500 to 700 degrees, draws 15 amps at 120 volts, and has an all-metal construction — no asbestos, no open flame. It's the easiest, cleanest, and best-designed paint-stripping tool we know.

## The 1983 OHJ Buyers' Guide Catalog

☐ Comprehensive buyers' guide to over 9000 hard-to-find products and services
12   for the old house. This "Yellow Pages" for restoration and maintenance — 11% larger this year — is the most complete, up-to-date sourcebook available.
*Softcover. $11.95 — $9.95 to current OHJ subscribers.*

*Please fill out this section even if you're ordering only a gift.*

## Send My Order To:

Name _____

Address _____

City _____ State _____ Zip _____

Amount enclosed: $ _____
              *NY State residents please add applicable sales tax.*

## Old-House Journal Yearbooks:
## The Restoration Encyclopedia

Each Yearbook is a compilation of a full year's worth of OHJ issues, packed with the restoration and maintenance techniques we're known for. The softbound volumes each have a Table of Contents and an Index.

76 ☐ 1976 — $10      81 ☐ 1981 — $16

77 ☐ 1977 — $10      82 ☐ 1982 — $16

78 ☐ 1978 — $12

79 ☐ 1979 — $12      90 ☐ The Full Set — $59.95
                                  *All seven Yearbooks at only*
80 ☐ 1980 — $12             *2/3 the price. You save $28!*

## or Send Gift To:

Name _____

Address _____

City _____ State _____ Zip _____

*We will send a gift announcement card with your name to the recipient.*
*Note: Please allow 8 weeks for your first issue to arrive.*

### The Old-House Journal

NOTE: If your order includes books or merchandise, you must give us a STREET ADDRESS — not a P.O. Box number. We ship via United Parcel Service (UPS), and they will not deliver to a P.O. Box.

*Please clip this page and mail together with check payable to The Old-House Journal to THE OLD-HOUSE JOURNAL, 69A Seventh Avenue, Brooklyn, NY 11217.*

All prices postpaid, and include fast UPS shipping.

YBK82

---

References are to
Month and Page of issue.

# C

---

KEY

(B) = Book Review or Literature Listing

(L) = Letter From the Readers

(P) = Product Listing

(RN) = Short Item (Restorer's Note-
      book, Ask OHJ, etc.)

KEY

(B) = Book Review or Literature Listing

(L) = Letter From the Readers

(P) = Product Listing

(RN) = Short Item (Restorer's Notebook, Ask OHJ, etc.)

References are to
Month and Page of issue.

# S

# T

# U

## KEY

(B) = Book Review or Literature Listing

(L) = Letter From the Readers

(P) = Product Listing

(RN) = Short Item (Restorer's Note-
        book, Ask OHJ, etc.)

# V

# W

References are to
Month and Page of issue.